M000199362

THE DETECTIVE IN HOLLYWOOD

Other books by Jon Tuska

Author

THE FILMS OF MAE WEST
THE FILMING OF THE WEST

Author/Editor

CLOSE-UP: THE CONTRACT DIRECTOR
CLOSE-UP: THE HOLLYWOOD DIRECTOR
CLOSE-UP: THE CONTEMPORARY DIRECTOR

THE DETECTIVE
IN HOLLYWOOD
by Jon Tuska

DOUBLEDAY & COMPANY, INC., GARDEN CITY, NEW YORK
1978

Library of Congress Cataloging in Publication Data

Tuska, Jon.
  The detective in Hollywood.

  Includes index.
  1. Detective and mystery films—History and
criticism. 2. Moving-pictures—United States—History.
I. Title.
PN1995.9.D4T8   791.43'0909'352
ISBN: 0-385-12093-1
Library of Congress Catalog Card Number 77-80915

Copyright © 1978 by Jon Tuska
All Rights Reserved
Printed in the United States of America
First Edition

Book design by Beverly Gallegos

For *Samuel Dashiell Hammett*, who brought contemporary America to the detective story—

And for *Roman Polanski*, who brought the vividness of Hammett's vision to the screen.

ACKNOWLEDGMENTS

This is a most important part of any book of this nature, but, to read most acknowledgments, you would never know it. There are many names cited below, many more even than there were for my book *The Filming of the West*. But one thing has been different from what it was then. For typing the manuscript, assisting in the selection of photos, for handling film prints, arranging interviews, editing the manuscript, remembering when I forgot, watching all the films, taking all the notes, traveling halfway around the world and back, living in hotel rooms in countless cities for nearly a year wherever our subject took us, for doing research when I was unable, for providing critiques, and for devoting herself as much to this book as indeed I did, I have to thank my secretary/companion, Vicki Piekarski. Not that she didn't complain. She would remind me of the number of people I once thanked for doing *all* of these things in the past. And now there was only one to thank. And so, in all honesty, I do thank her. But maybe most of all I owe to her the fact that as many times as she made me very angry with her, there were many more times she made me laugh. There is nothing so important as that.

Nor can I forget Barbara Hale, who wanted so much for this to be the best possible book and who worked so hard to help me achieve that end. She would come up with a suggestion that I interview someone and she would try to set it up. "What's the worst that can happen? It won't happen. Right?" I told her, as now I must tell the reader, this book is owed primarily to the women, like Vicki, like Barbara, and like Gail Patrick. Gail was responsible for bringing me together with many people, Barbara among them.

Then there is that *véritable ami* Joe Abruscato, of Columbia Pictures Television, who could perceive so many possibilities in what I was doing and who went to such extremes in striking prints where none existed and finding prints where none were known to survive. The release to television of a package of detective films, many of them for the first time, in conjunction with the publication of this book in the United States and the United Kingdom was initiated by Columbia Pictures and Joe Abruscato.

In what follows, I have undertaken to separate professional from distribution people. I think this is only fair. There are those who worked on the films and those who currently control their availability. Some have retired, indicated by an (r.) after their names; others have passed on, indicated by a (d.) There is also a third category, individuals associated with archives or writers around the world who have been of invaluable assistance. And there is one fine painter, S. Macdonald-Wright, and one film director, Sam Peckinpah, who were a comfort as well as an assistance.

Creative

Robert Altman
Leon Ames
Ralph Bellamy
Sally Blane
Hillary Brooke
John Cromwell
Angie Dickinson
Edward Dmytryk
Gordon Douglas
James Flavin (d.)
Norman Foster (d.)
Lorraine Gauguin (d.)
Maurice Geraghty
Howard Hawks
Alfred Hitchcock
Jack Hively
H. Bruce "Lucky" Humberstone

John Huston
Frieda Inescort
D. Ross Lederman (d.)
Keye Luke
Robert Montgomery
Patricia Morison
Chester Morris (d.)
Lloyd Nolan
Roman Polanski
George Raft
Dick Richards
Lizabeth Scott
Lesley Selander
John Wayne
Billy Wilder
Jane Wyatt

Distribution

COLUMBIA PICTURES TELEVISION
Bob Nilson
Ken Page
Alan Press
Sid Weiner (r.)

JANUS FILMS
Bill Becker

METRO-GOLDWYN-MAYER
Carla Davidson
Norman Kaphan

UNIVERSAL PICTURES
Dan Bishop (d.)

PARAMOUNT PICTURES
Joe Moscaret

TWENTIETH CENTURY-FOX
Marc Pevers
Frank Rodriguez
Jack Yaeger

MCA TELEVISION
Audrey Foster (r.)
Ernie Goodman
Irving Weiner (d.)

NATIONAL TELEFILM ASSOCIATES
Bud Grosskoff
Joanne Harris
Ken Harris
Donald Havens
Virginia Lisser

UNITED FILMS
Bill F. Blair

WARNER BROTHERS
Al Ashley
Bob Burriss
John Whitesell

FILMS, INC.

Allen Green

UNITED ARTISTS TELEVISION

Bart Farber

Literary

Leigh Brackett

Leslie Charteris

Frederic Dannay (Ellery Queen)

Jean Gardner (Erle Stanley Gardner)

Kenneth Millar (Ross Macdonald)

Francis M. Nevins, Jr.

David R. Smith

David Wilson

I also have to acknowledge the assistance of David L. Parker, at the Library of Congress, Washington, D.C.; Janus Barfoed at the Danske Filmmuseum, in Copenhagen; Jeremy Boulton and Michelle Snapes at the British Film Institute, in London; the Museum of Modern Art in New York; and the Motion Picture Academy in Beverly Hills, California. Nor can I forget the Wisconsin State Historical Society and its archivist, Sue Dalton.

Lastly, since this is an expensive book, I wish to express my gratitude to my publishers in New York and London for the faith they have shown in this project.

Los Angeles, California
December 7, 1976

CONTENTS

PROLOGUE

I have chosen to call this book *The Detective in Hollywood*. It is the second volume in my proposed trilogy on the American cinema.

When the initial volume first appeared, *The Filming of the West* (Doubleday, 1976), I was widely interviewed on radio and television in cities throughout the United States. I would warrant I had every conceivable question put to me, and the majority of them, at least, I tried my best to answer. One particular question, however, stopped me cold. The interviewer asked me: "What is a Western?"

It's such a simple and direct question you would think I had been asked it a dozen times, but I hadn't. And you might also think I had a ready answer, but I didn't. I had to think about it, begging off and discussing other things, until I finally formulated a response.

I do not wish to encounter any such difficulty here. The most effective detective stories, to my mind, whether written or put on the screen, may surprise, thrill, excite, but more than that they ought to provide a sudden shock of revelation. For the sake of the game, all of these effects may be achieved through cognitive processes or by intuition, but in strictly mechanical terms they are best accomplished by the most dramatic means possible.

When I was most recently in London, I saw the stage play *Double Edge*, written by Leslie Darbon and Peter Whelan. It is a three-person play. Margaret Lockwood was in the lead. She played a professor assigned by a publisher to do a book on an assassination attempt on the life of the Prime Minister, in which, through apparent inadvertence, the woman the Prime Minister was talking to was shot instead. Alone in her apartment, the writer is visited first by a Communist agitator, suspected by everyone, and then by the Home Secretary. The passing lamp of suspicion falls on all three characters. The whole business is so entertaining that you are quite entranced; even the writer is made to appear guilty. But two thirds through the second act, the masks are suddenly removed and the truth revealed. The audience can only gasp. After all, for better than an hour one interpretation of the events after another had been set forth and each had seemed more credible than the last. Now here was the truth, visible from the beginning, but observed by no one. Whenever you experience this effect, you have the very essence of the detective story at its most successful. Appearances have been reduced to the reality behind them.

The Detective in Hollywood has to do with three different aspects of the same phenomenon: the popular detectives and the authors who created them; how those detectives changed when they were brought to the screen; and the lives and personalities of those who played in detective films, or adapted them for the screen, or directed them. Through it all, from beginning to end, emanates that generating line in the treatment and perspective of the detective himself from what it was once in *Sherlock Holmes Baffled* (Biograph, 1900) to what it has become in Roman Polanski's *Chinatown* (Paramount, 1974).

I can breathe a sigh of relief about one thing. No player in detective films will ever be irked at me if I say of him that in his personal life he very little resembled his image on the screen. The same cannot be said of actors who portrayed cowboy heroes. Many of them took offense at how I tried in *The Filming of the West* to penetrate behind the Hollywood illusion, even when I knowingly and discreetly did not penetrate very far. Somehow the identification was all-encompassing. A cowboy player, I have had reason to learn, wants most to be remembered as he was on the screen, as if that projective fantasy had really existed.

One Western veteran's wife broke into tears because I hadn't included a portrait of her husband in his cowboy outfit. William Boyd once told me that he wanted to be remembered as Hopalong Cassidy. Gene Autry insisted I preserve the screen fiction and ignore entirely the real human being. Ken Maynard berated me because I once mentioned he drank. Fortunately, Humphrey Bogart did not think of himself as Sam Spade any more than Peter Lorre regarded himself as Mr. Moto or George Sanders confused himself with the Saint or the Falcon. Detective films do not lock their participants into mythic views of life without which they are all better off.

My exposure to detective fiction has been desultory on the whole. I possess nothing like the encyclopedic knowledge of so many who talked with me in my various travels as I was putting this book together. Because of the focus on films, an author like Rex Stout, whom I have read avidly for years, can preoccupy me only briefly, since only two Nero Wolfe films were ever produced. Others, like R. Austin Freeman, who wrote the Dr. Thorndyke mysteries, I have had to pass over with only a cursory mention. Still others I have had to exclude entirely.

Almost all detective fiction has been written to formula. This has never struck me as an adequate excuse for much of it to be abominably written, but such has frequently been the case. So, perhaps, it is just as well if I do not get sidetracked into any pretense at literary criticism. Some rather eminent critics have recently undertaken to approach this form of creative endeavor with metaphysical or sociological interpretations. I confess I am not up to it.

I recall when I arranged a screening of *The Dragon Murder Case* (First National, 1934) for Lucky Humberstone, who had directed the picture nearly forty years previously, about midway through he leaned over to me in the projection room where we sat at the Burbank Studios.

"Do you know how this thing comes out?" he asked.

I told him that I did.

"Don't tell me. I know I directed it, but I've forgotten who did it."

A good part of detective fiction, and therefore an abundance of detective films, falls into this category of story intended for people who primarily like surprises. But the shock of revelation need not be in discovering who committed a crime. There is another kind of detective story, the kind that becomes increasingly prevalent toward the end of this book. Here, who did it, or even why, is not as important as the environment in which the crime was planned, then executed, the infinite corruption indigenous to the American way of life in which, finally, even the detective hero is corrupted. When you cannot escape from corruption, nor successfully deal with it, all you can hope to do is to depict it.

For a number of detective story writers, their lives, often the settings for their stories, or the incarnation of their detectives converge and intersect in Hollywood. This is not only because a series of motion pictures was inspired by their characters or stories. Often it goes beyond that insofar as the milieu in which the detective is set is that of the uninhibited, frank, frequently bewildered society of Southern California. I am not altogether sympathetic with the view, currently so much in vogue, that if you want to know what Southern California is really like you should read Raymond Chandler.

Leigh Brackett, who worked on the screenplays for Chandler's *The Big Sleep* (Warner's, 1946) and *The Long Goodbye* (United Artists, 1973), commented to me as we sat in her cozy desert home, "You know where Ray got most of his characters, don't you? He went to the movies in the Twenties and Thirties. So many of his characters aren't real at all: they're movie conceptions of people."

Too many American detective story writers have come from the East or from the Middle West. Whether they have only visited Southern California or have in fact settled there, they have valiantly resisted becoming natives. I find myself in accord with Ross Macdonald: "Everything good *and* bad begins in California," he once said. "Then it moves East."

I do not know, as I have said, all there is to know of the subject of detective fiction; and certainly I would remark the same about detective films. What I have discovered is contained in this book. It would be pointless, of course, to mention every detective film ever made in Hollywood, or in Europe. It would be as pointless as attempting a critique of every detective story ever written. I am aware there are books which purport to accomplish the latter. With some delight I have read reviews which prove that the author or authors of these mammoth tomes have not read *every* book they criticize and have even cribbed some of their assessments from other sources. The reader may reasonably assume I have seen all the films which I cite in passing.

I am not one to mention a title of a film merely somehow to include it if I have nothing more than that to say about it. I admit the scope I have given myself in this book also affects the films or stories about which I may make comment. I do not believe you can come to any understanding of a storyteller's art or a filmmaker's craft without at the same time coming to terms with the man. How a director or a player or a screenwriter goes about achieving the results he does, and what goes on during the process, are of the greatest importance to me. Such an approach must have its inherent limitations. A film of particular merit may not be emphasized as much as one of little critical or financial consequence. But if, in the end, the various routes I have chosen bring me closer to my objectives, then more will have been accomplished than might ever be possible by an indiscriminate and encyclopedic chronicle of title after title, or praising again films which have often been praised.

In dealing with the Western, this approach meant that I had more to say about John Ford's first Western feature *Straight Shooting* (Universal, 1917) than I did about his later masterpiece, *The Searchers* (Warner's, 1956). Similarly, Ken Maynard's life explained more about the transformation of Western production in the Thirties than could an account of the plots of a handful of classic Westerns produced during the same period.

It is the same in dealing with the detective film. So much of what Dashiell Hammett and Raymond Chandler attempted to do in their fiction cannot be understood save in terms of its context, a violent aesthetic reaction to the amazing popularity of Philo Vance. So, even while Vance and his creator, S. S. Van Dine, are virtually forgotten to modern audiences, the hard-boiled tradition that emerged in the Forties can better be grasped by reflecting on the trend it sought to contradict.

I do not arrogate to myself the assumption critics must make, that I am able to best determine what was good cinema and what was not, which films are worth watching, and which ones are best left neglected. Because it is cinema history I am intent upon, and not a platform setting forth my personal opinions, my course is determined by popular tendencies, not subjective evaluations.

In dealing with the screen Western, or almost any other kind of motion picture, it is possible to write film history without going as deeply into the lives of individual authors or their works as I have had to do in approaching the detective film. This is readily understandable when you reflect that, with the exception of authors like Clarence E. Mulford, Western novels are seldom concerned with series characters. Detective story writers, for the most part, expended great energy in creating their fictional detectives. Not only did their detectives become essential to the kinds of stories they wrote, but indeed it was the detective himself in most instances who earned popular favor and built a sustaining readership.

When the time came to bring these detectives to the screen, their respective creators were very anxious lest the screenplay destroy overnight what had taken them years to construct. Many authors, such as Erle Stanley Gardner and Rex Stout, became so disgusted with the Hollywood treatment of their characters they refused to license further photoplays featuring them. In other cases, Hollywood created wholly new characters from their fictional prototypes. These scored better, if not with the public, at least with the producers who didn't have to put up with irate and incensed authors. In still other cases, men like Dashiell Hammett and Raymond Chandler became involved in working on the screenplay versions of their own fictional work. Chandler was, if anything, very much a hindrance, but, as he himself said, Philip Marlowe, his detective, was really all he had to sell. And it is due to this tendency on the part of certain detective story authors to become scenarists that their detectives, their world view, their contributions to dialogue and plot treatment ended up having such a widespread currency among film productions of all kinds.

Somewhere I have read that the detective was originally a personification of the Enlightenment. He represented the forces of reason, truth, and justice in a more or less absolute sense. He was a popularized version of the scientist. However true this may have been, it diminished under the influence of American writers like Dashiell Hammett, Raymond Chandler, and others from the *Black Mask* school. Repeated questioning overshadowed all certitude with the dark cast of doubt. Truth and justice, if not reason, may have remained the domain of the detective, but society became his opponent and who actually committed a crime was at best ambiguous.

William Ruehlmann has written an interesting book on the detective called *Saint with a Gun* (New York University Press, 1974). It is an indictment of American detective fiction. The detective, he tells us, is most often conceived as an avenger; justice is confused with revenge. Far from supporting order in a chaotic world, the detective becomes his own law and administers justice according to his own bias. But, as impressive as this may sound at first, it overlooks the rather sad fact that truth and justice are determined by money and power and not some abstract principle or some eternal, incontrovertible ideal. The detective who makes his own justice is doing nothing different than the judge whose opinion was bought long before he ever assumed the bench or the policeman who is victim to a system that gives him a daily quota of arrests to make if he wants to keep his job. Accepting all that Ruehlmann says, what I am compelled to come back to again and again is that the detective, no matter how outlandish his behavior, is but the victim of a corrupt social order and not even he can hope to escape from it untarnished. "The law is a funny thing," Sam Peckinpah has his Billy the Kid observe. It is. It can make a gangster a hero in a day. It can do it as easily as it can make a hero a gangster.

"Didn't it strike you as curious," I asked John Huston, as we talked together in his suite at the Beverly Hills Hotel, "that you should have directed *The Maltese Falcon* in 1941 and that Sam Spade emerged such a hero, only now to have played the villain in *Chinatown*, where money, and power, and influence alone rule the day?"

Huston leered at me and leaned forward, his features grimacing into a consummate smirk.

"It wasn't any different when I made *The Maltese Falcon* than it is now," he said. "It's only that we were less able or willing to accept it then."

He leaned back in his chair, relaxed, and puffed on his cigar.

Human nature is self-deceptive. In living our lives most of us find this a difficult state of affairs with which to deal. It definitely isn't the simplest task to write a mainstream novel that is successful without sympathetic characters. Noel Coward once said of his good friend W. Somerset Maugham that in a long literary career he never managed to draw a sympathetic character. Maugham loved detective stories. I suspect this was because detective stories rarely, if ever, contain sympathetic characters other than the detective. Maugham solved the problem in his own work by writing in the first person. Many detective stories use this device, whether they are narrated by a Watson figure or the detective himself.

A detective is by nature suspicious. He expects everyone to lie to him. We know this to be true of our fellow men, even if their supposed sincerity is merely the product of self-delusion; but it is many times knowledge we would prefer not to have and so tend to close it out of our minds. Detective fiction permits us a catharsis in which we can at once admit the deceit of humanity and still hold to the fond belief that not all men are so, because the detective is an exception. The anger incited in those cases where the detective is revealed to be the culprit is almost pathetic. We cannot really arrive at the identity of the wrongdoer on the printed page or on the screen without being nearly pathologically vigilant and cautious about believing anyone. "Watch them," Robert Montgomery says into the camera, playing Philip Marlowe in *Lady in the Lake* (M-G-M, 1946), "they're tricky." And so they are.

The author of a detective story is under no obligation to make us like his characters. He can expose them or kill them off and indulge us in an antisocial orgy that might, under other circumstances, be found morally suspect. But he has to achieve more than this to earn lasting favor. He must conjure ideal characters. And "lasting" for any writer is the span of his lifetime. If his favor outlasts him, future generations may become as interested in the writer as readers were once interested in his creations.

The principal charm of Conan Doyle's stories is the touching friendship between Holmes and Watson. It has been the same on the screen. Or witness that amazing professional association between Perry Mason and his loyal, enthusiastic Della Street and his friendship with Paul Drake of the Drake Detective Agency. This peculiar set of emotional affinities accounts, I imagine, for the enduring fascination of certain kinds of detective stories.

It can be otherwise. The rapport between Myrna Loy and William Powell in the Thin Man series is only one aspect of detective cinema. Particularly during the sound era, the detective in film has also been a loner with the audience as his only intimate companion. When romance enters the story in the form of a girl friend, she may, as often as not, be a suspect. In the Forties especially, she might very well be the murderer. Isolation follows upon universal suspicion, and a detective's life is necessarily a lonely one. Existential separation remains one of the dominant cinematic themes. But then, is not one of the highest pleasures in reading or in films learning to deal with our loneliness, our separation?

The detective traditionally has been a truth-seeker. Almost everyone else he deals with, to a greater or lesser extent, is a variety of truth-hater. Resentment of the truth-seeker is one of the oldest human dramas. It is the tension between the natural desire to conceal the truth and the daring impulse to expose it which provides the detective genre with its fundamental *raison d'être*.

The Age of Reason asserted that knowledge is power. The contemporary world in which we all live has shown us that knowledge is a source of suffering, despair, sickness unto death, reminding one of the pessimism of Ecclesiastes. Power is money. And because money consorts with greed in a society dominated by economic pressures of all kinds, the lack of it has become irremediably confused with the emptiness and dissatisfaction inevitable when romantic myths fail.

The Enlightenment neglected the maxim that "in much wisdom is much grief; and he that increaseth knowledge increaseth sorrow." Knowledge, for the detective, as for all of us, imposes a permanent loneliness. The Enlightenment placed the highest value of all on human life. Individual, premeditated murder is a deep-seated taboo that, for all its commonness, prompts sufficient emotional turmoil to sustain interest. Too many and too much have brought about a transition from a brave and open willingness to arrive at the truth, to a clandestine at first, then a brazen consent to reject it, or not discover it at all. The detective over the years passes through his phases, from inspiring awe and security to where he now stands, despised of all men, an offensive intrusion even to those who propose to employ him.

I am totally incapable of nostalgia. I do not know exactly why this is so, but so it is. All I need do is change my physical surroundings, move to a different city far away, establish a life amid new friends, and I think hardly at all of where I once lived, nor do I in any sense miss it. Life is kindest to us when, every ten years, we can begin it anew. I have heard that the past, collectively and individually, can be best used to instruct us. Usually it doesn't have that effect at all. If the detective story is to be believed, the individual past is most often filled with anguish which somehow cannot be forgotten. This is part and parcel of the detective story, since it takes us back in time, starting with a crime and attempting to reconstruct from the past how the crime came about.

One thing you would notice if, as I have suggested, you were to change your physical surroundings completely, and then return to your former setting: the people who were close to you when you lived there are still wound up in the same emotional and psychological circles they were in when you left. They seem strange to you because you no longer are a part of it. That same impression of strangeness is embodied in modern detective stories, as the past is unraveled through investigations and interrogations; patterns are revealed and you become aware of the powerful emotional grasp of the past, be it fantasy or reality.

I suppose, having said all this, it is only right that I conclude with a personal reminiscence. Reading has been the keenest pleasure of my life. I can only think of how insubstantial and bleak existence would be without it. Yet, I was all of eleven years of age before I read a book on my own initiative. Since earliest childhood I had begged my mother, who invariably read to me, to get a mystery story from the library which was less than half a block away from where we lived. She consistently refused to do this. Finally, I was forced to take matters into my own hands. I went to the library myself and, after much deliberation, drew out two books, *Murder within Murder* (Lippincott, 1946), by Frances and Richard Lockridge, and *The Lone Star Ranger* (Harper & Bros., 1915), by Zane Grey. I enjoyed neither. It might well have ended there had I not next tried *The Bishop Murder Case* (Scribner's, 1929) by S. S. Van Dine. I became caught up with Philo Vance.

I was a very poor reader. I did not know many words. I began memorizing the meanings to every word I did not know. I found the effort exhilarating. I read one detective story after another. In the summer months, when we had gone to live with my maternal grandmother in her large home, I would sleep all day. At night I would watch detective films on television on her screened back porch. Afterward, from late at night until dawn, I would read a detective story.

When I learned that S. S. Van Dine had assembled a library of some two thousand detective stories in 1923, I set out to duplicate his record. I got library cards for several of the surrounding counties so their shelves of mystery and detective fiction would be available to me. I did not want to purchase books that weren't pleasing to my taste. Once on a stay with my great-aunt in her Los Angeles home, she took me on the Pico Avenue streetcar to visit a dozen second-hand bookstores as part of my quest. I never completed the project.

Nor do I read many detective stories any more, although I have had to read many again while writing this book. When the notion for *The Detective in Hollywood* came to me in 1970, the only thing I had written on detective fiction was an exercise for my own amusement, begun in 1964, about S. S. Van Dine. I managed to screen all the Philo Vance movies and transformed the exercise into an essay which was published in *Views & Reviews* magazine. Bowling Green University Popular Press then brought out the essay, along with others I compiled by other authors, in pamphlet form, Van Dine thus becoming the first author in their popular writer series. I had tried to elucidate Van Dine's personality from the detective stories he wrote. I knew virtually nothing about him. The reader may readily surmise my astonishment, then, when I learned from Van Dine's brother and daughter, neither of whom I had known existed, that my portrait had been uncannily accurate. In revised form, that essay constitutes what I have to say here about Philo Vance.

In reading reviews of the essay, I was dismayed to find that some critics objected to my revealing the identities of murderers. I felt this essential to do in order to treat the plots as plots.

When I was married, my wife had a peculiar habit. Although she had hundreds of books to choose from, when she came to read, she preferred to read one or another of the books I was reading at the time. I complained bitterly, but never more so than when I happened to be reading *The Mad Hatter Mystery* (Harper & Bros., 1933), by John Dickson Carr. It had been my custom for some years to read detective stories before retiring; I am addicted to reading in bed. I was certain she was not the least inclined to read the Carr book. Before going out one morning, I remarked to her that I was within a few chapters of finishing it and that I was convinced I knew who had done it. When I returned, she greeted me with a knowing smile.

"You're wrong," she said.

"About what?"

"About the murderer. He didn't do it."

"How do you know?"

"I read the book." She triumphantly tossed her head. "Dr. Fell admits in the final chapter that the crime is best left unsolved."

I was irked. I never finished the book, so I cannot inform the reader if she was correct. Yet, I can only pray that when I must reveal a murderer's identity for the sake of what I have to say, it will not have a similarly adverse effect. My hope for reclamation rests on the circumstance that, if and when I do so err, it may be judged as having been in a worthy cause.

NOTE

The author wishes to thank W. W. Norton & Company, Inc., for permission to quote from police transcriptions reproduced in *Helter Skelter*, by Vincent Bugliosi with Curt Gentry; G. P. Putnam's Sons for permission to quote from *Step Right Up!*, by William Castle; and Charles Scribner's Sons for permission to quote from *To Have and Have Not*, by Ernest Hemingway.

Negatives for all the original illustrations appearing in this book were made by Eddie Brandt's Saturday Matinee, Box 3232, North Hollywood, CA 91609. Copies of any of them can be obtained by writing to Eddie Brandt.

NOTE

"Sue people like that and they're likely to be having lunch with the judge who's trying the case."

Roman Polanski's *Chinatown*

A sticker on the rear bumper of the Cadillac read, "Honk, if you love Jesus." The children's dark eyes looked out at me in solemn question. Was this the promised land?

Ross Macdonald, *The Underground Man*

ONE:

The Reichenbach Falls Caper

*An examination by experts leaves little doubt
that a personal contest between the two men
ended, as it could hardly fail to end in such a
situation, in their reeling over, locked in each
other's arms.*

from "The Final Problem"
by Sir Arthur Conan Doyle

I

The detective story in fiction had its birth in April 1841, when Edgar Allan Poe's "The Murders in the Rue Morgue" appeared in *Graham's Magazine*. Poe's detective was C. Auguste Dupin. He was French, lived in Paris, and preferred the night hours. He solved nearly all his "problems," as he called them, through ratiocination, which did not require him to leave the shuttered rooms he shared with the anonymous narrator of his exploits. In all, Poe published only three Dupin stories. "The Mystery of Marie Rogêt" appeared first in November 1842. It embodied Poe's attempt, using Dupin, to explicate the actual circumstances of a contemporary murder based on newspaper accounts; Poe and the official investigators did not agree. The third, titled "The Purloined Letter," is considered by critics to be his best. It was published in 1845.

The detective film began with Sherlock Holmes, that most famous and popular sleuth created by Sir Arthur Conan Doyle. The picture was titled *Sherlock Holmes Baffled* (Biograph, 1900). It opens to a burglar robbing the silverware. A man enters the room smoking a cigar, obviously Holmes. He espies the burglar. Through trick photography, the burglar vanishes. The cigar explodes and

Nigel Bruce as Dr. Watson. Basil Rathbone as Sherlock Holmes.
PHOTO COURTESY OF UNITED FILMS.

the burglar reappears. Holmes shoots at him and, once again, the burglar vanishes. When he next reappears, Holmes grabs the loot.

That's how it began. The cameraman was Arthur Marvin. The film was forty-nine feet in duration.

Conan Doyle was born May 22, 1859, in Edinburgh, Scotland. He studied at Jesuit schools, including a year in Austria, before he was accepted at the University of Edinburgh. After earning his bachelor's degree in 1881 but before receiving his medical doctorate in 1885, to earn extra money Conan Doyle spent seven months on a whaler in the arctic as a ship's doctor and, later, four months as a medical officer on a steamer going to Africa. In 1882, after a brief and unsuccessful medical partnership, Conan Doyle opened his own medical practice in Southsea, Portsmouth.

Conan Doyle began his writing career with historical fiction. Having read Poe's tales of detection and the early detective novels of French author Émile Gaboriau, he decided to try a detective story of his own, producing *A Story in Scarlet* in 1887. The book made him little money initially. He followed in 1890 with *The Sign of the Four* and then two dozen short stories which ran in *The Strand* magazine. His detective Sherlock Holmes won a large following almost immediately. Conan Doyle was rather nettled by this sudden popularity accorded to his detective fiction while his other works languished. In 1894, in a story he called "The Final Problem," Conan Doyle hoped to put an end to Holmes's career by telling of how, having captured the archcriminal Professor Moriarty, the two of them engaged in fatal combat and plunged to their deaths from a high precipice overlooking the Reichenbach Falls, near Meiringen, Switzerland.

The public furor, in retrospect, seems almost comic. Avid followers of the Holmes saga were unwilling to permit the detective to be treated in this fashion. Readers, editors, and publishers kept after Conan Doyle to write a sequel in which Holmes would be found safe and alive. Conan Doyle was reluctant to do this.

When Biograph made *Sherlock Holmes Baffled*, Holmes was still officially dead. I am sure this abbreviated film appearance did nothing to influence Conan Doyle to change his mind. But in 1902 he did publish a novel, *The Hound of the Baskervilles*, an adventure which had supposedly occurred early in Holmes's career. In *The Sign of the Four*, Conan Doyle had married Watson off to Mary Morstan, whom Holmes's able detective work saves from jeopardy. When Conan Doyle came to write the short stories preceding "The Final Problem," he had then to deal with Watson's marriage. He didn't know quite what to do, so he kept sending Mary Watson off on holidays or vacations, giving Watson an opportunity to return to the lodgings at 221B Baker Street, which he had once shared with Holmes. In *The Hound of the Baskervilles*, by recording an early adventure he could show Holmes alive without actually resurrecting him, and he didn't have to bother about Watson's wife, since the story took place chronologically before Watson's marriage.

Maurice Costello was cast in the role of Holmes in the film *The Adventures of Sherlock Holmes* (Vitagraph, 1903). It was more substantial than *Sherlock Holmes Baffled*, running 725 feet to the earlier film's 49.

The public wasn't to be put off. Conan Doyle in his characterization of this scientific detective, a man of strange, eccentric habits, of terrific mental acumen, but drawn sympathetically with many human failings, had an ever-widening appeal. By narrating the stories from the point of view of Dr. John Watson, unquestionably Holmes's closest friend, this touching, masculine friendship gave the stories an unusual luster that had been lacking in detective fiction prior to Holmes's appearance; through this, combined with the claustrophobic weather of London, the intriguing nature of ˉthe problems brought to Holmes for elucidation, and the solid comfort of Victorian England near the turn of the century, Conan Doyle had created a world so vivid and enticing that most readers seemed to prefer it to the real world in which they lived. The profound desire to believe that Holmes and Watson were actual persons has become so powerful over the years that societies such as the Baker Street Irregulars have been founded to do little else than meet, discuss and dissect the stories, and publish articles "proving" in what year Watson married and in what year Holmes retired to raise bees (for that's what eventually happened). Conan Doyle weakened enough to publish another collection of short stories in 1904, titled *The Return of Sherlock Holmes*, in which he recounted how Holmes had almost miraculously escaped injury in his plunge with Professor Moriarty and, after a time poking around in obscure parts of the world, he returned to the security of his abode on Baker Street. Watson became even a more inattentive husband and, until 1927, when the last story collection was published, he went on to share nearly all of Holmes's more interesting adventures with him.

Sherlock Holmes is probably the most international among cinema detectives. Whereas nearly every other fictional detective has had his exploits told exclusively by Hollywood, or possibly has been shared between American and British film companies, Holmes pictures were made throughout Europe while Conan Doyle was still alive, and seemed to attract their own following in a wide number of non-English-speaking countries.

Michael Pointer, in *The Public Life of Sherlock Holmes* (Drake, 1975), has recorded all of Holmes's appearances via the five entertainment media of stage, screen, radio, television, and phonograph recordings. It is an impressive listing. Yet Conan Doyle, especially after he was in the grips of his probings into spiritualism, that happy lunacy of his middle and old age, seemed indifferent, to put it charitably, to the expanding interest in Holmes. In none of the many biographies published about Conan Doyle is there any mention that he was even aware of the innumerable film exploits of his detective, beyond pocketing the royalties.

Perhaps the most important early Holmes films were those made in Denmark starring Viggo Larsen. Born on August 14, 1880, Larsen entered the military at fourteen and was sent to the Belgian Congo. When he saw an advertisement for the Nordisk Film Kompagni, he applied and so became one of the first actors and directors employed by the firm. After working in short films portraying Sherlock Holmes at Nordisk, he immigrated to Germany in 1910 and stayed there until 1945, appearing in some two hundred pictures. He died on January 6, 1957. Larsen continued in the role of Holmes for several German-made productions.

In Great Britain, in the Teens, Georges Treville starred in a series of twelve Sherlock Holmes films which were also released in the United States. This series was nowhere as significant, nor as financially lucrative, as the subsequent series produced by Stoll Picture Productions, Ltd., beginning in 1921. The Stoll pictures featured Eille Norwood as Holmes, probably Holmes's most effective impersonator during the silent era. Hubert Willis played Dr. Watson. Many of these Stoll productions survive at the British Film Institute. They slavishly reproduce the short stories on which they are based, and make no effort to adapt the fictions to the screen. In *The Man with the Twisted Lip* (Stoll, 1921), William J. Elliott is credited with the screenplay. It is done with contemporary London settings—as of 1921—with establishing shots of the beggar through the arch of Barclay's Bank on Regent Street at Piccadilly Circus. *The Beryl Coronet* (Stoll, 1921), with the same principals, narrates most of the story through a reconstruction handled by flashbacks. *The Dying Detective* (Stoll, 1921) has this same flashback formula. These are all short films, but they were very popular with British and American audiences alike.

The Hound of the Baskervilles (Stoll, 1921) was Eille Norwood's first full-

Viggo Larsen playing Sherlock Holmes after he immigrated to Germany. His characterization made Holmes appear more a Prussian aristocrat than a British sleuth.

PHOTO COURTESY OF THE DANSKE FILMMUSEUM.

length feature. While the picture opens on the moors, it soon moves to Holmes in London. The hound is presented through a flashback, using special effects as Allen Jeayes, playing Dr. Mortimer, narrates to Holmes the Baskerville legend. In contrast to the 1939 version with Basil Rathbone demanding at the fade, "The needle, Watson," Norwood concludes by asking for a whiskey and soda.

The Sign of the Four (Stoll, 1923) cast Arthur Cullin as Dr. Watson, replacing Hubert Willis. The whole thing retained the modern format of the shorter films with cars and lorries. The heavy reliance on flashback typical of this series did not let up any when Isobel Elsom as Mary Morstan tells Holmes, by this means, about her father's mysterious death and his previous life in prison. By the last reel, Eille Norwood and a Scotland Yard man are in a speedboat chasing the man with a peg leg and his dwarfish assistant. At the end, the camera does a close-up of the announcement of Watson's marriage to Mary.

Between the release of the first Norwood feature and the second the best Holmes film of the silent era, I think, was made by an American company, *Sherlock Holmes* (Goldwyn, 1922), directed by Albert Parker. John Barrymore starred as Holmes, with Roland Young as Watson. Gustav von Seyffertitz played Professor Moriarty.

However, other than the many Holmes films, very few silent detective films were produced. Detectives did appear in chapter plays and occasionally in fea-

John Barrymore on location overlooking the Thames while filming *Sherlock Holmes* (Goldwyn, 1922).   PHOTO COURTESY OF VIEWS & REVIEWS MAGAZINE.

tures, but their roles were generally comic. When Buster Keaton came to spoof a detective in *Sherlock, Jr.* (Metro-Goldwyn, 1924), Holmes was the only one he *could* parody; even Charlie Chan's appearance was in a serial, and he was scarcely the central character. It took S. S. Van Dine's talkative Philo Vance stories with their drawing-room settings to provide Hollywood with an acceptable alternative to the more physical and dramatic Sherlock Holmes, and, simultaneously, offer a format in which the emphasis was clearly on what the various characters had to say. There was one exception to this: Howard Hawks's silent version of *Trent's Last Case* (Fox, 1929).

Imitators of Conan Doyle, like R. Austin Freeman's scientific detective Dr. Thorndyke, retained as much as they could of Conan Doyle's formula. E. C. Bentley, who published *Trent's Last Case* in 1913, cut his own course. His detective was a bumbler. S. S. Van Dine praised Bentley's book in his introduction to the anthology *The Great Detective Stories* in 1927. When, in 1933, Doubleday asked W. Somerset Maugham to edit an anthology entitled *Traveller's Library*, a collection of novels, short stories, poems, and essays, Maugham chose to end the book by reprinting *Trent's Last Case*. Alfred Knopf had reissued the novel in 1930 to cash in on the added publicity afforded by the film. Maugham, in his prefatory note, reviewed what he considered to be the conventions of the detective story and the literary requirements the genre imposed. For all that he said, he could have been paraphrasing S. S. Van Dine's "Twenty Rules" for writing detective fiction, which appeared about the same time. Maugham thought Bentley's novel nearly perfect. Bennett Cerf, after he took over the Modern Library from Horace Liveright, included *Trent's Last Case* in his own collection of murder classics.

With all this going for it, plus a sound remake of the story in 1953 for Republic Pictures, I am somewhat hesitant to confess that I simply do not like the novel *Trent's Last Case*, neither its style, nor its characters, nor above all its plot.

Howard Hawks wasn't exactly pleased with the novel either. In 1928, he had signed a six-picture contract with Fox after directing four pictures on a per-picture basis for Sol Wurtzel, Fox's general manager. He was to be paid $30,000 each for the first three and $40,000 each for the second three. *Trent's Last Case* was Hawks's fourth picture on the contract and, following it, he was fired. As unenthusiastic as he was about the novel, in the film he managed to sustain moments of extraordinary brilliance almost unattainable for anyone else during the silent era confronted with a cinematic detective story.

"A detectve story depends on dialogue," Howard once told me. "It is essential to it. When I was given *Trent's Last Case*, we actually had a scenario for a talkie, but Fox couldn't get rights to make it as a talking picture. I had to shoot it as a silent. It was quite a challenge to tell a story that depended on dialogue while keeping dialogue at a minimum."

Casting had a lot to do with Howard's success with the picture. For the role of the villain, Sigsbee Manderson, Howard chose Donald Crisp, who deserves much of the credit for his villainous portrayal. The viewer has to be convinced that Crisp is singularly vicious and lunatic enough to shoot himself so as to blame his death on his secretary by planting the most incriminating circumstantial evidence. Apparently all those who have held Bentley's novel in such high esteem have had no trouble accepting this rather incredible scheme.

Howard Hawks couldn't. Scott Darling worked on the screenplay. In the novel, Sigsbee Manderson was dead at the beginning of the story. He becomes very much a character in Hawks's photoplay and is seen plotting out and implementing his plan at every step of the way. Petite and charming Marceline Day was cast as clubfoot Crisp's wife. The sophisticated silent comedian Raymond Griffith played the detective Trent and was successfully capable of realizing the inept quality Trent manifested in the novel. Edgar Kennedy was Inspector Murch. At one point, Murch and Trent collide, doing a double pratfall. Raymond Hatton had the part of Crisp's uncle, and it is so construed that, by accident, Hatton interrupts Crisp during his elaborate preparations and, in the resulting struggle, Crisp is shot by accident. Trent comes to the correct solution only when Hatton whispers it in his ear, right in the midst of Trent's attempt to pin the crime on the secretary.

Hawks, aptly, thought the best way to handle this material was in a light comic vein, and that is one reason it comes off so well. He went further, though, and created extremely interesting personality studies with his characters while never permitting the suspense and excitement to flag; the fast pacing true of Hawksian comedies in succeeding decades was already evident.

Hawks's film constitutes an intriguing contrast with the subsequent sound version of *Trent's Last Case*. The remake was originally a British-Lion release, produced and directed by Herbert Wilcox. Anthony Collins, the British conductor known for his interpretations of Jean Sibelius' music, did a stirring musical score. Margaret Lockwood, in her first important role in years, played Manderson's unfortunate wife (why she ever married him, considering how sweetly she is depicted by both Marceline Day and Margaret Lockwood, is never adequately explained in either film). Michael Wilding was Trent, this time a newspaper reporter who rejects the inquest findings of suicide. Orson Welles portrayed the crazed Manderson in flashback. I must admit that Welles brought off the role, in his brief time, as well as Crisp did—which is saying a lot. Pamela Bower's screenplay followed the book and the case opens after Manderson is dead. Yet the film fails, and for precisely the reason you would least suspect: it is too garrulous. Everyone talks and talks. There is no action. Hawks's version moves at all times, even if it is only from suspenseful episode to sheer comedy. The sound remake was a logical extension of the theories of Hollywood producers in the early sound era who felt that patrons would like detective stories because of the constant talking among characters. Even though he recognized there was some truth in this notion, Howard Hawks retains the distinction, uniquely, I believe, of having filmed a uniformly interesting and effective *silent* detective story.

Perhaps one of the reasons Conan Doyle did not take greater interest in the films based on his Sherlock Holmes stories was that he found them no more entertaining than we would today. But, even if true, there was more to it than that. Conan Doyle remained active in countless other areas, besides the various kinds of fiction he preferred writing to detective stories. He engaged in efforts to give men falsely accused, or wrongly imprisoned, an opportunity for a second hearing and, as a consequence, won them acquittals. He was knighted for his active pamphleteering on behalf of the British cause during the Boer War and wrote what is still regarded as the definitive history of that skirmish in the annals of the British Empire.

Conan Doyle was an outstanding figure in his time, and not even his later obsession with the occult diminishes the influence he exerted. I wouldn't say he ever completely reconciled himself to the way in which Sherlock Holmes overshadowed everything else he wrote, but he wasn't wholly displeased by it, either. He died in the presence of his family in 1930, anxious to make what he honestly felt was a voyage into another world from which he could communicate with the living through one or another medium.

II

Just before Conan Doyle's death, Clive Brook, who had made his first film in England in 1921 and was under contract to Paramount in 1929, received a cable. He was aboard the *Olympic* on his way to the States. He was told that *The Return of Sherlock Holmes* (Paramount, 1929) was to be his next film. Basil Dean was the director. H. Reeves Smith played Watson. The photoplay was filmed at Paramount's Astoria studio.

"We had a lot of trouble during the shooting of the film," Brook recalled. "The director's work had hitherto been confined to the theatre, and he had little experience of movies, and how they are made; and he was misguided enough to try to teach the studio personnel their job. He insisted on having four-sided sets constructed, to assist the actors in a feeling of reality, not understanding that cameramen and sound-recordists could not operate in such a set-up. Finally, he left before the picture was completed and I finished directing the film myself. . . . I very much enjoyed Holmes. I characterized him larger than life and this permitted much comedy."

It was an incredible film, to say nothing of it being intolerably, painfully dull. Watson has a flapper daughter who is getting married. Holmes is retired from practice. The dialogue, now that Holmes was given a chance to actually speak on the screen, was much like this:

HOLMES: And the motive wasn't simply robbery, either, Watson.
WATSON: How do you know that?
HOLMES: I deduced it.

Holmes spends two middle reels reconstructing what the viewer has already seen in the first reel. Donald Crisp played Colonel Moran, "the second most dangerous man in England," and Harry T. Morey was an incompetent Professor Moriarty. Moran's first literary appearance had been in Conan Doyle's "The Adventure of the Empty House."

Paramount played up the identification of Clive Brook as Sherlock, but a better series was already starting in England at Twickenham Film Studio. *The Sleeping Cardinal* (Twickenham, 1931) starred Arthur Wontner in the role of Holmes and the actor Ian Fleming (not the James Bond author) as a very polished Dr. Watson. Minnie Rayner was cast as Mrs. Hudson. The plot had Holmes foiling a bank swindle through counterfeit bank notes; at the bottom of it, of course, was Colonel Sebastian Moran played by Louis Goodrich. Wontner looked the part almost as much as Norwood had. His delivery was reserved, his bearing thoughtful, his characterization dignified. Leslie Hiscott directed.

"The studio wasn't much more than a big tin shed, really," Wontner once remarked of Twickenham, "not like film studios today. We used to start filming early in the morning, and continued until pretty late at night, with very few breaks. Of course, we had to stop shooting quite often when a train went by, because of the noise. But we couldn't afford much time for retakes, and there were no elaborate rehearsals or anything like that."

The Sleeping Cardinal was released in the States under the title *Sherlock Holmes's Fatal Hour*. It won the New York Cinema Award as the best mystery drama of the year and just happened to be shown at the same time as William Gillette was touring the country in a farewell engagement of *Sherlock Holmes*, the play written by Conan Doyle and Gillette, which had brought fame to the actor's portrayal of the detective early in the century. In March 1975, when I went to see the play in its Broadway revival, the house was packed, had been for weeks previously, and was sold out weeks in advance. The play, critics say, is so bad that it's good; at least, it's funny to modern audiences.

The Speckled Band (British & Dominion, 1931, for which studio George Sanders later worked) starred Raymond Massey in the Holmes role. Like *The Hound of the Baskervilles* (Gainsborough, 1932), with Robert Rendel as Holmes, the picture hoped to cash in on the new market for detective thrillers and the resurgence of interest in Holmes. Both films were excessively slow-moving.

Twickenham continued production with Arthur Wontner and Ian Fleming in the leads. *The Missing Rembrandt* and *The Sign of the Four* were both released in 1932. RKO Radio in the States bought *The Sign of the Four* for domestic distribution. Rowland V. Lee, the American director who at Paramount was directing Warner Oland in the Dr. Fu Manchu films, was credited as the production supervisor. This, in my opinion, is the finest Wontner/Holmes vehicle. When Sholto is murdered, the effects are appropriately eerie. Holmes wears a modified fedora. His detection sequences are among the very best in any Holmes film. Holmes disguises himself briefly as an old sea captain, and the picture concludes with a thrilling fight.

Back in the States, Clive Brook was drafted again. ". . . Fox asked Paramount for me for a Holmes film and I foolishly thought—Sherlock Holmes, fine! I'll do it—and I didn't have a script, which was unusual for me," Brook commented. "I usually read a first copy of the script to see what I was doing. I got on the set and began reading this thing and I discovered that it was ghastly from my point of view, bringing it up to date with gangsters from America, and Holmes engaged to that girl. . . ." That girl was played by Miriam Jordan. After their marriage, Holmes is going to retire from detecting and start a chicken farm. Bertram Milhauser did the screenplay and William K. Howard directed. Ernest Torrence plays Moriarty, who, once he escapes from jail, imports Chicago mobsters to assist him in his reign of terror.

A Study in Scarlet (WorldWide, 1933) was worse. Edwin L. Marin directed. Reginald Owen plays a very weak Holmes, who helps Alan Mowbray, as Inspector Lestrade, find a murderer preying on members of a secret society because the society is heir to a rich estate. Watch for this plot; it occurs over and over in subsequent films.

The Triumph of Sherlock Holmes (Real Art, 1935) was made in conjunction with a Hercule Poirot production for that year. The picture was supposedly based on the novel *The Valley of Fear*, but Wontner as Holmes and Fleming as

Arthur Wontner, pictured here in a scene from *Silver Blaze* (Twickenham, 1937), a quieter, more reserved Holmes.   PHOTO COURTESY OF VIEWS & REVIEWS MAGAZINE.

Watson were up against Lyn Harding as Moriarty, as was customary. Where the novel comes in is about four reels into the picture when Holmes is investigating a murder and the murdered man's wife tells of how they met long ago in the United States. It was a better entry for all concerned, Leslie Hiscott directing, than *Silver Blaze* (Twickenham, 1937) turned out to be. Lyn Harding was back as Moriarty, despite the number of times he was definitely killed off, interpolating himself into a murder supposedly perpetrated by a race horse.

III

Gene Markey, a screenwriter and an associate producer, Gregory Ratoff, the actor/director, and Darryl Zanuck, head of production at Twentieth Century-Fox, joined in conversation at a dinner party. As Basil Rathbone later told the story, "Out of the blue Markey said, 'You know, someone ought to film Conan Doyle's classics, *The Adventures of Sherlock Holmes.*' Zanuck . . . immediately agreed but asked who should play Holmes, to which Markey replied, 'Basil Rathbone—who else?' Ratoff agreed enthusiastically but said they would need a Watson to complete the team. Thereupon Markey came up with my old friend Nigel Bruce. Then and there at the table the matter was settled and within a matter of days Nigel Bruce and I were both signed up to create these famous characters on film."

Rathbone was born in Johannesburg, South Africa, on June 13, 1892. He had worked for years on the stage, preferring Shakespearean roles, when he made his sound film debut in *The Last of Mrs. Cheyney* (M-G-M, 1929). Except for playing Philo Vance in 1930, Rathbone had built a substantial reputation as a calculating, coldhearted villain. Off screen, he was infinitely charming, totally wrapped up in his second wife, Ouida Bergère Rathbone, who had formerly been married to film director George Fitzmaurice. She managed Rathbone's career and specialized in giving the most elaborate parties in Hollywood. One example should suffice. A joint guest of honor party was thrown by the Rathbones for pianist Artur Rubinstein and symphony conductor Leopold Stokowski at their Beverly Hills home. The dining area to seat fifty-four extended for the occasion out into the garden. On the mirrored surface of the largest table was a Lucite grand piano and a couple of Lucite violins. From the piano stemmed lilies of the valley and forget-me-nots. Scattered above were dubonnet flowers. Place cards were one continuous scroll of silvery-gray material inscribed with the names in dubonnet lettering. Between the names ran the score of one of Chopin's polonaises, also in dubonnet. A vast dubonnet rug covered the entire floor. Silver lamé flashed from the walls. Just below the ceiling ran a three-foot frieze of cellophane scored with black notes. Over the fireplace was a banner of red cellophane declaring "The world of Music knows no boundaries."

Rathbone spent his money as quickly as he earned it on this sort of thing. He preferred the company of musicians, poets, and painters. In his autobiography, *In and Out of Character* (Doubleday, 1962), long out of print and now avidly sought by collectors, Rathbone remarks, "Had I made but the one Holmes picture, my first, *The Hound of the Baskervilles* [20th-Fox, 1939], I should probably not be as well known as I am today. But within myself, as an artist, I should have been well content." Rathbone died of a heart attack in New York at the age of seventy-five. He was anything but happy about the course his career had followed and, far more than Conan Doyle, was bitter about the response Sherlock Holmes had brought forth from audiences. He felt that the identification with Holmes led to the circumstance that the public completely overlooked his gifts as an actor and dwarfed his reputation as a performer.

Since Nigel Bruce's parents were traveling at the time he was born, his birthplace is given as either Ensenada, Mexico, or San Diego, California, or somewhere in between, like Tijuana. The date was February 4, 1895. His parents returned to the British Isles, and, after schooling, he started on the British stage working in plays like *Bulldog Drummond* with Sir Gerald du Maurier. Bruce was known to his friends as Willy. His film debut was in *Coming-Out Party* (Fox, 1934) and in his very next picture he played a detective.

The 1939 *Hound* was superior to all that went before it, and most that came after it. Irving Cummings was originally set to direct it, but he was replaced by Sidney Lanfield. Casting was very effective, with Richard Greene as the Basker-

Basil Rathbone joking with Charles Chaplin during one of Rathbone's memorable Beverly Hills parties. PHOTO COURTESY OF VIEWS & REVIEWS MAGAZINE.

Rathbone and Bruce in period costume, the way Holmes ideally should be treated, in
The Hound of the Baskervilles (20th-Fox, 1939).

PHOTO COURTESY OF TWENTIETH CENTURY-FOX FILM CORPORATION.

Rathbone with his forward hair style as an updated Sherlock Holmes being menaced by George Zucco and Henry Daniell in *Sherlock Holmes in Washington* (Universal, 1943).   PHOTO COURTESY OF UNITED FILMS.

ville heir and Lionel Atwill as Dr. Mortimer. Baskerville Hall was constructed in its entirety on a Fox sound stage and left standing once the film was completed. The staginess, oddly enough, only increased the sense of terror, and the presentation of the vicious hound was more horrifying than it was certainly in the silent version for Stoll, or in the later version for Hammer Films.

As fine as it was, I do not believe that *Hound* is the equal of *The Adventures of Sherlock Holmes* (20th-Fox, 1939), which came next. Like *Hound*, *Adventures* is set in period. George Zucco is intensely menacing as Professor Moriarty and, if only I say so, I think the best Moriarty of the whole lot. Ida Lupino gave a convincing performance as the heroine, threatened by a clubfooted gaucho as part of a decoy plot to keep Holmes off the scent of Moriarty's real scheme, theft of the crown jewels from the Tower of London.

These were both major productions. MCA, the talent agency representing Rathbone, put together a package for Universal Pictures coupled with the weekly radio series. Universal announced in the trades in March 1942 that it had just concluded a deal with Denis P. S. Conan Doyle, son of the author, purchasing screen rights to twenty-one of the Holmes stories. The deal called for three pictures to be made a year, with year-to-year options for seven years.

Holmes was updated for this series and suffered greatly for it. In *Sherlock Holmes and the Voice of Terror* (Universal, 1942) Holmes wore his hair swept forward to his face. Rathbone's portrayal was as poised as ever, but the screenwriters at Universal increasingly wrote Nigel Bruce's Watson character as a buffoon and comic sidekick. The plot found Holmes battling to save England from a Nazi invasion. Lionel Atwill portrayed Professor Moriarty in *Sherlock Holmes and the Secret Weapon* (Universal, 1942), which, like the previous film, was preoccupied with patriotic dialogue and Moriarty only too ready to sell the coveted invention of a scientist to the Nazis. John Rawlins directed the first entry. Roy William Neill directed the second and from then on was retained as the director of the remaining Universal films.

The entries for 1943 began with *Sherlock Holmes in Washington*, in which Holmes comes to the States to oppose George Zucco's attempt to get a secret microfilm. *Sherlock Holmes Faces Death* had a more traditional setting in an old mansion turned into a rest home for wounded soldiers. Hillary Brooke, who had been in *Voice of Terror*, had a stronger role in this entry. I visited Hillary at her home down the coast from Los Angeles where she lives in retirement with her husband, Ray Klune, formerly an executive with Twentieth Century-Fox,

Mary Gordon seemed born to play Holmes's housekeeper, Mrs. Hudson. She followed the Rathbone/Bruce series to Universal.   PHOTO COURTESY OF UNITED FILMS.

who had begun in the business as D. W. Griffith's secretary. Hillary didn't look much different than she had when she played Charles Farrell's girl friend in the "My Little Margie" television series. She was at work on a cookbook as a church project.

"Basil and Willy knew each other off the set," she said. "They were very good friends and it came across on the screen. Basil loved ice cream cones and he would frequently go to the Universal back lot to look at the animals they kept there when he had a free moment. Basil and Willy made up a lot of scenes as they went along, although our director, Roy Neill, knew the scripts and knew both what he wanted and how he could get it on the budget he had. Every afternoon while we were shooting we would stop for tea at four o'clock. It was all very English."

The 1944 season began with *Spider Woman*, starring Gale Sondergaard as the master villain, using a rare spider to induce suicide in men naming Sondergaard as their insurance beneficiary. *The Scarlet Claw* was probably the second-best entry in the series, with an ingenious murderer and an extremely effective group of night scenes, at the river and, above all, the murder of Miles Mander. *The Pearl of Death* rounded out the year. Howard Benedict left as the executive producer on the series after *The Scarlet Claw*, and now Neill became the producer as well as the director. In *Pearl*, Miles Mander plays an expert jewel thief who has Rondo Hatton, a deformed and grotesque giant, commit his murders for him. Mary Gordon, who had first played Mrs. Hudson at Fox, was retained in this role throughout the Universal series. Dennis Hoey was a regular as the somewhat unimaginative Inspector Lestrade.

The House of Fear was the first entry in 1945. Holmes is called in to prevent the continuing murders of members of a private club known as The Good Comrades. He exposes the plot by the end. None of the men are dead: it was an insurance swindle. In *The Woman in Green*, Henry Daniell was cast as Professor Moriarty, Hillary Brooke as his assistant. He has an intricate blackmail racket going. At one point, Hillary has to hypnotize Holmes with Moriarty looking on. Both she and Basil broke out into laughter while this improbable sequence was being filmed. *Pursuit to Algiers* was the slowest film in the series, with virtually all the action taking place on board a ship, Holmes acting as bodyguard to the heir to the throne of Rovenia. Morton Lowry, who had played Stapleton in *Hound*, was here cast as the heir.

Terror by Night was the first entry for 1946 and in many ways the finest of all twelve. It is set completely on a train with Alan Mowbray in the cast, supposedly Watson's old military friend from India, but in actual fact the notorious Colonel Sebastian Moran. *Dressed to Kill* (Universal, 1946) was last. Patricia Morison was cast as an enterprising female villain who very nearly manages to kill Holmes.

Patricia, who is also a painter, was touring the country in a Noel Coward review when I first talked to her.

"Basil told the most marvelous jokes on the set," she said. "He was a very warm man, but, you know, he was also very high strung, jittery. He could never relax."

Attractive Patricia Morison, here being comforted by Nigel Bruce, turned out a dangerous adversary in *Dressed to Kill* (Universal, 1946).

PHOTO COURTESY OF UNITED FILMS.

As might only be expected, Rathbone's Holmes incorporated these same qualities, as opposed to the more placid approach of Arthur Wontner.

Darryl Zanuck, when he was released from the service, set about to wrench control of Twentieth Century-Fox from Bill Goetz. Louis B. Mayer assisted Goetz in founding International Pictures, which merged with Universal in 1946. With Goetz in charge of production, it was announced that Universal would no longer be making "B" pictures, Westerns, or serials. The Holmes series was canceled. Roy William Neill, who had four years to go on his seven-year contract,

The four principals of *The Seven Percent Solution* (Universal, 1976): Alan Arkin as Freud, Nicol Williamson as Holmes, Robert Duvall as Watson, and Vanessa Redgrave.   PHOTO COURTESY OF UNIVERSAL PICTURES.

settled with the studio and went on vacation to England, where he died of a heart attack. Rathbone was happy about this situation and went East to return to stage work. He refused a seven-year contract to continue the Sherlock Holmes radio programs. It became a point of contention between him and Nigel Bruce from then on. Rathbone, at his death, left an estate of less than $20,000. He might have made more had he continued in the role, but that wasn't what he wanted and he was probably happier for it.

Little if any distinction attaches to subsequent Holmes films before *The Seven Percent Solution* (Universal, 1976). *The Hound of the Baskervilles* (Hammer 1959) was a British entry, with Peter Cushing as Holmes and André Morell as Watson. Its only attribute worth mentioning was that it was made in color. The hound was laughably tame.

When I asked Billy Wilder what, in retrospect, he thought of his *The Private Life of Sherlock Holmes* (United Artists, 1970) with Robert Stephens as Holmes and Colin Blakely as Watson (the film implies that Holmes may be the victim of sexual perversion), Wilder looked at me sharply, snapping, "Can't we change the subject?"

A Universal executive invited me to a prerelease screening of *The Seven Percent Solution* while I was in New York. I found the picture excellent and could have predicted its favorable reception. Herbert Ross was the director. His use of a flash forward device to prepare the viewer for Freud's later dramatic revelation of Holmes's complex is effectively executed. Nicol Williamson makes a remarkably capable Holmes, Robert Duvall an admirable and *believable* Watson, and Alan Arkin a splendid Sigmund Freud. The plot of *Solution* is camp, but it is better realized in the film than it is in the book. It is encouraging, I think, after the abortive *Hound of the Baskervilles* that Universal made for television with Michael Rennie as Holmes, that the company could turn around and make such an effective *theatrical* film.

TWO:
The Philo Vance Murder Case

The world, of course, knows the external facts. For over a month the press of two continents was filled with accounts of this appalling tragedy; and even the bare outline was sufficient to gratify the public's craving for the abnormal and the spectacular. But the inside story of the catastrophe surpassed even the wildest flights of public fancy. . . .

from The Greene Murder Case
by S. S. Van Dine

I

Few people remember Philo Vance today, neither the popular novels nor the motion pictures based on them. This is sad. No other personality of whom I will write had so bright a moment as a detective story writer, eclipsing so suddenly and completely, as did S. S. Van Dine. He was a most interesting man.

Van Dine was born Willard Huntington Wright in Charlottesville, Virginia, on October 15, 1888. The younger of two sons, he came from a good family. He was educated at Pomona College in California, and elsewhere. During the first semester of 1906–7, he was accepted as a special student at Harvard. Willard was intolerant of professors. He took to selective studies, psychology under Münsterberg and English under Copeland. He was expelled from Harvard for attending classes with a small glass of absinthe perched on his student chair to assist the lectures down his throat.

Stanton MacDonald-Wright, Willard's older brother, together with Morgan

S. S. Van Dine with the inevitable Régie cigarette in his Park Avenue apartment beneath his brother's painting *New China*.

PHOTO COURTESY OF STANTON MACDONALD-WRIGHT.

Russell, became the co-founder of the Synchronism art movement in Paris before the Great War and remains, quite probably, the most important Post-impressionist painter in the United States. Willard and Stanton, when children, would lie awake mornings and describe the monsters which their youthful imaginations conjured before their eyes; frequently the imaginings were identical. Willard was very dependent on his mother, Annie Van Vranken Wright, and she always protected him. She was rather conventional and, later, when he was engaged in hackwork, he ambivalently used her maiden name as a pseudonym, writing as Frederick Van Vranken.

Willard wanted to be a poet as Stanton wanted to be a painter. Curiously, Willard had little facility for languages, a weakness which so nettled him that later, in the Philo Vance stories, he invariably introduced foreign words and phrases to give the impression that he was far more versed in European languages than he was. When it came to making a living, Willard compromised. He did what he felt, ideally, poets shouldn't have to do: he became a journalist. After leaving Harvard, Willard got a job on the Los Angeles *Times* in 1907 as a cub reporter and assistant literary critic. By 1910, he was writing under his own byline and was considered a literary authority of considerable merit. Willard's father had been a railroad contractor and owned many hotels and depots across the country, and Willard watched over his father's real estate holdings while in California. He was compelled to leave work early one day in 1910 with the onset of a sudden migraine headache just minutes before the *Times* building was dynamited as a terrorist act in a labor union struggle. Many were killed. It was the first time that Willard's fitful nervous disposition would bring truly good fortune into his life. It would again. But in the end it killed him. He died at fifty-one of coronary thrombosis on April 11, 1939.

Willard was a man who very much longed for success but who lacked the trained discipline of the scholar. He wanted fame, wealth, and his mental acumen applauded. While still a literary critic for the *Times*, he reviewed a book on the German philosopher Nietzsche by H. L. Mencken. Mencken thanked him and a correspondence sprang up. It was through Mencken's efforts that Willard was contracted to succeed Percival Pollard as editor of the magazine *Town Topics*. By October 1912, Willard came East. Besides his editorship at *Town Topics*, Mencken also secured him a position as a subeditor of the *Smart Set*. John Adams Thayer, who started in the magazine business with the Munsey publications, purchased the *Smart Set* for a dear price with the hopes of creating a journal of letters that would appeal to a more sophisticated audience. It wasn't very long before Willard's cleverness overwhelmed him to the point where Thayer agreed to give him the *Smart Set* editorship for a year and guaranteed him carte blanche freedom as to contents. H. L. Mencken was the *Smart Set*'s book reviewer, George Jean Nathan the drama critic.

Willard talked Thayer into financing a trip to Europe for himself and Nathan. The two were to join with Mencken in writing a series of essays for a book to be titled *Europe After 8:15*. Mencken, who had already been to Europe, was to contribute his share from American shores. Willard had Stanton, who was living in Paris, show them around to the better bawdy houses. Within six months, Willard had totally altered the tone of the *Smart Set*. But the book on Europe, published by John Lane Company in the summer of 1914, proved a bust confronted by the outbreak of hostilities. Thayer began to get cold feet when he was ostracized by long-time acquaintances and hard-won advertisers canceled their contracts. Willard was released before his editorship was scheduled to terminate, receiving a cash settlement after much haggling.

Willard and Stanton again became close. Stanton possessed much the same vituperative wit and audacious mixture of obscenity and erudition which made Willard such an iconoclastic editor. Willard plunged into a series of articles for *The Forum* and other publications on the futuristic tendencies in painting. He tried composing pieces for the piano in imitation of Debussy. He became addicted to opium. In England, with Stanton, he sealed himself in a hotel room in hope of overcoming the habit. He failed. But he wrote his first novel, *The Man of Promise*, which John Lane published in 1916. H. L. Mencken in *The Forum* lauded the book. It did not sell. Nor did it later, after Willard's fame as S. S. Van Dine.

Willard published *The Creative Will: Studies in the Philosophy and the Syntax of Aesthetics* the same year. It was praised. This followed his earlier book in 1915, *Modern Painting, Its Tendency and Meaning*. Stanton returned to the United States and lived with Willard in New York, assisting Willard in researching these books. Willard laughed at him and, sometimes, refused to feed him. Alas, for both of them, aesthetics proved to be no science in the sense of the Idealist philosophers, and no one much cared, one way or the other.

Willard was appointed editor of the literary page for the New York *Evening Mail* in 1917. Boni and Liveright commissioned him to edit *The Great Modern French Stories* for Modern Library. In 1937, Willard again would edit a book for Modern Library, *The Philosophy of Nietzsche*. The German philosopher had a considerable impact on him. Willard had married Katharine Boynton when he was eighteen, and she had accompanied him to California when he went to work for the *Times*. He left her behind in Glendale at the time he came East to edit the *Smart Set*. Willard believed Nietzsche's philosophy that when a man goes to a woman he must go armed with a whip. His life style in New York brought him into contact with a number of high society flappers who took an interest in him; he was not above forcing them to stand in a corner for several hours if their talk irritated him. Yet, at this point, women did more to support Willard than his writing did.

Willard published a series of articles, more an exposé, of the eleventh edition of the Encyclopaedia Britannica in *Reeder's Magazine*, later appearing as the book *Misinforming a Nation* (Huebsch, 1917). Then the blow fell. War hysteria was at fever pitch. The witch-hunting phenomenon so prevalent after the Second World War was also present during the war years of 1917–19. When Willard learned that his pro-German sympathies had made him a suspicious character, his zany sense of humor prompted him to dictate a wholly fictitious letter to the Washington correspondent of the *Evening Mail* concerning projected sabotage for "our glorious Kaiser." Willard's secretary had been instructed by the Creel Press Bureau, which acted as a federal intelligence agency, to carbon copy all his letters. He surprised the girl doing it and actually chased her out of the building into the street, cornering her in a drugstore. The incident received maximum publicity and both Willard and the *Mail*'s Washington correspondent lost their jobs. Mencken and Nathan blamed Willard as the cause for their friend with the paper in Washington losing his position, and would have nothing further to do with him. Willard was effectively ostracized from most newspapers and periodicals.

Willard had no choice but to return to California. He was forced to write movie reviews for *Photoplay* and other magazines under various pen names. He even descended to copy-desk work with long hours and low pay. Nervous fits returned and he relied increasingly on sedation and opium to quiet his agitated condition. Finally, in 1923, his health broke completely. He was a hopeless addict. He was sent to Paris by his mother to take a cure at a French clinic. He was kept in solitary confinement for six months, during which time he could read nothing more taxing than detective novels and stories. He devoured them by the thousands, and despair gave way to the desire to write.

When he recovered, Willard assessed himself and his desperate financial condition. "My books," he later recalled, "had never brought me a sufficient income to live on. And all my literary life I had been compelled to eke out my royalties with magazine articles, stories, editorial work, translations, teaching, etc.,—the sort of things that tear an author's heart out of him and keep his nose to the grindstone day and night. The war had cut into my earnings deeply; my ebbing strength during 1921 and 1922 had curtailed my output; and the kind of books I wrote had little sale during the aftermath of the great world struggle. My collapse in 1923 had practically cut off all my income, and when, two and a half years later, I began to struggle back to life, with little more than skin, bones, viscera as my physical capital, my skies were black with discouragement. . . . 'Why,' I asked myself, 'if other writers, with far less experience and training than I have had, can achieve success at this kind of fiction, can't I? I've studied the detective novel, and I understand its rules and techniques. I know its needs, and have learned its pitfalls.' "

Willard already had written three ten-thousand-word synopses of as many books—a method of working he would maintain throughout all of his novels—when he visited Maxwell E. Perkins of Charles Scribner's Sons. Perkins was an ingenious editor. He recognized and promoted literary talent where he found it, and often, as in the case of Thomas Wolfe, he literally wrenched it free of excessive verbosity, whereas another, less talented editor would have fallen back on a rejection slip. Perkins brought F. Scott Fitzgerald to prominence and very early perceived a remarkable quality in Ernest Hemingway and is probably to be thanked for much of Hemingway's finest work, which frequently his prodding alone saw through to completion.

"The books are just what we want . . ." he told Willard. "We'll take all three."

Willard chose S. S. Van Dine as his pen name. Years later, his mother asked him about his *nom de guerre*, as he termed it. "Because," Willard responded, "the steam ship initials summarized my desire to travel and I hoped that *dine* would at last turn into a verb. I had lived so many years without having had it in my vocabulary at all."

The Benson Murder Case (Scribner's, 1926) came first. The first edition was sold out the first week. *The "Canary" Murder Case* (Scribner's, 1927) was serialized in *Scribner's Magazine* and broke all publishing records for detective fiction, including those of Sir Arthur Conan Doyle at the time. From then on, it was an uninterrupted ascent to wealth and acclaim. In 1927, under the name Willard Huntington Wright, Van Dine edited *The World's Great Detective Stories: A Chronological Anthology*. He wrote a lengthy introduction to it which became his own credo. The only collection of short detective fiction that has rivaled Willard's anthology since, I suspect, is Ellery Queen's *101 Years' Entertainment: The Great Detective Stories 1841–1941*. Willard dedicated his anthology to Jacob Munter Lobsenz, his personal physician, who would virtually move in with him during Willard's last years to watch at Willard's wake. Willard championed the intellectual aspects of the genre. "There is no more stimulating activity than that of the mind," he wrote, "and there is no more exciting adventure than that of the intellect." Yet, in view of his own intimate association with the cinema during the Thirties, this very premise rather curiously led Willard to conclude that "the detective story, in fact, is the only type of fiction that cannot be filmed."

As S. S. Van Dine, Willard published his "Twenty Rules for Writing Detective Stories" in *The American Magazine*, which structured his formulas for detective stories. He insisted on working on the dialogue for the Paramount production of *The Canary Murder Case*, the first Philo Vance story brought to the screen, and signed with Warner Brothers to script an original motion picture. He moved from his apartment in a remodeled house to a Park Avenue penthouse, lived plushly, ate lavishly, was seen at the best places, hobnobbed with high society, raised Scottish terriers, got a literary agent to represent him when he least needed an agent, and spent money at a fantastic rate. From 1926 to 1939, his work inspired twenty-seven motion pictures. The magazine serializations, book revenues, and reprints brought in a fortune.

Willard originally sought to keep his identity a secret, but Harry Hansen, literary critic for the New York *World*, ruined his scheme. In his column, Hansen suggested that the author of *The Benson Murder Case* and *The "Canary" Murder Case* was not an inexperienced novice but indeed an illustrious name with a sterling reputation. He proceeded to make a few guesses, mostly of people better known than Willard. The search was on and Scribner's got to take advantage of it. The nation became "detective" conscious. In those days, you could afford such pleasant diversions. Finally, Bruce Gould, a columnist for the New York *Evening Post*, wrote an article conclusively proving Willard to be S. S. Van Dine. "We submit," Gould wrote after having been taken to lunch at the exclusive Pierre's by Willard, "that no writer of cultural subjects, such as Mr. Wright is, could ever make enough money in America to lunch with friends at Pierre's. Therefore we can only conclude that Mr. Wright has become very wealthy at the expense of his close friend, S. S. Van Dine."

Once his identity was revealed, articles appeared about Willard in newspapers and magazines. He was interviewed on any number of subjects, for the press and over the radio. Two Presidents of the United States declared him to be their favorite detective story writer. University bulletins were devoted to analyses of his novels, and they were translated into most foreign languages, including Russian, Croatian, Serbian, and Japanese. The Book-of-the-Month Club recommended *"Canary"* and picked *The Greene Murder Case* as its first alternate. An ice-cream sundae was named after the *"Canary"* and so was a rather potent cocktail. (I was interested enough in the drink to find out its ingredients from Allen J. Hubin, an avid reader of detective fiction and editor of *The Armchair Detective*, an amateur publication of criticism on detective fiction. Allen claimed the recipe was printed in a book entitled *So Red the Nose or Breath in the Afternoon*, whichever you may prefer. It's a good drink if you like Courvoisier or martinis or orange juice. *The "Canary" Murder Case* cocktail consists of ½ jigger dry gin, ½ jigger cognac, ½ jigger yellow vermouth, 1 jigger orange juice, 1 dash of orange bitters, all to be shaken well and served in chilled glasses.)

When Raymond Chandler put together a collection of his short stories in 1944, he dedicated the book to his mentor, Captain Joseph Thompson Shaw, editor of *Black Mask*, "with affection and respect, and in memory of the time we were trying to get murder away from the upper classes, the week-end house party and the vicar's rose garden, and back to the people who are really good at it." The Philo Vance stories are the purest varieties of exactly what Chandler was lampooning, with Agatha Christie running a close second.

Christopher Ward did a parody of Van Dine's technique for *The Saturday Review of Literature* in 1929. In 1930, Corey Ford wrote a book-length parody of the Vance stories which Scribner's published, calling it *The John Riddell Murder Case*. Van Dine was so taken by the book that even he contributed to it. Should this strike the reader as a bizarre happenstance, perhaps it is best accounted for by the fact that Willard's detective novels were themselves little removed from satire. Here is how he opened *The Scarab Murder Case* (Scribner's, 1930).

"Scarlett almost dashed through the portières of the library when Currie had pulled back the sliding door for him to enter. Either the Courvoisier had added to his excitement or else Currie had woefully underrated the man's nervous state.

"'Kyle has been murdered!' the newcomer blurted, leaning against the library table and staring at Vance with gaping eyes.

"'Really, now! That's most distressin'.' Vance held out his cigarette-case. 'Do have one of my *Regies.* . . . And you'll find that chair beside you most comfortable. A Charles chair; I picked it up in London. . . . Beastly mess, people getting murdered, what? But it really can't be helped, don't y'know. The human race is so deuced blood-thirsty.'"

Van Dine once gave Alex King, a New York literary friend, a Scottie to tend while he went to Europe for a month. The dog was trained to squat whenever he heard the name "Alex." Van Dine's Philo Vance stories are filled with the same wild and slightly cruel sense of humor.

Yet for all his success, Willard lived, not dangerously as Nietzsche instructed, but desperately. He chain-smoked his Régie Turkish cigarettes. He substituted cognac for opium and became equally addicted. His pose was that of a product of an exhausted, waning culture, shortly before the deluge. Despair hung on him palpably.

"You have sensed his feelings of utter futility and despair during the last years of his life," Stanton MacDonald-Wright wrote to me after reading an earlier version of this chapter. "Of course, you have known that his death was really a suicide. The last time I saw him—1932, I believe—he could think of nothing but the uselessness of human life, its aspirations and even its accomplishments. He would harangue me for hours on the subject, pointing out the idiocy of what I do . . . the impermanency of everything and the stupidity of conceiving of anything as significant or important. My rejoinder that we had to act *as though* we knew something and accept the results as did Arjuna, he pooh-poohed with bitter irony, accusing me of a bourgeois faith. I would argue with him about his method of self-destruction. . . . He had his butler place a pony of Napoleon brandy at his side every half hour—he was playing for Bright's disease, but the other got him. . . . Need I say he was the perfect example of what the poets have said about the hope that one never achieves in one's age, the desires of one's youth?"

At the very height of his dizzying success, Willard plunged into the deepest depression. "The demand . . . for the fictional avoidance of the facts of life has diminished," he had written in *Smart Set* in 1913. "The reader of today demands truth." His fame and wealth were based on the very principles he abhorred most in America.

Willard married for the second time in 1931, to Claire Rulapaugh. He instructed his first wife, Katharine Boynton, who was still living in California, to divorce him. This she obediently did. Claire didn't get on at all with Stanton when he came to visit; the visits ended.

"Why did you marry Claire?" Stanton asked Willard during that last visit of theirs in 1932. They were sitting in Willard's terrace garden, surrounded by potted palm trees, high above the New York skyline, sipping Napoleon brandy. Willard paused to light a Régie in an ebony holder. He was in a satin dressing gown. Behind them, lights burned in his study with his oval writing desk, his ceiling-high bookcases crammed with volumes, a gaudily decorated fireplace above which hung Stanton's painting titled *New China*. Frank Tuttle, director of the Philo Vance films at Paramount, had purchased another painting from Stanton, its companion, *New Japan*. Willard inhaled deeply. Like Vance, he wore a monocle in his right eye. The scent of fresh flowers in vases everywhere permeated the evening air.

"Because," he replied, "I liked her legs. We were aboard ship and the captain wouldn't stand for carryings-on between the passengers. I asked him to marry us at sea."

As Willard's life ebbed, his books lost their magic, their passion, their luster. He wanted to die. He chose to chart his death scientifically as it daily stole upon him. He had his personal physician, Dr. Jacob Lobsenz, who was very concerned about Willard, move in with him at his apartment to watch the dying process. His demise, as far as he was concerned, was concisely planned, however much it may have shocked other people. It proved fortuitous to him in that it preceded by only a few years the inevitable rejection of the kind of detective fiction Willard had written and the literary milieu he represented. Like so many of his murderers, he gambled on a means to success; and when it came, when he had won all he had hoped for and more, he lost. It wasn't enough. He left behind only $13,000.

"Some day," Willard wrote in 1936, "I shall take a long vacation and rest. Will I make a walking tour through Norway, or live a *dolce-far-niente* life on some South Sea isle? Frankly, I don't know. All I know at present is that I'll go far away from crime, police departments, and circulating libraries, and imitate the lowly vegetable. Then, having bidden farewell to 'Philo Vance' and 'District Attorney Markham' and 'Sergeant Heath' I shall return to my other literary labors. Ah, but when will that be? Again, I frankly confess I do not know. Just now I crave nothing beyond a good *filet de sole marguery*, a bottle of 1904 Amontillado, and one of the later Beethoven sonatas." He never did finish his scholarly books. Rather, he attributed them to Vance as works the amateur sleuth and young social aristocrat had written. He was working on detective stories right up to the day he died.

II

The executives at Paramount in 1929 had mixed feelings about making *The Canary Murder Case* as a silent. On January 24, 1928, Willard had granted Paramount an option on his first Philo Vance novel, *The Benson Murder Case* (Scribner's, 1926) for $17,500 with a provision that, should they exercise the option, they could also purchase screen rights on both the *Canary* and *Greene* murder cases. Paramount acted quickly on all three once *The Bishop Murder Case* (Scribner's, 1929) made the best-seller lists and stayed there for months. *Canary* went into production first.

For the role of Philo Vance, by some unusually sensitive stroke of casting, Paramount chose contract player William Powell, in violent contrast to the curiosity of perceiving Clive Brook as Sherlock Holmes or Warner Oland as Dr. Fu Manchu.

William Powell was born in Pittsburgh in 1892, the son of an accountant. When the family moved to Kansas City, after trying a university education and the telephone company, where he worked as a clerk, he enrolled at the American Academy of Dramatic Arts in New York. Powell made his New York debut in 1912 in a play called *Ne'er do Well*. The next year he had a major role in *Within the Law* and went on tour with the show for two years. His first Broadway success was in 1920 in the play *Spanish Love*. He was offered the part of Forman Wells in Samuel Goldwyn's production of *Sherlock Holmes* and readily found that he preferred motion pictures to the legitimate stage. With

Romola (M-G-M, 1925), he started being cast in villainous roles, and that year Paramount Pictures placed him under contract. Powell appeared in the studio's first all-talking picture, *Interference* (Paramount, 1929), in which he murdered Evelyn Brent and which included Clive Brook in the cast. Pleased at how well his voice recorded, Paramount decided in one of those rare and apt moments of inspiration to star Powell as Philo Vance in *The Canary Murder Case* (the movie dropped the quotation marks around the "Canary").

Malcolm St. Clair was the director of *The Canary Murder Case*. The picture went into production as a silent, but was changed at the last minute into a talkie. It seemed an obvious inference that a film with long sequences during which nothing happened other than interviewing suspects was best handled in the new medium. Louise Brooks was cast as the "Canary," a Broadway musical star who is little better than a professional tart, once married (according to the screenplay) to ex-convict Ned Sparks, and systematically blackmailing the society men with whom she has gone to bed. After shooting her part but before recording her lines, Brooks left for Germany to appear in a G. W. Pabst production, *Pandora's Box*, which, among certain film critics, won her enduring acclaim. But it put Paramount in a bind. Margaret Livingston was called upon to dub Brooks's voice. In its final release version, *The Canary Murder Case* was a curious hybrid product, some of it silent with sound intercuts for dialogue, or, in brief scenes, voices dubbed. Willard worked on the dialogue at Paramount's Astoria studio.

The cinematic Philo Vance was nothing like his literary counterpart. The exaggerated British accent, the posturing, the erudition were replaced by Powell's rather clipped, precise movements and mannerisms of speech. Eugene Pallette, cast as Sergeant Heath, took so well to the role that for many moviegoers he became inextricably associated with the part even when other studios sought to recast the role. Director Malcolm St. Clair achieved an exquisite Expressionist poetry as he had the incomparably beautiful Brooks swing out over her theater audience, the camera focusing from the rafters on the distressed countenances of her blackmail victims watching her in lecherous awe from below. (By the end of the Thirties, Hollywood could only offer Louise Brooks the opportunity of fitting her shapely bottom into tight slacks for *Overland Stage Raiders* [Republic, 1938], a Three Mesquiteers Western starring John Wayne, a part which of necessity kept Brooks's backside to the camera more than her face.)

Willard became instant friends with William Powell. Later, when Willard came to Hollywood and Powell was under contract to Warner Brothers, Willard insisted that the actor escort him to all the best bawdy houses. Frank Tuttle, who subsequently directed the next two Paramount Philo Vance entries, also became a cohort of Willard's, gaining a considerable reputation until the House Un-American Activities Committee branded him a subversive after the Second World War and he was confined to work as an art director.

But I fear this all has allowed me to get ahead of myself. *The Benson Murder Case* did not have a critical success commensurate with its commercial popularity. Dashiell Hammett, in his review of the novel for *The Saturday Review of Literature*, complained about the naïveté of Van Dine's plot. But the novel, whatever its technical shortcomings, did promulgate Van Dine's aesthetic and philosophic theories of how a crime, like a work of art, bears the indelible imprint of its creator's personality and temperament. The methodology Philo Vance employs to catch the murderer, eased by Van Dine's caricature of the police and deliberate blunting of their scientific routines, permits the reader to experience an acute sense of pleasure when, suddenly, he perceives a generating line through the miasma of misleading information and conflicting evidence. Willard did not wholly desert his artistic proclivities when he became S. S. Van Dine; instead he wove them adroitly into a finely textured psychological fabric of crime and pursuit. The reader doesn't have to labor beneath the needless complexity of odd clues, nor must he resort to endless fanciful speculations which ratiocination cannot suggest but only confirm after the fact, as was frequently the practice later with Ellery Queen's novels. Rather the crime and its generation are grasped as a unity. Our appreciation is aesthetic in character, and the appeal is more to the sensibility than to deductive mental processes. Van Dine retained this formula through the first nine Philo Vance stories.

One of Van Dine's favorite means of reading personality was a man's relationship to gambling and, specifically, to poker. In *The Benson Murder Case*, in conversation with one of the suspects, Vance examines carefully the attitudes toward gambling true of each of the other suspects. In *The "Canary" Murder Case*, Van Dine took the theory a step farther and permitted Vance to actually engage the leading suspects in a poker game. The film techniques of the time, and the direction of St. Clair, weren't particularly suspenseful when this episode was brought to the screen, but Van Dine saw to it that it was included in the photoplay. In both the novel and the film, the ploy allows the reader to construct a diagram of the murderer's personality and put it to the test.

I will not say much more about the early novels. But if, like myself, the reader should interest himself in them to the extent of reading them, I think he will share with me the regret, when contrasting the books with the films based on them, that one character is sadly absent from the screen that has a viable existence throughout all the books: the city of New York. This is New York during one of its golden eras when it was the hub of American cultural and artistic expression. The ease and polish of life, the contrasts among the upper classes at the time Van Dine wrote, give you as vivid an impression as any you might have of Paris, its society and intellectual sympathies, from the great French journalists of the nineteenth century. The gallery showings, the concerts, the clubs and restaurants, the amusements, games, crafts, interests, and aesthetic passions of New York in the Twenties and Thirties, interlaced as they are with brokerage houses, Broadway shows, horse races, the parks, sights, buildings, reveal a mighty, exhausting tapestry of a city of endless riches and extravagances. That New York is gone, never to return. The fashions, sartorial displays, the tastes in tobacco, wine, and food of that period, the weather, sounds, and personalities of New

William Powell was a moody, serious, polished Philo Vance.

PHOTO COURTESY OF VIEWS & REVIEWS MAGAZINE.

York as Van Dine knew and wrote of them are as distant from us today as Vance's aesthetic ponderings on criminology. It is the same with Conan Doyle's London or Raymond Chandler's Los Angeles. But unfortunately Van Dine did something the others didn't: he shows us only the rich, the well-to-do, the accomplished (or unaccomplished), disengaged wealthy, those for whom life is essentially meaningless and whom we see only in terms of what they possess, their hobbies and enthusiasms. In this marvelous feeling for a great city you see only the lights of skyscrapers from a penthouse garden and never the people in the streets, the sordid, the lonely, the degenerate, the frustrated, the poor, the corrupt, the criminal.

Van Dine really believed that motive was fallacious as a tool in detection and so presented his cases as to make it irrelevant. In this fashion he further removed crime from any basis in reality, however fanciful had been its treatment by Conan Doyle and R. Austin Freeman in their scientific approaches. Van Dine

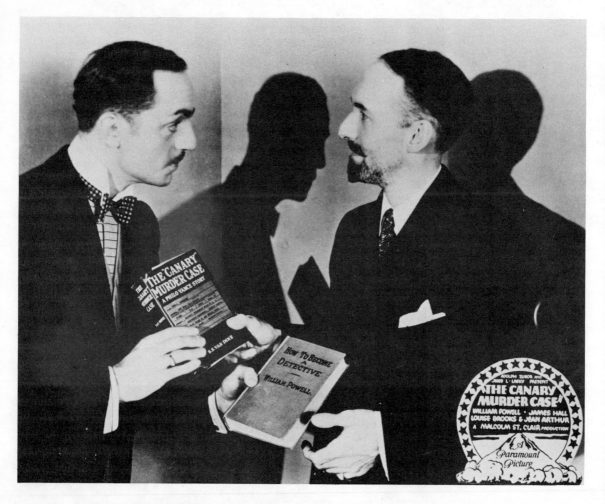

Willard and Bill Powell became friends during the filming of *The Canary Murder Case* (Paramount, 1929).   PHOTO COURTESY OF VIEWS & REVIEWS MAGAZINE.

likened detective stories to puzzles, but he did not write puzzles, rendering instead with *élan* paintings of personality, reducing detection not to clues but to an instinctive sensitivity to temperament. For Van Dine human behavior really was inspired by caprice or perversity.

The Greene Murder Case (Scribner's, 1928) was the third Philo Vance novel, but the second photoplay. Paramount rushed it into production right after *The Canary Murder Case* and it was released the same year. In the novel, Van Dine amused himself with the prospect of murdering a whole book of suspects. Jean Arthur played the little killer in the film version. A replica of the Greene mansion was built on a Paramount sound stage. Frank Tuttle, who directed, managed more effectively than St. Clair to create an atmosphere of suspicion and suspense.

Van Dine was enamored of the Cinderella fable, but with a variation: Cinderella as more evil than her stepsisters. This is the way Van Dine conceived Ada Greene in the novel and this is the way Jean Arthur played her on the screen. The compelling scene that brings the film to its climax is of the angelic Jean Arthur transformed into a fiend. She kicks and hacks at the second-story awning bar onto which Florence Eldridge is clinging for dear life until Vance can rescue her. Through a series of close-ups, Jean Arthur's face assumes a crazed frenzy that makes her perpetration of the murders believable, something not so convincingly portrayed in the novel.

Paramount did a good job on *The Benson Murder Case* (Paramount, 1930), third and last of the three Van Dine novels on which they owned an option. The plot, however, was altered substantially from what it was in the novel, after an almost literal adherence in both the *Canary* and *Greene* cases. Opening with a fine montage of descending values, margin desperation, sellouts, and ruin at the stock exchange, a cast of curious suspects is congregated at the victim's river lodge. Paul Lukas, who would eventually play Philo Vance at Metro, was cast as a gigolo and a check forger.

Probably one of the reasons Paramount didn't expend even more effort on *Benson* was that Van Dine had sold screen rights to his most popular book to date, *The Bishop Murder Case*, to Metro-Goldwyn-Mayer. It was announced in the trades that British character actor Basil Rathbone had been assigned the lead as Philo Vance.

S. S. Van Dine loved to caricature his mother. Crazy, oppressive, stifling, eccentric mothers recur repeatedly in the novels. There's old Mrs. Greene, and the hunchback's old mother in *Bishop*, and later old Mrs. Stamm, old Mrs. Llewellyn in *The Casino Murder Case*, old Mrs. Garden (poisoned with radioactive potassium). I could go on. I wouldn't bring up the subject at all except that directors of the Vance pictures seemed to enjoy these characters best of all and went all out in their treatment of them in the respective photoplays. Nick Grindé directed *The Bishop Murder Case* (M-G-M, 1930). Metro pushed the picture through production so it actually beat *The Benson Murder Case* into theaters by three months. But, regrettably, the Metro cinematic techniques were even more stage-bound, when it came to bringing a detective story to the screen, than were those at Paramount. David Burton was selected to direct the

The incomparably beautiful Louise Brooks in the plumes of the "Canary" confronted by a determined Jean Arthur.   PHOTO COURTESY OF VIEWS & REVIEWS MAGAZINE.

actors and their elocution. Basil Rathbone had as yet only very limited experience before the camera, and this picture did nothing for him. His delivery of dialogue was incredibly, if not purposely, trying. The visual effects were nonetheless quite good and the presentation of the various murders was handled with a flair for the grotesque.

The picture met with praise from critics on its release. Increasingly, motion picture companies were becoming convinced that detective stories were a wise investment. Because of their inherent static interrogatory scenes packed with little action and much dialogue, they proved extremely cheap to manufacture in addition to fully utilizing the novelty of the sound medium.

No one seems to have much liked *The Scarab Murder Case*. Paramount didn't exercise its option on it until mid-decade. The novel's plot relied on the device of the culprit deliberately fabricating such overwhelming evidence in favor of his guilt as to divert all real suspicion. This could only work in Van Dine's abstract and aesthetic fictional realm. In life, had Markham been a truly aggressive district attorney, he would have clapped this obvious suspect in jail and convicted him, innocent or guilty, at a splendid trial.

The innate stupidity and incompetence of the American court system to accomplish anything but a perpetuation of re-elected political figures who are both comfortable and corrupt in their abuse of justice was the farthest thing from Van Dine's world view. Dashiell Hammett had been writing this kind of realistic detective fiction for some years, but his stories were published in pulp magazines and weren't fashionable on Park Avenue.

Van Dine spent two years preparing *The Kennel Murder Case* (Scribner's, 1933). In the first place, he had commented often that a detective story writer had only six good detective stories in him; this was his sixth. Moreover, Willard had been hired and transported to Hollywood by Warner Brothers to script twelve two-reel mystery shorts for their Vitaphone short subject series and to work on an original story for a feature film. Willard left New York in early spring, 1931, and didn't return until late in summer. Paramount had made a Spanish language version of *The Benson Murder Case*, titled *El Cuerpo del Delito*, released in Argentina in June 1930. In *Paramount on Parade* (Paramount, 1930), William Powell and Eugene Pallette appeared in a short skit as Vance and Sergeant Heath. Around this time Warner's staged a raid on Paramount's contract players and directors. The move certainly didn't help Paramount's flagging fortunes. William Powell, who on June 26, 1931, married pert, outspoken Carole Lombard, was among those they signed. Jack Warner set about purchasing screen rights to Van Dine's next two Philo Vance stories even before they were written, in which he intended to star Powell. Despite Metro's lone entry, in the popular mind William Powell was still intimately identified with the role. Van Dine had spent many years in California and was certainly pleased at the prospect of returning. In 1929, Willard had made his final attempt to break the pattern of what his life had become. He had Scribner's reissue his novel *The Man of Promise*. When it failed a second time, he set to editing the S. S. Van Dine detective library in 1930, virtually the finest longer detective stories written to that time, published in a handsome, matched set. In 1931, Blue Ribbon Books reprinted *The World's Great Detective Stories* under the S. S. Van Dine pseudonym, reinforcing in everyone's mind, including Willard's, that as S. S. Van Dine he was internationally renowned, creatively and critically, as the dean of detective story writers, but that as Willard Huntington Wright he was still of little consequence.

The Warner Vitaphone shorts were not Philo Vance vehicles, although Van Dine wrote all the stories. Many of them starred Donald Meek and were directed by Joseph Henabery, who had played Lincoln for D. W. Griffith in *The Birth of a Nation* (Epoch, 1915). Typical of these shorts is *The Campus Mystery*, with Van Dine credited for the story and Burnet Hershey for the adaptation and dialogue. To Hershey the short probably owes the perceptive interchange between John Hamilton as Inspector Carr and Harriet Hilliard as Wanda Terry:

CARR: Everyone's guilty until proven innocent, ma'am.

TERRY: Or influential.

Girl Missing (Warner's, 1933) was directed by Robert Florey and starred Ben Lyon and Glenda Farrell. It was based on Van Dine's original story *The Blue Moon Murder Case*, in which Willard hoped Walter Huston would be given the leading role. The picture was shot in twelve days on a budget of $200,000. Willard disowned it, but he made enough money from the Warner Brothers' transaction to indulge his fancy in breeding Scottish terriers. Van Dine used this as one of his themes in *The Kennel Murder Case*, actually the most complexly plotted of all his books. It ran serially in *Cosmopolitan*. All in all, the really fantastic element of the story is neither the Scottish terriers nor the Chinese porcelain about which Vance prattles endlessly. It is the incredible circumstance of the victim leaving the room in which he was fatally stabbed, entering his bedroom on the second floor, where he expires, only to be murdered when dead by his brother, who had also planned his murder.

When Philo Vance was unable to secure a conviction of the murderer in *The Kennel Murder Case*, Van Dine had him executed by a Doberman Pinscher tearing out his throat. Vance could then calmly proceed to explain the mechanics of the crime. In the Warner's photoplay, this incident was altered so that the murderer was only frightened into confessing. William Powell, naturally, was Philo Vance. Michael Curtiz, fortunately for all concerned, was assigned to direct the film. The Warner Brothers' tendency in detective films from this period to offer a reconstruction of the crime through flashbacks perpetrated one bit of absurdity due to the screenwriter's confusion over Van Dine's plot. Vance was supposed to go into great detail in his reconstruction, even using miniature models of the Coe residence and the adjacent apartment house to demonstrate how the murderer must have seen Archer Coe enter his bedroom from a window in the apartment house. In the novel, Raymond Wrede, the murderer, lives in an apartment in the adjacent building, so the explanation makes sense. In the motion picture, he is living with Archer Coe, his bedroom on the same floor as Coe's, only farther down the hall. Under these circumstances, it would have been unlikely for him to have been in an apartment house across the way observing Coe, nor is any explanation offered for his presence there. Apparently no one at Warner's

Basil Rathbone as Philo Vance in *The Bishop Murder Case* (M-G-M, 1930),
searching Professor Dillard's attic, with Clarence Geldert (left) as District Attorney
Markham and gentle Alec B. Francis (right).

PHOTO COURTESY OF METRO-GOLDWYN-MAYER.

caught the incongruity, and so it stands. The literal unraveling of the crime,
however, is so singularly peculiar that it is trying enough to the imagination
without this, and perhaps it was felt not particularly important.

Earlier that year, Michael Curtiz directed Powell in *Private Detective 62* with
a screenplay by Rian James, based on a story by *Black Mask* author Raoul
Whitfield. Like *Kennel*, it moved swiftly, but the story had more potential for
character development, and it remains a better detective film for Powell than
any of his Philo Vance entries.

Jimmie Fidler, the Hollywood columnist, went drinking with Powell and became the recipient of some rather startling confessions. Powell confided to
Fidler that he was cursed with an inferiority complex; that he was afraid of

strangers; that he was ill-at-ease in the company of women; that he was uncomfortable turning his back when leaving a crowded room; that he was a poor conversationalist and not the least bit witty; and that in real life he was anything but the *bon vivant* he was pictured as on the screen. Fidler published the story in *Photoplay* in October 1932. It didn't make any difference in Powell's estimate of his professional abilities. Warner Brothers had bribed him with $6,000 a week to get him away from Paramount; when the studio went on a Depression economy drive, this was reduced to $4,000 a week. Powell grew very unhappy and insisted on more money.

There are critics who feel *The Kennel Murder Case* to be the cinematic highwater mark in the Philo Vance films. Warner Brothers didn't think so. The pic-

Robert Wade as Markham and Eugene Pallette as Sergeant Heath listen to one of Philo Vance's characteristically long explanations in *The Kennel Murder Case* (Warner's, 1933). Such explanations were William Powell's favorite part about playing detectives.   PHOTO COURTESY OF VIEWS & REVIEWS MAGAZINE.

ture made nowhere near the kind of money that Powell's name as a drawing power was supposed to ensure. It was decided by mutual agreement that William Powell should leave. Jack Warner announced to the trades that the reason was that Powell wanted to free-lance, but in truth Warner just didn't think Powell worth the money he was asking. Powell's agent entered into negotiations with Columbia Pictures, rather smug after their success with *It Happened One Night* (Columbia, 1934) and agreement was reached that Powell would star for them in four pictures. Meanwhile, W. S. Van Dyke was directing *Manhattan Melodrama* (M-G-M, 1934) for Metro, and he contacted Powell to play the governor, who was the best friend of Clark Gable and who places his political responsibilities before personal ties and permits Gable to be executed. Myrna Loy was cast as Powell's wife. Powell and Loy worked so spiritedly together that Van Dyke insisted on putting them right into *The Thin Man* (M-G-M, 1934). Metro had purchased screen rights to Dashiell Hammett's latest (and, as it turned out, last) novel, based on Hammett's fun-loving association with Lillian Hellman (I will have more to say about this in a later chapter). The two M-G-M pictures succeeded in making William Powell a bigger star than ever. Metro wanted him under contract so badly that the studio bought up his Columbia contract and even project rights to a film about Florenz Ziegfeld that was in the planning stages at Universal and for which Powell had signed an option. Powell was immediately teamed with Loy again for *Evelyn Prentice* (M-G-M, 1934). But Powell was crafty. He refused to sign with Metro for more than two or three films at a time. The studio gave him the ultimate in star treatment. A series based on the Hammett characters was planned and, inevitably perhaps, S. S. Van Dine was contracted for his next two novels to be turned into photoplays with Powell in the lead as Philo Vance.

All of which left Warner Brothers holding the bag with rights to *The Dragon Murder Case* (Scribner's, 1933), without William Powell. Hal B. Wallis, in charge of production at the time, selected Warren William, a character actor from the Warner's roster, to enact the part of Vance. He next set about lining up a contract director to do the picture. He asked Michael Curtiz, who turned it down; then Archie Mayo, but no go; then Mervyn LeRoy, but still nothing doing; finally, in desperation, Wallis approached Alfred Green but was rebuffed.

H. Bruce Humberstone (he has refused for years now to tell me what the "H" stands for) had been an assistant director for over ten years. His friends have always called him Lucky Humberstone. The first picture Lucky directed was *Strangers of the Evening* (Tiffany, 1932) for Samuel Bischoff, an independent producer on Poverty Row. It starred Zasu Pitts and Eugene Pallette. In it, Pallette played a police sergeant; unlike his portrayal of Heath in the Philo Vance films, little of the comedy was at his expense. The picture was shot in nine days. Lucky followed it with *The Crooked Circle* (WorldWide, 1932) because Zasu Pitts, who was starring, asked the picture's producer Joe Brandt if Lucky could direct her again. It was supposed to be a mystery-comedy with Ben Lyon, C. Henry Gordon, and James Gleason as a motorcycle cop. Gleason injected so much comedy that the mystery theme receded into the background.

C. Henry Gordon was cast as a swami who was actually a secret service man in disguise. The picture required fourteen days to make.

After a brief stint at Paramount during which time he worked on the George Raft segment of *If I Had a Million* (Paramount, 1932), Warner Brothers signed Humberstone for a two-picture deal. Lucky's first picture for them was *Merry Wives of Reno*, a comedy about divorce starring Margaret Lindsay. Hal Wallis was impressed with what Humberstone could do with a script; he really had a flair for visually interesting cinema with a high comic tone. Wallis summoned Humberstone to his office and gave him the screenplay of *The Dragon Murder Case*. "This is going to be your next picture," he told him confidently.

Humberstone took the script home and read it. He showed up the next day and told Wallis, no. He knew that Curtiz, Mayo, LeRoy, Green, and company had turned down the picture; and, more, he knew why: it was a terrible story. He was just getting started in Hollywood as a director. This kind of a picture at this moment could be disastrous. Again, no. Humberstone vanished from the studio and went on a short vacation. While resting in a hotel, Wallis called him. He said that the writers had gone to work on *The Dragon Murder Case* and had really improved it: Lucky should return to the lot at once. He did.

When he walked into Wallis's office, he was handed the same yellow-covered script he had been given before. "I won't do it," he protested, whereupon Wallis arranged for him to see Jack L. Warner. When he was ushered into Warner's office, Warner eyed the new director skeptically.

"How much are you making?" he asked.

"Seven hundred and fifty dollars a week," Humberstone replied.

"How old are you?" Warner asked.

"Twenty-nine," Humberstone said.

"Do you know how much I was making when I was your age?" Warner asked. "Twenty bucks a week, selling meat." He paused for emphasis. "So, why don't you want to make this picture?"

"Because it's a lousy story," Humberstone responded.

"Listen," said Warner, "I don't care if it *is* a lousy story. You're going to make this picture. Do you think it matters that it's lousy? That picture, with my theater chain, is going to make me fifty thousand dollars, good story or not. So, you're going to make it for me. Or," he paused again for emphasis, "or you're never going to direct another picture in this town."

Humberstone agreed to direct the picture.

Van Dine had dedicated the book to his second wife, Claire, and fancied tropical fish as part of the setting. Rudolph Stamm, at whose estate the series of murders takes place, has a large collection of such fish. In one chapter Vance, Markham, and Heath are guided through the aquarium rooms and are shown many rare and unusual varieties brought back from dark, obscure corners of the globe. In 1934 collecting tropical fish was almost unheard of in California. Humberstone searched far and wide, but no one could be found whose fish tanks and displays might be used as props. Being a stickler for details, Humberstone was resolved that fish had to be included. Then, as luck would have it, he came upon what could only be described as a fish "nut," a fellow working at the

Warren William as Vance, Robert Wade as Markham, Lyle Talbot, and Eugene Pallette as Heath outside the aquarium room in *The Dragon Murder Case* (First National, 1934). PHOTO COURTESY OF VIEWS & REVIEWS MAGAZINE.

Weber Showcase Company, in the San Fernando Valley, who not only collected tropical fish but had one of the most extensive arrays in the country. Humberstone worked out the arrangements for Warner Brothers to borrow the entire collection for use in the picture.

Neither Lucky Humberstone nor Van Dine anticipated the results of *The Dragon Murder Case*'s impact on the public. Such was the popularity of the Philo Vance stories and concurrent photoplay series that a "fish craze" swept the nation. Shops started specializing in tropical fish displays and an entire industry sprang up. Even Lucky became an enthusiastic breeder of fish for many years.

Eugene Pallette had appeared as Sergeant Heath in *The Kennel Murder Case* and returned in the role for *Dragon*. Robert Barrat, cast as Archer Coe in *Kennel*, played Stamm in *Dragon*. And Etienne Girardot, who generally portrayed Dr. Doremus, the Medical Examiner, although he had infinite trouble with his lines and cost dozens of retakes, was more or less retained throughout the series as it traveled from studio to studio.

Whatever Jack L. Warner's cavalier attitude toward the picture, *The Dragon Murder Case* was still an "A" feature, with a budget of $320,000. Van Dine wanted the novel to advance the theory of the perfect alibi. Lucky had the plot somewhat revised for the screenplay. In the novel, all of the suspects save Rudolph Stamm go swimming in the Dragon Pool on the Stamm estate. Sanford Montague dives into the water and does not come to the surface. Nearly a day later his mutilated body is discovered some distance from the estate in an ancient pothole. Rudolph Stamm, presumably, was too drunk to join the swimming party. But since he is the only suspect with an opportunity to commit the murder, his guilt is overly obvious, all the other suspects being constantly within each other's sight. The photoplay removed one of the suspects from the vicinity of the pool before Monty's fateful dive, and the camera, combined with the direction, created so much confusion around the water's edge and within the Dragon Pool itself with the search for Montague that some of the transparency was lost.

The motion picture contains, of all the Philo Vance photoplays, the finest example of the intuitive experience Van Dine sought to create in the denouements of his novels. At a certain point in the film, the mechanics of the murder, and the murderer's identity, suddenly dawn upon the viewer, almost as a revelation, and the entire plot becomes evident. For this reason most of all, I suppose, I hold it to be among the best detective films made during the Thirties.

The Dragon Murder Case was the last book Willard wrote in the style and according to the structure that had made him world-famous. The characters exuded a loss of all significance. Willard may have had several more years to live before his death in 1939, but a substantial part of him had already receded beyond reclaim. For Humberstone, the picture based on this novel also proved a turning point. At the premiere, he had his agent invite most of the noteworthy producers then in Hollywood. The film was extremely well received. Jack Warner collared him afterward, saying, "Don't sign with any of these guys. We want you." But a contract didn't materialize, although a succession of assignments did at Twentieth Century-Fox, which led to Lucky's working extensively on the Charlie Chan series.

The Casino Murder Case (Scribner's, 1934) adhered to the format but lacked the intensity and conviction of previous books. The plot used a device Van Dine had already used in *The Greene Murder Case*. Lynn Llewellyn poisons himself, much as had Ada Greene, to cast suspicion away from himself. Moments of visual brilliance invaded the narrative, such as the descriptions of Kincaid's gambling casino or Vance's surreptitious entrance into Kincaid's heavy-water distillery housed in the cellar of his Closter hunting lodge. The characters were still vivid, the setting imaginative, but the mechanics of the crimes and the emphasis on detection, which Willard felt were so distinctive to the genre, became secondary to the dramatic qualities of the story.

Metro cast Paul Lukas as Philo Vance. William Powell was by this time being promoted as Nick Charles and the studio didn't want to interrupt its publicity campaign, although Powell was loaned out to RKO to play a private detective opposite Ginger Rogers in *Star of Midnight* (RKO, 1935). Yet the casting of Lukas was odd, when you stop to consider that he spoke all his lines with a heavy Hungarian accent. Lucien Hubbard, long associated with scripting motion pictures and a sometime director, produced the film on a scale far more lavish than that of any prior entry. The screenplay was by Florence Ryerson and Edgar Allan Woolf, a team that would work together on several pictures after *Casino;* both, at different times, had contributed to the cinematic versions of Sax Rohmer's Fu Manchu novels. Donald Cook played Lynn Llewellyn; Alison Skipworth was his mother; Rosalind Russell played Skipworth's personal secre-

Keye Luke does a sketch of director Edwin L. Marin while in costume on the set of *The Casino Murder Case* (M-G-M, 1935).   PHOTO COURTESY OF KEYE LUKE.

tary. It was the intention at Metro to try to build the same sort of screen rapport between Russell and Lukas that existed between Powell and Loy. Even the publicity for the picture called it a successor to *The Thin Man*. Philo Vance was depicted as a man with romantic ardors.

At Paramount, both in the initial three films and later in *The Gracie Allen Murder Case* (Paramount, 1939), Vance was given an Oriental butler. In *Casino*, Eric Blore was cast as Currie, the English butler of the novels, giving Vance's home life some depth. Dimitri Tiomkin's musical arrangements helped considerably in providing smoothness and gentle transition to many scenes while highlighting the drama.

There is little reason to disbelieve Van Dine, in the stories, when he repeatedly ridicules the police. Doubtless he really felt them to be utterly incompetent. But his bias came from too little experience; too much experience might have reinforced it in a wholly different direction.

Louise Fazenda, wife of producer Hal B. Wallis, is confronted by Paul Lukas playing Philo Vance in *The Casino Murder Case* (M-G-M, 1935).

PHOTO COURTESY OF METRO-GOLDWYN-MAYER.

Except for *The Benson Murder Case*, where the culprit is arrested in Markham's office after being exposed by Vance, a murderer never survived till the end of the book. Many of the suicides and contrived deaths are the weakest parts of the narratives. In *The "Canary" Murder Case* the murderer is permitted to shoot himself. Ada Greene takes poison. The murderer in *The Bishop Murder Case* is inadvertently poisoned through Vance's intercession. In *The Scarab Murder Case*, an Egyptian servant does the murderer in after he hears Vance's explanation. I have already told of the fate of the murderer in *The Kennel Murder Case*. Lynn Llewellyn in *Casino* is shot by Kincaid in the book and Heath in the film. Stamm is killed by a boulder falling on his head. In *The Garden Murder Case*, about which I will have more to say presently, the murderer in the novel jumps over a parapet, while in *The Kidnap Murder Case* the murderer shoots himself in full view of the remaining suspects. *The Gracie Allen Murder Case* has the murderer die by smoking a poisoned cigarette given him by Vance, although the murderer is arrested in the film; and in *The Winter Murder Case*, again, the murderer takes poison. Ending a murder case with a suicide was a convention with Van Dine. It gives one pause when recounting how Van Dine dealt with his creation as the Thirties drew to a close, as did Van Dine's life.

III

Van Dine took to dictating his books. He engaged a secretary, Y. B. Garden, who took down his dictation and typed triple-spaced manuscript copies. While typing up her notes, Miss Garden was free to interpolate her own ideas above the lines. "I was free to do this at any time," she recalled, "and of course he was free to accept or reject such suggestions." Willard named his next book after her, *The Garden Murder Case* (Scribner's, 1935).

Gambling fever spread in *Garden* to include the race track. Philo Vance, consistent with the new tone of Van Dine's life, was now a famous sleuth, well known at parties and in the best circles for his interest in crime. After all, hadn't Parker Bros. just issued the popular parlor game Philo Vance? It replaced Bulls and Bears in public demand and for a time rivaled Monopoly. Van Dine, who had spoken disparagingly against romantic interest in the detective story in his Third Rule for their writing, found himself dictating in *Garden:* "Up to that time I had never considered Vance a man of any deep personal emotion, except in so far as children and animals and his intimate masculine friendships were concerned. He had always impressed me as a man so highly mentalized, so cynical and impersonal in his attitude toward life, that an irrational human weakness like romance would be alien to his nature. But in the course of his deft inquiry into the murders in Professor Garden's penthouse, I saw, for the first time, another and softer side of his character. Vance was never a happy man in the conventional sense; but after the Garden murder case there were evidences of an even deeper loneliness in his sensitive nature."

In the 1936 film Metro advanced the romantic element until it became a centralized theme, with Virginia Bruce playing the Zalia Graem of the novel opposite Edmund Lowe as a charming, debonair, but scarcely intellectualized Philo Vance. Very little of the original plot was retained save for the general setting of horse racing; one of the minor characters of the novel was magnified into a major role enacted by Gene Lockhart. H. B. Warner, a fakir from the East, not based on a character from the novel, inveigles Vance into a semihypnotic trance and leads him to mount a parapet overlooking the city far below via rear-screen projection. But before he can persuade him to jump, Vance turns on him, not hypnotized at all, and exposes his plotting of the murders. Nat Pendleton as Sergeant Heath intervenes, much as he did in *The Thin Man*, shooting Warner before he can lunge at Vance. The film ends with Vance and Zalia in a clinch.

Benita Hume, later married to Ronald Colman, played Nurse Beeton in the film; in the novel, Beeton was the murderer. Together with Frieda Inescort she added feminine glamour to the already lavish sets and customary M-G-M polish.

By 1936, Willard realized that trends were changing in detective fiction. This alteration in perspective was reflected in *The Kidnap Murder Case* (Scribner's, 1936), which alone was the only book in the series not made into a motion picture, a situation which prompted Van Dine to specifically write his last two books as the result of definite motion picture assignments. Willard's asking price for film rights had gone up to $25,000. He really tried in *Kidnap* to appeal to the new spirit, having Vance and Heath match their acumen in a harrowing gun battle at the gangsters' hideout.

One evening in early January 1938, a Paramount executive sat down to relax and tuned in the Burns and Allen radio show. In the episode, Gracie played a detective. The executive had an idea. Paramount had just made *A Night of Mystery* in the United States and *The Scarab Murder Case* in Great Britain with Wilfred Hyde-White as Vance on a supposed sojourn to England, where Kathleen Kelly as Vance's secretary ends up falling in love with Donald Scarlett, played by John Robinson. Kathleen Kelly, in fact, received top billing. The idea the executive had was to combine S. S. Van Dine with Gracie Allen. The next day the story department went to work.

Willard was contacted by Paramount. The studio requested that he prepare an outline of approximately three thousand words to be "used as the basis for the development of a detailed treatment and/or continuity, with dialogue, suitable for reproduction as a motion picture photoplay of feature length in which Mr. George Burns and Miss Gracie Allen and/or Mr. John Barrymore properly could appear." Since Van Dine in *The Benson Murder Case* had described Vance as resembling John Barrymore, the suggestion may have pleased him, although he probably didn't care to break his reliance on six-letter titles for his books because Wright had six letters in it. By the time a contract was signed, Willard was guaranteed $25,000 for the project. Harold Ober, Willard's literary agent, supervised the signing.

Burns and Allen met with Willard only once, for a lunch early in 1938. Van Dine wanted their permission to use them as characters in his book. "And that was all there was to it," George Burns later recalled, "as far as we were concerned. He retained all the rights, and we took advantage of the publicity."

Edmund Lowe and Virginia Bruce caught by the camera relaxing on the set of *The Garden Murder Case* (M-G-M, 1936). PHOTO COURTESY OF VIEWS & REVIEWS MAGAZINE.

Willard set about dictating a first draft to Y. B. Garden. When he came to publish the book version of *The Gracie Allen Murder Case*, he included a long chapter describing an interview between Vance and "Owl" Owen, who was dying of a cardiac disorder. "Owen began speaking of old books, of his days at Cambridge, of his cultural ambitions as a youth, of his early study of music," Van Dine wrote. "He was steeped in the lore of ancient civilizations and, to my astonishment, he dwelt with fanatical passion on the Tibetan Book of the Dead." Elsewhere in the same conversation, Owen asked Vance, "You think that either of us willed this meeting? Man makes no choice. His choice is his temperament. . . . But why do I even bother, this shadow between two infinities? I can give only one answer: the obscene urge to eat well and live well—which, in turn, is an instinct and, therefore, a lie." Van Dine had put his own despair into the mouth of a gangster.

The novelette which Van Dine wrote for Paramount, originally 20,000 words,

An older Warren William perplexed by Gracie Allen on the set of *The Gracie Allen Murder Case* (Paramount, 1939).   PHOTO COURTESY OF VIEWS & REVIEWS MAGAZINE.

and which he expanded into the shortest Philo Vance novel until that time, showed Vance somewhat mellowed with age. The book drags, the murder scheme fails to sustain interest, and Gracie Allen, at best, is a somewhat irritating intrusion into what one had come to expect a serious business. There is only "Owl" Owen, whose crime is killing another gangster, immersed in his distorted philosophical ramblings, the setting of a gangland cafe, a poisoned cigarette as the murder weapon, and Gracie Allen as Vance's assistant to remind us how far we have come since 1926.

But if the original novelette underwent changes in becoming a novel, it underwent even greater changes becoming a screenplay. *The Gracie Allen Murder Case* (Paramount, 1939), which Willard did not live to see, was a vehicle for Gracie Allen. George Burns, whom Van Dine had included, was replaced by Kent Taylor. "It was a personal decision on our part for me not to appear," George Burns remarked. "Gracie had always appeared with me, and we were anxious to see what the reaction would be if she appeared with another actor, and this seemed an appropriate time. It was the only time we were not together, except for once or twice with Jack Benny on his television show." Burns's response to what the public's reaction was prompted him to comment, "Well, it was so good that I never let her work with anybody else again." Yet, in an interview for the Washington *Evening Star* of November 5, 1941, Gracie stated that *Mr. and Mrs. North* (M-G-M, 1941), which she was then filming, was the first picture she had done without George's assistance. "I played without him in *The Gracie Allen Murder Case,*" she said, "but he was around all the time to help me."

Saddest of all is what happened to Philo Vance, if we remember how first he looked when William Powell projected him on the screen. Warren William was again given the part, not the Warren William of *The Dragon Murder Case,* but an older, wearier man, with signs of too much high living, totally indifferent to his characterization. Throughout the picture Gracie refers to him as "Fido" Vance and the satire is topped off when Markham and Heath, played respectively by Donald MacBride and William Demarest, in keeping with the ending to Christopher Ward's parody of a decade before, mistakenly arrest Vance as the murderer. The critics panned the whole enterprise as beneath Vance's standards. He summarized the case himself when he said in the book: "The goddesses of Zeus' Olympian menage never harassed old Priam and Agamemnon with the éclat exhibited by Gracie Allen in harassing the recidivists of that highly scented affair. Amazin'."

It had been Van Dine's custom, when preparing a detective novel, to write three drafts. The first was a ten-thousand-word synopsis containing all of the events and most of the conversations of the final version, sans the many side issues, literary and philosophic excursions, and depth of personality description. After he had expanded the synopses to thirty thousand words, the novels were ready for a final ten-thousand-word amplification, giving them the scholarly apparatus and the characters their substance.

Van Dine left behind him at his death a thirty-thousand-word synopsis to *The Winter Murder Case* (Scribner's, 1939). The plot came about as a result of a suggestion to Willard by Julian Johnson in a letter of August 24, 1938. Willard had written for Johnson under the name Van Vranken when Johnson was editor of *Photoplay*. Johnson later became an associate editor of *Cosmopolitan* before being appointed head of the Fox Story Department in 1932, a post he held until his retirement in 1957. Despite all the haggling back and forth about money and suitable story ideas, both with Johnson and Harry Joe Brown, an associate producer at Fox and guardian for the screen use of Sonja Henie, Willard died two days after completing the synopsis and the idea was shelved. Scribner's published it as a book with a special preface by Maxwell Perkins which Perkins did not sign.

Perkins felt deeply Willard's own despair during his later years, and a cognizance of that despair appears in his tribute. After all, it was the passing of a literary era. F. Scott Fitzgerald had brought what was left of his pained sensibility to the world of Hollywood, which was consuming him, and which saw print in the unfinished *The Last Tycoon* (Scribner's, 1941); Hemingway was in Spain enmeshed in the Civil War. The decade of the Thirties was winding up to a terrible holocaust. "There were other influences at work on him perhaps," Perkins observed. "But no one who knew Willard and the purity of his perceptions in art, and his devotion to what he thought was the meaning of our civilization as expressed in the arts, can doubt that the shattering disillusionment and ruin of the war was what brought him at last to a nervous breakdown which incapacitated him for several years. He would never have explained it so, or any other way. He made no explanations, or excuses, ever, and his many apologies were out of the kindness of a heart so concealed by reticence that only a handful ever knew how gentle it really was. So at last all that he had done and aimed to do seemed to have come to ruin, and he himself too."

Warner Brothers sought to cash in on Van Dine's passing by remaking *The Kennel Murder Case* as *Calling Philo Vance* in 1940. It was a comedy, not altogether intentionally. In the late Forties, Eagle-Lion got hold of the Philo Vance property and made three films. Alan Curtis was Vance in *Philo Vance's Secret Mission* (Eagle-Lion, 1947) and in *Philo Vance's Gamble* (Producers Releasing Corporation, 1947); William Wright was Vance in the final entry, *Philo Vance Returns* (Producers Releasing Corporation, 1947). Vance was now more in the mold of the Falcon at RKO than anything from the Thirties. In *Secret Mission*, he married Sheila Ryan at the fade, but was back as a bachelor in *Gamble*, finally tracing the murders to his girl friend, Terry Austin. There wasn't even a value left in the name.

I visited Stanton MacDonald-Wright at his home in Pacific Palisades. A giant mural he had designed at eighty-one covered the front of his house. The only windows were in the enclosed court and in his studio, which overlooked the ocean. I asked about the absence of windows. He said many of his neighbors had binoculars and examined minutely each new acquisition as it was being moved inside. This way they could see nothing.

Stanton resembled a much older version of Willard. The furnishings were reminiscent of the many years of austerity he had grown accustomed to while living in a Buddhist monastery. He was well-to-do. His paintings were selling for tens of thousands of dollars. Having once surrounded himself with fine *objets d'art*, he had obeyed C. G. Jung's admonishment to unload after forty, subsequently selling off many of the treasures of his collection. On the studio walls he kept several of his most powerful and provocative paintings, a flood of color and emotion—emotion necessarily detached from any particular, for he had learned that abstract emotion must seek its own timber and hue. He had a painting by Morgan Russell dating from their Synchronism period in Paris. It strongly attracted me. I asked him how much it cost. Stanton remarked that when Russell painted it he had sold it for $500. It had cost Stanton $11,000 to buy it. Now it was worth perhaps $13,000.

Stanton was smoking an American cigarette. I remarked on it. He responded that it was he who had first introduced Willard to Régie Turkish cigarettes.

The ocean could be heard in the courtyard and a dampness clung to the rocks and earth. But here in Stanton's studio, it was warm and very dry. As Stanton talked on about Willard's peculiar romanticism, Edna St. Vincent Millay's lines came to me from the opening stanzas of *A Few Figs from Thistles:*

> *My candle burns at both ends;*
> *It will not last the night;*
> *But, ah, my foes, and, oh, my friends—*
> *It gives a lovely light.*

I cannot with any confidence say to the reader that Philo Vance was in any way a perfect likeness of his creator, as I have the heard others comment, much less a self-parody. Beyond it all Willard was a sensitive soul, bewildered and frustrated, impeccably dressed, capable to a fault, cynical, confused, divided between the desire to live well and the desire to influence men's minds, and yet somehow cheated by life, which held for him, as for so many, too much and too little. It says in the Bible, "All things are double, one against the other." Might it not be said of Willard?

Van Dine was what critics of the detective story call the last of the great traditionalists. With his emphasis on personality and temperament, he made way for a later generation of writers with whose methods he was at a loss. Perkins saw in the man the disillusionment with the world which Hammett in the Twenties and Chandler in the Forties articulated indelibly, a world in which only gangsters, violence, and oppression prospered and money alone was the operative principle by which both justice and the American political system were enervated. The new philosophy of survival through character true of the *Black Mask* writers was not a feasible solution for Willard, for, you see, he didn't survive. He lived only long enough to murder Philo Vance.

"This is not a creative, but a commercial age," he once said, "in which all ardent and conceptual ideas in the arts are dominated by a spirit subversive to their operation." Yet, considering Van Dine's lavish tastes and extravagances, I doubt very much that he would have lived otherwise no matter what had happened. He wore his financial success both flagrantly and dispiritedly. He lived as best he could, in keeping with his own temperament. He wrote detective stories with rare *élan*, at least in the beginning, and no one should ask more of a writer than that he do his best.

THREE:

The Detective at Large

*If I'm not having fun writing a book no one's
going to have any fun reading it.*

—Rex Stout

I

If what I have to say in the following pages seems to reveal an unconcealed
preference for Rex Stout's Nero Wolfe mysteries, I might as well admit that I
have enjoyed his books more than those of any other author of detective stories.
I have enjoyed Hammett and Chandler, but I have enjoyed Stout more. I admire
Erle Stanley Gardner, as will become apparent when I write of him, as one of
the best plot artists and the finest champion of justice the detective story has
known. I am charmed uncommonly by the Miss Marple mysteries by Agatha
Christie and the Dr. Thorndyke adventures by R. Austin Freeman. But I am addicted to Rex Stout.

Conan Doyle, the reader will recall, stumbled into most of the pitfalls that
later writers of detective fiction have wisely tended to avoid. He murdered his
detective and married his narrator. Later, when Dashiell Hammett and Dorothy
L. Sayers had their detectives marry, they had reached the nadir of their productive contributions to the genre. Chandler, too, attempted marrying off Philip
Marlowe, his detective, with tragic results. Rex Stout made no such mistake. He
created a fantasy world, one with sufficient co-ordinates with the real world in
which you and I live that we aren't always aware of it. Agatha Christie narrated
Hercule Poirot's death and she showed Miss Marple ravaged by old age. Neither
Nero Wolfe nor Archie Goodwin ever ages. They cannot. This was part of
Stout's literary compact. He was not going to let Wolfe develop a cardiac disor-
der any more than he was about to expose Archie to venereal disease. Archie's

Edward Arnold glowering as the fat genius in *Meet Nero Wolfe* (Columbia, 1936).
PHOTO COURTESY OF VIEWS & REVIEWS MAGAZINE.

life is his job and he is so little troubled by urges and emotions that one can almost accept his reluctance to ask no more of life than to occasionally show up Wolfe.

In the beginning, Stout, a prodigy of the Depression, put all of his passion and vituperative dissatisfaction into his stories. This became less pronounced after the Second World War. Later it was immersed in the boredom he found in his formula. This was only to be expected. A reader may reasonably ask an author not to age his characters or alter their life-style, but he cannot expect an author to prevent these things from happening in himself.

Wolfe's house and his life are like a persistent dream, one man's romantic vision of a life of order, freedom from interruption, and, within its confines, peace. It's a wholly masculine environment. This of itself is very unusual, when you think about it. Women do read Rex Stout's books, but they do not read him anywhere as avidly as they have read Erle Stanley Gardner or Agatha Christie. Women are the readers in modern civilization: any publisher will tell you as much. Since women buy and read more books and story collections than men, they have every right to request that an author address himself specifically to women, at least some of the time.

Stout, years ago in one of his satirical essays, suggested that Dr. John H. Watson may have been a woman. He acknowledged Archie's sexual needs when he introduced rich, beautiful, capable Lily Rowan into the stories during the Second World War. Archie and Lily have kept company, on and off, ever since. Conversely, Wolfe's intense dislike of women and female hysterics has kept his home a masculine paradise with a Belgian chef, a German gardener who tends Wolfe's ten thousand orchids, and, of course, Archie.

I have always been astonished at the number of virgins in their early and mid-Twenties in Stout's fiction of the Forties and Fifties. He made the remark in one of his novels, *Death of a Dude* (Viking, 1969), that he suspected a lot of little old schoolteachers and librarians read his novels, and he may have been correct. I do not know how many crimes of passion can be traced to the lamentable confusions engendered by sexual congress in and out of marriage, but this is certainly responsible for a great many of them. It wasn't until publication of Stout's next to last book, *Please Pass the Guilt* (Viking, 1973), that Wolfe's attitude toward women and their sexual needs altered. Orrie Cather, an operative who has long assisted Wolfe, was falsely imprisoned in *Death of a Doxy* for having supposedly murdered a Park Avenue whore. We meet Orrie's grief-stricken fianceé in *Death*. By the time of *Please Pass the Guilt*, Jill, an airline flight attendant, and Orrie are married. Orrie investigates at least two Continental Air Network female researchers by taking them to bed on Wolfe's expense account.

For whatever the reason, until *Please Pass the Guilt*, Stout for the most part ignored probing too deeply into questions such as who is sleeping with whom. In *Guilt*, Wolfe instructs Archie to "seduce" the two leading, attractive female suspects, and Archie comments breezily that there is "no evidence that either of them has any chastity to surrender." As it turns out, neither of them has, although Archie has sexual congress with neither.

So skillful is Stout as a humorist that you never once realize that Nero Wolfe is actually a prisoner of his own fantasy, that the basis of his existence is a confession of the utter bankruptcy of love, of life in the world; it represents a cynical despair in one's fellows and all social structures; it is a retreat from the pressures, inadequacies, frenzies of reality. We can best laugh at life when we are least susceptible to being hurt by it, but we remember our former pain in our enjoyment, or when we have insulated ourselves within our own being to such an extent that we cannot easily be hurt by it again. Laughter is our release in the face of the inescapable futility of all that we do. It comes above suffering, before and after it, and it tells us that human relationships at their base can be funny because they are ultimately meaningless. A man who makes you laugh does so by telling you half a story, but half a story is only one side of reality and not the whole of it.

The more conscious you are, the more aware you become of each man's separateness. Think of Theodore Horstmann in the plant rooms, encased in a chrysalis of glass, as he was in the early novels before Stout moved him out, with a tiny sleeping chamber enclosed by brownstone right next to the potting room, his cot, his flowers, which he does not own, and Wolfe four hours a day. Archie doesn't tell it like this, because if he did the compact would break, and the compact is supposed to keep us amused. But that's Horstmann's life. He's like a happy lunatic I once met when visiting an insane asylum whose one joy consisted in scrubbing out ashtrays that had been soiled. I see her now, old, gray-headed, hobbling about, flashing me a quick, fleeting, impatient smile, and pointing mutely at the ashtray beside me, supplicating, would I please finish with it?

Rex Stout was born at Noblesville, Indiana, on December 1, 1886. In many ways, his life was as extraordinary as any of the fiction he wrote. Following his birth, his parents, John Wallace Stout and Lucetta Todhunter Stout, moved to Topeka, Kansas. One of nine children, Stout was very precocious, having read the Bible twice by the time he was four; by the time he was thirteen, he was spelling champion for the state. He was a voracious reader. At eighteen, he joined the U. S. Navy and became a warrant officer on the *Mayflower*, President Theodore Roosevelt's yacht, a post he held until he left the Navy in 1908.

He checked the want ads in New York City and found employment as a bookkeeper for *Pharmaceutical Era and Soda Fountain* for eighteen dollars a week. The job proved short-lived because he was found to be hustling advertisements on the side. He roamed the country as an itinerant bookkeeper, becoming a cigar salesman in Cleveland, a salesman of Indian baskets at Albuquerque, a guide to the Indian pueblos near Santa Fe, a barker for a sightseeing bus in Colorado Springs, a bookstore clerk in Chicago, Indianapolis, and Milwaukee, and a stable hand in New York. In four years he held thirty jobs in six states.

He had his first literary experience during these years. When he was twenty, he wrote a poem which was accepted by the *Smart Set* and for which he was paid fourteen dollars. He wrote another poem, and it was likewise accepted. He wrote a third, and it was accepted. He wrote a fourth, and it was rejected. He had enrolled in law school. With the rejection, he quit school, and he quit poetry, going to work in a cigar store. That was while he was living in Cleveland.

Perhaps Stout's greatest success was an article he sold to the New York *World* analyzing the palm prints of William Howard Taft, then running for the Presidency, and Tom L. Johnson, a prominent Democrat. That earned him $200.

It was probably on the basis of these efforts that Stout decided, in 1912, to become a magazine writer. Until 1916, he concocted and sold reams of fiction and articles to *Munsey's* and other popular magazines. Finally, he determined that this was getting him nowhere. He wanted to write serious fiction. In order to do this, he felt he would have to accumulate at least $200,000, so as not to be interrupted by economic pressures. He devised and proceeded to implement the school banking system which was eventually installed in four hundred cities and townships across the country. The notion was so successful he raised his goal to $400,000. He took time off to explore the high Rockies in Montana with two cowboys and thirty packhorses; these annual excursions would usually take three months during which time Stout fished, read, and walked. He went to Europe, and there he walked, once 180 miles to see Thermopylae. Back in the States, he would visit schools on Bank Day and address the students on behalf of thrift.

When he felt he was near enough his goal to try it, he went to Paris to live for two years. His first novel, *How Like a God*, was published in 1929. It was praised critically. He followed it with four more novels, all of which have been forgotten. By that time he had made a fundamental discovery about himself. "I was a good storyteller, and I would never be a great writer."

He had a tremendous fondness for Conan Doyle's Sherlock Holmes stories and would reread them almost as often as he reread Shakespeare's sonnets. He became a Baker Street Irregular.

The financial panic of those years dissipated his fortune. At forty-eight, he wrote his first Nero Wolfe novel, *Fer-de-Lance* (Farrar & Rinehart, 1934), which was run serially in *The Saturday Evening Post*. The book proved to be popular, and screen rights were purchased nearly at once, but for very little money, by Columbia Pictures. Before I say something about the motion picture Columbia made, if it should happen that you haven't read the novel but may have read one or more of Stout's later books, you may wonder how different Wolfe and Archie were in 1934. The answer is: not much. Horstmann slept near the orchids in the glassed-in greenhouses on the roof of Wolfe's brownstone. Fritz Brenner, the Belgian chef, slept across the hall from the plant rooms; he later moved to the basement. Archie and Wolfe were sleeping on the second floor; Archie later changed his bedroom. Archie kept a bottle of rye whiskey in his closet from which he would nip when particularly frustrated with Wolfe, and Archie liked smoking cigarettes. No doubt Wolfe's grousing about cigarette smoke made him cut down in future years. Harry Foster was the man at the *Gazette* who helped Archie with information; Lon Cohen only did so later. Ten thousand pages of the saga had been written before Wolfe and Archie made their final appearance in *A Family Affair* (Viking, 1975). Not very much was altered about them in all those years; we just got to know them better, or know them under varying sets of circumstances. Stout was eighty-eight when he wrote his last book. He liked his characters and he liked the world in which they lived. It was for this reason, and no other, that he was disgusted by what Hollywood did to them.

Meet Nero Wolfe (Columbia, 1936) cast Edward Arnold in the role of Wolfe. Arnold was born in New York on February 18, 1890. He was five feet eleven inches and weighed in at two hundred pounds when he assumed the role, which scarcely made him the requisite one seventh of a ton. Lionel Stander played Archie Goodwin. The picture went into production under the title *Fer-de-Lance*. According to the screenplay, Archie is about to marry Mazie Gray,

Lionel Stander as Archie and Arnold as Wolfe talking in the plant room in *Meet Nero Wolfe*.   PHOTO COURTESY OF COLUMBIA PICTURES INDUSTRIES.

played by Dennie Moore. Joan Perry played Ellen Barstow, daughter of the college professor who is murdered on the golf links by a pin that is shot from the handle of his golf iron. Rita Cansino, later to be known as Rita Hayworth, had a bit part. Victor Jory was one of the suspects. John Qualen was Olaf, Wolfe's Scandinavian chef. Herbert Biberman directed. The screenplay was by Howard J. Green, who was extremely well known at the time, Bruce Manning, and Joseph Anthony. B. P. Schulberg, who had been terminated at Paramount when that company nearly went into receivership, was the producer.

Edward Arnold as Wolfe, Rita Hayworth, and John Qualen as Wolfe's chef, Olaf, together in the hot room amid the plants (not orchids!).

PHOTO COURTESY OF COLUMBIA PICTURES INDUSTRIES.

The film was one of the finest detective films produced in the Thirties. Unfortunately, it has not been seen since its original theatrical release. Arnold's characterization is superb; he may not keep Wolfe's hours in the plant rooms, but he's there much of the time, and, atypically, that's where he solves the case with all the suspects gathered together.

Walter Connolly was the next actor to be cast as Nero Wolfe in *The League of Frightened Men* (Columbia, 1937). Connally was born on April 3, 1888, in Cincinnati, Ohio, and was educated at St. Xavier College in that city and at the University of Dublin. He married Nedda Harrigan, who later was in many pictures, including *Charlie Chan at the Opera* (20th-Fox, 1936). Connolly was very successful on Broadway, but in 1932, Harry Cohn at Columbia Pictures persuaded him to come to Hollywood for the summer months. Connolly was featured in pictures like Frank Capra's *Lady for a Day* (Columbia, 1933) and *A Man's Castle* (Columbia, 1933). He liked working in films so much he signed a long-term contract with Cohn. He was put into top-ranking pictures like Capra's *It Happened One Night* (Columbia, 1934) and Howard Hawks's *Twentieth Century* (Columbia, 1934).

Unhappily, Lionel Stander's Archie in *The League of Frightened Men* is far too much of a bungler. The plot follows the novel, which ran initially in *The Saturday Evening Post*. A group of ten men is threatened by one of their number, and murders begin. Eduardo Ciannelli is the logical suspect, since he was crippled in a hazing while the men were all in college. The love interest was delegated to Irene Hervey and Allen Brook. Alfred E. Green was the director. The film was in no way the equal of its predecessor.

In 1930, when he returned from France, Rex Stout put what was left of his money into building High Meadow, his home on a thousand-foot elevation at Brewster, New York, fashioned after a palace he had seen on the Mediterranean which belonged to the Bey of Tunis. It was a concrete structure in a U-shape with fourteen rooms. Together with nine men and "three and a half boys," all amateurs, he worked on it for fourteen hours a day for months. On the surrounding fifty-eight acres, he grew all manner of things, but principally flowers (none of them orchids).

Rex Stout was of a liberal mind, much like Dashiell Hammett but without the stigma of socialism. He wrote propaganda for the necessity of American involvement in the Second World War, in favor of preparedness, and, once war came, for Lend-Lease and the draft. He was the master of ceremonies for the Council of Democracy's radio program "Speaking of Liberty" and chairman of the Writers' War Board. He became chairman of the Writers' Board for World Government in 1949, and in 1943–45 he was president of the Authors' Guild. He was president of the Authors' League of America from 1951 to 1955, vice-president from 1956 to 1961, and then president again in 1962. He lobbied in Washington on behalf of copyright revision. If his efforts in this direction weren't so successful that a writer is better off having produced a book than having built an apartment house, new legislation at least promises him a slightly longer claim to his property before he must throw open the doors to public tenancy.

Stout in his lifetime wrote some thirty-three novels and thirty-eight novelettes about Wolfe and Archie. "The Adventures of Nero Wolfe" was a radio series, beginning in 1943, with Santos Ortega in the role of Wolfe; a later radio series featured Sydney Greenstreet as Wolfe and Everett Sloane as Archie. Stout's distrust of movies and then television made any series in these media impossible after the initial two Columbia entries. But what does it matter, after all? We have his books, which are such a splendidly humorous commentary on life. In the Nero Wolfe stories he constantly exposes hypocrisy and artifice. The detective form was the perfect vehicle for him to do this; by its conventions, he could assemble a widely divergent assortment of people who, under an external and inexorable stimulus, were forced to show themselves for what they were. Sex, greed, and vanity prompt nearly all human behavior. Stout specialized in ridiculing vanity. This was the impulse of his muse and it explains, I think, the delight we take in reading his narratives. Most of us cannot admire a man we cannot laugh at occasionally. Such laughter reminds us of our common humanity. We are absentminded enough about it, unfortunately, that we stand in need of frequent reminders. If he did nothing else, Rex Stout did provide us with that.

II

Herman Cyril McNeile, the son of Captain Malcolm McNeile of the Royal Navy, was born in 1888 and educated at the Royal Military Academy. At nineteen he joined the British Army and served for twelve years until he retired in 1919 as a lieutenant colonel. McNeile had been in the Royal Engineers and, while still in the service, was writing military adventure stories. He had a restless and excited imagination. His first book featuring his most famous character, *Bulldog Drummond*, was published in 1920. Originally, he wrote under the pseudonym Sapper, British vernacular for an engineer.

Drummond as a hero proved extremely popular with the British reading public, but it took the motion picture appearance in the role of Ronald Colman in 1929 before the character caught on with American audiences. George H. Doran was McNeile's American publisher. When Doran merged with Doubleday in 1927, the firm published all the McNeile books in a matched set, in conjunction with Colman's second cinematic adventure in the role. You don't hear much of Drummond anymore; to my knowledge the books have been out of print for years.

In the novels, Drummond has a number of friends and cohorts who join him in his various escapades in search of thrills. Most of these characters, such as Peter Darrell and Ted Jerningham, never made it into the movies. Those who

Sydney Greenstreet, surrounded here by beer and orchids, playing Nero Wolfe on radio. PHOTO COURTESY OF VIEWS & REVIEWS MAGAZINE.

did include Algy Longworth, a friend who can always be counted on, James Denny, Drummond's valet whose name was changed to Tenny, and Colonel Neilson of Scotland Yard. Phyllis Benton, to whose rescue Drummond comes in his first recorded exploit, had her name changed in the movies to Phyllis Clavering; they marry after Drummond dispatches master villain Carl Peterson in the 1920 novel. It required a lot more time for this to happen on screen.

McNeile probably did not intend to write a series of books about Hugh Drummond. His first was in every way a transition book, keeping alive the wartime spirit of camaraderie of the British soldier after the Great War, coupled with the love for melodrama which preoccupied British writers from Edgar Wallace to the much later Leslie Charteris. However, *Bulldog Drummond* (Hodkinson, 1922) was made the basis for a British photoplay with Carlyle Blackwell in the lead, adhering closely to the plot of the book. McNeile wrote *The Black Gang* and published it the same year the film was released. The group referred to in the title was Captain Hugh Drummond's unofficial militia, which specialized in rounding up Communists and other such nonpatriotic evildoers, mostly foreigners. This concept was but a variation on a theme Edgar Wallace put forth in *The Four Just Men* (Tallis, 1906), in which four men take it upon themselves to prevent, through murder, certain events from occurring. They are justified in the murders because of the uprightness of their cause. The four (although in reality only three, since one dies before they begin in earnest) are determined to see justice done where the law cannot, or will not, do anything about it. If you take Wallace's just men and combine them into one, as with Hugh Drummond and his black gang, you come up with modern counterparts like Mickey Spillane's Mike Hammer or Ian Fleming's James Bond. Wallace featured his just men in an entire series of books which were continuously popular.

One of the regrets I have in writing this book is that I cannot give more space to Edgar Wallace. His books, more in the crime fiction and mystery field than detective stories, probably inspired more films than the work of almost any writer in the genre. In 1959, long after he was dead, the four just men, with the fourth member brought back, was made into a thirty-nine segment half-hour television series.

It was to Wallace, more than to anyone else, that McNeile had to look for having provided him with a ready audience for the type of fiction he preferred to write. McNeile's third Drummond book, *The Third Round*, was filmed the same year it was published, 1925, under the same title in Britain, with Jack Buchanan in the Drummond role. McNeile wrote three more Drummond novels between 1926 and 1929, but by 1921 his first book had already been translated into a stage play that had a successful London run followed by an impressive Broadway opening.

Samuel Goldwyn was in search of a property suitable for his first all-talking picture and which, simultaneously, could be used as a vehicle for Ronald Colman, who was under contract to him. Goldwyn's story editor, Arthur Hornblow, went to New York to find a stage play. The theory in Hollywood was that audiences for sound pictures wanted talking and plenty of it. Hornblow was taken with *Bulldog Drummond*. He inquired into the rights and found that, for a *sound* film, the property was available. Next he engaged Sidney Howard, a distinguished playwright who had had two extravagant Broadway successes in the Twenties and who was an admirer of Colman, to do the screen treatment. Goldwyn was pleased with the whole idea, doubly so because *Bulldog Drummond* (United Artists, 1929) might be made to combine talking *and* action. Voice tests done on Colman proved excellent.

Goldwyn insisted on an innovation in preparing *Bulldog Drummond* that later became customary in the manufacture of talking films: he held exhaustive rehearsals *prior* to filming, shot on the elaborate sets he had built. The melo-drama of the picture was embodied in its action, but the dialogue, which was witty and spontaneous, maintained the accelerated pacing Goldwyn wanted. Screening rushes one day, Sam asked the director, F. Richard Jones, what the word "din" meant. Jones told him it meant the same thing as noise. Sam couldn't

Carlyle Blackwell (left), Warwick Ward, and Evelyn Greely in a dramatic scene from *Bulldog Drummond* (Hodkinson, 1922).

PHOTO COURTESY OF THE NATIONAL FILM ARCHIVE.

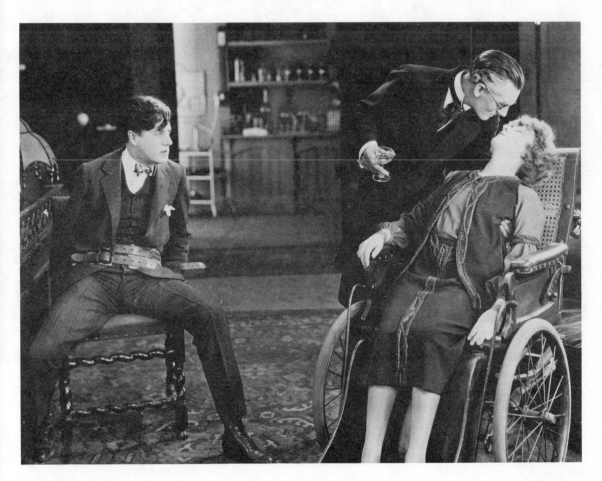

Ronald Colman is in trouble, but Joan Bennett will save the day in *Bulldog Drummond* (United Artists, 1929).   PHOTO COURTESY OF THE NATIONAL FILM ARCHIVE.

understand why, if din meant noise, it wasn't noise in the dialogue. He spent an additional $20,000 to have the scene reshot with the word substitution.

When *Bulldog Drummond* opened at the Apollo Theatre in New York, Colman was requested by Goldwyn to make a personal appearance after the film was shown. Colman agreed. He was literally mobbed by the audience, which had fallen in love with his voice as they had, in the silent era, with his eyes. The reviews were raves of enthusiasm. Colman infused such a lighthearted tone into his manner and delivery that audiences then didn't mind lines such as, "If you hurt but one hair of her head, I'll kill you." Or: "We'll see who laughs last, Bulldog Drummond," to which Colman quietly smiles.

If the film doesn't stand up today, it is primarily due to the overstatement of its plot and what now appear to be clumsy cinematic techniques. I doubt if anyone took the story seriously in 1929. But the film further fortified Colman's hold on the public as a dashing, romantic hero.

The Fox Film Corporation lost no time in attempting to duplicate Goldwyn's achievement. The company purchased rights to McNeile's latest novel, *Temple Tower* (Fox, 1930), and rushed it to the screen. Kenneth MacKenna was cast as Drummond, Marceline Day as the fearful heroine in distress, and Cyril Chadwick as Algy. Donald Gallagher directed. Henry B. Walthall was the villain and probably the only able performer in the cast. When this follow-up picture proved very much a failure, studio executives comforted themselves with the notion that only Ronald Colman could play Bulldog Drummond adequately.

Certainly this was Darryl Zanuck's reasoning when his newly formed Twentieth Century Pictures signed Colman to a contract. Zanuck's films were also distributed by United Artists, so all the changeover required of Colman was a switch of dressing rooms on the same lot. Zanuck cast Loretta Young as Drummond's love interest. The script by Nunnally Johnson ignored the earlier picture and Drummond's probable marital attachments. C. Aubrey Smith was cast as Inspector Neilson, Warner Oland performed slyly as Prince Achmen, the villain at the bottom of all the trouble, and E. E. Clive was cast as a British policeman. The picture was stolen for comedy by Charles Butterworth and Una Merkel, playing Algy and his new wife Gwen respectively. They are married at the beginning of the picture, with Hugh acting as best man; unfortunately, all of Hugh's adventures constantly interrupt their nuptial night and Algy is forever being pulled away before the union is consummated. Merkel and Butterworth established the right rapport between two newlyweds. One of the basic plot ingredients was the frustration Drummond has, and the viewer shares with him, when, every time he produces a witness to skulduggery, the witness disappears before Scotland Yard can take up the questioning. The picture, *Bulldog Drummond Strikes Back* (United Artists, 1934), proved to be only the first of a series of successes for Ronald Colman during his association with Zanuck.

The next year the British released their first all-talking entry in the series, *The Return of Bulldog Drummond*, based on the 1932 novel and starring Ralph Richardson. The plot was a swing back to the older books, however, and Drummond found himself the head of the Black Clan, making a crusade against wrongdoers and warmongers. The events, particularly the race by the Clan to save Drummond at the end, were quite similar to American matinee serials.

The same year *Bulldog Jack* (Gaumont-British, 1935) appeared, which was a satire of the Bulldog Drummond character and the melodrama of the escapades in which he found himself. Atholl Fleming played Drummond, turning over his part in the drama early in the film to Jack Hurlbert, who impersonates him,

George Regas, Warner Oland, and Mischa Auer gang up on Ronald Colman in *Bulldog Drummond Strikes Back* (United Artists, 1934).

PHOTO COURTESY OF THE NATIONAL FILM ARCHIVE.

rather after the fashion of the *Casino Royale* (Columbia, 1967) satire of James Bond movies with several Bond impersonations. Ralph Richardson was cast as a master criminal.

Paramount Pictures then negotiated a contract with McNeile for a ten-year license to film all the previously published books and any new ones he might write. McNeile died soon after the agreement was signed. Gerard Fairlie, a fellow writer and close friend of McNeile's all the years he was working on the saga, took over writing novels about Drummond with the approval of the estate.

Bulldog Drummond Escapes (Paramount, 1937) was the first entry in this new series, based, as had been the 1932 British entry, on *Bulldog Drummond Returns* (Doubleday, 1932). The story line also bore strong resemblances to the plot of *Bulldog Drummond Strikes Back*. Ray Milland, recently put under contract to Paramount, was selected to play Drummond. Heather Angel was Phyllis Clavering. The silent comedian Reginald Denny was cast as Algy, and Sir Guy Standing was assigned the role of Inspector Neilson, who prefers to be known by his military title, Colonel. This time much of the comedy derived from the fact that Algy is anxiety-ridden over the baby Gwen is about to have, but he is constantly being dragged off by Hugh in Drummond's efforts to rescue Phyllis. James Hogan directed and Edward T. Lowe wrote the screenplay. Gerard Fairlie was given joint screen credit with H. C. McNeile for the "Sapper" stories.

John Howard, born on April 14, 1913, in Cleveland, Ohio, was signed to a long-term contract by Paramount while he was still a student at Western Reserve University. Once he started working at Paramount, Howard moved his mother and father to Brentwood and lived with them, along with his collection of five hundred model ducks. He had to affect a slight British accent for the Drummond role. Paramount hoped the part would build him into a leading attraction. Perhaps Frank Capra's decision, earlier that year, to star Ronald Colman and John Howard as brothers in *Lost Horizon* (Columbia, 1937) was the impetus behind the idea. E. E. Clive had played Drummond's valet, Dobbs, in *Escapes*. In Howard's first picture, *Bulldog Drummond Comes Back* (Paramount, 1937), Clive was cast in the same role, but now named Tenny. John Barrymore got top billing as Colonel Neilson. Louis King was the director, and, again, Edward T. Lowe prepared the screenplay. Algy was played by Reginald Denny. Phyllis was changed to Louise Campbell, who had a certain physical similarity to Heather Angel. John Barrymore, joining into the spirit of the game, dons several disguises so he can shadow Drummond and his friends and watch over them. His disguises are outlandish, but he dissolves himself into these various identities with enthusiasm. All the reviews at the time singled out Barrymore's performance as notable, but otherwise did not find the picture up to the standards set by earlier films in the series. I say this because to a contemporary viewer, I would suspect, *Bulldog Drummond Comes Back* would appear superior to *Bulldog Drummond Escapes* and possibly, at least, to the Goldwyn picture with Ronald Colman.

Jack Barrymore continued to dominate *Bulldog Drummond's Revenge* (Paramount, 1937), although he had fewer scenes in it than in the previous entry.

John Barrymore added distinction to the Paramount series, shown here with John Howard in *Bulldog Drummond's Revenge* (Paramount, 1937).

PHOTO COURTESY OF THE NATIONAL FILM ARCHIVE.

Barrymore was no longer able to remember lines and it is interesting to see how, always with perfect timing, he will have it right on the button by looking at a paper on his desk or glancing off quite naturally in another direction. He was under contract to Paramount and the studio felt his name would not only help establish the series but give added class to the pictures. Louis King directed *Revenge*, with Edward T. Lowe on the script. Howard, Denny, Louise Campbell, and Clive kept their same roles. By this time, Howard's subtle, understated approach had taken command.

Hugh and Phyllis are off to Switzerland to be married, when the pilot of a plane with the inventor of a new explosive kills the inventor and bails out. Hugh is drawn into the case. Phyllis, in that characteristically shrewish cliché of female girl friends of detectives in the Thirties and Forties, wants him to try some other line of endeavor. Phyllis, at one point, packs up to leave for good. But she doesn't. Together, Barrymore and Howard apprehend the pilot.

Bulldog Drummond's Peril (Paramount, 1938) was directed by James Hogan. Stuart Palmer did the screenplay, basing it on McNeile's book *The Third Round*. As this picture opens, Howard and Louise Campbell are definitely getting married; the announcements are printed. Algy gives Hugh a penguin as a wedding present. Gwen Longworth, played by Nydia Westman, gives Phyllis one of the diamonds created by her father using a new synthetic process. The diamond is stolen and Drummond takes off after the thieves. There are two gangs of them in this case, with Porter Hall, himself a scientist, the head of the smarter gang.

Edward Dmytryk was the film editor on this picture, and the director, James Hogan, allowed him to be continuously on the set to see how the picture was

Louis King (with cigar) directing John Howard, Reginald Denny, and E. E. Clive in the pub sequence from *Bulldog Drummond Comes Back* (Paramount, 1937).
PHOTO COURTESY OF THE NATIONAL FILM ARCHIVE.

played so he would best know how to cut it. He would engage in word games, using an unabridged dictionary, with Jack Barrymore, Howard, and Hogan.

"Barrymore was excellent," Dmytryk recalled. "He had a huge vocabulary. Yet, strange thing, Barrymore had an unbelievably dirty collar. He didn't seem to care about things like that. After 6:00 P.M., Jack was usually drunk. Hogan would have to have someone watch him if he wanted to use Jack after that time. There was a dialogue director hanging around. Dialogue directors did nothing. Barrymore was drunk. It was after six. He told the dialogue director to hold the idiot card higher. He kept saying, 'Higher, higher.' An apple box was brought for him to stand on. 'Higher,' Barrymore ordered. Hogan finally had to call it quits that day since Barrymore was too drunk to continue."

McNeile, at the time of his death, had earned a reputed $400,000 from the Bulldog Drummond property. His last year he had collaborated with Gerard Fairlie in a new stage play called *Bulldog Drummond Hits Out*. Paramount was so pleased with the success of the series that, negotiating with McNeile's widow, they extended their ten-year option, which had been limited to only four photoplays, to an additional three photoplays for the same term. To give the reader some idea of the financial prospects of the series, *Bulldog Drummond Strikes Back* had cost $514,152.95 to make; it earned $714,651.76 in the United States and a foreign gross of $591,432, which includes revenue from the United Kingdom of $378,243. This gave the picture almost a million and a half in gross income.

Barrymore was no longer interested in the Colonel Neilson role, so he was replaced by H. B. Warner in *Bulldog Drummond in Africa*, (Paramount, 1938). Heather Angel returned to the series in her original role of Phyllis. The screenplay was by Garnett Weston and Louis King directed. Barrymore was missed in the picture, but *Africa* got good reviews on its own merits.

Arrest Bulldog Drummond (Paramount, 1939) found Hugh confronted, on the verge of his marriage, by George Zucco, who succeeds in stealing a death ray machine. Stuart Palmer did the screenplay and James Hogan directed. Hogan also directed *Bulldog Drummond's Secret Police* (Paramount, 1939), with a screenplay by Garnett Weston, which, somewhat wearily by this time, found Hugh about to marry when he learns of a fabulous treasure hidden beneath his castle coveted by Leo G. Carroll. The search leads the principals into an underground chamber of horrors before Carroll is subdued.

Paramount announced that *Bulldog Drummond's Bride* (Paramount, 1939) was to be the final entry in the Drummond series. Stuart Palmer and Garnett Weston collaborated on the screenplay and again James Hogan directed. Hugh agrees to help Colonel Neilson capture elusive bank robber Eduardo Ciannelli, asking Phyllis to meet him in France three days hence for their wedding. He's successful, of course, but this time on both counts. The long-awaited marriage at last puts an end to Drummond's bachelor roving.

Columbia Pictures decided to resurrect the Drummond property in the late Forties and starred Ron Randell, soon to become the last Lone Wolf in that series, as Drummond in *Bulldog Drummond at Bay* (Columbia, 1947). Phyllis, Tenny, and Colonel Neilson were nowhere in evidence, nor was Algy; Drum-

One of the horrors that Reginald Denny, E. E. Clive, Heather Angel, John Howard, and H. B. Warner encounter in *Bulldog Drummond's Secret Police* (Paramount, 1939).   PHOTO COURTESY OF THE NATIONAL FILM ARCHIVE.

mond is assisted by an old friend, Pat O'Moore, and a cub reporter. Sidney Salkow directed, but the picture was actually a remake of *Bulldog Drummond at Bay* (Republic, 1937), a lone entry occurring between Ray Milland's try at the role and John Howard's series for Paramount. The Republic film had a lot more action, and the villains, led by Victor Jory, had been international thieves, not mere racketeers. Anita Louise played the love interest in the Columbia film. Frank Gruber was credited with the screen adaptation. *Bulldog Drummond Strikes Back* (Columbia, 1947), the second effort with Randell, was little better. Frank McDonald directed. The plot bore no relationship to either the earlier picture or the novel.

Phyllis is finally successful in the film from which this lobby card is taken.

PHOTO COURTESY OF THE NATIONAL FILM ARCHIVE.

Edward Small Productions, operating through Bernard Small, had a financial interest in the two Columbia Drummond pictures. Small changed distribution to Twentieth Century-Fox, Bernard Small remaining the producer. Tom Conway, who had been dropped from RKO and had a definite following as the Falcon, possibly the most popular detective series of the mid Forties, was signed to play Drummond. The plots of the two Drummond films in which Conway starred were more complex than the Columbia entries had been, but Conway underwent no alteration in the way he portrayed Hugh Drummond from the way he had played Tom Lawrence, the Falcon.

The Challenge (20th-Fox, 1948) was first, with the screenplay by Frank Gruber and directed by Jean Yarbrough. 13 Lead Soldiers (20th-Fox, 1948) was directed by Frank McDonald. There's one asset in that Algy Longworth is back as a character in these two films, but in 13 Lead Soldiers his attempts at comedy, projected by John Newland in the role, were pathetic.

When Bulldog Drummond returned to the screen for his final bows to date —he was portrayed by Richard Johnson. Deadlier than the Male (Universal, 1967) was financed by Sydney Box and Bruce Newberry, produced by Betty E. Box, and directed by Ralph Thomas. Drummond and his swinging nephew are right out of the James Bond stories. Elke Sommer and Sylva Koscina—seen in mini bikinis—are deadly assassins who, the screenplay implies, are also lesbians.

The picture had an indifferent reception. The Rank Organization undertook to release a follow-up picture, *Some Girls Do*, in 1971. Betty E. Box again produced, and Ralph Thomas directed. This time Richard Johnson as Drummond is investigating a series of accidents befalling testing of a British supersonic jet. Carl Peterson is the master criminal with a flock of bionic super-lovelies as his allies. At least this could be said for Drummond, unlike so many others; he made his exit in a flurry of extravagance, rather than in a "B" series of descending production values.

There was one Drummond film which came between the last Conway film and the first Johnson effort, *Calling Bulldog Drummond* (M-G-M, 1951). It starred Walter Pidgeon as Drummond, an older man now, seasoned and retired, who is brought back into action by Scotland Yard to help battle a crime wave. Victor Saville directed. David Tomlinson was the comic relief, Robert Beatty the master villain, and Margaret Leighton the feminine interest. It was produced out of frozen funds in Britain but did not lead to a series. Mention of the picture brings up Walter Pidgeon and the effort to make him a screen detective a decade previously.

Robert Beatty, Margaret Leighton, director Victor Saville, and Walter Pidgeon sitting on the set of *Calling Bulldog Drummond* (M-G-M, 1951).

PHOTO COURTESY OF THE NATIONAL FILM ARCHIVE.

III

It was primarily because of the success of Bulldog Drummond at Paramount, and, coincidentally the Saint at RKO and the Lone Wolf at Columbia, that Metro-Goldwyn-Mayer decided to make its own detective adventure series. As the central character, the studio chose Nick Carter, a clean-cut super-hero of pulps who had been around since the turn of the century. Nick Carter was a corporate creation. His first recorded adventure was in the September 18, 1886, number of the *New York Weekly*. Ormond G. Smith, son of one of the founders of the pulp magazine syndicate Street & Smith, provided the outline for the story to John Russell Coryell, who wrote it and followed with two sequels.

The character proved a success, and a number of other writers over the intervening years wrote stories about him, signing the tales with a pseudonym such as "by Sergeant Ryan" or "by Nicholas Carter." According to the *Encyclopedia of Mystery and Detection* (McGraw-Hill, 1976), the most prolific contributor to the series was Frederick Van Rensselaer Dey, who wrote more than a thousand stories in the saga.

None of these were really high-grade fare. The emphasis was on outlandish physical achievements by Nick Carter. Stories in the saga are still being written today, although the character has definitely been updated and now he is a modern secret-service agent, a graduate of the Matt Helm and James Bond school.

Just why Metro struck upon this character is perplexing if the Bulldog Drummond films are not taken into account. Lucien Hubbard, who had produced Metro's later entries in the Philo Vance series, was credited with the idea and, as a reward, was placed in charge of production on the first picture. Bertram Milhauser, who later worked on the Universal Sherlock Holmes series, did the screenplay for *Nick Carter, Master Detective* (M-G-M, 1939). The title apparently was so unusual that when Columbia Pictures began their Ellery Queen series, rather than using their usual inaugural title for a new detective series, like *Meet Nero Wolfe* (Columbia, 1936) or *Meet Boston Blackie* (Columbia, 1941), they chose *Ellery Queen, Master Detective* (Columbia, 1940). The title was certainly more suitable for Ellery Queen, in terms of his portrayal in the Columbia screenplay, than for Nick Carter in the Metro entry.

Walter Pidgeon, born on September 22, 1898, in St. John, New Brunswick, was an M-G-M romantic contract player assigned the role of Carter. This was scarcely inspired casting and, when the series failed dismally after three entries he was better employed by Metro in that enchanting series of true love fantasies of the Forties where he co-starred with Greer Garson.

Jacques Tourneur directed the initial effort. Character actor Donald Meek was cast as Nick's sidekick. The plot required Meek to be comical, but neither the direction nor the dialogue gave him any assistance. Most of the last two reels is given over to a chase. Meek surreptitiously paints a large X on the culprit's automobile so Nick can easily pursue him from the sky. When the saboteurs take off in a motorboat through a heavy fog, this doesn't deter Nick. He flies right after them through the fog.

Phantom Raiders (M-G-M, 1940) came next with Pidgeon and Meek teamed up again. Carter works strictly for the fee he is paid, although he makes quite a fool of himself chasing every skirt who walks through the picture. Nick's employer is an English shipping firm. They want him to investigate a gang of saboteurs who, by means of a radio-controlled bomb device, are sinking their ships in the Panama Canal. Nick is there on vacation, but he enthusiastically accepts the assignment. There isn't much mystery left once Nick discovers that Joseph Schildkraut, playing a former Chicago gangster despite his German accent, is in the vicinity. From that time on, it's just a matter of getting the goods on Schildkraut. Nat Pendleton joined the cast to assist in the comedy, but neither he nor Meek, with or without Jacques Tourneur's direction, could bring it off. The improbable finish wasn't as exciting as it had been in the first film.

There were no new ideas in *Sky Murder* (M-G-M, 1940), although you have to hand it to Metro for stubborn persistence. In all the films, Donald Meek, at critical junctures, releases his pet bees. He does so here with predictability. Nick is requisitely flirtatious with Joyce Compton, and Kaaren Verne, playing a foreigner, is confused all her time on screen; as one reviewer suggested, it was probably an accurate portrait of her real state of mind. George B. Seitz was the director. He had been known for his exceptional work in Pathé action serials in the silent era, but too many Andy Hardy pictures had presumably blunted his approach to action films. The only memorable aspect of the film was the appearance of Tom Conway in a minor role. Surely it was with a sigh of relief that he went over to RKO and better things.

Never having thought much of the stories, perhaps I shouldn't have expected much more from the films, although evidently the public did. In any event, the series was canceled after *Sky Murder*. M-G-M finally did get its chance more than a decade later to put Walter Pidgeon in the Drummond role they wanted him for anyway, so perhaps all can be said to have ended well, even if it hadn't started out that way. In anticipation of a much longer-running series, by the time of its cancellation Metro owned screen rights to 1,261 Nick Carter stories dating all the way back to 1891.

IV

In *Sky Murder*, Joyce Compton played an amateur sleuth who was constantly getting in Nick Carter's way. Fortunately, for the sake of women in general, Hollywood was, upon occasion, far more charitable in its treatment of female detectives.

One of the best detective films of the early Thirties both in terms of direction and characterizations was *The Penguin Pool Murder* (RKO, 1932). It was based on a novel by Stuart Palmer and a story by Lowell Brentano, with the screenplay by Willis Goldbeck. Palmer was born in 1905 in Baraboo, Wisconsin. He was educated at the Art Institute of Chicago and the University of Wisconsin, all of which was of little help to him when he sought employment, working variously as an iceman, an apple picker, a sailor, a taxi driver, a newspaper reporter, an advertising copy writer, and, at last, with the publication of *The Penguin Pool Murder* in 1931, a detective story author. The novel featured a spinster schoolteacher named Hildegarde Withers and Inspector Piper, her unwilling associate in crime detection. The movie sale to RKO Radio Pictures led Palmer to a job with the studios as a screenwriter, principally for RKO, although he did contribute occasional scripts to Paramount like that for *Bulldog Drummond's Peril* (Paramount, 1938) and an entry in Columbia's Lone Wolf series.

Extremely good fortune prompted RKO to cast character actress Edna May Oliver as Miss Withers, with Jimmy Gleason's Inspector Piper as her ambivalent foil. Most reviewers at the time, and most cinema histories since, have described Edna May Oliver as "horse-faced." She herself was scarcely pleased with the appellation. She was born Edna May Nutter in Boston on November 9, 1884. Originally she wanted to be an opera singer, but lack of funds to pursue voice training in Europe compelled her to compromise and go on the stage instead. She had worked in the legitimate theater for nearly twenty years when, appearing in Chicago, she received a telegram from William LeBaron, who then was head of production at RKO. Her first motion picture appearance had been as early as 1923 at Paramount's Astoria studio, but no doubt LeBaron wasn't aware of it. He wanted actors for talking pictures with good stage voices. The telegram, in effect, asked her how much she wanted to sign with RKO.

"So I wired back what I wanted," Edna May Oliver told a *Photoplay* interviewer in 1931, "and LeBaron wired back 'nothing doing.' "

She remained on the stage. Sometime later, LeBaron wired again. This time her asking figure was greater. LeBaron wired his response: "All right. Button up your overcoat, come out and join the family."

Hollywood did many things for Edna May Oliver. For the first time in her life she could afford a home. When she was starting out on the stage, so little money came in that she used to hide in the wardrobe or behind a bureau when the landlord came to collect the rent. Now she had a house with a white picket fence surrounding the front lawn and the old-fashioned garden in the rear. She took up swimming and was accustomed to being driven to the ocean every day, rain or shine, summer or winter. She preferred to live alone, although in her early years in Beverly Hills she had a maid. She purchased a German shepherd to patrol her yard. She liked to sunbathe, water her posies, knit, or read outdoors. She took up horseback riding and frequently traveled the bridle path at Bel Air, in Los Angeles County. Her marriage to New York stockbroker D. W. Pratt lasted for all of three months and she divorced him, at his request, soon after arriving in Hollywood. The passion of her life remained music. "It's my inner life," she once said. "I couldn't live without it." She helped finance the Hollywood Bowl Symphony. She was invariably in her box under the stars in the summer months. She would play the piano and sing. She eventually bought an elaborate phonograph with speakers in many rooms so the entire house could be flooded with music.

Edna May Oliver off the set of *The Penguin Pool Murder* (RKO, 1932), looking at
one of the penguins being·fed by an attendant.

PHOTO COURTESY OF THE NATIONAL FILM ARCHIVE.

She made friends in the movies. Although she disliked going out, she would have friends join her for quiet dinners, Franklin Pangborn, Grant Mitchell, and Lynn Starling among them. When she went on a trip, she might wire a friend at the last minute to join her, with her paying the way. Her face was soon recognized by everyone. She had rather mixed feelings about it.

". . . [The] happiness is tinged with just a slight flavor of bitterness," she was quoted as saying, "because I know it's this face that makes them remember me. . . . Oh, well—why complain? I've found a measure of happiness, and let it go at that, face or no face. If any woman wants to be thought beautiful, let her surround herself with me, and she will be. As for me—if I ever have my own producing company, I'm going to surround *my*self with the most beautiful women I can hire. And then I'll at least stand out and be distinctive."

By 1939, however, her countenance underwent a gradual spiritualization; humanity and compassion radiated it. Yet it was undoubtedly on the basis of looks that she got the part in *The Penguin Pool Murder* (RKO, 1932). George Archainbaud was the director. The story had it that Mae Clark was intent on leaving Guy Usher. Richard Llewellyn sympathizes with Mae, because they were once lovers, and in a fit of temper knocks out Usher at the New York Aquarium. Hildegarde Withers is at the aquarium with her students. Shots of the sea life and fish in tanks are fascinating. While admiring the penguins, Guy Usher's body suddenly floats downward in the tank and into view through the glass partition. Jimmy Gleason is called in to investigate. Hildegarde is determined to keep him on the right track. Usher, it turns out, was murdered by having a hatpin stuck through his right eardrum while unconscious from the blow landed by Llewellyn. The dialogue is sparkling throughout, and the picture concludes with a trial sequence. Gleason, quite overwhelmed, proposes to Hildegarde at the fade, but she isn't about to marry him.

This set the tempo for the series. One of the most engaging aspects of the formula, of course, was the middle-aged romance between Hildegarde and Piper, as unusual in pictures of any vintage as it is enticing. *Murder on the Blackboard* (RKO, 1934) was next in production. Edna May Oliver was asked by RKO, as part of their austerity program, to take a pay cut; and she did. George Archainbaud again directed. Willis Goldbeck did the screenplay from a Stuart Palmer magazine serial. Hildegarde and Piper again join forces. If anything, the dialogue is even better than *Penguin* and more caustic in the best scenes.

Murder on a Honeymoon (RKO, 1935) was based on Palmer's story *The Puzzle of the Pepper Tree*. Interestingly, the picture was directed by none other than that lovable player from the later Boston Blackie series, Lloyd Corrigan. It had a splendid cast. Leo G. Carroll portrayed a motion picture director on location at Catalina Island. Willie Best, the Negro actor, was billed as Eat an' Sleep on the credits. Lola Lane, Chick Chandler, and George Meeker, along with Carroll and Edna May Oliver as Hildegarde are all on the seaplane to Catalina. A man thought to be the key witness at a forthcoming trial is murdered. Hildegarde sends for Gleason to help her out. There are many scenes set around the old casino on the island. Corrigan was fortunate in that Robert Benchley joined Seton I. Miller on the screenplay, and the humor was bright without stupidity.

Tully Marshall, Edna May Oliver, and James Gleason on the set of *Murder on the Blackboard* (RKO, 1934). PHOTO COURTESY OF THE NATIONAL FILM ARCHIVE.

One of the reasons, surely, for the successful advent of the series and the three strong entries at the outset was producer Kenneth MacGowan. He was born in Winthrop, Massachusetts, in 1888 and entered the industry through advertising and promotion for Samuel Goldwyn. MacGowan's hobby was reading detective fiction. He believed that detective stories could be entertainingly filmed while stressing the art of detection at the same time as building sympathy for the central characters and a concern for the story line. When Edna May Oliver fell seriously ill in late 1935 after *Honeymoon* was completed and RKO decided to continue the series without her, MacGowan chose to be taken off the pictures. He was replaced by William Sistrom, about whom I will have more to say later on in this narrative. Oliver was replaced by RKO contract comedienne Helen Broderick. Palmer's prototype for Hildegarde Withers was his high school English teacher, a Miss Fern Hackett, and, ostensibly, his father. *Murder on a Bridle Path* (RKO, 1936) was based on Palmer's story *The Puzzle of the Briar Pipe*. Dorothy Yost, Thomas Lennon, Edmund North, and James Gow were all given screen credit for the script, but none of them, and least of all Broderick, had anywhere in their heads the conception of Palmer's delicate creation. It was a bad picture.

Sistrom felt the problem was in the casting of Hildegarde—a rather elementary deduction. So, for the next picture, he tried Zasu Pitts. It wasn't really an improvement. Pitts was known primarily as a scatterbrain, an impression which most of her pre-1936 screen work served to augment, especially the Hal Roach short comedies she made with Thelma Todd, who had recently been murdered. Jimmy Gleason was given top billing, as if by this means RKO could hope to overcome the loss of Edna May Oliver, which in fact had spelled doom to the series. Pitts could in no way express the quiet authority and stage presence Oliver could, and it was senseless to make her try. When Edna May Oliver recovered, rather than return to RKO she signed a new contract with M-G-M and immediately went to work on David O. Selznick's *David Copperfield* (M-G-M, 1935) where she was brilliantly cast as David's Aunt Betsy. The New York *Times* put it more directly: "Miss Pitts is better as a midnight screamer during the unreeling of these detective epics than she is as an inquisitive and reliable amateur Philo."

Ben Holmes directed *The Plot Thickens* (RKO, 1936). The RKO Publicity Department decided to emphasize Jimmy Gleason as the star of the series, but most reviewers weren't fooled, nor has anyone been fooled since. The comic repartee had to be softened to permit Pitts and Gleason to work amicably together, but in the end it did no good.

RKO tried again with *40 Naughty Girls* (RKO, 1937) before throwing in the towel. According to the screenplay by John Grey, Zasu Pitts, fluttering her hands and letting off those bewildered sighs, is supposed to keep the police from blundering. She has one good line in the picture. When Marjorie Lord comments of the murder victim, "But everybody loved Windy," Pitts responds, "Somebody didn't."

In the Forties, Stuart Palmer joined Craig Rice, who was also working at RKO in the Story Department, and they wrote a series of short stories which united their detectives Hildegarde Withers and J. J. Malone respectively. M-G-M decided to make a film using the characters. But after purchasing the screen rights, studio rewrites altered the characters so that Hildegarde became Mrs. O'Malley, portrayed by Marjorie Main, in a backwoods role similar to her Ma Kettle characterization, while Malone was played by James Whitmore. The picture was titled, as you might expect, *Mrs. O'Malley and Mr. Malone* (M-G-M, 1950).

Just as the RKO series with its middle-aged heroine ceased production, on the other side of the spectrum Warner Brothers began to film the Nancy Drew mysteries with Bonita Granville in the leading role. The character was a creation of Edward L. Stratemeyer, who was born in Elizabeth, New Jersey, in 1862. After beginning in the pulp markets, in 1906 he founded the Stratemeyer

Literary Syndicate, which was to specialize in producing children's books. To date, the Syndicate has published some 1,200 titles. Stratemeyer himself supplied the plot outlines and edited almost 700 books before his death in 1930. His two daughters continued the Syndicate; one of them, Harriet S. Adams, still active, is now the head of the firm. In addition to successful series such as Tom Swift, the Rover Boys, the Bobbsey Twins, and the Hardy Boys, Stratemeyer launched the Nancy Drew series and wrote three of the novels about her. Harriet S. Adams has written the rest, now at forty-six titles in 1976, and selling between one and two million copies a year collectively.

Recently, there has been a campaign to "modernize" the older books. This means that ethnic groups such as blacks or Italians or Jews no longer talk like blacks or Italians or Jews. In the Thirties, youngsters in the United States were made vitally aware by means of books like the Nancy Drew mysteries of the richness and diversity of the different national and racial characteristics of Americans (although admittedly with a heavy leaning on stereotype). As long ago as de Tocqueville, Americans were warned that the single most dangerous national impulse, and one surely destined to have the most shattering long-term effect, was the drive toward uniformity. All that the special interest pressure groups have achieved, as evidenced in the Nancy Drew rewrites, is that now all the characters talk exactly alike, in fine, grammatical English and, more than ever, they all live alike and have alike outlooks. I wonder if this is really a preferable image for the "modern" youngster to have.

Reading habits have changed. The Nancy Drew stories used to appeal to girls between the ages of ten and fifteen. Now they are usually picked up at eight and put down at twelve. Nancy, on the other hand, has changed her age from sixteen to eighteen. Murder was never a subject to be investigated in the books. Warner's changed that, even though they hoped the new series would compete with Metro's Andy Hardy. Bonita Granville was born in New York City in 1923. She had appeared in a number of roles in Warner Brothers films in the Thirties but was typecast as a malicious brat by her Oscar-nomination portrayal of a schoolgirl in *These Three* (Warner's, 1936), based on Lillian Hellman's stage play *The Children's Hour*.

Nancy Drew, Detective (Warner's, 1938) began the series. John Litel was cast as Nancy's attorney father, who allows her the freedom to pursue the solutions to various mysteries she happens to come upon. Frankie Thomas played her boy friend, Ted Nickerson, altered from the Ned Nickerson of the novels. The original screenplay was by Kenneth Gamet and was based on a novel by the Syndicate's pseudonym, Carolyn Keene. When an old lady who has promised her school a large endowment disappears, Nancy investigates to find out what happened to her. William Clemens directed. He also directed *Nancy Drew, Reporter* (Warner's, 1939), which found Nancy working on a newspaper as part of a school assignment. She becomes convinced that a girl being held for murder is actually innocent.

Nancy Drew, Trouble Shooter (Warner's, 1939), again directed by William Clemens, showed Nancy coming to the assistance of one of John Litel's friends who has been wrongly accused of murder. *Nancy Drew and the Hidden Stair-*

case (Warner's, 1939) was last in the series. Nancy wasn't really old enough to be kissed by boys, much less, like Andy Hardy, to have innumerable romantic problems. But even murder plots weren't sufficient, evidently, to keep a juvenile audience interested.

Another series that Warner's launched in the Thirties with more success was that featuring the character Torchy Blane, created originally by Frederick Nebel, one of the best, if lesser known, contributors to *Black Mask.* Torchy was a tough, independent, wisecracking newspaperwoman wildly in love with Steve McBride of the police department. Her cases were always involved with murder, and frequently they were more adventure films than straight detective stories. Glenda Farrell played Torchy in seven of the nine entries.

All of which brings us to that curiosity of detective fiction which had such a strong appeal to feminine readers in the Thirties but whose melodramatic books seem to set most critics' teeth on edge, namely Mignon G. Eberhart. She was born on July 6, 1899, in a suburb of Lincoln, Nebraska. According to her testimony, when three years of college led to her marriage to Alanson G. Eberhart, a civil engineer whose work required him to travel greatly, she turned to writing to escape boredom and, believing mystery fiction paid the best, tried that. Her first books featured the team of Sarah Keate, a middle-aged registered nurse, and Lance O'Leary, a rising young police official. If this sounds a little familiar in view of the Hildegarde Withers setup, nonetheless in Eberhart's favor it must be reflected that she came first. Her second novel *While the Patient Slept* (Warner's, 1935), not only became the first film in the Warner Brothers series, but it also won her a $5,000 prize in the Doubleday, Doran mystery-of-the-year contest. Doubleday was a very enterprising publisher and saw immediate dividends from having a strong tie-in of novels with motion pictures. Long before anyone else recognized the value of performing rights, generous contracts were negotiated for the Cisco Kid property and for Hopalong Cassidy. Warner's eventually tied in their mysteries by declaring them Crime Club pictures in a subtitle which harked back to Doubleday's marketing scheme for detective stories.

With this as a background, I wish I could say something positive about *While the Patient Slept,* but in fact it was a dull picture. Aline MacMahon portrayed Nurse Keate and Guy Kibbee—of all people!—was Lance O'Leary. Obviously, Warner's hoped to capture the audience for the Hildegarde Withers pictures. Allen Jenkins and Lyle Talbot, contract players from the Warner's roster, were included in the cast. Ray Enright directed.

The Murder of Dr. Harrigan (Warner's, 1936) saw the idea of middle-aged romance scrapped and the series got down to the serious business of young love. Ricardo Cortez and Kay Linaker, now Sally Keating, find their hospital love affair interrupted by murder. The police are called in. Mary Astor was cast as a nurse who helps conceal the murderer. Cortez, frustrating an attack on Keating's life, finally has to explain the whole thing, which he does by means of a reconstruction aided by flashbacks. I hope you don't mind if I provide the hint that the murders were committed by a man overzealous in his desire to test a new formula.

Frank McDonald directed *The Murder of Dr. Harrigan* and he directed the next entry, *Murder by. an Aristocrat* (Warner's, 1936), which had Marguerite Churchill as Sally Keating and Lyle Talbot now back as an amorous physician. Nurse Keating has her hour when, via a reconstruction through flashbacks, she exposes the guilty party.

The series underwent a considerable improvement when Ann Sheridan was cast as Sara Keate (another name change) in *The Patient in Room 18* (Warner's, 1938). Sheridan was a very gifted actress with a genuine flare for comedy and drama which Howard Hawks drew upon later. But as it stood in 1938, Warner's did not know exactly how to use her any more than Paramount had in the early Thirties. Ann was thin, accentuating her height, which was slightly below five feet six inches. She could be hard and tough, but you would never know it from roles like Pat O'Brien's girl friend in *San Quentin* (Warner's, 1937), directed by Lloyd Bacon. In *Room 18* Cliff Clark played his typically bewildered but dyspeptic inspector from homicide. Patric Knowles was cast as Lance O'Leary, a private detective in the hospital recovering from a nervous breakdown. O'Leary has gone to pieces because of an inability to solve a case. Keate is his nurse. The screenplay, by Eugene Solow and Robertson White, was directed in a comic vein by Bobby Connolly and Crane Wilbur, but Ann Sheridan was the only rewarding aspect of the whole enterprise.

Evidently Warner's thought so too, since they put Sheridan in the next and final film in the series, *Mystery House* (Warner's, 1938). It was a partial remake of *Murder by an Aristocrat.* Dick Purcell played Lance. Noel Smith directed. There are only two murders in the picture, but the acting, except for that of Ann Sheridan, was so uniformly poor that, again, it really didn't matter.

Although, quite rightly, Agatha Christie and her Belgian detective, Hercule Poirot, will occupy me in a later chapter, it is here I should like to introduce Miss Marple. With the exception of the Edna May Oliver/Jimmy Gleason entries in the Hildegarde Withers series, Margaret Rutherford's four Miss Marple films for M-G-M's British studio in the Sixties are among the finest detective films in general and those featuring female investigators in particular.

Murder at the Vicarage (Dodd, Mead, 1930) was the first Miss Marple book Agatha Christie wrote. It isn't as fine, to my way of thinking, as any of the subsequent Marple books because in it the author depended on a first-person narrator, namely the vicar. The book was turned into a more successful stage play which opened at the Playhouse in London on December 14, 1949. I happened to see a revival at the Savoy in London in the spring of 1976 with Avril Angers cast as Miss Marple. In the program, there was an article about Margaret Rutherford by Matthew Norgate. ". . . one must admit that to this spinster-sleuth she seemed to add qualities which appeared essential to the character but which one felt might not have occurred to Agatha Christie." Avril Angers was not in the least influenced by the Margaret Rutherford films in her interpretation of the role, but I, for one, can never shake Dame Rutherford's characterization from my mind when I read one of the Miss Marple stories. While it may seem blasphemous to say so, I think Miss Marple is a more plausibly drawn, a more humanly inviting character than any of Agatha Christie's other detec-

tives, including Poirot. In fact, more often than not, I find Poirot insufferable. Not so with Miss Marple. However much of a busybody she may be, she is the kind of person you might like very much to know. Agatha Christie herself was enthusiastic about the idea of Margaret Rutherford playing Miss Marple in the photoplays, and I cannot help but suspect that with books like *The Mirror Crack'd* (Dodd, Mead, 1962), which Dame Christie dedicated to Margaret Rutherford, the screen interpretation effected subtle changes in the fictional characterization, especially in terms of Miss Marple's attitude toward the oncoming of old age, her indomitable will, her inflexible determination, and her eccentric but insatiable curiosity about human nature.

Margaret Rutherford was born in London in 1892. When her mother died, she was raised by an aunt. She became a singing and elocution teacher in London. In 1924–25, she attended the Old Vic School of Acting and made her stage debut at the age of thirty-three as the fairy with the long nose in *Little Jack Horner*, a pantomime play. She continued to get parts in numerous London plays. In 1931, she met Stringer Davis when he was a leading man at the Oxford Repertory Company. Oddly enough, they weren't married until 1945. In the course of their consummately happy marriage, they adopted four children. One of them, George Langley Hall, when he was thirty-eight in 1968, underwent a sex change operation and assumed the name of Dawn Hall. The next year Dawn married a twenty-five-year-old black male at her home in Charleston, South Carolina. Margaret Rutherford, when queried, said she approved of the marriage except for the fact that the black was a Baptist.

Rutherford made her motion picture debut in a British film of 1936, *Dusty Ermine*. On stage, in 1939, she permanently established herself in the role of Miss Prism in Sir John Gielgud's production of *The Importance of Being Earnest*. She went to New York with the company in 1947. She loved reading poetry and all her life gave recitations in churches and manors, as is still the custom in the United Kingdom.

When Metro approached her to play the role of Miss Marple in a projected series of photoplays to be shot at the rate of two a year, she rejected the idea. "Murder, you see, is not the sort of thing I could get close to," she later commented. "I don't like anything that tends to lower or debase or degrade. But then a friend and I talked it over and she pointed out that it *could* be entertaining and might indeed have a moral value, of a sort. And one does like to throw one's weight in on the side of good, doesn't one?"

Murder She Said (M-G-M, 1962) was the first in the series and probably the best. "I see her as a dear spinster lady," Dame Rutherford remarked of Miss Marple, "very much like myself to look at, living in a small country town, who is able to apply her knowledge of human nature to any conceivable crime and come up with a solution, always just one jump ahead of the police. She is eccentric but her passion for justice is very real."

Ann Sheridan, seen here with Patric Knowles, was the only saving grace in the Nurse Keating series at Warner Brothers.   PHOTO COURTESY OF VIEWS & REVIEWS MAGAZINE.

She was seventy-one when she began in the role. Stringer Davis, who customarily would help her remember her lines (her eyesight increasingly was failing), was cast in the picture as Mr. Stringer, the local librarian, a role he had in all the films. On the set Dame Rutherford would walk purposefully to the mark under the lights and, adjusting a wayward fold in her dress, would nod to the director, George Pollock, "Ready when you are, George." Stringer Davis, if asked, would recall the time when they met and he was the leading man. "My wife started with the company in the same year as a bit player. Now, *she* is the star. I'm lucky if the newspaper columnists spell my name correctly." But he would rise at five in the morning, when they were working, and be glad of the fact that his wife was somewhat deaf "because then the alarm doesn't wake her and she can sleep until I bring her a cup of tea." They would go over her lines before she got out of bed. Seven years her junior, Davis was completely devoted to his wife. He would see that she had a constant supply of her favorite ginger chocolates or peppermint creams. He would order her lunch, usually soup, cheese, and biscuits, and see that it was sent to her dressing room. He would answer all her fan mail because Margaret Rutherford believed that "if people are kind enough to write, one should have the courtesy to reply."

Agatha Christie visited the set of *Murder She Said*. Afterwards, when interviewers would ask Dame Rutherford if she knew Dame Christie, she would recall that visit and add, "She's eighty-one, you know. Hers is the world of observation and the pen. Mine—well, it's speech. As I get older, I find I'm slower to pick up contemporary doings. I don't do a great deal of reading anymore." Beyond that she would not go.

The screenplay, by David Pursall and Jack Seddon, was based on the Miss Marple novel *4:50 from Paddington* (Collins, 1957). It showed Miss Marple getting on a train at Victoria Station. When another train passes the one she is on, she sees a man struggling with a woman, choking her. She reports the incident to the police. She is not believed because no body is found. Investigating on her own with the help of Mr. Stringer, Miss Marple suspects the body is hidden somewhere in the grounds of an estate alongside the railroad track. She hires on at the estate as a cook. A touchingly human relationship develops between Miss Marple and Master Alexander, played by Ronnie Raymond. It is one of the few instances in detective films, and I think the best, where there is depicted such a growing rapport between an old person and a youth. But then, among her special interests, Margaret Rutherford and Stringer Davis were parent-confessors at a boys' reformatory. Six murders take place before Miss Marple solves the case.

By the time M-G-M came to make *Murder at the Gallop* (M-G-M, 1963), the studio held exclusive contracts with Agatha Christie entitling them to screen rights on eighty books and four hundred short stories, as well as a contract with Margaret Rutherford. While she was filming *Murder She Said*, Rutherford was invited to Buckingham Palace to receive the Order of the British Empire from

Margaret Rutherford and Stringer Davis made the M-G-M-British Miss Marple series a delight.   PHOTO COURTESY OF METRO-GOLDWYN-MAYER.

Queen Elizabeth. "I have no desire to sit back and write my memoirs," she said presently on the set of *Murder at the Gallop.* "I like to make people laugh. I want to make them forget their troubles and it's what I can do best. After all, it's so easy to laugh at an old gal like me, isn't it?" She would frequently break up the cast by dancing a jig and when it came time for her to dance in the film she declined the waltz that director George Pollock had in mind, and insisted on doing the twist.

Murder at the Gallop was based on the Poirot novel *After the Funeral* (Dodd, Mead, 1953), with the screenplay by James P. Cavanagh, David Pursall, and Jack Seddon. While making a charity collection at an English manor, Miss Marple and Mr. Stringer find the owner dying. They also find a cat, which is curious because the owner of the manor was deathly afraid of cats. Inspector Craddock was played by Charles Tingwell. Despite his efforts to keep Miss Marple off the case and minding her own business, Miss Marple (with the blitheful comment to Mr. Stringer, "Have we ever read a thriller that stops with a single killing?") rents a room at Robert Morley's inn to observe the various heirs. In addition to riding about the countryside, Miss Marple does expose the murderer. "I didn't really ride that horse in *Murder at the Gallop,*" she said subsequently. "The only time I ever rode was when I was two or three in India. I had a white pony." But her riding sequences were among her funniest.

The same year, Margaret Rutherford appeared in *The V.I.P.s* (M-G-M, 1963), which starred Elizabeth Taylor and Richard Burton. She won an Academy Award for her performance.

Murder Most Foul (M-G-M, 1964) was based on the Poirot novel *Mrs. McGinty's Dead* (Dodd, Mead, 1952). David Pursall and Jack Seddon did the screenplay and George Pollock again directed. Miss Marple was on a jury. The police are certain of a conviction. Tingwell has got a promotion to Chief Inspector as a result of his record of arrests. It's a hung jury because of Miss Marple, who makes up her mind to investigate the murder on her own. A playbill among the murdered Mrs. McGinty's effects causes Miss Marple to join a small touring repertory company. One of the company is also murdered. "While it must irritate you, Inspector," Miss Marple tells Tingwell at one point, "women do sometimes have superior minds." She traps the culprit during a performance of the play they are all in.

Murder Ahoy! (M-G-M, 1964) was fourth in the series, but the Metro Sales Department thought it better than *Murder Most Foul.* Consequently, it went third into release. Since the picture culminated with a sword fight between Miss Marple and the murderer, Margaret Rutherford was given fencing lessons by Rupert Evans, who was accustomed to providing professional training to motion picture players. David Pursall and Jack Seddon came up with a wholly original screenplay for this picture. George Pollock directed. Miss Marple becomes a trustee on a board which trains youngsters in seamanship on an old sailing ship. Most of the action takes place on the ship, exteriors being filmed aboard an actual cadet training vessel on the Thames. In this entry, as in the others, the police are depicted not as being stupid but merely unimaginative.

Agatha Christie particularly did not like *Murder Ahoy!* "I kept off films for years," she said in an interview, "because I thought they'd give me too many heartaches. Then I sold the rights to M-G-M, hoping they'd use them for television. But they chose films. It was too awful. They did things like taking a Poirot book and putting Miss Marple in it. And all the climaxes were so poor, you could see them coming. I get an unregenerate pleasure when I think they're not being a success. They wrote their own script for the last one—nothing to do with me at all. *Murder Ahoy*, one of the silliest things you ever saw! It got very bad reviews, I'm delighted to say."

Dame Christie was undoubtedly too harsh on the Marple films. Metro wanted Margaret Rutherford to come to Hollywood in January 1964 to appear in the picture *Every Man Should Have One*, budgeted at $2 million. She didn't want to go to the United States. The next Marple picture scheduled was *The Body in the Library*, based on the Miss Marple novel of 1942. Metro scrapped its plans for making it and failed to renew Margaret Rutherford's option. In part, the Miss Marple pictures were not as successful with American audiences as the studio had hoped—they were released to the art theaters—and there was pique about her obduracy in not coming to Hollywood.

It suited Margaret Rutherford. She was recipient of the title Dame for her distinguished services to the acting profession in 1967. She and Stringer Davis lived in their fifth home since their marriage, Elm Close. On the surrounding lawns, the couple built a bird sanctuary, and it was their intention to have an open-air theater. In 1968, Dame Rutherford tripped over a rug and broke her leg while filming in Italy. Two hip fractures finally led to complications. She died on May 22, 1972. Stringer Davis survived her. "Old age?" she once said. "That's nothing to be ashamed of. I'm beginning to be rather proud of it." And it was in her old age that she won international recognition.

*"People that come to me don't come to me
because they like the looks of my eyes, or the
way my office is furnished, or because they've
known me at a club. They come to me because
they need me. They come to me because they
want to hire me for what I can do." She looked
up at him then. "Just what is it that you do,
Mr. Mason?" she asked. He snapped out two
words at her. "I fight!"*

from The Case of the Velvet Claws
by Erle Stanley Gardner

V

I do not know what your experience has been with attorneys, but most likely
you have had some experience with them. You really cannot get through life
without it.

For some reason I have never been able fully to determine, I am constantly
thrown into association with attorneys. While I have come to like several of
them, I would want to be a client only of a very few of them. And, at those
times when I have really needed an attorney, I haven't always been fortunate
enough to find one who was willing to give his all for his client. Most attorneys,
it would seem, prefer the easy way in connection with any lawsuit. They are
only too ready to settle, to compromise, to stress that their function is primarily
that of arbitrator, not advocate.

I don't know how many times I have been lectured by attorneys of all kinds
that only a hopeless nitwit would confuse the law, the practice of the law, or
the administration of the law with justice. Attorneys are worldly wise. Just as
college students study professors and not subjects to get grades, so attorneys
study judges. No case has any intrinsic merit. An attorney can instead give you
a reading as to how this judge will look upon the matter, or how that one will
decide.

Attorneys are usually experts in percentages. Unlike agents, they don't charge
by percentages, but they can examine a case, give you a percentage, based on
their knowledge of the judges, and will be inspired or dispirited in their ad-
vocacy on what they preconclude is the percentage of winning. Why fight it?
Settle. Why not just take it in stride? Write it off. It's the law. No one is interested in justice. You sound just like my wife. She keeps telling me that it's not
just. She doesn't understand law. What happens in the practice of the law has
nothing to do with justice.

If it weren't this way so much of the time, I seriously doubt Perry Mason

Erle Stanley Gardner in his study at his desk. Despite all the guns, he never killed
animals.   PHOTO COURTESY OF JEAN GARDNER.

would ever have become so popular. Perry Mason as an attorney is primarily and vitally concerned in securing justice, in discovering the truth, in defending his clients. Although technically a servant of the court, he knows that district attorneys are assessed in their effectiveness by the number of convictions they have had, not by their discerning ability to correctly interpret evidence.

The American public is rather contradictory on the subject. On the one hand everyone, apparently, is wholly willing to ignore the existence of organized crime, and on the other almost everyone campaigns for law and order. Just how law and order is supposed to coexist with organized lawlessness, I, for one, have never quite been able to determine.

Perry Mason is champion of neither upholding the law in all instances nor in supporting the police and the district attorney's office. Because his counsel is justice, Perry will go to dangerous lengths. He will sequester a witness, as he has done on at least nine different occasions. Perry has been careless about reporting a homicide; he destroys evidence and removes evidence; he breaks and enters; and he forges checks. He will plant objects to confuse the police and he will manufacture witnesses who seem to identify persons they never saw before. Whatever some attorneys may think of these techniques, the readers of Erle Stanley Gardner's books approve of them, just as they would like to believe in the existence of Perry Mason. It is precisely because people are more interested in true justice than the law that, at his height, Erle Stanley Gardner's books sold twenty thousand copies a day. I cannot think of a more deserved success. But Perry Mason, perhaps more than any other character, was the extension of his creator, not merely of his outlook on life and the world, but more importantly an embodiment of what is best, under necessarily ideal conditions, in the American experiment. If there was any tragedy at all in the creation, it is to be found in the fact that Perry Mason, when all is said and done, was a fantasy.

Erle Stanley Gardner was born in Malden, Massachusetts, on July 17, 1889. His father was a mining engineer and an expert in gold dredging, which led to Erle's attending schools in Mississippi, Oregon, California, and, in 1906, he spent several months in the Klondike. He completed high school in Palo Alto, California.

Erle was a youth of strong opinions. He was expelled from a school at Oroville, California, for cartooning a long-chinned disciplinarian. Also in Oroville he idolized a fellow named "Swede" Meyerhoffer, who eventually became famous as a stunt flier later killed in a plane crash. Swede announced that he was going to turn Erle into a prizefighter. I don't think Erle thought the whole business merely fun when one day, on his way to the Butte Athletic Club in Oroville, which Meyerhoffer had founded, he heard the clang of an ambulance and saw a warm-up fighter who had been projected out of a window by the contender imported from Sacramento to engage Erle in the ring. Erle, despite two black eyes and a cut-up face, managed to stay the limit. The two promoted a number of unlicensed matches which got Erle in trouble with the district attorney's office. After a lecture from a deputy district attorney on the consequences of what he was doing, Erle determined he would study law. He enrolled at Valparaiso University in Indiana, but he was expelled for slugging a professor.

Erle returned to Oxnard, California, and assumed the position of clerk-typist with a law firm. After reading law for an average of fifty hours a week, Erle passed his bar examination in 1911, at the age of twenty-one. On April 9, 1912, he married Natalie Talbert and, after trying law with several firms, settled at last in Oxnard. In 1916, he joined H. Frank Orr in law partnership in Ventura, California. Erle won a considerable reputation for championing the plight of the underdog, particularly through his defense of indigent Mexican and Chinese clients. Erle loved to relate years later, long after his fame as a novelist, that mysterious contributions would still appear on his bank statement, deposits made anonymously by one or another of the Chinese clients, now more affluent, he had once defended. Addressing juries, Erle always spoke in plain and simple terms, and his confidential, ingenuous manner won him their attention and respect.

The reader can readily discern that to practice law in this fashion, as fine as it was for the client, wasn't very lucrative. Erle quit law to go to work in San Francisco as a tire salesman in 1918. He really didn't expect to spend his life in sales work, but the money was better; for the moment, that's what counted, since Erle had decided he wanted to write. He started at it in 1920. In 1921, he returned to the firm of Drapeau, Orr, and Gardner with the understanding that he would be permitted time to adventure. He sold a story titled "Shrieking Skeleton" in 1923. He began turning out stories for pulp markets.

Erle's early marriage did not work out. But, curiously, neither he nor his wife sought a divorce. They had one daughter, named Grace. In 1927, Erle bought a camp wagon and occasionally would set out to gather material for use in his stories. He went to China in 1931, living with a Chinese family and writing all the time he was there.

Erle's working habits were ambitious. He practiced law all day long, reading law in the law library into the night; then, at his apartment, he would write until the early hours of the morning, setting himself the goal of turning out four thousand words a day. The year he spent in China, the dozens of stories he wrote under countless pseudonyms, earned him $20,525. In 1932, he wrote his first Perry Mason novel, *The Case of the Velvet Claws* (Morrow, 1933), in three days. He submitted it to several publishers and it was rejected. Thayer Hobson, the head of William Morrow, liked the book and suggested that Erle turn it into a series. Perry Mason became an immediate success. By the end of the Thirties, Gardner's titles were even on best-seller lists.

Erle owed much of his success to Hobson's constant attention to the proper promotion and sale of Gardner mysteries. The flyleaf on *Velvet Claws* had advised readers: "Perry Mason, criminal lawyer. Remember that name. You'll meet him again. He is going to be famous." Hobson knew that in publishing most often success is dependent on what the publisher does with a talented writer.

Gardner, for his part, was eminently fair in his dealings with Morrow. He felt an author should make his profits from sales to the reading public, not by way of excessive advances from the man who publishes his books. "An author should cement a personal relationship with his publisher," Erle once commented, "so that the publisher feels he has a *permanent* property in the author so long as the publisher can keep the author happy." The system obviously worked for the two men. When Hobson retired from Morrow, Gardner assigned administration

Helen Trenholme was a very amorous Della Street, seen here with Warren William as Perry Mason in *The Case of the Howling Dog* (Warner's, 1934).

PHOTO COURTESY OF UNITED ARTISTS TELEVISION.

of all his copyrights to a separate firm he set up with Hobson, which licensed Morrow with the titles of his books and concentrated on foreign sales.

Edward Dmytryk, the director, knew Gardner in the Thirties and was somewhat amused by his unusual life-style. Gardner lived alone in an apartment just down the street from his wife and daughter. Frequently Gardner would have parties with his family and invited guests, but, when it came time for the guests to leave, Gardner would leave with them.

Very shortly after Perry Mason's appearance in book form, Warner Brothers undertook to bring him to the screen. They purchased rights for *The Case of The Howling Dog* (Warner's, 1934) and cast Warren William in the role of Perry Mason. Warren William Krech was born in 1896 in Aitkin, Minnesota. After service in a field artillery unit in France, he went onstage with a troupe touring Army camps. He joined the road company of *I Love You*, a stage success with Richard Dix in the lead. Harry Warner signed William after seeing him onstage in New York in 1931.

It had been hardly a constant ascent for William. Between the touring show to Army camps and *I Love You*, he had been forced to return to Minnesota, where he entered newspaper work. The tour with the Dix play "blew up," but William managed to negotiate himself a position with an Erie, Pennsylvania, stock company. *Expressing Willie* marked his Broadway debut. He was frugal, as a result, with his amazing salary at Warner's, $1,250 a week. When the Warner salary cuts went into effect, unlike William Powell, who quit, or James Cagney (who, like William, was cut from $1,250 to $1,000 a week) and Ann Dvorak (who was cut from $250 to $210), who both went on strike, William stayed put. I suppose he agreed with Edward G. Robinson (who was cut from $2,500 a week to $1,975) that he could somehow make it on that salary.

I have already narrated how Warren William came to play Philo Vance. Once Metro-Goldwyn-Mayer took over production on the Philo Vance series, Warner's sought to compete with Perry Mason. It was natural that William should portray the attorney. Warner's expected it to become a series as success-ful in its way as the Philo Vance films.

Alan Crosland directed *Howling Dog*. Allen Jenkins was cast as Sergeant Holcolm. Helen Trenholme played Della Street. Mary Astor was cast as Bessie Foley, Mason's client. Ben Markson, the scenarist, didn't know how to handle the Paul Drake role, so it was dropped. Unlike the novel, Mason has a large law practice with several lawyers and numerous secretaries. However, the essential plot of the book is adhered to.

Gardner was very delicate in his treatment of the relationship between Perry and Della in the novels. Although, occasionally, Perry does kiss her, and a few times even proposes to her, she refuses. She is more devoted to her job than to marriage. She knows that Mason would only retire a wife and hire another sec-retary. She wants to share more of his life than any wife could.

While Gardner was still in law practice, he hired Jean Bethell and her sisters Ruth "Honey" Moore and Peggy Downs. He based Della Street on Jean Bethell. Over the years, she became as much a companion as secretary, managing all his affairs, organizing the activities of her sisters and other clerical people, and ac-companying him on all of his adventurous trips. Natalie would not grant Gardner a divorce and, presumably, it did not matter to him sufficiently to press the issue. When the actress Gail Patrick married Gardner's literary agent, she became fast friends with Erle. She remarked to me that, however tender and in-timate Gardner's relationship with Jean may have been, when he traveled on business he always made it a point that he and Jean had separate rooms on different floors of the same hotel.

The Case of the Curious Bride (Warner's, 1935) followed. Warner's subtitled it "A Crime Club Picture." Michael Curtiz, who in retrospect has come to be regarded as one of Warner's finest contract directors, directed the picture with even more *élan* and polish than had been true of his previous *The Kennel Murder Case*. Margaret Lindsay was cast as Rhoda. Claire Dodd was Della. Donald Woods had a supporting role. Allen Jenkins returned, not as the irascible Sergeant Holcolm of the novels, but instead as Spudsy, a sidekick of Mason's modeled loosely on Paul Drake. Errol Flynn appeared briefly in a flashback as the murder victim.

Perry is a gourmet in this picture. William's characterization differed dramatically from the rough and tumble Perry Mason of the novels. Della calls Perry "darling" and is shrewishly jealous of other women in his life. The picture was set in San Francisco. This time Perry has only a one-man office. The comedy routines got so absurd that in one scene Perry and Spudsy sob into their handkerchiefs under the influence of tear gas. Perry has a walk-in bar in his office. There is no trial; Perry exposes the murderer during a cocktail party at his home. One element Curtiz retained from his treatment of *Kennel:* Perry exposes the culprit by means of a detailed reconstruction, illustrated through flashbacks, of the commission of the crime. It was better handled than in most Warner's films.

Gardner wasn't at all pleased with what Warner Brothers was doing to his characters. He complained.

Lucile Browne and Margaret Lindsay when they were both ingenue players, lying on a Santa Monica beach.   PHOTO COURTESY THE LATE LUCILE BROWNE FLAVIN.

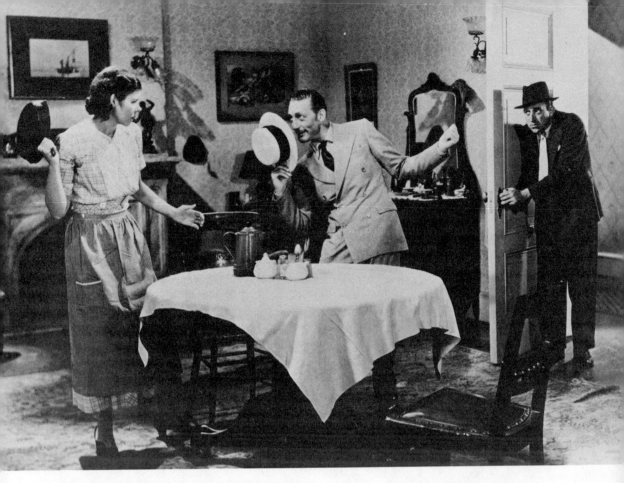

Perry's investigations were often comical as here, with Allen Jenkins in *The Case of the Lucky Legs* (Warner's, 1935). PHOTO COURTESY OF UNITED ARTISTS TELEVISION.

But Warren William was playing Perry Mason much after his own heart, and Warner's was pleased with William's performance. Hal Wallis, still head of production, offered him a new contract and an increase in salary, promising William that his next role would be Perry Mason in *The Case of the Lucky Legs* (Warner's, 1935). William bought an estate which became a showplace for tourists on their guided journeys past the homes of the stars. William liked to invent contraptions and went so far as to patent his lawn suction cleaner.

Brown Holmes, who had worked on the screenplay for *Curious Bride*, joined Ben Markson on scripting *Lucky Legs*. The picture opened with Mason being discovered sleeping rolled up in the carpet behind his desk. Porter Hall wants to hire him, but Perry is sadly quite hung over. He staggers over to his gigantic liquor cabinet and pours himself a healthy eye-opener. When Hall persists, explaining that it is a complicated case, Perry quips, "Good. I was afraid it was going to be so simple I couldn't swing any more of a fee out of it." At no point is Perry together enough to get his client's name right and he has his personal physician come in to give him an examination while Hall is telling him of his woes. Della for her part stays at the office playing solitaire and drinking while Perry runs around investigating. It's rather a good novel, although you could never tell it from the screenplay.

The only way Winifred Shaw can get Mason to represent her and leave the shrewish Claire Dodd as Della "Mason" is by holding a gun on him in *The Case of the Velvet Claws* (Warner's, 1936). Eddie Acuff is Spudsy Drake.

PHOTO COURTESY OF UNITED ARTISTS TELEVISION.

In 1968, two years before he died, Erle married Jean Bethell, Natalie having passed on a short time before. I visited with Jean at her spacious, airy home down the coast from Los Angeles in the direction of San Diego. Jean Gardner was petite, with blond hair and blue eyes. She had seven cats and one dog to keep her company. The conversation turned to the Perry Mason films.

"Oh," she said, horrified, "they were just awful. Erle would get so mad at what they were doing to his characters. He thought the pictures would turn readers away, not attract them.

"He had control on the television series," she continued. "He could say nothing at all about the Warner Brothers movies, except to continue complaining. Which he did."

The Case of the Velvet Claws (Warner's, 1936) opened to Warren William as Perry and Claire Dodd as Della getting married—a totally unacceptable abuse as far as Gardner was concerned. It gets even worse when Della shrewishly insists that Perry must give up his law practice so he can work full time being a devoted husband!

Warner's lost Warren William, due to circumstances I will mention later in connection with the Lone Wolf series at Columbia. He was replaced as Perry Mason by Ricardo Cortez in *The Case of the Black Cat* (Warner's, 1936), based on the Mason novel *The Case of the Caretaker's Cat* (Morrow, 1935). June Travis was Della Street. William McGann directed, with the screenplay by F. Hugh Herbert. Nothing improved very much. Although his office is filled with people, Perry is calmly behind his desk working on a crossword puzzle. Paul Drake is Mason's assistant, supposedly in charge of crossword puzzles and delving into people's backgrounds. The notice on his door indicates that Perry is both Attorney and Private Investigator. Guy Usher played District Attorney Burger. At least the picture ended with a courtroom scene, even if it was poorly staged, with Mason providing the court with a reconstruction of the crime by means of flashbacks.

Gardner wasn't pleased about Perry being portrayed as a Latin type. Another attempt was made.

The Case of the Stuttering Bishop (Warner's, 1937) was based on the 1936 novel of the same title, with Donald Woods, who had been a character actor in *Curious Bride*, now cast as Mason. Ann Dvorak, probably the best of the lot, played Della Street. William Clemens directed.

"What happened after *Stuttering Bishop?*" I asked Jean Gardner.

"Erle flatly refused to license any more Perry Mason novels to film companies," Jean replied. "He was making so much money from the books he didn't see why he should. If his readers couldn't go to a film and see Perry, Della, and Paul Drake the way he had drawn them in the novels, then he would rather they not see them at all."

Warner Brothers still retained screen rights to *The Case of the Dangerous Dowager* (Morrow, 1937). After much negotiation, the studio agreed to use the novel as the basis for a picture that had nothing to do with Perry Mason. It was released as *Granny Get Your Gun* (Warner's, 1940); as the title implies, it really wouldn't have worked as a Mason film.

It has not been my objective in these pages to make more than a cursory mention of television series based on fictional detectives. I beg the reader to allow me the indulgence, in the present instance, of going somewhat more than customary into depth on the "Perry Mason" series. It remains, I think, the best detective series ever made for television. It has certainly lasted the longest. Since it left the air in 1966, it has been seen almost continuously in reruns all over the country. I must have seen all but one of the 271 episodes many times (the one exception being the color pilot Gail Patrick produced at the very end of the series).

Ann Dvorak with blond hair was the best of the Della Street characterizations at Warner Brothers. Donald Woods with mustache was a mediocre Perry Mason. The scene is from *The Case of the Stuttering Bishop* (Warner's, 1937).

PHOTO COURTESY OF UNITED ARTISTS TELEVISION.

In the Forties, Perry Mason was on radio five days a week, broadcast by CBS. In the Fifties, when CBS wanted to televise the series, Gardner consistently turned them down. Gail Patrick urged him to reconsider. Finally, Gardner conceded, instructing Gail that she would have to be the producer on the series. She agreed to this.

Gardner was an independent man. He bought a thousand-acre ranch near Temecula, California, and named it Rancho del Paisano. He had a number of guest cottages built and loved to entertain his friends there. This whole project had started already in the Thirties, when a love for the desert first seized Gardner. His initial desert home consisted of a large general room where he would have his fleet of secretaries type and file, and Jean would cook. Gardner would dictate his stories, first using one Dictaphone and then another; later he switched to tape recorders. He employed a giant windmill to supply power for the installation.

Among his friends were fellow *Black Mask* writers, for it was in *Black Mask* that Gardner found one of his earliest markets. He knew Dashiell Hammett well, and Raymond Chandler, who long admired him, became a visitor at the

Rancho del Paisano. "He's a terrible talker," Chandler recalled, "just wears you out, but he is not a dull talker. He just talks too loud and too much. Years of yapping into a Dictaphone machine have destroyed the quality of his voice, which now has all the delicate chiaroscuro of a French taxi horn. His production methods amaze me (he can write a whole book in a week or ten days easily) and once in a while he does something pretty good."

Gardner liked to move about. In addition to the ranch, he had a home at Palm Springs, a cabin in the mountains, five house trailers, three houseboats, and a cruiser. Everywhere he went, he had a dictating machine. He would sit down and write a chapter; interruptions seldom bothered him. When he wearied of one place, he would go to another. He began in 1940 to write books under a pseudonym, A. A. Fair, about the Cool and Lam detective agency. He wrote a number of novels about Douglas Selby, a district attorney. In time, he called his production routine the "fiction factory."

Although Gardner would claim that once he dictated something he would never look at it again, his secretaries knew better. He would dictate in the morning, edit the previous work in the afternoon, and might easily dictate some more at night. His life was his work and he never tired of telling stories. He probably knew more about detective stories than anyone else who has ever written them. Jean Gardner showed me his "plot book," as he called it. Given Gardner's penchant for narrating a story primarily by means of dialogue and keeping all his characters two-dimensional, his plot book was a tool he could use repeatedly and brilliantly. He broke down a mystery plot into more than a hundred subdivisions and, from variations contained under each heading, could work out a plot speedily but effectively.

His staff not only would keep track of his voluminous correspondence, but would keep record books of every story and novel, and every cent it earned in any edition or language. Writing made Gardner quite wealthy, but not in terms of any one title; rather the accumulation of titles. He wrote more than seventy titles in the Perry Mason series, and his volume sales amounted to in excess of 200 million copies. And even now, after his death, the sales go on.

No one in the mystery field could match him for plots, nor, I imagine, for sales volume. His organization and the inestimable assistance Jean provided him made for much of his productive capacity, that, coupled with his keen knowledge of California law and a dozen other disciplines.

Gail Patrick's success in production as well as acting has given her a self-assurance and a proven capability possessed by very few, men or women. When I spoke to her, I told her that I felt casting had been the key to success in the "Perry Mason" series.

"Yes," Gail agreed, "but I had an angel on my shoulder."

Originally, Bill Hopper, Hedda Hopper's son, was supposed to be Perry Mason, and Raymond Burr was to be tested for the role of Hamilton Burger.

"Ray lost a hundred and twenty pounds so he could try out for the Perry Mason part. We tested him in some trial sequences. We knew at once that we had the right man."

Gail wanted Barbara Hale for the part of Della Street. When her husband,

Bill Williams, heard of the offer, he suggested she take it. Barbara objected that the role would be very demanding.

"That's just it," her husband told her. "No television series has ever gone for one hour week after week about one person. It can't possibly succeed. Sign the contract for its full term. It won't last more than ten weeks."

Nine years later, she was still playing Della Street.

Gail offered me a scotch whisky. I lit a cigarette.

"You really shouldn't smoke," she counseled.

"Well, it's an idea," I responded.

"Smoking certainly took its toll on 'Perry Mason.' Ray Collins, who played Lieutenant Tragg, died by inches, of emphysema. Bill Hopper died from smoking. William Talman, whom we had to suspend for a while because he was caught smoking marijuana, died of lung cancer."

"But not Barbara," I said.

"Whisky is better for you," Gail returned.

In the beginning, each episode cost $85,000. By the end, episodes were running $185,000. Raymond Burr was receiving a million dollars a year. Gardner read all the scripts and supervised how characters and plots were treated.

"Erle was concerned," Gail said, "that the courtroom scenes be kept authentic. So we had the same judges, bailiffs, and so on, so the viewers could concentrate on the proceedings."

"The courtroom scenes are the best thing about the series," I said. "I could only wish most courtrooms were conducted in such a manner."

CBS wanted to do the shows in color, but they refused to finance them adequately. In the final show, Gail had one line of dialogue and Erle Stanley Gardner himself portrayed the judge on the bench.

"You became close friends with Erle Stanley Gardner over the years," I said. "What kind of man was he?"

"His loyalty to his friends," Gail replied, "was boundless. He always wanted people to be happy, it seemed. He was sentimental and he loved the outdoors and animals. He was a short man, five feet seven, and he lived in his own world. If he knew he was right in an argument, he still wouldn't push the point. When you visited him, he was constantly trying to feed you. But you ended up doing more eating than he did, since he talked so much. Near the end, when he knew he was dying, of cancer, he never let you know it. You kept silent because you knew he was going to go on right to the end living just as he had always wanted to live, enjoying the things he enjoyed, until, suddenly, it stopped, and that was it."

Marshall Houts, who delivered the eulogy at Erle Stanley Gardner's funeral, recalling how his novels had made the public aware of the need for justice in the administration of the law, founding the Court of Last Resort, which had freed so many men wrongly indicted and sentenced, said of him that he "has contributed more to the cause of justice than any man of his generation."

In 1973, "The New Perry Mason" series of half-hour shows went into production. Gardner was dead and Gail Patrick had nothing to do with it. The series failed.

Barbara Hale insisted on getting the "Perry Mason" television cast together for this photograph, William Talman, Ray Collins, Barbara, Raymond Burr, and Bill Hopper. PHOTO COURTESY OF BARBARA HALE WILLIAMS.

"They thought they had to update the characters," Jean Gardner told me.

"I can understand that," I responded. "Today you would have to have Perry and Della living together, at the very least."

I remembered Barbara Hale regarding me with a wry smile when I reminded her that never once had Perry so much as patted her shoulder, much less any other part of her anatomy.

"I suppose you're right," Jean Gardner sighed. "I guess we've changed too much for it to be the way Erle wrote about the relationship."

The change goes deeper than that, I fear. We've lost his concern with justice. That, in the long run, will probably have a more dismal effect than Perry's and Della's loss of innocence.

FOUR:

"*Chinatown, My Chinatown*"

"*Little things tell story.*"
—Charlie Chan in London

I

It is somewhat regrettable that Earl Derr Biggers did not live long enough to realize the full measure of fame and bounty earned through his creation of Charlie Chan. He was born in Warren, Ohio, in 1884, and graduated from Harvard in 1907. Apparently his professors were shocked by his irreverence for the classics. He preferred storytellers like Rudyard Kipling and Richard Harding Davis to Oliver Goldsmith. His affinity for the poetry of journalist Franklin P. Adams prompted his classmates to request he leave the room when, at twilight, they elected to read Keats to one another.

Biggers found employment writing a humorous column for the *Boston Traveler*. He didn't care much about it. He was promoted to drama critic. He offended so many people with his devastating critiques of plays he didn't like that he was fired. He then tried a novel, titled *Seven Keys to Baldplate*. It was published in 1913 by Bobbs-Merrill and, subsequently, became the basis for three motion pictures. The novel was both romantic and melodramatic and initially enjoyed an encouraging trade sale. *Love Insurance* (Bobbs-Merrill, 1914) and *The Agony Column* (Bobbs-Merrill, 1916) followed. They were all in the same style and met with increasing public enthusiasm.

Once *Seven Keys* was accepted for publication, Biggers married Eleanor Ladd, who also worked on the *Boston Traveler*. They migrated to New York. Many years after his death, Eleanor Biggers commented that her husband employed no secretaries, notes, or research files; and he never kept copies of his work. Biggers next turned to playwriting with even greater success. His sentiments were aptly in correspondence with the inclinations of his time. He really

Peter Lorre as Mr. Moto.   PHOTO COURTESY OF THE LATE NORMAN FOSTER.

believed in his characters as people. "To be human always," he summed up his literary objective, "to write of human beings, real people though they carry the bright banner of romance."

Biggers grew bored with stage plays. He moved to Pasadena, California, when his health needed a more temperate climate. He had received offers of motion picture work.

The House Without a Key was his first Charlie Chan novel. It was serialized by *The Saturday Evening Post*, beginning in the issue of September 24, 1925. It had not originally been Biggers' intention to make Charlie the central character in the novel. He isn't to be seen at all in the first *Post* installment. Ever since Biggers had visited Hawaii years before, he had wanted to write a mystery novel set there. While preparing *House*, he perused several Honolulu newspapers and came across a reference to a police case effectively solved by two Honolulu policemen named Chang Apana and Lee Fook. He decided to make the policeman in his novel a Chinese.

Charlie Chan captured the public's fancy. Biggers rapidly produced a sequel in *The Chinese Parrot*. Senator Charles C. Cook, of Connecticut, had shown Biggers the beauties of the California desert which Biggers used as the setting for the novel. The *Post* serialized the book in 1926 and Bobbs-Merrill published it in a cloth edition. Toward the end of the novel, Biggers had occasion to describe a movie company on location. Charlie, who is disguised as a cook, is offered a career in pictures.

It was prophetic. Pathé had already purchased *The House Without a Key* as the basis for a silent chapter play in ten episodes. Allene Ray and Walter Miller were a tremendously popular serial team. Pathé thought Biggers' tale an ideal property for an action-mystery adventure. Frank Leon Smith, chief scenarist for Pathé serials, did the screen adaptation and Spencer Gordon Bennet directed. George K. Kuwa was cast as Chan, twelfth in the credits.

I recall one visit with Spencer Bennet at the old Columbia Pictures lot on Gower Street.

"No prints of *House Without a Key* are known to survive," I told him. "I guess I'm going to have to rely on your memory."

"Well, I can tell you this, Jon. It was no Charlie Chan picture. Chan was just a detective. He wasn't that involved in the action. In fact, we were a couple of chapters into the story before he even made an appearance."

"Warner Oland didn't suggest himself to you for the role?"

"Not to me, no." Spencer shook his head. "Of course, he specialized in playing Orientals, usually villains. I was at Pathé in New York when he worked on *The Yellow Arm* [Pathé, 1921]. I remember I was given the job of finding him when he disappeared. Warner was a heavy drinker and might vanish for days on end. I spent nearly a week going through every bar on Third Avenue before I finally found him. We were then able to sober him up and shoot his scenes. He was a splendid actor. The part in *House Without a Key* would have been too small for him, even if somebody had suggested he be cast for it."

Kuwa, the first Chan, was Japanese. When Universal Pictures bought screen rights to *The Chinese Parrot* (Universal, 1927), Kamiyama Sojin, another Japanese, was cast as Chan. J. Grubb Alexander did the screenplay, and this time Charlie was a major character. Paul Leni, the German director, was given the picture as his second directorial assignment in Hollywood. Sojin's performance was praised in the trades, but Universal expressed no further interest in making Chan films.

Biggers' third novel was *Behind That Curtain* (Bobbs-Merrill, 1928). Charlie's identity was emerging in the novels. It was certainly different from the characterization depicted on the screen, even in the best films. Charlie was of Chinese descent, but an American. He was drawn as a man struggling with the opposing values of the Occidental world and his Oriental heritage. Fox filmed *Curtain* with E. L. Park as Chan.

The fourth Chan novel was *The Black Camel* (Bobbs-Merrill, 1929). The title was inspired by the old Eastern maxim, "Death is the black camel that kneels unbid at every gate." The plot involved the fatal stabbing of actress Shelah Fane in her pavilion in Hawaii. Behind her death is the unsolved murder of a Hollywood actor three years before. The actor's murder has an intentional resemblance to the actual circumstances surrounding the death of movie director William Desmond Taylor, a crime not officially solved to this day. Charlie, who has his share of prejudice against the Japanese, is given Kashimo, a Japanese detective, as an assistant. Kashimo fulfills the same function here as Charlie's various offspring served subsequently in the films.

In this scene from *The House Without a Key* (Pathé, 1926) Walter Miller and Allene Ray flank archvillain Frank Lackteen while George Kuwa (right) observes.

PHOTO COURTESY OF VIEWS & REVIEWS MAGAZINE.

The Black Camel was not brought to the screen at once. *Charlie Chan Carries On* (Fox, 1931), based on Biggers' fifth novel, was the next Chan film. The *Post* ran the novel serially. *Post* artist Henry Raleigh illustrated it with drawings of Chan in which he was fatter than in previous *Post* sketches, with his eyebrows more dramatically sloped, but most important, for the first time Charlie sported a mustache.

Fox Film Corporation purchased screen rights to *Carries On* and cast Warner Oland in the Chan role. Oland was born on October 3, 1880, in Umeå, Sweden. He came to the United States when he was thirteen, making his stage debut with Sarah Bernhardt's company. Following a season with Nazimova, he lost his sav-

Bela Lugosi and Warner Oland straddle Dorothy Revier's body in *The Black Camel* (Fox, 1931).   PHOTO COURTESY OF TWENTIETH CENTURY-FOX FILM CORPORATION.

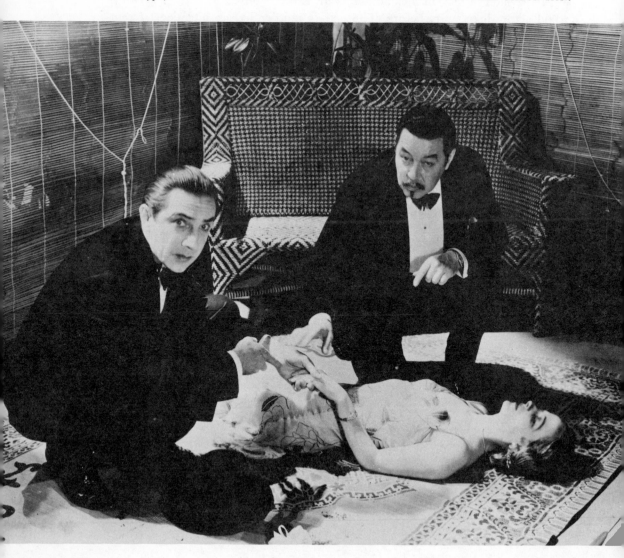

ings producing his own plays at the Hudson Theatre in New York. He drifted into films starting with *Jewels of the Madonna* (Fox, 1909), which starred Theda Bara. While he worked for several companies in varying roles, much of his movie work during the silent era was for Fox. He was cast as the satanic devil doctor in *The Mysterious Dr. Fu Manchu* (Paramount, 1929), starred again in *The Return of Dr. Fu Manchu* (Paramount, 1930), and did a cameo as Fu Manchu in *Paramount on Parade* (Paramount, 1930).

Charlie Chan Carries On (Fox, 1931) does not survive. This is unfortunate because it makes prohibitive any comparison of the growth and development of his characterization as the series progressed. The plot followed the novel and Charlie didn't appear until midway through the picture. Oland was credited third. Marguerite Churchill was the headliner, and William Holden and George Brent both had roles. I don't suppose it matters at this late date, and in view of the inaccessibility of the picture, if I divulge to the reader that the script indicated the series of murders on a world cruise to have been perpetrated by C. Henry Gordon in an effort to revenge himself on Jason Robards, Sr., because Robards stole the affections of Gordon's wife years before the story opens. Biggers liked to detail the solutions to his mysteries in past adventures obscured by the passage of time. This ingredient was one of the first to go when Fox began producing original screenplays.

The New York *Times* was rather positive in its approval of Oland. "Mr. Oland's conception of Chan's manner of speaking is quite acceptable," Mordaunt Hall reported in his review, "and he relies on very little change in his appearance to play the part." Hamilton MacFadden directed. Philip Klein and Barry Connors did the screenplay. Charlie's pearls of wisdom, the Chanograms, were apparently present from the very outset. At one point, Charlie declares, "Only a very brave mouse will make its nest in a cat's ear." He later asserts that "he who feeds the chicken deserves the egg" and that "only a very sly man can shoot off a cannon quietly." The *Times* reviewer had to remark that the Chanograms so charmed the audience that "one could have listened to Charlie Chan for an hour longer." At the end of the picture, in a gesture so typical of him, Warner as Charlie took the audience into his confidence. He said of the young hero and heroine, "Pam and Mark are to be one—more later."

The film was an immediate success. Fox bought rights to *The Black Camel* (Fox, 1931) and adapted it for the screen so as to make Warner's Charlie Chan the central character. Dorothy Revier played Shelah Fane. The *Motion Picture Herald* liked her enough to find her a "compelling love interest" in *The Avenger* (Columbia, 1931), a Buck Jones Western released simultaneously, and "convincing" in the role of Shelah Fane in *The Black Camel*. But Oland dominated the picture, with Bela Lugosi's portrayal of the psychic Tarnaverro the only really competitive characterization. Prints of *Camel* do survive and it was even screened at a Charlie Chan film festival at the Museum of Modern Art in New York in 1968, although there is a rumble in the sound track. Hamilton MacFadden again directed. C. Henry Gordon was included in the cast as a red herring. In making Shelah the murderer of the celebrated actor in the book, changed to a director in the photoplay (an even stronger analogy with William

Desmond Taylor's murder), both Biggers and the Fox screenwriters were hinting at a solution to the real-life crime which was then whispered all over Hollywood: silent screen comedienne Mabel Normand had murdered Taylor in a lovers' quarrel.

The Keeper of the Keys (Bobbs-Merrill, 1932) was Biggers' last novel. Charlie made an appearance on the second page. His penchant for aphorisms seems to have increased through his creator's exposure to Warner on the screen. The book was adapted for the legitimate stage, although, somewhat curiously, it was never made into a photoplay. One of the reasons for this might possibly have been the play's short run. It opened on October 18, 1933, with William Harrigan in the lead role. It closed three weeks later.

Biggers died of heart disease. Warner Oland, who had recently appeared as an Austrian officer in *Shanghai Express* (Paramount, 1932) with Marlene Dietrich, expressed his sincere regret that he had never met Biggers. But for Oland the Chan role was becoming so much a part of his intrinsic personality that he began increasingly to limit his screen work to Chan films. Biggers himself had been no less enchanted with the character. He went so far as to inscribe his books with Charlie's signature, much different from his own. On his Charlie Chan New Year's card, he had told friends: "For the New Year I warmly wish you plenty rice—since even the sunrise is without beauty to the hungry; plenty health—since even the road down hill is hard for the sick; and plenty peace of mind—since trouble follows the restless like flies in the fifth month."

Biggers was still alive when *Charlie Chan's Chance* (Fox, 1932) was released. It was a remake of the first Fox entry in the series, *Behind That Curtain*. There was a lot of talk and little suspense. H. B. Warner played a Scotland Yard inspector, Marion Nixon a masked dancer. More than ever, Oland's personality and his philosophizing held up the picture. John Blystone directed.

Fox acquired rights to *The House Without a Key*, which formed the basis for the only entry the next year, *Charlie Chan's Greatest Case* (Fox, 1933). The screenplay by Lester Cole and Marion Orth was still in slavish acquiescence to the novel's plot, and Chan was introduced only after considerable preliminary background. But the trades, by this time alert to Oland's popularity, recommended that exhibitors stress his presence. The *Motion Picture Herald* felt that Oland's Chan was "one of the most generally lovable of all screen detectives, with his quaint speech and his subtly phrased aphorisms."

Prints do not survive of *Chance* or *Greatest Case*, nor of *Charlie Chan's Courage* (Fox, 1934), based on *The Chinese Parrot*, for which property Fox acquired rights from Universal. With this entry, however, John Stone was appointed associate producer for the series by Sol Wurtzel. He was delighted by Oland's characterization and felt more should be done with the portrayal and the series. Production was increased to three Chan films a year. Fox had originally intended to make only four Chans. Oland was supposed to be paid $10,000 a picture. He did receive $10,000 for the first one. The popular response prompted him to ask $12,500 for the second one. He wanted $20,000 for the third, but the studio kept him at $12,500 an entry until *Charlie Chan at the Circus* (20th-Fox, 1936), at which time he contracted to do three Chans at $20,000 a picture.

When his option was picked up again, he signed for his last three Chan films at $30,000 a picture.

John Stone was born in New York on September 12, 1888. He began in the industry as a screenwriter with Fox, specializing in Westerns. He wrote several exceptional stories for Buck Jones and, during his two years with the Tom Mix unit, he did the screenplay for the splendid *Great K&A Train Robbery* (Fox, 1926). Producer Stone, as much as anyone, was constantly thinking up new Chanograms. Seton Miller, the scenarist on *Courage*, followed the novel. Warner was able to impersonate a Chinese cook in the course of the film, adding to the complexity of his performance.

Stone next came up with the idea, now that the Biggers originals were exhausted, of starting Charlie on a round-the-world trip of murder investigations. *Charlie Chan in London* (Fox, 1934) was the first stop. Fox Film Corporation was in serious financial trouble due to the stock manipulations of William Fox in his attempt to seize control of Metro-Goldwyn-Mayer. Eugene Forde directed *London*. E. E. Clive appeared as a Scotland Yard inspector, and a young Ray Milland was among the suspects. *London* was the longest film in the series, with a running time of eighty minutes. While it was slow-moving at times, it introduced several new ingredients to the formula. Instead of Charlie tricking the guilty party through ruse or physical action, the suspects were now gathered together for a reconstruction of the crime. Charlie's presentation of the evidence would conclude with the verbal confrontation: "You . . . are . . . murderer." A love interest between two of the suspects, always a staple of Biggers' novels, became secondary and, eventually, unimportant. One reason for this was the appearance of a new character in *Charlie Chan in Paris* (Fox, 1935).

Keye Luke was born near Canton in 1904. He was thirty-one years old when in *Paris* he appeared as Charlie's son, Lee Chan; he looked twenty. He had as yet no desire to be a detective; he was not Number One son; he referred to Charlie as Dad, and not Pop; instead of stealing Charlie's collar button, as he later did in *Charlie Chan on Broadway* (20th-Fox, 1937), in one scene he bent down to take off Charlie's shoes.

Keye was almost seventy when first I met him in Hollywood. I had talked to him previously over the phone at the Warner Brothers Burbank studio. He had been on Sound Stage 7 shooting *Kung Fu*, a movie for television that generated its own series of successors. On the phone, he sounded precisely as he had on the screen opposite Oland. At home Keye was surrounded by his books on art and on the walls were hung samples of his fine, meticulous pen drawings. He had begun with Fox as an artist and, later, moved on to RKO Radio. He had once studied under S. S. Van Dine's brother at the University of Southern California when Stanton MacDonald-Wright was artist-in-residence there. At RKO, he was made a technical adviser on Chinese films and was cast in two-reelers. He appeared in W. Somerset Maugham's *The Painted Veil* (M-G-M, 1934) with Herbert Marshall, George Brent, and Greta Garbo before being selected by John Stone for the role of Lee in *Paris*. When he joined the series, the story line was tightened up. Charlie uttered fewer aphorisms, but they were more to the point. Detective story writer Philip MacDonald wrote the original screenplay for *Paris*. Keye's interaction with Oland was more serious than comic, but at once it furthered the humanization of the Chan character, giving him a dimension beyond mere sleuthing.

No one remarked on the potential charm of the relationship between Oland and Keye until after *Paris* was released. Certain plot ingredients strike a modern audience as ineptly funny, particularly when in *Paris* Charlie undertakes to protect Mary Brian's reputation when she is found in the apartment of a murdered man. *Charlie Chan in Egypt* (Fox, 1935) was made without Keye. But once Stone became aware of audience and critical reaction, Keye was immediately put under contract and was cast in all but one of the remaining Oland films. *Egypt* was the last Chan film before the merger between Fox Film Corporation and Twentieth Century Pictures.

Joseph Schenck, brother of M-G-M president Nicholas Schenck, set up Twentieth Century early in 1933 and recruited Darryl F. Zanuck from Warner Brothers to be head of production. Louis B. Mayer's money was behind the venture. Over lunch at the Brown Derby on April 18, 1933, Joe Schenck closed the deal by giving Zanuck a check for $100,000 signed by Mayer. Mayer already had one son-in-law, David O. Selznick, working for him at Metro, and wanted William Goetz, his other son-in-law, to become involved in his own production company. Goetz's official position was that of Zanuck's assistant.

Joe Schenck was president of United Artists. Since the founders of the company—principally Charlie Chaplin, Mary Pickford, and Douglas Fairbanks—had cut back on new production or ceased altogether, it was now up to Samuel Goldwyn and Darryl Zanuck to provide the bulk of the pictures for United Artists' releasing schedule. Zanuck's films, with a single exception, were extraordinarily successful. Schenck, restless at United Artists, approached Sidney R. Kent, president of the failing Fox Film Corporation. Fox had one of the finest distribution networks in the country. The Chan films, the Shirley Temple pictures, and Will Rogers' two pictures a year were virtually supporting the studio. The two companies merged, becoming Twentieth Century-Fox. Zanuck was in charge of "A" picture production. Sol Wurtzel, who had been with Fox in various capacities since 1915, took over supervision of the "B" units.

Despite Keye's absence, *Charlie Chan in Egypt* is the best Chan film Oland was to make. Comic relief was provided by Stepin Fetchit, Will Rogers' frequent foil. It was by the curious circumstance of linking a Chinese, a black, a Jew, and an Egyptian with several Europeans that a rather unusual commentary on life, death, and racism resulted. The plot of the film had a complicated origin, but it is worth recounting because of the light it sheds on the tremendous social impact of the cinematic detective in the Thirties.

Throughout the latter part of the nineteenth century interest had run high in the discoveries being made in Egypt and the preparation of a consistent history of ancient Egypt which continued excavations by European-sponsored expeditions made possible. This interest became so consuming that variously both Great Britain and France exercised powerful political influence over Egypt, culminating in its being annexed to the British Empire as a crown protectorate. In the Twenties Egyptologists agreed that most of the tomb treasures had been exhausted; political control lessened with the ceasing of hostilities on the Continent, while foreign museums became glutted with their shares of the great finds.

Howard Carter originally came to Egypt while still in his teens apprenticed to P. E. Newberry, the famous Egyptologist. He served as an assistant to Flinders Petrie in 1892 and, under Gaston Maspero's second tenure as director of antiquities, began his first excavations in the Valley of the Kings. An American, Theodore Davis, who held the excavation concession in 1914, went on record declaring the valley definitely exhausted of tombs. The concession was duly passed on to George Herbert, the fifth Earl of Carnarvon. Carter managed to

Warner Oland's Charlie Chan stands before young Tommy Beck, his hands joining the hieroglyphic symbols for life and death as the reach of man. Stepin Fetchit is in the background. *Charlie Chan in Egypt* (Fox, 1935) was perhaps the finest entry in the series.   PHOTO COURTESY OF TWENTIETH CENTURY-FOX FILM CORPORATION.

convince the earl, based on several minor finds he had made while employed by Davis, that a tomb was not accounted for, that of Tutankhamen, a young king of the Eighteenth Dynasty whose life and times, in the wake of heretic king Amenhotep IV, better known as Akhnaton, remained in shadow. Carnarvon financed Carter's expedition, which lasted several years. By 1921, with no results, the earl was tempted to withdraw his support. He was persuaded to persist only when Carter himself offered to finance another expedition if the earl didn't. Scarcely a week after reopening the campaign, on October 28, 1922, a flight of steps was laid bare. It wasn't until 1928, amid worldwide publicity and talk of ancient curses, that Carter finally penetrated to the Pharaoh's sarcophagus and succeeded in opening to the light, after four thousand years, the tomb of solid gold. It has become the best known of all the Egyptian discoveries.

"Slowly, desperately slowly it seemed to us as we watched," Carter described the dramatic scene, "the remains of passage debris that encumbered the lower part of the doorway were removed, until at last we had the whole door clear before us. The decisive moment had arrived. With trembling hands I made a tiny breach in the upper left hand corner. Darkness and blank space, as far as the iron testing-rod could reach, showed that whatever lay beyond was empty, and not filled like the passage we had just cleared. Candle tests were applied as a precaution against possible foul gases, and then, widening the hole a little, I inserted the candle and peered in, Lord Carnarvon, Lady Evelyn, and Callender standing anxiously beside me to hear the verdict. At first, I could see nothing, the hot air escaping from the chamber causing the candle flame to flicker, but presently, as my eyes grew accustomed to the light, details of the room within emerged slowly from the mist, strange animals, statues, and gold—everywhere the glint of gold. For the moment—an eternity it must have seemed to the others standing by—I was struck dumb with amazement, and when Lord Carnarvon, unable to stand the suspense any longer, inquired anxiously, 'Can you see anything?' it was all I could do to get out the words, 'Yes, wonderful things.' Then widening the hole a little further, so that we both could see, we inserted the electric torch."

Charlie Chan in Egypt called on Carter's book relating these adventures. Reproduced almost exactly at the opening of the picture is that joy of discovery, the electric torch illuming a room of long-buried treasure and everywhere gold sparkling in the shadows. Robert Ellis and Helen Logan, who worked on the screenplay and most successfully collaborated on many subsequent entries, borrowed heavily from the best sources in detective fiction. R. Austin Freeman's *The Eye of Osiris* (Dodd, Mead, 1911) was one of the six volumes selected for reprint by Scribner's in their S. S. Van Dine Mystery Library. One of Freeman's finest mysteries, *Osiris* concerns itself with the disappearance of an Egyptologist of independent means named John Bellingham. Dr. Thorndyke, Freeman's scientific investigator, brings his search for the missing body to a small chamber off the fourth Egyptian room at the British Museum. It is here that, with the aid of a gigantic X-ray apparatus, Thorndyke demonstrates conclusively to the museum officials and the police that the body wrapped in a mummy case presented to the museum by the late John Bellingham, far from being Sebek-Hotep, is in fact the desiccated remains of none other than Bellingham himself. While the ancient Egyptians were quite familiar with dentistry in a primitive fashion, not only fillings but even an artificial tooth show up on the X-ray. Metal sutures in the victim's kneecaps, the result of a serious injury, also show up. Ellis and Logan snatched this moment for *Charlie Chan in Egypt*.

Van Dine was equally taken by the subject of Egyptology. He introduced it as a background for his fifth Philo Vance story, *The Scarab Murder Case* (Scribner's, 1930). A man named Kyle, who has financed several expeditions into the Valley, is found dead in the Bliss Museum in New York, his head crushed beneath a statue of Sahkmet, the god who protected the Egyptian dead. Ellis and Logan lifted this element and transposed it, so that in the film Professor Arnold's son is permanently crippled when a tomb wall guarded by a statue of Sakhmet collapses on his leg. Although Paramount had purchased screen rights to *The Scarab Murder Case*, the subsequent film was delayed. *Charlie Chan in Egypt* scooped them and remains the most intriguing detective film to have an Egyptian setting.

In *Egypt*, Charlie's philosophy rises to the occasion. When Oland and Tommy Beck, playing an American Egyptologist, are inspecting the inner chamber to the high priest Ameti's tomb, Charlie asks what the hieroglyphics on the walls mean. Tommy explains that the lines around the top represent Ameti's prayer to Sakhmet for protection and the others are the alternating symbols for life and death. Charlie traces the symbols, muttering, "Story of man very simple . . . life, death, life, death." Then he straddles the two symbols with his arms, turning to face Tommy. "Am reminded of ancient sage, Confucius, who say: 'From life to death is reach of man.'" Later on he tells a different character, "Theory like mist on eyeglasses—obscures facts."

On one level *Charlie Chan in Egypt* may be regarded as a racial analogue, for it is a plodding Chinese and a seemingly inept black who are the true heroes of the film. The Europeans are arrogant, self-assured, wasting their time, in a sense, digging up treasures of an ancient civilization primarily for material gain rather than for any cultural or spiritual enrichment. The lives they lead are without real reason or purpose, while Tommy Beck, the American, is innocent, head-strong, handsome, but a somewhat simple-minded scholar who can translate Egyptian hieroglyphics while remaining insensitive to their meaning. The murders are committed for possession of a treasure that, by rights, should belong to the Egyptians, but about which they, embodied in a brilliant characterization by Nigel de Brulier, care very little except to keep it out of others' hands. Charlie and Stepin Fetchit, whose traditions meet on an inverse plane, the one with an ancient history, the other with no tradition at all, are united by their lack of greed and their interest in truth and justice. Both Warner and Lincoln Perry, who took the name Stepin Fetchit, are parodying on screen the white man's postures and conceits toward the nonwhite races. Only in a strict genre piece, such as *Egypt*, would this have been possible in 1935, and perhaps only there, precisely, is it most effective today, when too much consciousness has replaced too little.

A Jewish guide in *Egypt* is constantly trying to get Stepin Fetchit to give him what money he has so that he can excavate the remains of his great-, great-, great-, great-, great-grandfather. Stepin Fetchit tells Chan that according to a fortuneteller in Mississippi his ancestors came from Egypt. They may, of course, have been Nubian kings, but the implication is more likely they were slaves. Somehow Stepin Fetchit cannot become as enthusiastic about ancestory and the discovery of remains as the Europeans are, financing great and expensive expeditions. Just as Chan can make wise sayings, so Stepin Fetchit can make pithy comments, as when he tells a black Egyptian girl friend: "Come back to Mississippi with me. You don't have to worry about no job dere. Ah knows a lot of white folks that'll keep you working." Chan, Stepin Fetchit, and the whites comprise three different attitudes toward the ancient Egyptians, Chan in his respect for the past, Stepin Fetchit baffled by the passion of the whites, and the whites anxious to unearth hidden wealth. At the conclusion of the film, directed by Louis King, brother to Henry King, Stepin Fetchit chooses to follow Chan, for the expedition has brought only murder, sadness, and ultimate frustration to the white men. Chan is wiser. He is following the life force which, like a feather, floats on the water and follows the current.

When *Egypt* was released, Warner Oland took a trip to the Orient. He was mobbed when his ship disembarked at Shanghai. The Chinese mayor of Shanghai invited him to a celebration in his honor, attended by all the luminaries of the international quarter. "Am so happy," he commented in his afterdinner speech, "to be once again in the land of honorable ancestors." Fox publicity was sufficiently impressed by Warner's reception by the Chinese to write the scene into his next film, *Charlie Chan in Shanghai* (20th-Fox, 1935). Oland lavished on his role as Chan all of his talent as an actor and created an idealized human being: sensitive, wise, cautious, humorous, and gentle. Charlie neither smoked nor drank, although Oland did both. That he was a Chinese detective helped immensely to transform the image of the Oriental in America's eyes, as well as in the world's. You must remember that at the time Oland visited Shanghai, the British, who policed the international quarter, still had a sign hanging over Shanghai Park instructing: "Neither Chinese nor dogs allowed."

Keye Luke's role was much expanded in *Charlie Chan in Shanghai* from what it had been in *Paris*. Edward T. Lowe and Gerard Fairlie wrote the screenplay. In a charming opening scene, Oland is on board ship en route to Shanghai. He sings a Chinese song about "Ming Loh Fuei" with a reference to the Emperor Fu Manchu. When he concludes, he reflects, facial expression and intonation adding significantly to the words, that he is "sixty summers young, sixty winters old." At a reception, ostensibly in Shanghai, Oland recites an address in Chinese which he had rehearsed beforehand with Keye. An inquisitive reporter asks another what all that means. "Thank you so much" is the response. Keye got a chance to draw a sketch in the context of the story and there were many pleasant interchanges between the two of them. Of course, the culprit is still the least suspected person. Charlie resorts to a trap to flush him out.

Robert Ellis and Helen Logan were back for the screenplay to *Charlie Chan's Secret* (20th-Fox, 1936). Keye Luke was not in the cast. The plot was altered somewhat from the by now customary story line with Charlie being engaged to find a missing heir. At the Lowell family estate, amid eerie goings-on, Charlie has an opportunity to expose a couple of phony mediums after a spooky séance. The suspects are gathered together at the end for an explanation.

In the July 1937 issue of *Modern Screen*, a columnist named Faith Service wrote a long biographical article on Warner Oland and his identification with Charlie Chan. The reporter began her story by lunching with Oland at the Fox commissary, where they had mandarin chicken chow mein and yellow tomato juice. Commenting on his reticence to give interviews, Oland remarked, "Don't talk too much. Words like sunbeams. The more they are condensed the more they burn." The reporter was astonished that Oland was so into the part that he actually spoke in Chanograms.

Warner Oland married Edith Shearn, who was ten years his senior. They had met in New York when Warner was playing in Ibsen's *Peer Gynt* at the Keith and Proctor Theatre. Edith Shearn was a portrait painter who had written a one-act play. Upon meeting, it was—according to what they told columnist Faith Service—as if they had known each other all their lives. Edith was so impressed with Warner's modesty, his humility and sincerity, that she canceled all her appointments just to talk. "It is a marriage," Warner said, speaking objectively as Charlie Chan, "which is enduring because it is joined by the treasures of the mind which neither rust nor corrupt. They are as much married in their tastes and interests as in their affections." Warner increasingly was coming to look on everything, including himself, as Charlie Chan would. "He has habit, for instance," Warner continued, still talking like Charlie Chan about some third person, "of putting his lighted cigarettes—at all times he resembles a lighted chimney rather than a portly gentleman of some 200 pounds—on desks, tables, ancient books, choice prints. Accidents occur. I would like to tell him that he should pay attention to detail. Insignificant molehill sometimes more worthy of notice than conspicuous mountain. He does the same with wet fountain pen. Mrs. Oland does not believe in Occidental wifely habit of nagging. As Oriental wife, she bears and forebears; she permits him to blot and burn."

The Olands then lived quietly on their ranch in the Carpenteria Valley near Santa Barbara in a farmhouse facing the sea on one side, the Santa Barbara hills on the other. They also had a farmhouse in Southboro, Massachusetts, and a seven-thousand-acre ranch on the wild Mexican island of Palmetto de la Virgin. "Now and then he does some gardening himself. But he is an indolent fellow, this Oland," Charlie summed up the Warner Oland side of his personality. "He spends much time walking by the sea and in the hills. He calls this 'refreshing his soul.' He also sits before the fire, meditating and reading Chinese philosophies. As the years go by, he is becoming more and more steeped in Oriental literature and the ancient wisdoms. But he says, sadly, that not all his reading will 'capture the sea of literature in the thimble of man's brief span of time.'"

Oland's drinking was becoming a very serious problem. "Pop imbibed immoderately," Keye Luke once put it. "Sometimes he was really lit. It made him benign, with a perpetual grin on his face. You couldn't help but love him." Yet the studio and Mrs. Oland were concerned. When he was shooting *Charlie Chan at the Circus* (20th-Fox, 1936), a private nurse named Miss Ryan was assigned to him to see to it that he didn't drink. Oland started bringing his lunch in a metal lunch box. He would eat with Keye and take out two thermos bottles. "For Number One son," he said, "good split pea soup." Then, looking over his shoulder to make sure the coast was clear, he poured out a martini from the second thermos. "For honorable father, tiger tea."

Circus was a consistently entertaining picture. Daniel Clark, who had been Tom Mix's personal cameraman, was the cinematographer. Robert Ellis and Helen Logan did the screenplay, and Harry Lachman directed. Lachman was both engaging and personable, but he was a taskmaster on the set. A real circus was used. J. Carrol Naish, who much later would portray Charlie Chan in an abortive television series, was cast as a snake charmer who committed the murders dressed in an ape suit. All twelve of Charlie's children were in attendance at the circus, as was Mrs. Chan. Wade Boteler played an impetuous rather than a dumb cop, as was generally the lot of the policemen in the series. Much was added to the grace and interest of the picture by the skillful inclusion of the capable midgets, George and Olive Brasno. Lachman liked to tease them on the set. Keye Luke responded by reproving Lachman. Lachman called Sol Wurtzel and complained about Keye. These episodes were incidental. Charlie's interplay with the midgets was quite touching.

At this point, Lucky Humberstone entered upon the scene. Sol Wurtzel had

The entire Chan family as pictured in *Charlie Chan at the Circus* (20th-Fox, 1936) with Keye Luke at the left end and Warner Oland at the right end.

PHOTO COURTESY OF TWENTIETH CENTURY-FOX FILM CORPORATION.

engaged Lucky some six months after release of *The Dragon Murder Case* (First National, 1934) to direct *Ladies Love Danger* (Fox, 1935). It was a detective film in which Gilbert Roland starred as a playwright and amateur sleuth with Mona Barrie and Donald Cook in support. Lucky followed it with *Silk Hat Kid* (Fox, 1935) with Lew Ayres and Paul Kelly. After directing *Three Live Ghosts* (M-G-M, 1936), with Richard Arlen and Beryl Mercer for Metro, Wurtzel summoned Lucky back to Fox to direct *Charlie Chan at the Race Track* (20th-Fox, 1936).

Lucky was a devil's advocate. While shooting the exteriors for the racing sequence at the Santa Anita track, Oland disappeared and the entire crew set out to find him. He was in a dead sleep in the track restaurant. Lucky wanted an intercut shot of Oland supposedly watching the horse race, but Oland kept dozing off. Lucky solved the problem by having extras around Oland to bolster him up.

"I know you can't see anything," Lucky told Oland. "But just turn your head with the sound."

It worked.

Yet, for all that, Lucky encouraged Oland to drink before doing his scenes. Screening rushes, Oland had to agree with Humberstone that alcohol improved his characterization. As fine an actor as he was when sober, he recited his lines too quickly; alcohol fogged his memory, and it seemed, on screen at least, as if the Oriental detective was grappling with a difficult, alien language when he was only groping for a line. Lucky started casting Jimmy Flavin regularly as a cop in his films, regarding Jimmy as a sort of good luck charm. *Racetrack* did business and was well received. Wurtzel used Lucky again to direct *Charlie Chan at the Opera* (20th-Fox, 1936).

It was Lucky's idea to cast Boris Karloff as an amnesiac opera singer in the film. Sol Wurtzel initially resisted the notion because of the additional expense. Karloff had gained a considerable reputation since his early appearance in *The Black Camel* (Fox, 1931). Lucky won out. A subtitle to the picture read "Warner Oland vs. Boris Karloff." Oscar Levant composed an operatic sequence called "Carnival," based on a confluence of styles without being overly distinguished. The picture proved a hit.

In the production, Lucky used several of the elaborate sets Zanuck had had built for E. H. Griffith's *Cafe Metropole* (20th-Fox, 1937). Griffith had shot most of his scenes in extreme close-up. When Zanuck saw the production value the sets brought to *Opera*, he remarked to both Wurtzel and Bill Dover, Darryl's right-hand man: "This son-of-a-bitch Humberstone is making my 'A' directors look sick turning out a 'B' that looks like this. Put him under contract." Wurtzel, too, made his contribution to the completed film. After seeing rushes of Nedda Harrigan as an opera singer, he emerged from the projection room.

"Humberstone," he said in a thick Jewish accent, "tell me something. Does a *lady* fuck?"

"What?"

"You heard me, Humberstone. Does a *lady* fuck?"

"I suppose she does."

"Well, this one doesn't look like she does. Shoot it again."

From left to right: John Stone, the producer on the Chan series, Warner Oland, William Demarest, and Lucky Humberstone discussing the script of *Charlie Chan at the Opera* (20th-Fox, 1936).   PHOTO COURTESY OF LUCKY HUMBERSTONE.

Layne Tom, Jr., was cast as Charlie's Number Two son in *Charlie Chan at the Olympics* (20th-Fox, 1937). It was an entertaining film with varying locales and expert use of stock footage interpolations of everything from the airship *Hindenburg* to the Olympic games in Germany in 1936. C. Henry Gordon was prominently cast as a murder suspect. Only Keye Luke's performance, incessantly trying to spout Chanograms, was a little heavy-handed. Again, Lucky directed.

The Chan films were being shot in four weeks with an extra week for retakes. Budgeted at $250,000 to $275,000, they were netting a million dollars each upon release. Oland rented a bungalow at the Beverly Hills Hotel while in production. Shortly after the *Modern Screen* story about the marital bliss of the Olands appeared, Edith Oland sued her husband for separate maintenance. She couldn't take the drinking.

The nurse wasn't much help. Keye Luke would visit with Oland in Oland's dressing room. Oland would tiptoe to the closet where he kept a bottle hidden.

"Nurse smart," Oland said, "but honorable father smarter."

Oland's mind was deteriorating. While Lucky found the fumbling for words an asset to the character, it would require a dozen takes to get out a single line. In *Charlie Chan's Secret*—a rather appropriate title under the circumstances—Henrietta Crosman and Oland did a scene in which Oland had to trudge up a flight of steps, speaks his line, and she'd answer with hers. Henrietta always got her line. Oland always blew his. On the twenty-third take, Oland finally got it right; but Henrietta was so shocked she blew hers! Oland would resort to excuses, "Honorable father not in marks" or "Honorable father picked up wrong object."

After his separation, Oland moved into the Beverly Hills home of his agent, Jack Gardner. Nurse Ryan went along. Keye visited him one New Year's Day to find him waltzing to music from the radio during a broadcast of the Rose Bowl game.

"We had a grand visit," Keye said to me as we talked in his Hollywood apartment, "and it was good to see Pop in such good 'spirits.' Everyone loved him. He had a crowd around him whenever he went out. Once he called me up.

In *Opera*, as in most of the pictures where he appeared as Lee Chan, Keye Luke helps Warner look for clues.

PHOTO COURTESY OF TWENTIETH CENTURY-FOX FILM CORPORATION.

'Honorable father invite Number One son to go for ride.' Sure enough, he stopped out front in his limousine. We rode around the Hollywood hills. When we came to the Oriental Gardens, Pop had the car stop. 'Must pay respects,' he said, getting out. People began to notice us. When a crowd started in our direction, Pop turned toward a bush. 'Try to make yourself inconspicuous,' he said.

"But," Keye went on, laughing, "he loved it. He was mobbed everywhere. 'Charlie Chan,' people would say, 'it's Charlie Chan.'"

William Demarest had played an anti-Chinese cop in *Opera*. Early in the film, he exclaimed to his superior, "You're not going to call in Chop Suey, are you?"

Peter Lorre stopped by the set of *Charlie Chan at the Opera* and lit Boris Karloff's cigarette. PHOTO COURTESY OF VIEWS & REVIEWS MAGAZINE.

Lucky Humberstone (beneath camera) and the crew assembled to shoot a scene with
William Demarest and Warner Oland. Humberstone was a "devil's advocate."

PHOTO COURTESY OF LUCKY HUMBERSTONE.

Harold Huber (with hat) became a familiar face in the Chan series with Warner
Oland. Donald Woods, Keye Luke, Warner Oland join Huber in discussing the
murder in *Charlie Chan on Broadway* (20th-Fox, 1937).

PHOTO COURTESY OF TWENTIETH CENTURY-FOX FILM CORPORATION.

Harold Huber played a New York cop in *Charlie Chan on Broadway* (20th-Fox, 1937), which brought director Eugene Forde back to the series. Huber did a lot of talking, so much talking, in fact, that Oland's dialogue even in the denouement could be kept at a minimum. Audiences had such a positive reaction to Huber that he was cast again in the next entry as a French prefect. Joan Marsh played a pert and curvaceous freelance photographer in *Broadway*. Donald Woods, who had had a sympathetic part in *Charlie Chan's Courage*, had one less so. Leon Ames played a sophisticated gangster. Louise Henry, the glamorous murder victim in *The Casino Murder Case* (M-G-M, 1935), was done in once more. When Charlie's boat docks in New York, Huber, not knowing the Chinese national anthem, has a police band play "Chinatown, My Chinatown" by way of greeting.

Charlie Chan at Monte Carlo (20th-Fox, 1937) was Oland's last Charlie Chan film. The trades declared it his greatest success to date. At least a third of the dialogue was in French, but it actually added polish to the exposition of the plot. Eugene Forde directed. Huber handled most of the interrogations.

Charlie Chan at the Ringside went into production on January 10, 1938. Oland's condition had worsened considerably. He had been found in the early hours of the morning wandering aimlessly far from Hollywood and unable to say who he was. It was seventy-seven degrees in the shade when he insisted it was too drafty on Sound Stage 6 at the Fox lot on Western Avenue. The number on the stage was changed. Oland wasn't fooled. He walked off the picture again. When he quit on director James Tinling for the fourth time on January 17, Darryl Zanuck scrapped the picture, partially completed, at a cost of $100,000. Oland was put on suspension. The rest of the cast was paid off. Although Keye Luke had been tested for a series tentatively called "Son of Chan" in case of emergency, the Fox executives agreed that Oland was too closely identified with the role for any substitution to be made.

Oland was reportedly suffering from a nervous breakdown. The collapse of his marriage certainly had affected him deeply. It made national headlines when a photograph was taken of him sitting on the running board of his limousine throwing away his shoes.

"Honorable father must go to Europe," Oland told Luke. "Must see once more the chestnut trees of Florence."

Oland was hospitalized in February. By March, he was released. He signed a new contract with Darryl Zanuck to make three Charlie Chan films for the 1938–39 season. Zanuck agreed that an ocean voyage might be a good idea before resuming work.

Warner and Edith talked of reconciliation prior to Oland's sailing. It was never consummated. On an excursion to Stockholm, Oland fell ill with bronchial pneumonia.

"Life," Oland had once said, "like piece of delicate jade, difficult to create, easy to destroy."

Sol Wurtzel was three days into production on the first Chan film under the new contract when the news came. He had previously cabled Oland to return at once so the picture would stay on schedule. But on August 6, 1938, wire services all around the globe carried the message that Warner Oland was dead. He had passed away quietly, reposing in his mother's bed. "Life, death, life, death," he had remarked to Tommy Beck. Now Oland's life at fifty-seven had reached its span. Wurtzel gave the crew the rest of the day off. Edith long survived her husband. She died in 1968, fully expectant of making it to a hundred. "No use to hurry," Oland once said, "unless sure of catching right train."

Warner Oland's death did not kill Charlie Chan, however; the inscrutable Chinese detective had many more years of screen detecting before him.

II

John Marquand was born in Wilmington, Delaware, in 1893. Like many people, he married too young and regretted it, but he compounded his error. After receiving a divorce from one incompatible woman, he married another one, even worse.

From early childhood, Marquand's values were distorted by the peculiar New England emotional climate in which he was raised. Attending Harvard certainly didn't help. He found employment with the J. Walter Thompson advertising agency but proved unsuitable for a business career. By then it no longer mattered: he was selling short stories to *The Saturday Evening Post*. He was a naturally gifted stylist with a vividly melodramatic imagination who also happened to be wholly in tune with the popular sentiments of his time, much as was Earl Derr Biggers. He served during the Great War and was repelled by the wanton slaughter he witnessed in the trenches in France.

Marquand discovered that he could dictate his stories to a stenographer. He also tended to fall in love with his stenographers, a proclivity that apparently was not applauded by either of his wives. On a number of occasions, Marquand remarked about the loneliness writing imposed on him. Perhaps this wasn't least among the reasons behind his preference for writing by dictation. Yet, such an attitude strikes me as a curiosity. Can the company of one's fellows ever equal the solitary solace of being alone, watching the sentences slowly form on a page? This, it would seem to me, is the most acutely real pleasure a writer can have. When I commented as much to Ross Macdonald in conversation, he said not at all.

"Writing is painfully lonely." He paused. "But I make sure I'm not alone the rest of the time."

Marquand spent the better part of his life trying to prove himself, first to his fellows at Harvard, then to the parents of Christina Sedgwick, who was to be his first wife, then to Christina herself, whom he finally did marry in 1922 after a prolonged courtship, then to the critics. Had this not been the dynamic of his personality, he might very well have written entirely different books.

Whatever the anguish marriage to Christina caused him, it is to her that we owe the Mr. Moto stories. Unquestionably, interest in the Far East ran high among Americans between world wars, particularly those who frequented the pages of large-circulation slick magazines. Ray Long, editor of *Cosmopolitan*, negotiated a staggeringly lucrative agreement with Somerset Maugham for a series of short stories with exotic settings similar to those in Maugham's travel book *On a Chinese Screen* (Doran, 1922). Long hankered after a detective story, but the closest Maugham ever got was "Footprints in the Jungle," a tale that was nearly all true. All but two of Maugham's one hundred and four short stories, several of them among the finest of their kind, appeared in *Cosmopolitan*.

George Horace Lorimer, who edited the *Post*, had much the same close working relationship with Marquand that Long had with Maugham, and almost every month there was a Marquand story or serial in the *Post*. Marquand wrote superficial fiction and could title a story that began in the January 20, 1934, issue "Winner Take All" less than a year after Hemingway prefaced a collection of his short fiction titled *Winner Take Nothing* with the words: "Unlike all other forms of butte and combat, the conditions are that the winner shall take nothing; neither his ease, nor his pleasure, nor any notions of glory, nor if he win far enough, shall there be any reward within himself."

When Earl Derr Biggers died, Lorimer wanted to continue the by now traditional *Post* annual serial with an Oriental setting and, ideally, an Oriental detective. Hearing about Marquand's marital problems with Christina, he proposed a long holiday in the Orient without her, with the *Post* paying Marquand's expenses. Lorimer went on to suggest that while there Marquand should put his mind to inventing a successor for the popular Charlie Chan.

It was a worthwhile investment. Marquand's mainstream novel *Ming Yellow* was serialized in the *Post* beginning with the issue of December 8, 1934. The first Mr. Moto novel, *No Hero* (Little, Brown, 1935), began its serialization in the *Post* under the title "Mr. Moto Takes a Hand" in the March 30, 1935, issue. Marquand's creation of the dapper, intelligent, obsequious Japanese secret agent was an immediate success with *Post* readers.

Marquand had an awkward tendency, even in his best fiction, toward melodramatic overstatement. It was no different, really, in the Moto stories; it was merely more acceptable there. *No Hero* was dictated to Carol Brandt, the wife of Marquand's literary agent. In one of those strange relationships which in life are so commonplace and yet so preposterous when you encounter them in fiction, Marquand eventually began a long-term affair with Carol Brandt only mildly disapproved of by her husband. The trip to the Orient had another effect. Marquand met the heiress Adelaide Ferry Hooker, with whom he did not get along and whom, once he was divorced from Christina, he married. The rest of his life, almost, was spent trying to get finally clear of Adelaide.

Marquand was a heavy drinker, as I suppose are most writers for some reason I have never been able to determine. Dictation would begin in the morning and last for about four hours. Then a tray of martinis would arrive. Woe be to the secretary who wouldn't join Marquand for the cocktail break, although the afternoon had to be spent editing material already transcribed.

Thank You, Mr. Moto (Little, Brown, 1936) came next, and was followed by *Think Fast, Mr. Moto* (Little, Brown, 1937) and *Mr. Moto Is So Sorry* (Little,

Brown, 1938). By the time of *So Sorry*, Adelaide was already meddling in Marquand's work, an intrusion that quixotically led even to her sharing copyright notices on four books. She felt the Moto stories beneath him. Marquand wasn't decided in his own mind. He wanted to write truly serious fiction, but he returned to the little Japanese twice more over the years that saw him publish novels like *H. M. Pulham, Esquire* (Little, Brown, 1941) and *Women and Thomas Harrow* (Little, Brown, 1958). *Last Laugh, Mr. Moto* (Little, Brown, 1942) was run serially in *Collier's* during the Second World War and showed Moto getting outwitted, consistent with the anti-Japanese feeling of the time. In a nostalgic frame of mind, he wrote *Stopover: Tokyo* in 1956 for the *Post* before it came out in a cloth edition.

"Naturally," Marquand once recalled concerning his creation of the Moto character, "I did a great deal of poking around in Chinese cities and eventually wandered to Japan. There I was constantly shadowed by a polite little Japanese detective. Suddenly, it dawned on me that he was just the protagonist I was looking for—and while my shadow did his duty very conscientiously, Mr. Moto, the shrewd, the polite, the efficient sleuth was born." Whatever his origin, Mr. Moto in the novels remains at all times as shadowy and one-dimensional as his prototype must have been. This was by design. Marquand wanted to stress the lives and interrelationships of his main characters with Moto darting in or out of the narrative at strategic points. Biggers had done this with Charlie Chan in at least two of his novels, but, however brief his appearances, Charlie's personality had more substance than Moto's, which is probably why Charlie has become an American folk hero and Moto has not.

Moto was courteous, precise, amazingly competent, crafty, and so vague you could never be sure what he was thinking or would do next. It is this vagueness we have to thank for the rather short-lived popularity the novels enjoyed. They have been out of print for years now, and nothing about their slick style and romantic plots can any longer captivate even the nostalgic reader who might still be inclined to read Earl Derr Biggers. It was therefore probably inevitable that when Moto was brought to the screen little could be done by Peter Lorre, who was assigned the role, to give the character additional depth.

But that was only part of the problem confronting Sol Wurtzel when he decided to star an actor with a German accent in the role of a Japanese detective. Lorre was born on June 26, 1904, in Rosenberg, Hungary. He was the eldest of four sons born to Alois and Elvira Lorre. Alois made a living selling wood off the land he owned, until that played out and his wife died. He moved with his family to Vienna and eventually became a manager for the Steyr automobile company. Alois did not approve of his son's desire to become an actor. He discouraged him so adamantly that Peter ran away from home shortly after the Armistice of 1918. I think it is safe to assume that, from the beginning, the younger Lorre had the exophthalmic eyes, diminutive stature, and delicate voice which became his most memorable attributes as an actor. He was, apparently, also from a very early age rather peculiar emotionally. All of this he turned to his advantage when he assumed psychopathic roles. But initially—let's admit it— it must have been something of a handicap.

During the inflation of the early Twenties in Germany, Lorre took to sleeping on park benches at night and looking for work during the day. He tried one-man performances, giving readings illustrated with pantomime. For a brief time, he got into banking but was soon terminated for being irresponsible. He landed a small job in Breslau in the stock company there, which was directed by Leo Mittler, later a film director. He got acting jobs in Zurich and Vienna, and finally ended up at the Volksbühne (People's Theater) in Berlin. He played, among other things, a sex fiend and the adolescent Moritz Stiefel in Wedekind's *Frühlings Erwachen*, who commits suicide when he finds himself unable to deal with his sexual urges. Fritz Lang saw him in the latter role. The German director went backstage and asked Lorre how he would like to be in pictures. Lorre, reflecting on his physical endowments and the role he was playing onstage, was perplexed by the question.

But Lang was right. Lorre was rehearsing in Bertolt Brecht's *Mann Ist Mann* at the Berlin Staatstheatre when Lang offered him the starring role of a psychopathic killer in *Mörderer Unter Uns*, released as *M* (Nerofilm, 1931). While the picture was in production, Lorre commuted between the makeshift studio outside Berlin to the Staatstheatre and back again. Brecht was personally directing his play, which opened and closed after two days. *M* scored better. It became a masterpiece of the German cinema and its reputation spread abroad, typecasting Lorre as an unbalanced and haunting screen personality. UFA in Germany signed Lorre to a contract. Lorre himself preferred comedy roles: his contract afforded him opportunity to appear in humorous roles amid the predictable assemblage of heinous villains.

The rising tide of National Socialism interrupted Lorre's stage and screen career. He was convinced that his name was on one of the lists of persons the Nazis intended to eliminate. He fled to Vienna three days before the Reichstag fire. For all that, as long as they were broadcast, Lorre seldom missed Hitler's radio speeches despite their upsetting effect on him. Sam Spiegel, Universal Pictures' representative in Germany, put Lorre in a poorly scripted program picture that persuaded him he might do better elsewhere; he went to Paris, where he lived in a boardinghouse with, among others, Billy Wilder the screenwriter, Franz Waxman the composer, and Paul Lukas. Despite his impossible French, Lorre landed a job dubbing Lukas' voice on a French voice track.

Times were bad and got worse when Lorre immigrated to England having no money and speaking no English. Sidney Bernstein, a producer, introduced Lorre to Alfred Hitchcock, who had once been an assistant director at UFA. Hitchcock cast him as the anarchist in *The Man Who Knew Too Much* (Gaumont-British, 1934). Cecilia Lvovsky, whom Lorre had met in Berlin, played a Russian aristocrat in the film. They were married.

Years later, Lorre recalled his initial meeting with Hitchcock. "Hitch talked," he said, "and I leaned forward looking intelligent but not understanding a word. By following his gestures, I'd guess when he was coming to the gag-line and I'd laugh out loud. I got the role and it was two weeks before Hitch found out I spoke no English. I must say he got a big kick out of it."

When I visited Alfred Hitchcock at his office on the Universal lot, *The Family Plot* (Universal, 1976) had only just been released.

"Photographs are forbidden here," he said.

These were his first words to me. As I was not carrying a camera anywhere on my person, I had no idea at all what prompted him to make the remark. But he was genial, his skin possessing a healthy reddish tint. In the course of our conversation, once we sat down, I brought up Peter Lorre's reminiscence of their first meeting.

"I had no idea at all," Hitch drawled, "that Lorre was Hungarian, so, when we met, I spoke to him in German. I had to learn German when I worked in Germany as an art director ten years earlier."

In Hollywood, Josef von Sternberg decided to cast Peter Lorre as Raskolnikov in his cinematic presentation of Dostoyevsky's *Crime and Punishment* (Columbia, 1935), another ideally psychoneurotic role which Lorre accepted with alacrity, and he departed England for the States. Before production could begin, Lorre was loaned out to Metro to play a bald maniac in *Mad Love* (M-G-M, 1935) directed by Karl Freund. It was a remake of the 1924 film *Orlacs Hände*, which originally featured Conrad Veidt.

Among the best stories Somerset Maugham wrote are those included in *Ashenden, or the British Agent* (Doubleday, 1928). They grew out of Maugham's experiences in the British secret service during the Great War. One of the most unpleasant characters Ashenden meets is a hairless Mexican. When, in 1936, Alfred Hitchcock brought the literary property to the screen, he hastened to cast Lorre as a curly-haired hired killer, comically enough based on Maugham's hairless Mexican.

Lorre considered the whole business an inside joke and, of course, proved splendid in the role. He later reported that, as a prank, upon departing England for the States the second time he purchased an entire pet shop of canaries and had them shipped to Hitchcock's home. But, according to Lorre, Hitchcock had his revenge. He began cabling Lorre aboard ship every fifteen minutes, night and day, telling him how he had named each of the canaries and giving him moment-by-moment details as to what each of the canaries was doing. It was so continuous that Lorre was unable to sleep.

I asked Hitch if that, indeed, had ever happened.

"No," he said.

We talked of other things. Finally, our meeting nearly over, I let out a sigh. Hitch looked at me with curiosity.

"I frankly wish that story about the canaries had been true," I said. "It makes such a fine anecdote."

Hitch smiled quietly.

"Why don't you say my memory is bad," he drawled, "for it is sometimes. Let's just say, I don't remember it as having happened."

In November 1936, convinced by his screen work that Lorre was a valuable player, Twentieth Century-Fox put him under a three-year contract. Malcolm St. Clair, who had directed *The Canary Murder Case* (Paramount, 1929), directed Lorre in his first picture under the new arrangement, a spy drama called *Crack-up* (20th-Fox, 1936). Lorre appeared in two more nondescript films when he found himself in the midst of a Sol Wurtzel brainstorm.

Before I can go farther, I really must introduce Norman Foster. There is a detective film so obscure I don't imagine anyone is likely to have seen it. It's called *Fire Trap* (Majestic, 1937) and starred Norman Foster and Evalyn Knapp. The plot concerns Sidney Blackmer's collusion with Oscar Apfel in an insurance swindle. Foster is the young, not-to-be-put-down insurance investigator who is working for Blackmer and who both steals Blackmer's girl—Evalyn Knapp in skin-tight gowns and dresses without support garments—and exposes Blackmer as a villain. The dialogue was often satirical and the picture gave Foster, whose career as an actor was not altogether thriving, an opportunity to participate in the direction.

Foster, who had been married and divorced from Claudette Colbert, was by this time married to Sally Blane, Loretta Young's older sister. Sally had been working on the Fox lot and was now pregnant. No matter, the two were intent on going to New York to find stage work. Sol Wurtzel intervened.

My first conversation with Norman Foster was by telephone from my home when I was in the process of screening the Moto films. Norm had laryngitis. Sally handled the call, relaying my questions and Norm's answers.

"Sol really did us a favor," Sally said. "He asked Norm, 'How does Sally feel about going to New York with a baby?' 'She doesn't like it,' Norm told him. Sol suggested that Norm become a director at Fox and Norm took him up on it. He started for $350 a week, when he had been getting $2,000 a week as an actor."

"Lorre complained toward the end of his life that the Moto characterization did nothing for him," I said.

"Well," Sally said, "he didn't talk that way so much when he was making the pictures. Peter and his wife were frequently our guests. He was a gentle . . . What was that, Norm?"

There was a pause.

"Oh yes," Sally resumed, "Peter did once say to Norm, after their first couple of pictures together, that 'we're like a husband and wife who have been living together for too long.' "

"Did Norm have any trouble directing him?" I asked.

Sally put the question to Norm, who croaked a response.

"Not," Sally said, "if you take into account that he was an actor with a German accent playing an Oriental. Sometimes he would get temperamental and have a complete breakdown, sobbing and totally unable to work."

"He would just start sobbing?"

"Yes." Sally paused. "What was that, Norm?" There was another pause while Sally listened.

"Norm says that you have to remember that Peter was in a rest home at the time Sol cast him, recovering from drug addiction. When they began filming, he had a dressing room on the set where a doctor would come daily to give him a shot. He was very thin and frail then compared to later years. He had suffered from malnutrition when he was small, and his teeth were rotten."

"How much did Lorre really contribute to the characterization?"

"I don't know. Norm had a lot to do with it. He talked over the character with John Marquand and, besides directing, he worked on the screenplays."

"Sally," I said, "I suspect Wurtzel started the Moto series to keep Warner

Oland in line, the way he once promoted Buck Jones to act as a brake on Tom Mix's salary demands. Do you know why Fox dropped the series?"

"Originally, it wasn't supposed to be a series, but the first picture was such a success that Sol kept making them. I guess he got angry at Peter . . ."

"Or Lorre at the part," I interrupted.

"Maybe both. Sol just stopped. He was like that. He was a wonderful man. But if he became angry at someone, that was it. He just stopped. Norm always blamed it on horse racing. Sol would sit in his office, feet up on his desk getting a haircut, manicure, and shoeshine while talking on the phone to his bookie."

Marquand's third Moto novel was made the basis for the first picture, *Think Fast, Mr. Moto* (20th-Fox, 1937). Norman Foster directed *Fair Warning* (20th-Fox, 1937) for Sol Wurtzel and was then assigned to direct the Moto film. Fox publicity dreamed up a catch phrase for promoting the film and Lorre, terming Lorre "Europe's One Man Chamber of Horrors." But the script did not reveal Lorre to be a ghoul. He was soft-spoken, wily, very much the enchanting little character of the novels. Possibly Lorre was apt for the role precisely because he left the personality of Moto unaffected.

Think Fast did change the plot of the book somewhat. The setting was altered from a gambling house in Honolulu as a blind to sneak Chinese money into the Japanese colony of Manchukuo to the theme of smuggling in general. Although it opened in San Francisco, much of the action took place in Shanghai. Tommy Beck and Virginia Field supplied the love interest.

While *Mr. Moto Takes a Chance* (20th-Fox, 1938) was fourth to be released, it was second in order of production. It was previewed under its working title *Look Out, Mr. Moto*. Lou Breslow and John Patrick did the screenplay based on an original story by Willis Cooper and Norman Foster. Foster directed. The setting was the Cambodian jungle. Third in order of production and second into release was *Thank You, Mr. Moto* (20th-Fox, 1937). The screenplay by Willis Cooper and Norman Foster was based on the Marquand novel of the same title. Again the plot was altered. Instead of stealing Chinese art treasures, which was the plot of the book, seven scrolls are supposed to give the whereabouts, when pieced together, of Genghis Khan's hidden wealth. Sidney Blackmer was in the cast, joined by Tommy Beck, Pauline Frederick, Sig Rumann (who had been in *Think Fast*), John Carradine, and two players who had also been in *Charlie Chan at the Opera*, Nedda Harrigan and the fantastic John Bleifer. After much intrigue, Moto gets the scrolls and burns them, thus leaving the Khan's booty undisturbed.

Fourth in production, but third into release, was *Mr. Moto's Gamble* (20th-Fox, 1938), which began as the Chan picture in production at the time of Warner Oland's death. James Tinling, who had been assigned to direct *Charlie Chan at the Ringside*, stayed on as director. Since so much footage had been shot of Keye Luke, Sol Wurtzel instructed the writers to give him a role. John Stone remained the associate producer, although he had not previously been involved in the Moto series. Harold Huber was a New York policeman. When a fighter is poisoned in the ring, Moto investigates with Luke as Lee Chan and Huber as his comic assistants. Not surprisingly, the Chan formula was crossed with the Moto formula in this picture. Wurtzel was pleased with the results.

Norman Foster was back contributing to the screenplay (with Philip Mac-Donald, who had worked on Chan films) and directing for the fifth entry, *Mysterious Mr. Moto* (20th-Fox, 1938), obviously one of the most ambitious films in the series. The picture opens to a map of Devil's Island and the escape of two criminals, Leon Ames and Moto. Moto becomes Ames's houseboy in London, where Ames attaches himself to Harold Huber's assassination ring. Henry Wilcoxon is their next victim. He's a Czech industrialist who plays Chopin at the piano while dictating business letters to his secretary, with whom he is in love. Moto foils the plot and discovers the identity of the ring's secret leader.

I was already in the booth I had reserved at the Brown Derby in Hollywood when Leon Ames walked in the door. I recognized him at once. We talked about Peter Lorre.

"I've visited Norman Foster since I've been out here," I said. "He told me that Lorre would listen to Hitler's speeches in his dressing room and then come racing out with an insane look on his face, nose running, saliva coming from his mouth, shouting, 'How can you want me to make pictures when the world is falling apart?'"

John P. Marquand (center) joins Norman Foster and Peter Lorre on the set of a Mr. Moto picture.   PHOTO COURTESY OF THE LATE NORMAN FOSTER.

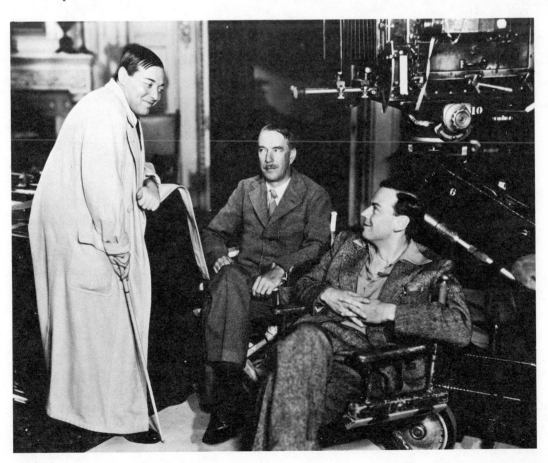

The setting was supposed to be Peiping (Peking), but it was actually the Fox back lot on Western Avenue.   PHOTO COURTESY OF THE LATE NORMAN FOSTER.

"He was quite a character," Ames said, smiling as he remembered. "He had the foulest breath because of his teeth. He later had them taken out. But he was fond, when we worked on those Moto pictures, of going up to girls and saying, 'Could you get used to my body, you think?' He relished being gnomelike. But he was an expert at matching scenes. When we'd stop shooting and then begin again, he knew exactly what he had been doing, where he was standing, and how he was holding his body."

"Do you have any idea why the series was dropped?" I asked. "Was it Sol Wurtzel?"

"Actually," Ames replied, "there were four Wurtzels working on that lot when I came to Fox. I remember it was a studio joke that there was a girl under contract for the last three years who had yet to make a picture because she was sleeping with the wrong Wurtzel."

Ames continued, "I think the pictures just got boring. I recall when we were doing that Devil's Island sequence together, Lorre and I had to go through the swamps at night in order to escape. It was shot on the Fox back lot. We were wading in mud up to our necks. There was a tiger in a tree, supposedly chained. But when we got close to it, I saw that there wasn't anything like a chain around him, not even a small rope. We then had to crawl into a small boat and we get shot at. Foster had sharpshooters out there, using real bullets. That's when I rebelled. I told them to stop everything. The tiger had been bad enough, but I wasn't going to get shot at for the sake of any picture."

"Norman Foster did tell me one interesting thing," I said. "He met Peter Lorre many years later, and Peter looked at him and commented wryly that it was too bad Norman didn't know him now."

Philip MacDonald again collaborated with Norman Foster on the screenplay for *Mr. Moto's Last Warning* (20th-Fox, 1939). Foster directed. When Warner Oland had his nervous breakdown during the 1937–38 season, Wurtzel reduced the number of Chan releases from three to two and with *Mr. Moto's Gamble* from the next season had in effect increased Moto production from three to four pictures a year. Even when production later resumed on the Chan films for the 1938–39 season, Wurtzel kept them at two a year, the Motos at four. In *Last Warning*, the setting is Port Said and the attempt of conspirators to sabotage the French fleet. Moto saves the day, centering his suspicions on Ricardo Cortez. John Carradine was in the picture. So was George Sanders, only Sanders didn't want to be. He took it out on Foster by running up large restaurant bills and charging them to Foster's account. One night, they were shooting late. It was Foster's birthday and the script girls had got together and bought him a quart of expensive bonded whiskey. Sanders, who had a scene to do, found the bottle first and drank all of it. Norm was so angry he shot the sequence with Sanders in his inebriated condition. Sanders just smirked. The next day, screening the footage, it had to be scrapped.

Next in production, although last in release, was *Mr. Moto Takes a Vacation* (20th-Fox, 1939). MacDonald and Foster did the screenplay with Foster directing. The casting was strong with Joseph Schildkraut, Lionel Atwill, and Virginia Field in major roles. The trades at the time were agreed as to Norman Foster's very capable direction, but faulted the screenplay. The story still doesn't make sense at this late date. Schildkraut finances an expedition to find the crown of the Queen of Sheba. Moto watches over the crown all the way back to San Francisco. It is rumored that a famous criminal, long thought dead, will steal the crown. This criminal in the end turns out to be none other than Schildkraut himself, who scarcely would have had to resort to theft to possess the crown.

Because of the cutback in Chan production, John Stone had another Moto picture added to his complement for the next season. It remains a tribute to him because it is undoubtedly the best in a surprisingly good series. Although released three months before *Vacation, Mr. Moto in Danger Island* followed it in production by three months, starting as *Mr. Moto in Puerto Rico*, then *Terror Island*, and at last *Danger Island*. Herbert I. Leeds directed. Peter Milne did the screenplay, based upon story ideas by John Reinhardt and George Bricker and a novel by John W. Vandercook. Richard Lane, soon to be in the Boston

Leon Ames and Peter Lorre while making good their escape in *Mysterious Mr. Moto* (20th-Fox, 1938).　　PHOTO COURTESY OF TWENTIETH CENTURY-FOX FILM CORPORATION.

Blackie series for Columbia, is a police commissioner. Jean Hersholt, Warren Hymer, Leon Ames, and Douglas Dumbrille are all prominently in the cast. Warren Hymer as a wrestler is sort of a sidekick for Moto. It may have been Wurtzel's intention to give Moto a foil equivalent to the Chan sons, but more likely Stone adapted the character from a script originally intended to be a Charlie Chan entry.

From February 1937 until December 1938, Peter Lorre appeared in eight Moto pictures. He deported himself like the Moto of the novels, and he talked like him: "I am so very, very happy" or "Not ever again, I am thinking" or "You must not make a sound, please." The films were so well mounted, the casts filled with such entertaining and polished players, the stories filled with intrigue and action, you never really notice how insignificant the Moto character is when compared to Warner Oland's profound impact in the Chan series.

Lorre rebelled at being kept in a "B" series, and Sol Wurtzel shut down production. Peter was idle for three months before he asked to be released from his Fox contract. Wurtzel dropped the three Motos scheduled for the 1939–40 season with the same shrug of the shoulders with which he responded to Lorre's checking off the Fox lot. But between Lorre and Oland, Sol had certainly had his hands full with emotionally distraught actors playing Orientals. Like Boris Karloff, who shied away from such roles after the Wong series (discussed further on in this chapter), Lorre went on to become even more important in the history of the genre as a heavy than he was as a detective. For Lorre, Mr. Moto was only a beginning.

I mentioned that John Marquand wrote a last Moto novel near the time of his death. Twentieth Century-Fox purchased screen rights to it. But the character of Moto was deleted from the screenplay of *Stopover Tokyo* (20th-Fox, 1957), which starred Robert Wagner and Joan Collins.

The Return of Mr. Moto (20th-Fox, 1965) in typical Hollywood style did not happen for many years, and when it did it proved a disappointment. Produced by Robert L. Lippert and Jack Parsons and directed by Ernest Morris, Henry Silva appeared as Moto, playing with a cast of relative unknowns. The plot had to do with the murder of an oil magnate and an effort to seize the leases he held on fields in the Persian Gulf. At one point, Moto is thrown into the Thames in a weighted sack. He cuts himself loose, much as Peter Lorre once had in a similar scrape. But there the similarity ended. A new era had found new heroes. Mr. Moto proved as outdated as *The Saturday Evening Post*. James Bond now articulated the popular conception of an international spy.

Marquand lived to see none of this. One summer morning in July 1960, Marquand's houseman brought him his breakfast, dropping the tray when he realized that John Marquand wouldn't be waking up. Marquand's son rushed to his side; it was too late. He had died in his sleep. He may have been all written out, but he had written a last book, *Timothy Dexter Revisited* (Little, Brown, 1960), which he had wanted to write sheerly for his own amusement. He had got rid of Adelaide. He died at sixty-six, not a long life-span, to be sure. His youngest son, Lonnie, who was staying with him, thought nothing of it when Marquand remarked over dinner the previous night that he thought he would have another heart attack. He patted the boy on the head and retired early. He was living alone and sleeping alone and, as his biographer Stephen Birmingham pointed out rather cruelly, he died alone.

III

On January 15, 1935, Monogram Pictures Corporation released *The Mysterious Mr. Wong*. It starred Bela Lugosi as a low-budget imitation Dr. Fu Manchu. The plot was based on "The Twelve Coins of Confucius," by eccentric mystery writer Harry Stephen Keeler. William Nigh directed. If you have been fortunate enough not to have seen such wholly meretricious Lugosi films as *Voodoo Man* (Monogram, 1944), it is conceivable that you might think Lugosi incapable of such a bad picture. *The Mysterious Mr. Wong* is so bad it isn't even funny; there's no relief from the tedium. As he expires, Lugosi grabs a doorknob. Other characters talk about his dashed hopes to be a Chinese warlord as, one after the other in very slow motion, Lugosi's fingers uncurl from the knob; his hand is supported now by only two fingers, then one, then it collapses to the floor.

I wouldn't mention the film at all save to forewarn the reader that it is *not* a picture featuring James Lee Wong, the Chinese detective, and thus spare the reader the possible displeasure of watching it.

Yet I would not wish to imply that the subsequent Mr. Wong series was a whole lot better. It was based on a series of short stories by Hugh Wiley published in *Collier's*. William Nigh directed all five of the Wongs starring Boris Karloff. Nigh was unhappily a rather unimaginative director. Even Karloff must have been bored, since he made no effort at a charming or in any way memorable characterization. The only thing Chinese about him, other than the fact that he was named Wong and drank tea, was his execrable make-up. But even this was dropped in the 1940 films. The stories were sufficiently farfetched to be as unintentionally comic as the dialogue.

The series began with *Mr. Wong, Detective* (Monogram, 1938). Here's a precis of the plot. John Hamilton, Hooper Atchley, and William Gould, all traditional heavies, are business partners in a chemical plant that manufactures poison gas. When Hamilton is gassed in his office, Wong, assisted by Grant Withers as browbeating, overbearing Captain Street, discovers the gas is being made from a formula the three stole from John St. Polis, who is jailed for the murder. Atchley then gives a party for the entire cast except for Withers and, of course, St. Polis. During the festivities, Atchley gets a note from St. Polis threatening his life. He barricades himself in his library and calls Withers. Atchley is gassed. Withers, having raced to Atchley's home, sirens blaring, after viewing the body races back to the jail to grill St. Polis with idiotic questions, not so much as pausing to interview any of the suspects at the scene of the crime. William Gould is the third to go.

In *Charlie Chan in Egypt* (Fox, 1935) one of the murder devices was a sealed vial of poison gas inserted beneath the soundholes of a violin. When the victim

Boris Karloff mildly made up for his role of Mr. Wong.

PHOTO COURTESY OF THE NATIONAL FILM ARCHIVE.

played the violin at a certain pitch, the vial broke, releasing the gas and causing instant death. Houston Branch, the scenarist on *Mr. Wong, Detective*, borrowed this notion. St. Polis is a mad genius. He makes three glass spheres filled with gas and plants them in Hamilton's office, Atchley's library, and Gould's living room. The glass is such that it only shatters when a police siren blares outside. Hence, Withers with his siren is the unwitting foil. Luckily for St. Polis, Withers' siren was the only one to be heard in these vicinities for several days.

Nor did matters improve in later pictures. *The Mystery of Mr. Wong* (Monogram, 1939) had a screenplay by Scott Darling and depended on dialogue such as the boy friend of the intended murder victim's wife shouting into the camera: "I won't stand by and watch the woman I love torn to pieces." I happen to have seen outtakes from this picture. Maybe they should have been left in. At

Karloff as Mr. Wong talking to a frustrated Grant Withers in *Mr. Wong in Chinatown* (Monogram, 1939). PHOTO COURTESY OF THE NATIONAL FILM ARCHIVE.

one point, in the released version, Wong opens the victim's safe to extract a letter written before he died in which he states the name of his would-be murderer.

"The door is open," Karloff observes, opening the safe door.

In the outtakes, Karloff walks over to the safe.

"The door is open," he observes. He tugs at the door. He tugs some more. Then he turns to the director. "The goddamned door won't open!" He resumes tugging. William Nigh calls: "Cut!"

Mr. Wong in Chinatown (Monogram, 1939) added Marjorie Reynolds to the series as news reporter Bobbie Logan. Her one beat, apparently, is Grant Withers' office. She sits on his desk, rides in his car, listens to all the conversations he has, and phones in to her paper to report every expletive. At least twenty minutes of screen time is devoted to her sparring with Withers. The remainder of *Chinatown* is about the death of a Chinese princess, her maid, and, offstage, Angelo Rissito, a grotesque dwarf. They are all shot in the neck with a Chinese hand-operated bamboo blowgun loaded with giant-sized poison darts. All you need know to solve this one is that the princess had a million dollars on deposit at a San Francisco bank. Once a banker is introduced as a suspect, especially at Monogram, it follows automatically that his bank is short of funds. But just why he should prefer this clumsy death apparatus to simpler methods is never explained. Confronted by Wong with the truth, the banker jumps off the ship they're on and splashes about two inches away from the side of the boat before Grant Withers' double jumps directly on top of him for a split-second action arrest.

I suppose the reader may have concluded (as I confess I did seeing these films and imagining how Scott Dunlap, head of production at Monogram, must have cringed at thought of the scathing reviews) that the series was quickly upgraded and the plots made more plausible. Not at all. Dunlap was so impressed with these plots that, at his suggestion, *Mr. Wong, Detective* was remade as *Docks of New Orleans* (Monogram, 1948), a Charlie Chan film with Roland Winters, and *Mr. Wong in Chinatown* was remade as *The Chinese Ring* (Monogram, 1947), another Chan opus.

Doomed to Die (Monogram, 1940) featured the trio of Karloff, Withers, and Reynolds. It opened to stock footage of a freighter burning. The shot had the ship moving right to left. It was extremely short, so the film was reversed and the ship burned some more, this time moving left to right. An entire scene between Karloff and Richard Loo was lifted from *Mr. Wong in Chinatown*. Guy Usher's son is fighting with the owner of a shipping firm while Usher is in the outer office. The son is told to get out. At this point, the murderer opens a door, shoots the owner, and throws the gun in alongside the body. The son is so shocked to see the owner fall it doesn't occur to him to look in the direction of the murderer. In this way, the case can only be solved by Mr. Wong.

Midway through the picture, Kenneth Harlan in an offbeat role as a chauffeur is caught prowling around on the fire escape in broad daylight by Wong and Withers.

"It's a pleasure to meet you," Wong comments.

"The pleasure is all yours," Harlan replies.

"What were you doing on the fire escape?" Withers asks.

"Parking the car."

The Fatal Hour (Monogram, 1940) could have been plotted any of a dozen different ways. Grant Withers tries most of them out while hassling various suspects. Marjorie Reynolds got to go a few more rounds with him in between. But it's the worst of all the plots that Wong finally uncovers as the truth.

It would have been all up early in the game if Jason Robards, Sr., had had a chance to talk. He was sitting in a crowded waiting room outside Withers' office. The murderer entered, stole a long metal fingernail file from the desk sergeant, and plunged it into Robards' neck. Robards did not cry out, so no one knew he was being stabbed. It is left to Wong to tap Robards on the shoulder only to have him topple dead to the floor.

At Monogram, rather than avoiding scenes likely to be expensive to create for the camera, in view of the niggardly budgets, the screenwriters seemed to delight perversely in writing them in. Two characters go out to dine at a swank night club. However, this is Monogram, not Metro-Goldwyn-Mayer. There is no orchestra, not even a juke box. The tables are made of bamboo with postage-stamp tablecloths. When the script needed to establish that there was gambling going on upstairs, to save on costs one character simply remarked to another: "A little gambling, eh? I can hear the poker chips." No one bothered to insert such a sound on the track.

Not that it concerned Karloff. His Monogram contract ran out before the final Mr. Wong picture could be rushed into production. Scott Dunlap's pleading fell on deaf ears. Karloff was relieved that the entire business was over at last.

Monogram had presold three Wong pictures for 1940, and one was still unmade. What to do? The solution was obvious. What was always done in the Forties when, for whatever the reason, a producer needed a Chinese actor fast? The answer was inevitably Keye Luke.

The screenplay for *Phantom of Chinatown* (Monogram, 1940) was by Joseph West, based on an original story by Ralph Bettinson. But you cannot be taken in by the title. There was no phantom in the picture. Luke was scarcely suited to the role and even with a mustache looked too young. Grant Withers was unacquainted with him until a third of the way into the story. Lotus Long played a Chinese secretary to an explorer returned from an expedition to the Gobi desert; she was also a secret agent for the Chinese government. The explorer has a map showing the location of an oil deposit in Mongolia, but he is poisoned drinking a glass of water while narrating a filmed travelogue of his adventures. Withers has a plush office and doesn't berate a single suspect. Luke and Withers expose the culprit by means of the old hospital routine, where Luke is confined to his bed and catches the murderer when he tries to sneak into his room. At the fade Luke sails off for China with Lotus Long.

Phil Rosen directed this final entry. I do not know how much he was to blame. I have come to believe that Monogram was incapable of producing a well-made detective story. If the Wong series cannot prove it, then one need only survey their subsequent efforts with Charlie Chan.

IV

Some four days after Warner Oland's death, *Variety* reported that Twentieth Century-Fox was canvassing exhibitors for possible replacements for the Charlie Chan role. J. Edward Bromberg, who had been tested when Oland first fell ill, was rated as having the best chance, with Noah Beery, Sr., rated a strong contender because of his resemblance to Oland. A total of thirty-four actors were tested before a final choice of Sidney Toler was announced on October 18, 1938. Toler was born at Warrensburg, Missouri, in 1875. He was nearly sixty when he started in the role. He began in films with *Madame X* (M-G-M, 1929) after working on the stage. Despite his subsequent identification with Charlie Chan, his best parts as an actor were in non-Chan roles, above all in Westerns for producer Harry Sherman at Paramount. Production on *Charlie Chan in Honolulu* was slated to begin on October 24, 1938.

"Look," Sol Wurtzel had once commented to Keye Luke, "with this team, there's one smart one and one dumb one. You're the dumb one." Luke asked to be excused from his role in the Chan pictures and released from his contract. He didn't feel that anyone could really replace Oland and he resented the pay cut he received when Oland died. Fox subsequently cast Victor Sen Young as Charlie's Number Two son, Jimmy Chan, the screenplay of *Honolulu* explaining that elder son Lee was away at art school. Sen Young, whose real name was Sen Yew Cheung, had been a chemical salesman who thought he might like to be in pictures. It suited him, apparently, and as recently as *The Killer Elite* (M-G-M, 1975) Sam Peckinpah cast him as a Chinese underworld tough.

Lucky Humberstone was called upon to direct *Honolulu*. After the first few days of shooting, he found Toler's performance awkward and wooden. Flaring at Sen Young's inexperience, he would rage, "Get Keye Luke back." But for Toler he had more practical advice.

"I knew Sidney was a heavy drinker," Lucky confided to me. "I told him I wanted him to take a few stiff belts before he started work the next morning. Sidney could hardly believe his ears. But he did it. He loosened up and gave a better characterization."

"Aww," Jimmy Flavin remarked to me, "all those Chans were drunk while making those pictures. You'd have to be drunk just to talk that pidgin English." Jimmy played a cop in *Honolulu*.

John Stone opined correctly that the only way to really compensate for Sidney's shortcomings was to devise scripts of strong intrigue and unusual interest. Most of the plots of Toler's Fox Chans are superior to those of Warner's films. *Honolulu* was definitely no exception. The picture opened with Charlie at table with his wife and twelve children. A murder aboard Robert Barrat's ship and its solution run parallel to the delivery of Charlie's first grandchild. George Zucco was cast as an eccentric psychologist who pretends to be hard of hearing and who carries about with him the brain of a Chinese criminal which he keeps alive in a chemical concoction. Because Lucky was directing, much in the picture was played for comic effect. A great many wild animals in cages were supposedly aboard ship, and Oscar, a tame lion, got involved in several humorous situations.

Charlie Chan in Reno (20th-Fox, 1939) was based on *Death Makes a Decree*, a novel by Philip Wylie. Frances Hyland, Albert Ray, and Robert E. Kent supplied the screenplay. Norman Foster directed. Louise Henry was back as a bitchy divorcée who is murdered. Charlie investigates. Slim Summerville was cast as a rustic sheriff. Hamilton MacFadden, whom the reader may recall as directing some early Chans, was still under contract and was given a role. The trades seemed unanimous in praising the complexity of the plot structure.

Reno was such a success that the studio almost outdid itself with the next entry, *Charlie Chan at Treasure Island* (20th-Fox, 1939). Edward Kaufman, who had just joined Fox as an associate producer after leaving Warner Brothers, assembled an exceptional cast to enact an engaging story by John Larkin. "Favorite pastime of man is fooling himself," Charlie observes. Cesar Romero was cast as a magician named Rhadini. Douglas Fowley was a police reporter. June

Sidney Toler as Charlie Chan and Victor Sen Young as Number Two son, Jimmy Chan, became the new team in the Chan films.
PHOTO COURTESY OF TWENTIETH CENTURY-FOX FILM CORPORATION.

Gale, soon to be married to Oscar Levant, played Romero's wife. Douglas Dumbrille portrayed an insurance investigator (the previous year Toler had appeared as Dumbrille's sidekick in Harry Sherman's production of Zane Grey's *The Mysterious Rider* [Paramount, 1938]). Sidney liked Dumbrille and, perhaps not by accident, Dumbrille worked in several more Chan films. Trevor Bardette was the treacherous Dr. Zodiac's Turkish servant. Dr. Zodiac is a phony medium who uses his guise as a psychic consultant to blackmail his clients. There is a lot of plot here, much more than I am inclined to relate. Norman Foster rather ably directed such an assorted cast.

The setting of the old *Charlie Chan in Paris* inspired the story for *Charlie Chan in the City of Darkness* (20th-Fox, 1939). Robert Ellis and Helen Logan based their screenplay on a play by Gina Kaus and Ladislaus Fodor. John Stone was again the associate producer. There is much in this film to recommend it, but nothing more so than the state of urgency rampant in Paris as the world girds itself for another war. The title *City of Darkness* is derived from the blackouts which occur at strategic points, and the investigations are intermittently interrupted by the terrible drone of fighter planes flying overhead. The coming of a far greater catastrophe is nearly palpable in the oppressive opening to the film, featuring as it does news footage of the Czech crisis.

So popular was the Oriental detective in China that two illegal Chan films were made by the Hsin Hwa Motion Picture Company in Shanghai. The first was *Charlie Chan in Homeland* with Hsu Hsin-yuan in the role of Chan. It was followed by *Charlie Chan in Radio Station*. The pictures were done in Chinese and were never distributed beyond the borders of the war-torn mainland.

Charlie Chan in Panama (20th-Fox, 1940) was directed by Norman Foster. John Larkin wrote the screenplay. Espionage was the theme, with Charlie cast as an undercover agent sent to Central America to assist in protecting the Panama Canal and the U.S. fleet. Lionel Atwill played a British mystery story writer. Addison Richards was dispatched with a poisoned cigarette, beginning a series of daring crimes. The culprit was exceedingly well concealed for a Chan film.

Robertson White and Lester Ziffren returned to the screenplay of *Charlie Chan Carries On* for the next entry, a remake titled *Charlie Chan's Murder Cruise* (20th-Fox, 1940). This time Charlie was in the picture almost from the beginning. The plot device of two characters using a disguise to protect each other was revived from *Charlie Chan in Paris*. Layne Tom, Jr., was back, this time as Willie Chan, Charlie's seventh son, with Sen Young as the Number Two son Layne had presumably been in *Charlie Chan at the Olympics*.

Although interestingly directed by Eugene Forde, Sol Wurtzel announced after release of *Murder Cruise* that it was Fox's intention to drop the Chan series from the production schedule for the 1940–41 season. A sudden change of heart led to a new contract being negotiated with both Toler and Sen Young. It called for three new Chan films a year, definitely for the new season and with a renewable option for succeeding seasons. Probably the two best films Toler made as Charlie Chan came in the 1940–41 season, with *Murder over New York*, still a strong entry, between them.

Addison Richards after he smokes the poisoned cigarette in *Charlie Chan in Panama*
(20th-Fox, 1940). PHOTO COURTESY OF TWENTIETH CENTURY-FOX FILM CORPORATION.

Charlie Chan at the Wax Museum (20th-Fox, 1940) came first. Lynn Shores
directed and John Larkin did the screenplay. Walter Morosco and Ralph Dietrich were the associate producers. The plot was excellent, filled with atmosphere and suspense, but the Chanograms had been diminishing during the Toler
years. The best the script could do was to quote an old screenplay when Charlie
observes, "Only very foolish mouse makes nest in cat's ear."

The plot of the novel *Behind That Curtain* was updated for its third cinematic version in *Murder over New York* (20th-Fox, 1940). Harry Lachman's direction, with its stunningly effective use of close-ups for facial studies, made up
for the deficiencies in Lester Ziffren's screenplay. Sol Wurtzel, who had obviously gone to bat to save the series against Darryl F. Zanuck and other executives, was billed as the producer. The idea of poison gas in a glass sphere, a once

Sidney Toler as Chan interrogating versatile character actor Leo G. Carroll in *Charlie Chan's Murder Cruise* (20th-Fox, 1940).

PHOTO COURTESY OF TWENTIETH CENTURY-FOX FILM CORPORATION.

original concept in *Charlie Chan in Egypt*, was again the means of murder in a sabotage effort. This was well after Monogram's writers had already used it for *Mr. Wong, Detective* (Monogram, 1938), nor by any means was this the end of it. Jimmy Chan, a law student in the former picture, was now a chemistry student. "Favorite son, Jimmy," Chan introduces him, "without whose assistance many cases would have been solved much sooner."

Harry Lachman intensified his use of lighting, shadows, and close-ups for eerie effects in *Dead Men Tell* (20th-Fox, 1941). To these he added sound. The plot, on the face of it, was fantastic and probably wouldn't have been convincing no matter what the screen treatment, but it does illustrate that compelling cinema need not be convincing. Lachman made unusual use of a parrot's screeching voice and the thumping of a wooden leg.

The war in Europe and the Far East had increasingly cut off the foreign market. The Chan films owed a large percentage of their profitability, even with Toler in the role, to worldwide grosses. Wurtzel, in an effort to open a new foreign market, made a tour of South America, returning to Hollywood the same month *Dead Men Tell* was released, March 1941. Sol gave out a press notice that the next Charlie Chan would be set in Rio de Janeiro. But the screenwriters didn't knock themselves out for *Charlie Chan in Rio*. Instead it was a remake of *The Black Camel*, this time with Victory Jory in the old Bela Lugosi role. Hamilton MacFadden, who had directed *Camel*, was in the cast. Harold Huber was back as a Spanish-speaking policeman. Harry Lachman directed. There were even some well-staged musical numbers. I think Wurtzel was really trying his best, but as a detective film *Rio* was hopelessly dull.

Lachman also directed *Castle in the Desert* (20th-Fox, 1942). More than anyone, Lachman realized the limitations of Toler's Chan characterization. It was becoming more inflexible and lifeless as Toler himself aged. Lachman attempted to compensate for this by choosing economical yet interesting sets. *Castle* used the Fox Western set and the mansion that had served as Baskerville Hall in *The Hound of the Baskervilles* (20th-Fox, 1939). The story was a loose remake of *The Chinese Parrot*. Douglas Dumbrille had a strong part, as did Henry Daniell. Lachman intended for the story to carry the show. To an extent it did, but not to South America.

Sol Wurtzel canceled the Charlie Chan series with *Castle* as his own career ended, making a last venture into a new series with the comedy team of Laurel and Hardy, featuring pictures like *A-Haunting We Will Go* (20th-Fox, 1942), reusing all the magic props from *Charlie Chan at Treasure Island*. *The Big Noise* (20th-Fox, 1944) even had the boys pretending to be detectives. In his career Wurtzel had supervised twenty-six Charlie Chan pictures.

The loss of foreign markets was only one problem. The Federal Government had filed an antitrust suit against motion picture producing companies that also owned theater networks. Exhibitors preferred to book major productions. All of the major producing firms began to cut back on "B" series and stress "A" product. Universal, Columbia, and RKO didn't. Nor did small companies like Monogram and Producers' Releasing Corporation. Originally Fox had scheduled production on *Castle* to commence on September 15, 1941. Lucky Humberstone ran longer than expected on *I Wake Up Screaming* (20th-Fox, 1941), for reasons I will explain later, and *Son of Fury* (20th-Fox, 1942) also ran over schedule, so production was postponed ten weeks. When Toler received word that Chan was being canceled, he immediately negotiated for screen rights to the character with Eleanor Biggers Cole, the author's widow, now remarried. It was his intention to find financing and let Twentieth Century-Fox distribute. Everything went according to plan except for the financing.

It wasn't until May 1943 that Toler succeeded in lining up a production outlet. Philip N. Krasne and James S. Burkett, who had purchased screen rights to the Cisco Kid property from Fox, did the same with Charlie Chan. Since Toler had screens rights to the character, he was signed to star. Scott Dunlap on behalf of Monogram Pictures agreed to finance and release the new series. Dunlap

Lynn Shores (holding script) directing Sidney Toler while surrounded by the crew and some of the cast on the set of *Charlie Chan at the Wax Museum* (20th-Fox, 1940).

PHOTO COURTESY OF THE NATIONAL FILM ARCHIVE.

figured that by lowering the budgets from $200,000 to $75,000 and with the return of the world market following the war, the studio had a good chance of coming out.

Toler was if anything even more aged. He shuffled through most of his scenes. *Charlie Chan in the Secret Service* (Monogram, 1944) was the first entry. The biggest problem was Monogram Pictures. The company's writers had no sense of story; no production standards were combined with the cheapest possible sets; and Phil Rosen, a veteran of the lowest grade pictures, directed. Monogram always had that amazing facility of making a bad picture worse just because it was Monogram. George Callahan did the screenplay.

The plot cast John Elliott as a scientist working on explosives in his home. Benson Fong (who now is in the Chinese restaurant business) played Chan's Number Three son, Tommy; Marianne Quon was Charlie's daughter Iris Chan, and because Monogram had strong distribution in the South, Mantan Moreland was cast as Birmingham, Charlie's Negro chauffeur. Moreland's contribution to the series consisted primarily of rolling his eyes and acting absurdly frightened at the sight of a corpse. Unlike Stepin Fetchit, Mantan did a disservice to black

Norman Foster (with his arm over the chair) and the crew and some of the cast while directing a scene from *Charlie Chan in Reno* (20th-Fox, 1939).

PHOTO COURTESY OF THE LATE NORMAN FOSTER.

actors; you always knew Stepin Fetchit was parodying the white man's attitude toward the blacks, while Moreland was just an uncomplicated noodnik.

When Elliott is murdered, all the suspects line up around the body. Useless footage is spent tracking in detail Chan's journey to the scene of the crime. For the remainder of the picture, the murderer takes potshots at Chan, after which all the suspects are dutifully herded together and questioned anew. In *The Birth of a Nation* (Epoch, 1915), D. W. Griffith included a close-up of Raoul Walsh's eye just before, as Booth, he shoots Lincoln. Phil Rosen was evidently so impressed with this device that he used it repeatedly in several of the Chan entries he directed, presuming, I suppose, that a close-up of an unknown eye could only enhance viewer suspense.

The Chinese Cat (Monogram, 1944) was little better. George Callahan did the screenplay; Phil Rosen directed. Benson Fong was the only Chan offspring in the cast. Mantan Moreland was now a taxi driver. A diamond theft leads to murder, and the jewel thieves hole up in an abandoned fun house. The last two reels of the picture are played for laughs with the gang chasing Chan and Moreland around the fun house.

Mantan Moreland gets Chan enmeshed in *Meeting at Midnight* (Monogram, 1944) when he takes a job as a butler in the home of a psychic medium. The picture was also issued under the title *Black Magic*. But under whatever title you may see it, the plot by George Callahan using the notion of bullets made from frozen blood carried in a refrigerated cigar case is patently ridiculous. Frances Chan plays one of Charlie's daughters. The medium naturally is a phony and a blackmailer. Toward the end, Rosen gives the viewer another close-up of the murderer's eye.

Monogram couldn't get Benson Fong for *The Jade Mask* (Monogram, 1945), so they drafted Keye Luke's brother, Edwin Luke, to play Charlie's Number Four son, Eddie. Since the beginning of the Monogram series, Charlie was working for the Government. In this picture, he is promoted to an inspector and exposes Jack Ingram as the murderer of a nasty scientist, shielding his identity by wearing a rubber mask that makes him look like another suspect, who is also done away with. Ingram is assisted in this fantastic scheme by his puppeteer wife, who has the corpses dance around on steel wires so as to appear alive after they've been murdered.

The Scarlet Clue (Monogram, 1945) is set for the most part in Stanford Jolley's radio station with Charlie, Benson Fong, and Mantan Moreland wandering around interviewing suspects between murders. The murder weapon is a poison gas hidden in a microphone which kills when mixed in the air with cigarette smoke. The gimmick for *The Shanghai Cobra* (Monogram, 1945) was stranger still: cobra poison is rubbed on a needle that is beneath the selection knob of a jukebox puncturing the victim's fingertip.

Phil Karlson directed *Shanghai Cobra*, one of his first pictures as a director. The script was no better than those previously, but Karlson obviously tried to do more with it than Phil Rosen would have done. He provided an interview for the editors of *Kings of the Bs* (Dutton, 1975) in which he said that Monogram "had their own distribution. They were very liquid, that company. They really

At Monogram, the entire crew of suspects kept following Chan around and so were conveniently grouped together every time some villainy occurred, saving on time and camera movement.   PHOTO COURTESY OF VIEWS & REVIEWS MAGAZINE.

were well organized and they knew how much they could spend. They would have their money back before they even started because they got so much money from their exchanges. Right from the exhibitors. And that's where we're going to be again. That's where the whole ball game is going back to. People say television is what killed our industry. This didn't kill our industry. What killed our industry was divorcement. Studios and theatres, that's what killed us. When they came in with the idea that this was a complete monopoly—the guy that's making the picture owns the theatre it's playing in and whatnot—that's when we got in trouble." Karlson has a point. When he began in the motion picture business, it was the fourth-largest industry in the United States. Today it is nowhere near that size. Perhaps studio management lacked a most essential attribute, which certainly the oil companies possessed: the willingness to put up unlimited funds to buy political favor. Conglomerates with more perspicacity now own the studios which, before government action, were once independent and prosperous.

Phil Rosen returned to direct *The Red Dragon* (Monogram, 1946), but Mantan Moreland was absent. Willie Best as Chattanooga supplied the necessary low Negro humor. Although the picture was set in Mexico City, a shot of the neon signs of night spots are all of Los Angeles clubs. The murder gimmick is a bullet in a metal case shot off by a remote control radio device. The best Charlie can do for a Chanogram is to remark pathetically: "Confucius could give answer to that. Unfortunately, Confucius not here at the moment."

I can readily sympathize with the reader should he become irritated at this point if I dwell on plots of pictures that, in all probability, he would have avoided seeing in the first place. Just so, they got worse. *Dark Alibi* (Monogram, 1946), directed by Phil Karlson, was about a love-sick prison guard who uses phony fingerprints to convict his beloved's father. *Shadows over Chinatown* (Monogram, 1946) was sustained if unintentional comedy. Benson Fong left the series with *Dark Alibi*, and Victor Sen Young returned to it, initially as Jimmy Chan, then changing suddenly into Chan's Number Three son, Tommy.

Terry Morse, who began as a film cutter at First National in 1923, took over as director for *Shadows* and also directed the next entry, *Dangerous Money*

Benson Fong became Chan's Number Three son at Monogram. Cy Kendall at left.
PHOTO COURTESY OF VIEWS & REVIEWS MAGAZINE.

(Monogram, 1946), which had too many characters and an excessive number of murders but did boast rather elaborate sets.

Sidney Toler was rapidly deteriorating. He doggedly dragged himself through *The Trap* (Monogram, 1946), which, for story and direction, hit an all-time low despite the fact that Howard Bretherton, a veteran director of above-average Westerns, was assigned to the picture. Victor Sen Young and Mantan Moreland didn't even try to be funny. The picture was released on November 30, 1946. On February 12, 1947, Sidney Toler died.

James Burkett, still producer of the series at Monogram, was hard pressed to find a speedy replacement. He began testing for the role.

Roland Winternitz was born in Boston on November 22, 1904. His father was a concert violinist. "I was restless when I was young," Winters recalled, "and was always looking for something exciting to do. I decided to become a sailor as a teenager and shipped out with the United Fruit lines for two summer trips, one to Central America and the other to the West Indies. When I was sixteen, a friend of mine got me interested in one of Boston's little theatre groups. This led me to working with many stock companies and eventually to Broadway in 1924. A classmate of my brother's was producing *The Firebrand* and so I landed a part in the play. The cast was loaded with other actors who, like myself, were to come into their own later on. Joseph Schildkraut, Edward G. Robinson, Allyn Joslyn, and Frank Morgan were the type of unknowns I worked with back then."

Winters continued in stock companies until 1931, when he became a staff announcer for WNAC in Boston, sportscasting 154 Braves and Red Sox games a season. He stayed in various aspects of radio until his film debut in *13 Rue Madeleine* (20th-Fox, 1947) with James Cagney. Winters previously had bit parts in a couple of silent pictures, including *Monsieur Beaucaire* (Paramount, 1924) with Rudolph Valentino. They led nowhere. There's no telling where the Cagney picture would have led had Burkett not asked Winters to test as a replacement for Toler. Winters was made up and did a trial scene. Burkett, who was watching the proceedings, told him right after the take that he had a job.

I have already mentioned that Scott Darling's screenplay for *Mr. Wong in Chinatown* was used again for Winters' first Chan film, *The Chinese Ring*, released December 6, 1947. The blowgun was switched to a European air rifle. The San Francisco setting was kept. The Grant Withers role was played by Warren Douglas with Louise Currie as the obnoxious female reporter. Victor Sen Young and Mantan Moreland were Charlie's assistants. Even several of the sets were the same. The lines were still bad and the acting no better, but the plot was at least an improvement over the final entries in the Toler series. William Beaudine, who was born in New York City in 1892 and entered the motion picture industry in 1909 at Biograph, directed.

The mechanism in *Docks of New Orleans* (Monogram, 1948) was switched from what it had been in *Mr. Wong, Detective* to poison gas hidden in radio tubes. If anything, the plot was made the more ridiculous because the release of the gas depended on the inventor persuading his prospective victims to tune in on a program featuring his wife singing operatic arias, her high-pitched voice bursting the tubes. Winters was certainly as good in the part as Toler had been in the Monogram series, but neither was more than a shadow of Warner Oland. Derwin Abrahams, who assisted on the later entries in the Hopalong Cassidy series, directed.

Burkett was so pleased with the initial box-office reception of Winters as Chan and Winters' relative youth he began to develop high hopes for the future of the series. He sought better scripts. He cleaned up the Moreland comedy routines and Sen Young was more often sober than lame-brained. Oliver Drake, a veteran Western screenwriter since the late Twenties, was hired to do the screenplays.

I often wonder how many original stories Drake did write in his long career. He had a tremendous penchant for reusing his previous material. It was no different with his Chan scenarios, although I doubt if Burkett suspected. Beginning with *The Shanghai Chest* (Monogram, 1948), directed by William Beaudine, Drake began adapting Three Mesquiteer and other Western properties he had worked on in the Thirties. *The Golden Eye* (Monogram, 1948) even kept the Western setting, with Chan going to Arizona to get to the bottom of a phony gold mine racket.

Beaudine also directed *The Golden Eye* and the next entry, *The Feathered Serpent* (Monogram, 1948). For *Serpent*, Drake used his script to *The Riders of the Whistling Skull* (Republic, 1937). By a fluke of casting, Robert Livingston, who had starred in *Riders* as Stony Brooke, turns out to be the culprit Winters exposes at the end. To maintain the trio concept of the original stories, Tim Ryan was cast as a police inspector in both *Chest* and *Eye*. He was replaced in *Serpent* by Keye Luke, who rejoined the series in its twilight, playing one of Chan's sons while Sen Young played another, and Mantan Moreland, staying on as Charlie's servant, was about equivalent to Max Terhune's dummy Elmer in the Mesquiteer Westerns.

The Chan unit was one of the very last to be working on the nearly deserted Monogram lot. In a move toward expansion and refinancing, the firm was soon to be absorbed into Allied Artists. Keye Luke appeared alone with Winters in his sixth and last Chan film, *Sky Dragon* (Monogram, 1949), which was directed by Lesley Selander, also an experienced director of Westerns and action films. Selander had started in the industry as an assistant to Woody Van Dyke at Fox in the Twenties, working on Buck Jones Westerns. Subsequently, Les had assisted Woody on the original *The Thin Man* (M-G-M, 1934) and assisted Edwin L. Marin on *The Garden Murder Case* (M-G-M, 1936).

When I met Les for breakfast at the Cafe Universal at the Universal-Sheraton in the summer of 1975 to review his career, he seemed in the best of health and spirits for his seventy-five years. His face was aglow beneath his fluffy white hair.

"To what do you attribute your remarkable physical condition?" I asked him.

"Travel," he said. He began rattling off the trips he had been on during the last decade. "Travel and two or three double whiskeys in the afternoon."

I told him that I had just been around to Keye Luke's apartment for another visit. Woody Van Dyke had studied Taoism with Luke in the Thirties. After the ill-fated Charlie Chan television series with J. Carrol Naish, Luke had finally had an opportunity to play Chan—or at least his voice—in the equally short-lived Hanna-Barbera cartoon series.

"He did the characterization the way Warner Oland had," I said to Les. "He recalled for me, laughing, how Oland had responded when Philip Morris approached him to sponsor a Charlie Chan radio program: 'Honorable father doesn't want to work that hard.'"

Instead Walter Connolly, Ed Begley, and Santos Ortega impersonated the Oriental detective on radio.

Les was glancing through his screen credits.

"You directed the last theatrical Chan picture," I said. "*Sky Dragon.* Elena Verdugo was an airline stewardess and the murderer. When she finished the picture, Monogram was going to shoot a couple of Chan pictures out of frozen funds in England. The deal fell through. Elena was cast as the lead in the 'Meet Millie' television series and, of all people, Roland Winters played her boss."

Keye Luke returned to the series during its swan song, with Roland Winters, seen here as Chan, and black comedian Mantan Moreland.

PHOTO COURTESY OF VIEWS & REVIEWS MAGAZINE.

Les was still paging through the onionskin sheets of his filmography.

"What year was that?" he asked.

"Nineteen forty-nine," I replied. "A funny thing. Keye Luke, who remembers so much about working with Warner, could scarcely recall anything about *Sky Dragon*."

"Are you sure of that title?"

Les's forehead was furrowed in concentration.

"Here it is," I said, going over my copy of his credits. "You've got it listed under its working title, *Murder in the Air*."

Les looked sheepishly at me. There was a silence.

"Jon," he said then, "I certainly wish I could help you out. But to be perfectly honest, I can't even remember having made that picture."

Perhaps it is best that when today Charlie Chan in the movies is recalled, it's Warner Oland who comes to mind, with his soft, pervasive reassurance to the viewer, "Not very good detective . . . just lucky old Chinaman."

FIVE:
The Black Mask

*I don't like eloquence; if it isn't effective enough
to pierce your hide, it's tiresome; and if it is
effective enough, then it muddles your thoughts.*

from "Zigzags of Treachery"
by Dashiell Hammett

I

If Dashiell Hammett is not the whole of the American detective story, he may well be the best of it. He was the first—and no one tried very strongly to second him—to demonstrate the intimate links between organized crime and politics on all levels.

There still is an amazing naïveté in the way this mutual coexistence is treated. It was accepted at the time with equanimity that Joseph P. Kennedy made a fortune in bootlegging, used part of that fortune to finance Franklin D. Roosevelt's presidential campaign, and should be rewarded with a tariff in perpetuity on the importation of scotch whisky to the United States. The efforts of Kennedy's sons on the floor of Congress to investigate criminal infiltration into labor unions were applauded, but what ever came of it? The leftover fear of Communism which promoted Richard M. Nixon into the White House was used by the Kennedys to oppose Fidel Castro's revolution in Cuba, but in fact the Syndicate's gambling operations in Havana were the greatest loss Americans suffered in the Communist take-over.

One of Dashiell Hammett's best short stories is "Death on Pine Street." Since it is among that body of his work which his executrix Lillian Hellman has seen fit not to reprint, I will provide the reader with its plot.

The story features the Continental Op, heavy-set and middle-aged, an experi-

For many, Humphrey Bogart was the embodiment of the hard-boiled detective
Dashiell Hammett brought to fame. PHOTO COURTESY OF VIEWS & REVIEWS MAGAZINE.

enced, tough, professional detective. He is sent out by the agency to talk with Mrs. Gilmore, whose husband was found on Pine Street, shot to death. The only curious thing about the death is the angle of the bullet, which apparently penetrated the body when it was already in a prostrate position. Mrs. Gilmore tells the Op that her husband had a string of women over the years; his latest mistress is a Cara Kendall, whose apartment is very near where her husband's body was found. The Op goes to question the Kendall woman and learns nothing. He talks to the police in the form of Sergeant O'Gar, who tells him about the body being discovered by Kelly, a cop on the beat. O'Gar draws no conclusions because he's not paid to think.

The Op goes back to talk to Mrs. Gilmore. She's out. But the Gilmore maid tells him that Mrs. Gilmore followed her husband the night he left the house and was later killed. When Mrs. Gilmore returns, the Op confronts her with this information, not revealing its source, and she confesses that she did follow her husband but she didn't kill him. She also admits she tried to telephone Cara Kendall about the time of the murder, and that she didn't answer her phone. The Op goes back to interview Cara Kendall. This time she admits that it was Gilmore who called off their relationship. The Op doesn't get much further because Stanley Tennant arrives, using his own key in her front door. Tennant is an assistant city engineer. He doesn't like the case the Op appears to be building against Cara, who is now *his* mistress, so he pulls a gun on the Op. With the Op watching, he rips Cara's clothing and belts her in the face. He then tells Cara to call the police. She is to back his story that the Op tried to assault her with intent to rape while questioning her. With the pull he has in City Hall, he is convinced he can get the Op sent up.

The Op tries to physically fight his way out of the frame, but the girl gets hold of Tennant's gun and taps the Op a couple of times on the head, making Tennant's blows all the more effective. At police headquarters, the police are readily convinced by Tennant's story, backed by Cara Kendall's testimony; even O'Gar is wavering toward believing it. And why not? Here's an easy conviction in court. The Gilmore killing isn't likely to be solved. Everyone is ready to railroad the Op, but he's allowed to pull himself out of it by demanding to see Kelly, the beat cop who discovered Gilmore's body. He accuses him of the murder. Kelly confesses that it was an accident, that he saw Gilmore's shadow in a building archway, told him to stop, and pulled out his gun. He tripped. The gun went off. Gilmore was shot. The charges against the Op are dropped. Tennant wants to give the Op some money as they leave the station house. The Op, who's willing not to make trouble for Tennant because he doesn't want more trouble for himself, still isn't up to this. He slugs Tennant and feels good about it.

This short story illustrates many of the finest elements true of Hammett's best fiction. There is physical action all the way through, but the emphasis is not so much on it as on the closing circle of the legal, political, and judicial system in which the characters live. The tension isn't who committed the murder; the murder is of secondary importance to the reader, as it is—for different reasons —to most of the characters in the story. The tension derives from the reader's instinctive knowledge that American society is ever ready to nail a fall guy and not see justice done or discern the truth. The Op saves himself at the last possible moment, but it's too close a call for him not to be shaken by it, and the reader with him.

The narrative is economical. Much is handled by means of dialogue. Description, as in Hammett generally, is at a minimum. The plot has a fine, inevitable precision, flawless in design and always balanced in development.

Dashiell Hammett, for most of his life, was a heavy drinker. He said once it was caused by being "confused by the fact that people's feelings and talk and actions didn't have much to do with one another." He tried to articulate this confusion, and overcome it, in all of his fiction. He accomplished more in the objective style than Hemingway did. Hemingway, at some point, always lets us see what is going on inside his characters, how they really feel, how tough they are on the outside and how beaten and miserable they are within themselves. Charles Dickens wrote of the mysterious ways of the human heart, and Somerset Maugham claimed that one man could never know another man, one human being could never possibly perceive the inner workings of another human being. Human motivation in most fiction, and in detective fiction in particular, is usually made a function of the plot. Motives are made to coincide with the preconcluded course the plot will follow. Because of this conceit, readers are invariably led to believe that they understand why a character acts in such and such a way. Freud and Jung and their followers gave even more substance to this notion that human motives can be adduced or deduced from human behavior.

But can they? Why is it, if psychoanalysis is a science in the same sense as physics or chemistry, that with all our supposed "knowledge" about human motivation we can in no way make even clumsy predictions about human behavior in a given set of circumstances? Freud explained away this difficulty by saying that only neurotic behavior could be predicted, not normal behavior. But this proposition only leads to greater confusion, especially when you try to define the term normal, as opposed to neurotic, and do not wish to confine yourself to the particular premises, largely false, at the basis of every social order. Most fiction comforts the reader because it lets him in on a character's motivation. But in life, we actually know next to nothing about motive. Moreover, in life, motives have a tendency to change both suddenly and unaccountably.

For me, the finest literature we have must necessarily be ambiguous about motivation. The problem you run into here, however, is that, when motive is ambiguous, behavior tends, in fiction at least, to become preposterous; what we might accept with a shrug of the shoulders in everyday life, we question as incredible in a story.

Hammett tried to solve this difficulty by means of describing truthfully what his characters said and did, without ever taking us inside of them to speculate *why* they did it. Because he did this, and did it so well, I think he deserves his position as being the equal of Hemingway and Scott Fitzgerald in the Twenties and Thirties.

Very little is known about Hammett's life. Because of problems I will mention later in more detail, while an interested reader can acquire collected editions of Hemingway's and Scott Fitzgerald's complete works, Hammett is only collected, if at all, by resorting to the extremity I had to go in asking mystery fiction critic and author Francis M. Nevins, Jr., to survey all the collectors in the United States to supply me with photocopies of most of his stories from the twelve years during which he wrote fiction. Most of what can be assembled about Hammett's life from published sources is to be found in William F. Nolan's *Dashiell Hammett: A Casebook* (McNally & Loftin, 1969). I compliment the book highly for what it has done, but it does leave even the most elementary questions unanswered. I don't know how much Hammett assisted Hellman on her plays, but it is a fact that she never wrote a successful play before her association with Hammett, and no plays at all after his death. Hellman wrote *The Searching Wind*, which Hammett helped name, while he was in the Aleutians, and the critics at the time found it "simple-minded," "pretentious," "loose as a haystack," "more windy than searching," and even her biographer and admirer, Richard Moody, who feels that Hammett was Hellman's editorial conscience, terms this play "banal and inconsequential."

In the Introduction for *The Big Knockover* (Random House, 1966) an authorized collection of Hammett short stories by Lillian Hellman, she writes: "I don't know when Hammett first decided to write, but I know that he started writing after he left Army hospitals in the 1920's, settling with his wife and daughter—there was to be another daughter—in San Francisco. (He went back to work for Pinkerton for a while, although I am not sure if it was this period or later.)" This is needlessly vague. Yet no one, including William F. Nolan, sought to ask Hammett's ex-wife, Josephine Dolan Hammett. Divorced from Hammett in 1937, she moved to Los Angeles when Hammett went to work for Paramount in 1930 as a screenwriter and was living with Hammett's elder daughter, Mrs. Mary Jane Miller, when David Fechheimer of *City of San Francisco* magazine interviewed them in 1975, practically in Nolan's back yard.

It comes to this. When Hammett's life is written accurately, it will reverse almost everything that has been written about him up to the present time. It would take me too far afield, in what is already a very long book, to set the record straight here, but I can give the highlights of Hammett's life.

He was born May 27, 1894, in Saint Marys County, Maryland, the son of Richard Thomas Hammett and Annie Bond Hammett. He was baptized a Roman Catholic. His youth was spent in Baltimore and Philadelphia. He was twenty when he answered an advertisement and was hired as a Pinkerton operative. He had *Wanderlust* and so worked in a number of Pinkerton offices around the country. In June 1918, he enlisted in the service and became a sergeant in the Motor Ambulance Corps, stationed only twenty miles away from his home in Baltimore. When he fell victim to the wave of influenza, it was discovered that he had tuberculosis. This was the beginning of a lifelong battle with lung disease of various kinds.

Hammett was transferred to a veterans' hospital in Tacoma, Washington. While a patient there, he met a floor nurse, Josephine Dolan. As his condition improved, they went out of the hospital on dates to various restaurants or parks. Hammett was again transferred, this time to a veterans' hospital in San Diego. Josephine Dolan was transferred to the Cheyenne Hospital in Helena, Montana.

They kept in touch by letter. When Hammett was in the Ambulance Corps, he hit a protrusion in the road and dumped all the patients in the ambulance into a ditch. He refused ever to drive a vehicle again for the rest of his life. The ambulance had been pulled by mules. When Hammett was released from the hospital in San Diego, he went to San Francisco and reapplied to the Pinkerton agency. When he was rehired, he wrote to Josephine and asked that she join him. She took a room at the Golden West Hotel on Powell Street. Hammet lived around the corner at the Woodstock Rooms on Ellis Street. De Chiel was a family name. Hammett was known then as Sam Hammett.

The couple were married in St. Mary's Cathedral on Van Ness Avenue. They rented a furnished apartment on Eddy Street for forty-five dollars a month: living room in front, a small room with a folding bed, and a kitchen. It had steam heat. Their landlady was a bootlegger, and the police were among her customers. Hammett did the cooking. He preferred hamburger, when they could afford it. Pinkerton detectives were paid six dollars a day, every day of the year. Work was irregular. They might have off two or three days and then be out on a job for a week. Paul Haultain, who also worked as a Pinkerton operative, described Hammett in those days as "tall, thin, smart as a steel trap. He knew his business. He wasn't a drinking man. . . . But he used to smoke like hell. Rolled his own cigarettes."

The San Francisco agency was run by a man named Phil Geaque, who later entered the Secret Service and became a bodyguard for President Roosevelt. He was short, bald-headed, and, like Hammett's Continental Op, a heavy smoker of Fatima cigarettes. Among others, Hammett worked on the Fatty Arbuckle case, which had created a stir in San Francisco, and for a time tailed Fanny Brice hoping to locate her second husband, who was wanted for theft. Hammett was expert at shadowing and was usually given this type of assignment. He found in his everyday experience that drinking is unrelated to trustworthiness in bonding a man, that fingerprints are almost useless, that burglary provides so poor a living that most burglars end up living off their women, and that the best way to beat a rap in court is to deny *everything*.

When the Pinkerton agency was retained by the mining companies in an attempt to suppress the International Workers of the World, Hammett was sent to Butte, Montana, to participate in strikebreaking. At one point he almost sailed for Australia in connection with another case, but he found the cache of stolen bullion before the ship left the San Francisco harbor. He later confessed to his daughter, Mary Jane, to whom he became particularly close, that he didn't care if his clients were bums, he was strictly out to do his job—an attitude which all his detectives in fiction retained. Life was hard and there was seldom any money. Hammett would take Mary Jane with him to speakeasies and let her drink sparkling water in a champagne glass. He used to sit with her on his lap, during his days off, and read to her. Hammett loved books. At Christmas, he would spend hours with Mary Jane decorating the tree.

Hammett wanted to be a poet. He wrote in his spare time, but his poems were universally rejected. San Francisco is a very damp, fog-laden city, and Hammett's shadowing jobs kept him outdoors and, frequently, near the docks. He started hemorrhaging again. He wouldn't complain, but he would say, "I've become ill" or "I've had a very nasty day." Then he wouldn't eat at all. He would stay in bed and just sit there, night and day, night and day. He quit Pinkerton's and found employment as an advertising manager for Albert Samuels, who owned a jewelry store on Market Street. Samuels was responding to a "Work Wanted" ad Hammett ran in the San Francisco *Chronicle*. Hammett met a lot of people through his work at the jewelry store. He started drinking. "He'd write copy for me all day," Samuels recalled, "then go home to his apartment and drink during most of the night, sobering up enough to report in the next morning. Yet he was a man of honor, and he always did fine work. I remember particularly his 'romantic' approach, which was ideal for us." Hammett's contention to one side—about drinking to assuage his confusions about people—he drank mostly to control the irritation of excessive smoking and the pain of recurrent coughing. He was often sick, and Samuels would pay him during his periods of recuperation. Hammett would go to the library every afternoon and read. He discovered pulp magazines at the library. He told Mary Jane that he could write better than that. He set out to try it.

Hammett was never moody. He had no temper to speak of. He would walk away from a fight. He was the antithesis of the aggressive, greedy dynamic which he perceived as propelling most human activity.

George Jean Nathan and H. L. Mencken began publishing *Black Mask* as one of three pulp magazines in early spring of 1920. Some of the best stories in American fiction were run in its pages, although nobody knew it at the time.

Hammett's first short story, "The Barber and His Wife," appeared in the December 1922 issue of *Brief Stories*, at the same time as his first story for *Black Mask* appeared in the December issue of that magazine, "The Road Home." Both were signed "Peter Collinson." Hammett took the name from "Peter Collins," slang for a nobody. He wanted to keep his real name for his poetry. In 1923, Hammett, writing under the Collinson pseudonym, wrote two more stories for *Brief Stories*, two for *Saucy Stories*, one for the *Smart Set* called "The Crusader," signed as being written by "Mary Jane" Hammett, another for the *Smart Set* under his own name, one for *Pearson's Magazine*, and seven for *Black Mask*. It was with the fourth story that year for *Black Mask*, "Crooked Souls," that Hammett began using his middle and last name as his nom de plume. From then on, with one exception, which I will come to later, Hammett signed all his stories, and then his novels, Dashiell Hammett. Only when he went to New York in late 1929 and to Hollywood in late 1930, where he wasn't known, did people call him, and did he call himself, Dash Hammett. In San Francisco he was still simply Sam Hammett.

Hammett's physical condition worsened. He would line up chairs from the bed to the bathroom so he could support himself on the way to the toilet. Josephine would hassle him about his smoking and his drinking. All Hammett wanted to do was write. When a second daughter was born, Hammett shipped Josephine and the two children off to stay with relatives in Montana. A penny a word wasn't a living wage when you wrote the way Hammett did, at a typewriter in the kitchen, writing over and over and over again. Writing came hard, even though he drew on personal experience to give the stories verisimilitude. Hammett was convinced that he could cure himself of lung disease by making a success of it as a writer and by drinking large doses of scotch whisky, which was very expensive because it was illegal. Hammett supported this theory by the observation that, when things were going well, when a story turned out the way he wanted it and when it was accepted by a magazine, he didn't cough so much. His problem, he felt, was that his memory was too accurate; he remembered too much, and what he remembered hurt. It was more important to him to be a good writer than to be a good father or a faithful husband. The only things he wrote when he wasn't drinking were a handful of short stories after 1932 and *The Thin Man* (Knopf, 1934), considered unanimously by critics to be his least important work. If it did nothing else, whisky did dehydrate him.

Hammett would write all night. He gave up sleeping, and it told on him. His family stayed in Montana for six months in 1925. During this time, Hammett rented a cheap room on Pine Street. He made acquaintance of the girl across the hall and would sleep with her when he felt it necessary to relieve his sexual congestion. He worked sporadically for Samuels, who was surprisingly understanding. He found another girl on Grant Avenue to fill in when the girl across the hall was otherwise engaged. If he ate at all, he ate cheap food; mostly he lived on soup, coffee, scotch, and cigarettes. In the years 1924–25, following this regimen, he wrote twenty-three short stories, published in *Black Mask* and elsewhere.

In the latter part of 1925, Hammett consulted a physician who declared his lung ailment cured. He had more money now. He rented lodgings at 620 Eddy Street in a four-story apartment building, erected shortly after the famous earthquake, which he used as the setting for Ned Beaumont's rooms in *The Glass Key* (Knopf, 1931). He wrote in the living room, near the fireplace. He listed himself in the city directory as an "advertising manager" at Samuels'. He was given an office on the second floor of Samuels' store and was permitted to hire an assistant, Peggy O'Toole, on whom he based the characterization of Brigid O'Shaughnessy in *The Maltese Falcon* (Knopf, 1930).

In the autumn of 1924, Phil Cody had succeeded George W. Sutton, Jr., as editor of *Black Mask*. Cody started off by rejecting two Hammett stories, one of them "Death on Pine Street," which I have already retold. Hammett wrote an apologetic letter to Cody explaining the inferior quality of the stories and his intention to rework them. "The trouble is, this sleuth of mine has degenerated into a meal ticket . . . and recently I've fallen into the habit of bringing him out and running him around whenever the landlord, or the butcher, or the grocer shows signs of nervousness. . . ." Hammett thought it best to relieve himself of these pressures. Now, more than ever, he felt in control of the situation.

When Captain Joseph T. Shaw was appointed to edit the magazine in 1926, he knew nothing whatever about editorial work. But he, too, started out by rejecting one of Hammett's stories. Hammett became outraged and wrote Shaw a letter telling him that he would never write for the magazine again. Shaw read several of the back issues and decided that Hammett was exactly what he wanted in the pages of *Black Mask* and wrote Hammett an apologetic letter, requesting him to please do a story of novel proportions. He asked Erle Stanley Gardner, by this time another frequent contributor to *Black Mask,* to also intercede with Hammett. Gardner, living in California, had met Hammett at several local meetings of pulp writers. He urged Hammett to comply with Shaw's request. It wasn't until later, when Hammett was already associated with Lillian Hellman and would come to visit Gardner at his home in the desert, that Gardner noticed the changes that this relationship had had on Hammett, how it had made him indifferent to life and hopelessly despondent in his drinking. Gardner remarked on it to Jean Bethell after every visit. In 1926, Hammett still cared. He wrote to Shaw: "You've hit on exactly what I've been thinking about and working toward. As I see it, the approach I have in mind has never been attempted. The field is unscratched and wide open." The short novel *Blood Money,* one of Hammett's best, was the result.

Many of Hammett's *Black Mask* stories featured the Continental Op and almost all of them were set in San Francisco. Hammett, it seemed, couldn't set a story anywhere that he didn't know intimately. Unlike the later Raymond Chandler, who went even further in his attempt to characterize Los Angeles than Hammett did in writing of San Francisco, Hammett kept his descriptions simple, naming streets and buildings but not going into excessive detail. For this reason, Hammett's stories do not show their age, whereas Chandler's stories are hopelessly dated. In this, Hammett resembled Erle Stanley Gardner, who kept his descriptions so laconic that a Perry Mason novel from the Thirties can be read with no more difficulty than one from the Sixties.

Hammett had a brother, Richard Thomas Hammett, but they were not close. He also had a younger sister. He had few friends, but he would engage everyone in conversation about writing, from the mailman to the iceman.

Hammett talked to Gardner about his marital problems. He didn't feel his wife understood him, nor did she completely sympathize with his desire to become an important writer. Gardner told him that he had the same difficulty with his own family. For that reason, he lived apart from his wife and daughter. Hammett thought he would try it. In 1927, having changed apartments once already, he discussed it with Josephine and she moved with the two girls to live in San Anselmo, while Hammett remained in San Francisco, at 891 Post Street, writing. He completed what was to be in his first true novel, *Red Harvest* (Knopf, 1929), which ran first, serially, in *Black Mask.*

He loved his family, particularly Mary Jane, and so he had them move back to San Francisco, renting them an apartment near the cable-car line, while he moved to an apartment on Turk Street. Here he wrote *The Dain Curse* (Knopf, 1929), also run serially in *Black Mask.* Both novels featured the Continental Op. The better of them, by far, is *Red Harvest,* which put the Op directly in the midst of the corruption that Hammett saw as indigenous to the American way of life. The Op chooses to treat violence with violence. Then he realizes that it was a mistake. "This damn burg's getting to me. If I don't get away soon," the Op confessed, "I'll be going blood-simple like the natives. There's been . . . a dozen and a half murders since I've been here. . . . I've arranged a killing or two in my time, when it's necessary. But this is the first time I've ever got the fever. It's this damned burg. You can't go straight here. . . ."

Hammett was becoming restless in San Francisco. He had achieved his success there. In retrospect, he would be able to say he was his happiest there, but he felt the irrepressible urge to move on. In the apartment on Turk Street he started and completed his finest book to that time, and his most famous, *The Maltese Falcon*, of which I will have much more to say later on in this chapter.

"But you know," Mary Jane said of her father, "you could tell that he was at home in San Francisco, everywhere he went. He belonged. Some places, you can live there and never belong. But he belonged in San Francisco." Only Hammett didn't know that in 1930. He went to New York. His last apartment in San Francisco had been at 1155 Leavenworth. He started *The Glass Key* there.

In New York, Hammett lived in an apartment at 133 East Thirty-eighth Street. In addition to his stories and novels, while still in San Francisco, he had become a reviewer of detective fiction for Mencken's and Nathan's *The Saturday Review of Literature*. In New York, he completed *The Glass Key* and started a new novel called *The Thin Man*. What survives of the original book, before his relationship with Lillian Hellman, shows a better novel, featuring an unmarried San Francisco private detective, but he certainly lacked the plethora of commercial possibilities the Nick and Nora Charles combination inspired in terms of performing rights.

Hammett got a low-paying job as a reviewer of books for the New York *Evening Post*. He was doing a lot of drinking and socializing. Hammett's publisher, Alfred Knopf, was a very wary fellow with an advance, and *The Maltese Falcon* was still in prepublication. Needing money, Hammett went to the editorial offices of the *Detective Fiction Weekly* and presented the editor with a story he had written, in haste, and signed as Samuel Dashiell. He asked the editor to read it while he sat there in his office. When the editor finished, he informed Hammett he would accept it. Hammet demanded that since the periodical paid upon acceptance he wanted his check at once. After some talk, he was paid. However, the editor wanted some changes made. Hammett agreed to the changes and left with the check and the manuscript, insisting he would make the changes himself. He proceeded to go on a long drinking bender. The editor grew increasingly nervous as the publication date grew nearer and he had the story featured on the cover, but no Hammett. At the last minute, a taxi driver appeared with the altered manuscript. Hammett, in a speakeasy, had made the corrections and dispatched the cabby to make delivery. Lillian Hellman, when she heard Hammett relate this story, was so impressed with it that she tried a variation of it when attempting to get her first play produced. She sat there in front of the producer until he read it.

Paramount Pictures purchased screen rights from Knopf for *Red Harvest*. The terms were a pittance, but Hammett used them as the basis to negotiate himself a job in the writing department at Paramount in Hollywood.

Roadhouse Nights (Paramount, 1930), directed by Hobart Henley, with the screen adaptation by Ben Hecht, who had started the gangster film cycle with the script for Josef von Sternberg's *Underworld* (Paramount, 1927), bore only the loosest relationship to Hammett's original story. Charles Ruggles is a newspaperman, assuming more or less the role of the Continental Op in Hammett's novel. Helen Morgan debuted as the star, with Jimmy Durante as Daffy, her piano accompanist. It was a far cry from Hammett's profound and compelling novel of universal corruption in America!

Hammett's first original screenplay for Paramount was *City Streets* (Paramount, 1931), which remains a classic from that period in the cinema. Rouben Mamoulian was the director. Hammett, because it was his first job, was credited with the story, Oliver H. P. Garrett and Max Marcin with the script and adaptation. Clara Bow was originally to have starred, but a personal crisis prevented that. Sylvia Sidney replaced her at the last minute, an accident which projected Sidney into stardom. Sidney played Guy Kibbee's stepdaughter. Kibbee works for bootlegger William "Stage" Boyd. Sidney falls in love with a young Gary Cooper, cast as The Kid. She urges him to chuck his carnival job and join the rackets to make big money. The Kid doesn't welcome the idea. Kibbee knocks off familiar heavy Stanley Fields so Boyd can get Fields's girl friend, Wynne Gibson. Boyd covers for Kibbee. When Sidney refuses to finger Kibbee, the law railroads her to prison on a phony charge. That does it. The Kid joins the rackets to find enough evidence to spring her. When Sidney gets out of stir, she can't convince The Kid to quit the rackets. She tries to get Boyd to help her, but Wynne Gibson puts him away in the interim and blames Sidney for it. Sidney is taken for a ride, but The Kid comes to her rescue.

The film was touching in many ways, if melodramatic. When Warner Brothers purchased screen rights to *The Maltese Falcon*, Hammett felt he had "arrived." He sent for Josephine and the children to join him, setting them up in their own place in Los Angeles. He liked to spend time with his daughters. His carousing and his womanizing were all part of an ultimately futile effort to escape the sense of physical imprisonment and mental claustrophobia from which he chronically seemed to suffer. He might have gone on indefinitely, visiting his daughters, working on original stories for film companies, and writing fiction. But it was not to be. Something happened. It finished him first as the foremost author of action detective fiction. Then it finished him with the studios. Finally, it finished him altogether.

> *The underworld taught me that you could buy*
> *anything you want—cops, lawyers, judges,*
> *politicians—if you paid enough.*
>
> *—George Raft*

II

Back in the period when Hollywood made movies as a solace to the populace there were films about men who have no price; however, such men are seldom in public office except in the movies. In life, if they are in office, they are speedily removed one way or the other. The corollary, of course, is that when you are paying graft you cannot be too noisy about it, and you must be certain that it is *enough*. The gangster films of four decades tell a fanciful tale of woe. The mistakes that are made in these films—or what are considered mistakes according to the respective screenplays—are the most fanciful of all. Al Capone, a typical headliner in several films, was both too obvious and too flagrant. Those who have succeeded him have crept more quietly into the fabric of the nation's economic rhythm. Even Capone had a relatively light prison sentence and was finished by venereal disease rather than the vigilance of John Law.

The Godfather (Paramount, 1972) comes close to the record as the top-grossing film ever. It's about a fictional gangster, because real gangsters are more wary about exposing themselves than they once were. But for all that, Americans conceal a hidden admiration for them, sufficient for Hollywood to have produced hundreds of films about them.

Al Capone should have seen the handwriting on the wall when Howard Hawks directed *Scarface* (United Artists, 1932). Hawks ended the picture with Paul Muni as Scarface, joined by his sister, shooting it out with the police. The censors prevailed on Hawks to tack on a new ending to the film, showing Muni getting hanged by prison authorities. The censors' objections held up release of the film for nearly a year. In time, Hawks was finally able to take off the phony ending and conclude it the way he had originally intended.

While Hawks was still in production, several of Capone's associates came to the studio, requesting to preview the film. Hawks told them to relay to Capone that when the picture came out Al could buy a ticket just like everybody else. Capone's associates didn't like that. Under pressure, Howard screened a rough cut for them. They thought it was great and related their sentiments to Capone. Howard was invited to Chicago to meet Capone.

"They met me at the train," Hawks told me. "They were late. One of the fellows said, 'There was a killing last night and we had to go to the funeral.' I said, 'Do I have to ride with you if there was a killing last night?' They said I could ride in a different car. When we went into a cafe, they would sit with their backs to the wall and I had my back to the door. We had some damn good-looking girls with us, a bit brassy but very pretty. When I saw Capone, we had tea and he was dressed in a morning coat, striped trousers. I was with him for two or three hours."

The picture was only one in the cycle of gangster films of that era, and one of the very best. After it was released, it also was responsible for bringing George Raft to prominence (Raft had played Paul Muni's bodyguard).

When Howard was preparing the screenplay, together with Ben Hecht, he asked around town about visiting gangsters from the East from whom he might gain some information. He was at the fights one night when he ran into Owney Madden, whom he knew as one of the heads of the New York underworld. Madden had the young George Raft with him.

Raft was born September 26, 1895, in a family tenement building on Forty-first Street between Ninth and Tenth Avenues in New York City. The area was known as "Hell's Kitchen" because of the rampant lawlessness. Raft grew up in the streets, becoming a member of the reigning street gang. Shortly after a youth named Owen Madden from the slums of England moved into the neighborhood, he met Georgie Ranft, as Raft was then known, and the two became fast friends. Madden worked his way up in the Gophers, as the street gang was called, until he became one of its leaders.

In 1914, Madden, by then called Owney the Killer, was sentenced for ten to twenty years at Sing Sing for the killing of one Patsy Doyle. Over the years until his release in 1923, one of Madden's most frequent visitors in prison was Georgie Ranft. When Madden got out, he found a different world. Prohibition had done what probably nothing else could have done: it organized the gangs into a network, first controlling sections of cities, then entire cities, and, before long, vast parts of the country.

Georgie had changed his last name to Raft sometime earlier and was busy pursuing a career as a hoofer in New York night clubs. Nearly all the night clubs were speakeasies and most of them were owned by gangsters. Being a gangster was fashionable. The Volstead Act existed to be flouted. Owney Madden formed a partnership with Larry Fay. They paid the police protection for their brewery, and when the brewery couldn't supply enough they resorted to hijacking. In his off hours, Georgie drove reconnaissance for Madden's liquor shipments, which were delivered to Dutch Schultz or one of his mob. Madden saw to it that Raft got exposure in his clubs. He started financing Broadway and off-Broadway shows and got George parts where he could. Madden owned 50 per cent of Mae West's *Diamond Lil*, which opened at the Royal Theatre in New York for 323 performances before it went on the road. Raft was Madden's messenger who would appear nightly to pick up Madden's split of the box office. George met the play's star, Mae West.

Madden and Fay eventually split, Fay leaving for Miami with the main attraction of the El Fey night club, singer Texas Guinan. They tried to force Raft to go along with them, but he escaped. Madden formed an alliance with "Big Frenchy" de Mange. Between the two, they controlled the El Fey, the Parody, the Stork Club, and the Cotton Club in Harlem, which King Oliver and Duke Ellington were making famous. "Texas," came back, after a time, engaging in a torrid love affair with Madden. Warner's gave her an offer to go to Hollywood to make a musical based on cabaret life in New York. Madden sent Raft along to watch over her. George got a role in the production, *Queen of the Night Clubs* (Warner's, 1929).

By 1930, Raft was back in New York. "Mad Dog" Coll quit Dutch Schultz's gang and with a group of ruffians set himself up to challenge the others. He kidnaped "Big Frenchy" de Mange and demanded a ransom from Madden. Madden got "Big Frenchy" back, but he could see trouble brewing, probably an all-out gang war. Together with George Raft, the two left for California on vacation. Madden wanted to get his pal of more than thirty years into pictures. He felt he had talent, and looks, and he deserved a chance. Once he hit town, Madden made a number of telephone calls in Georgie's behalf to people he had met in his various clubs in New York. Madden registered at the Beverly Hills Hotel under an alias. Raft stayed at the Mark Twain Hotel on Wilcox, in Hollywood. When Owney went back East, he bankrolled George. One of the calls paid off.

Rowland Brown, the director, hearing that Raft frequented the Brown Derby, showed up there one day and offered George the part of a gangster in his forth-coming picture, *Quick Millions* (Fox, 1931). Raft went on a two-picture con-tract as a featured player. His next role was as one of the gang in *Hush Money* (Fox, 1931). A comic role in *Palmy Days* (United Artists, 1931) followed.

Owney Madden returned to see how his friend was doing. They went to the fights. After meeting Howard Hawks, the three men spent the evening together. When Raft left for his hotel, Hawks and Madden, who unlike Raft were both drinking men, went to Madden's suite. Hawks wanted to find out all he could about gang society.

Madden had promoted Primo Carnera into a wholly fraudulent championship and was about to start the fighter in a round-the-country tour with a carnival. He offered Raft a job with the carnival. Howard Hawks called Raft. He wanted him to come over to the General Service Studio. Raft arrived. Hawks asked him how he would like a part in *Scarface*. Raft said he already had a job with the carnival and would be leaving for Miami soon, so Howard would have to make it definite or not at all.

"How's this?" Howard returned. "You're on the payroll as of right now."

Howard suggested to Raft that he flip a nickel in all his scenes. Raft practiced at it for days until he could look at another player without his hand stopping the flipping action. Raft also found that Hawks and Hecht and others were con-stantly pumping him for information. Raft had met Capone on several occasions in New York at the crap game in the back room of the El Fey Club.

When the film played Chicago, Raft went there to make a personal appear-ance in connection with it. Capone had presented Howard Hawks with a minia-ture machine gun as a trophy. Now he sent for Raft.

George was escorted to the gangster's headquarters at the Lexington Hotel on Michigan Avenue. Capone sat behind a big mahogony desk and conducted most of the conversation as if it were an interrogation. When it came time to leave, Capone called Raft back from the door.

"Wait a minute, Georgie," he said. "I see you tossin' a coin all through the pitcher."

"Just a little theatrical touch," said Raft.

"A four-bit piece, huh?"

"No, it was a nickel."

"That's worse. You tell 'em that if any of my boys are tossin' coins, they'll be twenty-dollar gold pieces. See?"

George Raft was on his way up. When he signed what amounted to a lifetime contract with Paramount Pictures, he was promoted into the position of one of Hollywood's top movie personalities. Raft brought Mae West to Hollywood to work with him in *Night After Night* (Paramount, 1932). He had millions of fans, thousands of acquaintances, hundreds of co-workers who liked him. Owney Madden got sent back to prison for violating his parole. When he was released, the top mobsters in New York gave Owney a no-options offer to take the money he had made and move to Hot Springs, Arkansas. He would be given control of that state's gambling. Madden set up shop and eventually became a most respected citizen in Hot Springs. He lived there in comfort until 1965, when he died at age seventy-three of emphysema.

Big star, world celebrity, or not, when George Raft's mother died in July 1937, right in the midst of George's plans to bring her to Hollywood, none of the Hollywood or New York society people came to the funeral. But sitting there in the front row, paying their respects, were Owney Madden and "Big Frenchy" de Mange. Raft never forgot their loyalty.

With all this going beforehand, I must confess to the reader that, when I am preparing to interview someone for the first time, I make it a point to know as little as possible about him. However chaotic this may seem, I have found it effective. When George Raft and I, after a couple of talks on the phone, were set to meet at the Brown Derby in Beverly Hills, where he usually lunches, I made no preparations. I had not read the series of articles about his life which appeared in 1957 in *The Saturday Evening Post* with the by-line by Dean Jennings. Several studios at the time bargained for screen rights. Allied Artists purchased them and made a film, almost totally unrelated, called *The George Raft Story*, in 1961. The image of Raft which emerged in the magazine series was that of an intimate of gangsters, a man who knew or had met every important hoodlum that Prohibition produced, a scion of Owney Madden, whose Hollywood career had been initiated by underworld money. Raft himself claimed that the articles seriously misquoted him.

Nor had I read prior to our meeting *The George Raft File* (Drake, 1973) by James Robert Parish with Steven Whitney, although I did take the book with me because of its exhaustive filmography.

"That's not my official biography," George said, indicating the Parish book.

I can see now why he felt that way. Parish goes as far as he can in linking George Raft with the underworld and stresses that Raft may have been closely associated with several of Owney Madden's more redoubtable capers.

"I was going to fight that book," George continued, "but my attorneys advised me that fighting it would only draw attention to it. And that's something I definitely didn't want."

Nor had I yet read Lewis Yablonsky's *George Raft* (McGraw-Hill, 1974), the authorized biography. If Parish's concluding image of George was that of a lonely, sick old man who does nothing but watch television and dream of how it once was to be surrounded by the glitter of gangland easy money, or the sparkle of Hollywood stardom, or acting as a "front" for the international gambling Syndicate, Yablonsky, with Raft's help, presents an alternate image of an amiable dancer whose upward road was rather smooth and who from the tender age of twelve went to bed with a staggering number of women.

True, Raft proved attractive to women. At a party at Howard Hawks's house before going to New York to film, Raft was accompanied by Ann Dvorak. She wanted Raft to dance with her. When he wouldn't, she came over to him in her low-cut gown and did a sensuous, enticing sexual number that finally got George on his uppers. Hawks was so impressed with it he put it into the picture. Several of George's affairs in Hollywood in the early days were well publicized, but the succession of hookers at the rate of two a day, every day, didn't begin until he broke up with Betty Grable. Virginia Pine, with whom he carried on a relationship for years, taught him refinement; Norma Shearer, his next long-term engagement, taught him about the arts. But George used as his excuse his marriage to Grace Mulrooney, whom he'd married in a hasty moment in 1923 and who, supposedly, wouldn't give him a divorce. After nearly twenty years of being separated, George could have forced a divorce, but he never did. His promiscuity may have started out as a drive to prove himself, but it ended up being a protection of his fierce independence. However lonely he may have been, loneliness proved preferable to binding attachments. Not in all his life, however many social functions he might attend with women, however many he might go to bed with, did he ever *live* with a woman.

I didn't need this new image of George Raft any more than the old one. George Raft is the sweetest, gentlest, most charming man in all of Hollywood. But he has lived his life, for better or worse, by images. He never acted a part in any picture. He *was* the character, or he would have nothing to do with the picture.

In a sense, Prohibition made a way for George Raft in Hollywood, just as it made the private detective an anachronism even as his lively presence was first emerging. Prohibition created the milieu in which Dashiell Hammett set his stories and provided the insoluble human problems with which his detectives attempted unsuccessfully to grapple. It served as a background for the political futility, barrenness of quality in life, and empty despair which confronts the reader at the conclusion of Hammett's best novel, *The Glass Key*. George Raft appeared in the photoplay, made by Paramount in 1935, directed by Frank Tuttle. He played the Ned Beaumont character, with the name changed to Ed Beaumont, who could believe in nothing but his friend, political boss Paul Madvig, played by Edward Arnold, and when he could no longer believe in even him, he was left with nothing. The *néant*, or sense of nothingness, in *film noir* of the Forties and Fifties was only a recognition of the world of reality Hammett had drawn.

By this time not only had Hammett's novel *The Thin Man* (M-G-M, 1934) been brought to the screen, but in 1934 RKO Radio Pictures made *Woman in the Dark*, based on the Hammett short novel. Hammett hadn't been very accurately translated to the screen before *The Glass Key*. Most critics and audiences in general wanted to be amused by crime, not startled. Kathryn Scola and Kubec Glasmon did the screen adaptation with additional dialogue by Harry Ruskin. Almost all of the interconnecting links between politics and the underworld were toned down or removed. The plot was subtly altered so that Edward Arnold, forced to breathe life into a part made vapid by the story department, comes out more a reformer than one of the men who in city politics "pick" the candidates the electorate gets to vote on. The romance between Madvig and Janet Henry, played in the film by Claire Dodd, does not have the revealing underside it does in the novel, nor does she cotton to Arnold's shadow assistant, George Raft. There is a romantic spark played up instead between Raft and Rosalind Keith, portraying Opal Madvig. Raft as Beaumont comes along and breaks up the affair between Opal and the virtuous senator's son,

Taylor Henry, played by Ray Milland. The murder and its perpetrator stay the same as in the novel, but it means so much less. The best portrayal by far was Guinn "Big Boy" Williams as the brutal and sadistic Jeff. The scene of Raft's terrible beating, while being held prisoner by Jeff, wasn't diluted, nor Williams' final scene, choking Robert Gleckler, playing gangster Shad O'Rory.

Reviewers at the time were in agreement that George Raft gave his best performance in *The Glass Key* since he'd worked in *Scarface*.

Sitting across from Raft at his customary table at the Brown Derby, you would have no idea at all that he was eighty years old. He had undergone serious aneurysmal surgery early in 1976. That combined with his emphysema had weakened his condition.

"You can't tell it by looking at you," I said.

"Yeah. I asked my doctor if I was looking pretty good. 'Yeah,' he said, 'but not as good as you looked thirty years ago.'"

Raft was dressed in a dark sport shirt with a long collar and a gold, off-white

"Big Boy" Williams as the sadistic Jeff works over George Raft in *The Glass Key* (Paramount, 1935).   PHOTO COURTESY OF MCA-UNIVERSAL.

During all of his frequent suspensions from Paramount and then Warner Brothers, because he didn't like the parts he was offered, George Raft worked in radio, as here with Joan Bennett and Walter Connolly.

PHOTO COURTESY OF VIEWS & REVIEWS MAGAZINE.

and black-checked sport jacket. Although his hair was thinning, his face retained its smoothness and his eyes were very alive, watching girls' bottoms in tight-fitting slacks as they walked past us, or studying the faces of various patrons. We had been talking for some time. A man at a neighboring booth kept watching us.

"I think we're being watched," I said.

George smiled.

"When I had my trouble with England, I was watched by the FBI. I invited the guy into my apartment. I was doing the morning dishes. 'You're going to have a dull job,' I told him. 'I stay inside most of the time. I go out to eat. That's about all.' "

"Did you meet Hammett while you were making *The Glass Key?*"

"Yeah. He came on the set once. I didn't know much about him. I've never been much of a reader. I like horse racing, sports, that kind of thing. I wasn't very well educated. I didn't know very much. What education I got was in a Catholic school. You know what that's like. Hammett was a very distinguished man. I told him I hoped the picture turned out."

"How did you get on with the director, Frank Tuttle?"

"He was a great guy. I think he was afraid of me. He thought I was the tough guy I portrayed on the screen. I nearly got in trouble on that picture."

"How's that?"

"Tuttle's wife was a Communist. So was Frank. She was always selling tickets to Communist meetings. They were like benefits. I'd buy tickets from her. Why not? But I'd never go. What did I know about politics?"

"Why did you turn down the part of Sam Spade in *The Maltese Falcon?*" (This was one of several roles Raft had turned down. He didn't want to play in *Dead End* (United Artists, 1937) because he felt the part of the gangster was unsympathetic. He turned down the lead in *High Sierra* (Warner's, 1941) because he didn't want to get shot again and die in another picture. All three roles had gone to Humphrey Bogart.)

"I listened to my agent, Myron Selznick," Raft said. "Maybe I shouldn't have listened to him so much. But, like I said, I didn't know much, so I listened to guys who were supposed to know something. Selznick said the three women in the picture weren't that hot. So I said no. Besides, it [*The Maltese Falcon*] was John Huston's first picture. He was untried. 'An inexperienced director and three babes like this,' Selznick said. 'Turn it down.' It was a low-budget picture."

"You got your chance to work with Peter Lorre and Sydney Greenstreet in *Background to Danger* [Warner's, 1943]." Raoul Walsh was the director. The

Peter Lorre was supposed to be menacing George Raft in *Background to Danger* (Warner's, 1943), but off-camera it was a different story.

PHOTO COURTESY OF THE NATIONAL FILM ARCHIVE.

picture was based on a novel by Eric Ambler with a screenplay by W. R. Burnett.

"Yeah."

"How did you like Lorre?"

"I didn't."

"Oh?"

"Yeah. He stole my hat."

"He stole your hat?"

"Yeah. We all had our own prop wardrobe. I checked mine out. My hat was there. When I went back to get it, it was gone."

"How did you know Lorre stole it?"

"I saw him wearing it."

"What did you do?"

"I let him wear it."

"And for that reason you disliked him?"

"No. I had this scene where I enter a room and look around. I get hit on the head. I wanted to come back to that room when I search the place a second time. The director said no. He had me tied up. Lorre was sitting on a table in front of me. He was a mean little guy. Lorre blew cigarette smoke in my face. I didn't like it. Lorre grinned. We had retake after retake. Lorre kept blowing smoke in my face. He kept getting closer and closer to my eyes with that cigarette. 'Untie me,' I said, before the next retake. I grabbed Lorre. 'You keep that cigarette out of my face,' I said. Lorre ran away and locked himself in his dressing room. When they had me tied up again, he comes prancing out. He sits on the table. He blows smoke in my face. And he flicks the cigarette around, real close to my eyes. When I got untied, I slugged him. I told him he was a German spy. That upset him. But he didn't blow smoke at me again."

"And Greenstreet?"

"Bad at dialogue. He'd get it down two or three days ahead of time and then would never change a word of it. But he got along with Lorre."

"I liked *Johnny Allegro* [Columbia, 1949]."

"Yeah?"

"Yeah. You played an ex-con hired by the Treasury Department to get to the bottom of some counterfeiting."

"Yeah, I remember."

"It was set in Florida. Did you shoot it on location?"

"No. We shot some of it on Catalina."

"At the end, did George Macready really fire those arrows at you?"

"No actor fires arrows at George Raft."

"Did you have an expert?"

"Yeah. We had to. I did my own stunting, as long as I could."

"I also liked you in *Red Light* [United Artists, 1949]. When your brother, who's a priest, gets murdered, you set out to find who did it. It was on the order of *Johnny Angel* [RKO, 1945] where you were hunting down the murderer of your father, J. Farrell MacDonald."

"Yeah." George smiled. "Pictures in those days were too much alike."

"In *Red Light*, Raymond Burr was a vicious killer. In one scene, he knocks a semi-truck down on top of Gene Lockhart."

"I thought Burr had a lot of talent. He did a good job in that picture. But I didn't like the title. I thought it should be something else. It's like the dialogue I had in *Johnny Allegro*. I tell this government man that the racket is counterfeiting. He says, 'We know.' I tell him MacCreedy is behind it. He says, 'We know.' I tell him they're using old Nazi plates. He says, 'We know.' I asked our director on that picture, Ted Tetzlaff: 'If he knows all this stuff, why make me repeat it all for him?' It was too much dialogue. I should have fought harder. They left it in the picture."

"You don't smoke?"

"Not anymore. And I don't drink. But I used to smoke four packs of Lucky Strikes a day, all my life, until a couple of years ago. It's the smog, here. It irritates my emphysema. They should have let me stay in England. I wasn't bothered by it at all over there. Maybe it was the dampness."

George Macready, George Raft, director Ted Tetzlaff (with pipe) and Nina Foch discuss a scene for *Johnny Allegro* (Columbia, 1949).
PHOTO COURTESY OF THE NATIONAL FILM ARCHIVE.

"I thought dampness was bad for emphysema. I thought dryness best, like in the desert. Dashiell Hammett tried drinking. It kept his body dehydrated."

Raft smiled.

"Yeah. But I don't drink."

"What about that England business?"

"It was unfair. Sure, I knew people in the underworld. A lot of them took on my mannerisms. Like Bugsy Siegel. I loaned that guy a hundred grand, and I never saw it again. It was guilt by association. They still won't give me a hearing."

Raft was right. He had been unjustly discriminated against because Syndicate gambling interests had invested in the George Raft Colony Club in London. The British didn't like it.

The man at the neighboring table finally got up the courage to come over. He introduced himself.

Brian Donlevy played Paul Madvig in the second *Glass Key* (Paramount, 1942), visiting Alan Ladd in the hospital with Veronica Lake.

PHOTO COURTESY OF MCA-UNIVERSAL.

"Can I have your autograph, Mr. Raft?"

He pulled a card out of his card case and placed it before George on the table.

Raft signed it.

"I'm a federal judge," he said. "And I've always loved your movies."

He pulled out another card.

"Let me know if there is ever anything I can do for you."

George laughed.

"Where were you when I needed you?"

We all laughed.

The Glass Key, by the way, was remade by Paramount in 1942. It was done as a vehicle for Paramount's pint-sized romantic duo, hard guy Alan Ladd and peekaboo blonde Veronica Lake. Brian Donlevy was given the role of Paul Madvig. Stuart Heisler directed. Even though Jonathan Latimer did the screenplay, the film still wasn't faithful to even the spirit, much less the plot, of Hammett's novel. It was strong stuff, and the best way to deal with it was still thought to be through systematically ignoring it. This time Bonita Granville was Opal Madvig. Joseph Calleia played the gangster, now called Nick Varna. Veronica Lake was Janet Henry, but the stress on the Ladd-Lake relationship left little opportunity to play Ladd off against Donlevy or to discover in the Janet Henry character what costs Madvig the election. The best performance was again the Jeff role, this time assumed by Ladd's close friend, William Bendix. After the splash Ladd had made in *This Gun for Hire* (Paramount, 1942) as a cold-blooded, dedicated, crazed killer, much might have been expected. But, alas, with a second chance, Paramount still couldn't do it right.

III

Dashiell Hammett, because he was in Hollywood at the time, worked on the screenplay for the first *Maltese Falcon* (Warner's, 1931) without credit. "I followed Gutman's original in Washington," Hammett commented, "and I never remember shadowing a man who bored me so much. He was not after a jeweled falcon, of course; but he *was* suspected of being a German spy. . . . I worked with Dundy's prototype in a North Carolina railroad yard. The Cairo character I picked up on a forgery charge in 1920. Effie, the good girl, once asked me to go into the narcotic smuggling business with her in San Diego. Wilmer, the gunman, was picked up in Stockton, California, a neat small smooth-faced quiet boy of perhaps twenty-one. He was serenely proud of the name the papers gave him—The Midget Bandit. He'd robbed a Stockton filling station the previous week—and had been annoyed by the description the station proprietor had given of him and by the proprietor's statement of what he would do to that little runt if he ever laid eyes on him again. So he'd stolen a car and returned to stick the guy up again and see what he wanted to do about it. That's when we nabbed him."

Roy Del Ruth directed. Maude Fulton, Lucien Hubbard, and Brown Holmes worked on the screenplay. In my opinion, Ricardo Cortez is no more at home in the role of Sam Spade than he was later in the role of Perry Mason. Villain Walter Long was cast as Spade's partner, Archer. Bebe Daniels played Ruth Wonderly, the character in the Brigid role. Dudley Digges was Gutman, Una Merkel as Effie, Robert Elliott as Dundy, Otto Matieson as Cairo, Dwight Frye as Wilmer, and Thelma Todd as Iva Archer, the woman with whom Spade continues to carry on an affair after Archer is murdered.

I think Hammett intended the novel as a parable, demonstrating the corrupting influence of greed on the major characters. One can distinguish little difference between Spade and the men against whom he is set in the plot. This is the way Hammett wanted it to be. Spade is no hero: he's just smarter and his greed satisfies itself with being petty rather than monumental. Above all, he won't be played for a fall guy. He tells Brigid truthfully at the end that he's going to send her over, even though he will have some bad nights out of it, because all of him wants to set her free, "wants to say to hell with the consequences and do it—and because—God damn you—you've counted on that with me the same as you counted on that with the others." Brigid seemed to condense all of Hammett's disdain for and distrust of women.

The Maltese Falcon was remade as *Satan Met a Lady* in 1936 by Warner's as a vehicle for Warren William and Bette Davis. William Dieterle directed. It was the loosest kind of remake. William played a detective named Ted Shayne. Davis was Valerie Purvis. Gutman was changed to a woman, Alison Skipworth. Effie, Spade's secretary, became Murgetroyd, played by Marie Wilson. Brown Holmes did this new screen adaptation.

John Huston, because he was a screenwriter and because he both knew and admired Hammett, wanted to remake *The Maltese Falcon* as his first film as a director. Jack L. Warner had his reservations. Howard Hawks, talking to Huston about the project, suggested that if the picture was to be done, why not do it exactly as the plot is developed in the novel? This, wisely, was the course Huston followed. He had to humanize the Spade role somewhat for Humphrey Bogart—Hollywood wasn't quite ready for the notion of dubious heroes, enraptured as it was by the star system—but, otherwise, Huston could and did detail the novel with only minor changes. The film is probably more familiar than any other detective vehicle of the decade. Sydney Greenstreet, who had specialized in playing butlers on Broadway, was imported to portray Gutman. His relationship with Joel Cairo—the homosexuality themes were still held in reserve—proved sufficiently popular that Greenstreet and Peter Lorre continued to be featured in a number of films together, sort of a Laurel and Hardy of villainy, to paraphrase Lorre.

Huston wanted Geraldine Fitzgerald to play Brigid, but Warner's vetoed the idea in favor of Mary Astor. Huston's father, Walter Huston, appeared in a

Bebe Daniels, Dudley Digges, and Otto Matieson pore over the black bird in the first *Maltese Falcon* (Warner's, 1931). PHOTO COURTESY OF UNITED ARTISTS TELEVISION.

cameo role to bring his son luck. Huston had Mary Astor run around the set several times before he shot her scenes, to give her perpetual lying a breathless quality and to keep her nerves hypertensive.

"You originally wanted George Raft as Sam Spade?" I asked Huston.

"Yes," he said. "I did. I thought Raft would be perfect as Spade. If," and Huston leered, "the lines didn't prove too long for him. George liked his lines short. But he turned it down because it was my first picture as a director. So I took Bogart."

"Eddie Dmytryk told me that when he directed Bogart, he would have to wait for ten minutes before each of Bogart's scenes so he could cough his lungs out on one side of the camera. Bogart didn't want to cough in the middle of a scene."

"Now," Huston said, smiling, "I wouldn't know about that." He inhaled deeply on his cigar. "Because I was probably on the other side of the camera, coughing."

If *The Maltese Falcon* isn't Bogart's best picture, it is certainly one of his most endurable. It can be viewed repeatedly. The outcome isn't important. Huston managed to achieve in film what Hammett had achieved in fiction: he made us more interested in the characters than in the plot.

If it doesn't soften or make a vibrant testament a lie, Hollywood very often will destroy a rare good performance with a remake. *The Black Bird* (Columbia, 1975) starred George Segal as Sam Spade, Jr. It was supposed to be funny, but it wasn't. Those who were still alive from Huston's cast were called back into action, Lee Patrick again as Effie, Elisha Cook, Jr., as Wilmer. The setting is San Francisco in 1975. The falcon is again the source of murder and mayhem. David Giler directed and worked on the screenplay with a story by Don M. Mankiewicz and Gordon Cotler. Columbia took a financial bath with the picture's failure. But it does point up one thing. As enthusiastic as Hollywood was, and seemingly is again, about Dashiell Hammett, not one film, not even John Huston's *The Maltese Falcon*, saw filmmakers ready for the full impact of the world view contained in Hammett's fiction. In that world view, men and women live by deceit, presenting the world with a hard or soft front, but only a front. It was a world that recognized that economic necessity embraces all of us, and that financial exigencies prompt, if not motivate, most human behavior. Men are naturally aggressive; whatever their laws, there will be violence, because one man would dominate another. Women are predators. So are men.

Hemingway and Hammett, when they did meet, disliked each other. But Hemingway liked the way Hammett wrote. He was in Spain when *The Maltese Falcon* reached him. He had an eye infection and asked his wife to read the novel aloud to him. When he came to write *To Have and Have Not*, Hemingway must have remembered Hammett's description of Sam Spade as a blond Satan, because he described his central character, Harry Morgan, the same way,

Warren William and Bette Davis were at cross-purposes in *Satan Met a Lady* (Warner's, 1936). PHOTO COURTESY OF UNITED ARTISTS TELEVISION.

and in almost the same language. (Appropriately, Bogart played both roles on the screen.) In Hammett's novel, Spade is as much corrupted by his environment as the Continental Op was in *Red Harvest;* it's just a matter of degree. Hemingway wanted to take issue with Hammett, though. He wanted to show him that a tough hero doesn't come out at the end, no matter how tough he is. When *To Have and Have Not* was in galleys, Hemingway showed it to Lillian Hellman. He thought she'd easily make the connection, especially since she was sleeping with Hammett. She didn't. She relates that she was confused by the book and puzzled at Hemingway's comment that, as much as he would like to go to bed with her and she with him, there was somebody else.

Sam Spade appeared in three short stories by Hammett following publication of *The Maltese Falcon.* A radio series was begun in 1946 over CBS with Howard Duff in the role of Spade. It was canceled when Hammett and Lillian Hellman got into political difficulty. ABC sought to compete in a radio series that began in 1945 featuring a detective called Brad Runyon, known as The Fat Man, loosely based on the Continental Op. As each program began, he would step on a scale and inform his listeners that his weight was 237 pounds and that his fortune was danger. J. Scott Smart was cast in the role for *The Fat Man* (Universal-International, 1951), directed by William Castle. Julie London, Rock Hudson, and Jayne Meadows were also in the cast. It was one of Rock Hudson's early screen appearances. Castle got Bill Goetz, in charge of production at U-I, to agree to hire the famous pantomime clown, Emmett Kelly, as the villain. Otherwise, the film wasn't especially remarkable and a series did not result.

But neither film nor radio series did justice to the Op. He may well be Hammett's finest creation, a man who in fiction remains nameless because Hammett had known dozens like him. He is a hero because he does not succumb to either greed or vanity. Hammett himself, like the Op, wasn't an easy man to know outside his work; whatever his work might have been at the time, he tried his best at it because he knew no other way.

"He had two hemorrhages right in the store," Samuels the jeweler recalled. "Once we found him unconscious in a pool of blood. But he couldn't stop drinking." Once Hammett was successful in Hollywood, he had his driver (he owned a Rolls-Royce) drive him up to San Francisco to look in on Samuels. He was friendly and grateful. A part of Hammett was dying almost from his adolescence. It cut him off from the world, making him fundamentally unapproachable. He tried to make himself in living as closely as he could to his Op. "I see him," Hammett wrote of the Op, "a little man going forward day after day through mud and blood and death and deceit—as callous and brutal and cynical as necessary—toward a dim goal, with nothing to push or pull him to it except he's been hired to reach it." When everything is said or done, that was the sum total of motivation Hammett could see in life; all else was illusion.

When *The Maltese Falcon* was first filmed in Hollywood, the nation was starving. Newspaperman Colonel Robert R. McCormick, in his Chicago *Tribune,* called on every citizen to pay his taxes and declared his own taxable personal income was only $25,250, against which he was levied $1,515. He wasn't so badly off as Louis Florsheim, the shoe magnate, who paid only $90. J. P. Morgan called upon his employees to contribute from their wages to the national relief but himself paid no income tax in 1930, 1931, and 1932. A march of the unemployed on the Henry Ford plant in Detroit was met first with tear gas, then freezing water from fire hoses, then gunfire from revolvers, finally with fire from machine guns. A group of Russian technicians, visiting the plant to learn of Ford's production methods, observed the demonstration from the windows over Gate Four. And Hammett knew what happened to the money politicians did collect, that instead of serving only a few years with full-time careers elsewhere, as Jefferson and others had intended, politics was a lifetime vocation and as ready a way to wealth as the clergy had been in the Middle Ages. His Continental Op was the common man everyone had on his lips, as befitted the political slogan of the day. He stood between organized politics and organized crime. But he differed from his fellow man in one important respect: he refused to live by fantasies.

Director John Huston shaking hands with his father, Walter Huston, Bogart with his hand on the camera, outside the office door on the Spade office set while filming his masterful version of *The Maltese Falcon* (Warner's, 1941).
PHOTO COURTESY OF THE NATIONAL FILM ARCHIVE.

SIX:
Marriage and Murder

Her body was lean and tough as a whip,
With little of breast and little of hip,
And her voice was thin and hard as her lip.
And her lip was hard as bone.

—Dashiell Hammett

The question is frequently brought up by almost anyone who has the least interest in Hammett: Why did he quit writing? According to a great many people who knew him after he went to Hollywood, at least part of the answer lies in his having met Lillian Hellman.

Had Hammett not met her, I have been told, he might well have had several more productive years as a detective story writer. I do not know how true this is. But it is certain that by virtue of becoming Hammett's executrix, Lillian Hellman has refused to permit much of Hammett's short fiction to be reprinted.

When Hammett handed Hellman the manuscript of *The Thin Man* (Knopf, 1934), he said that Lillian was the model for Nora Charles, but also the model for the silly girl in the novel and for the villainess. Tuberculosis, alcoholism, and emphysema he could have lived with and still managed, at times, to write. But he couldn't survive the snobbish intellectualism and New York values and literary people his association with Lillian Hellman introduced him to; they all tended to make him think very little of what he had written and drove him to try writing something more serious, more artistic. In the end, he wrote nothing, except a fragment which has since been published, titled "Tulip."

When Hammett worked in the Paramount story department, he would occasionally attend a Hollywood party given by a fellow writer or some studio luminary. He talked very little at these affairs, and would mostly stand around, drinking. Midway through the party he was as likely as not to be found in the

William Powell, Myrna Loy, and Asta.
PHOTO COURTESY OF THE NATIONAL FILM ARCHIVE.

kitchen, still drinking, and having an animated discussion with a servant about detective fiction or world literature. Not a man to make friends easily, he never felt drawn toward most of the people he met at these parties enough to want to engage them in even small talk. He had a drinking booth at Musso & Frank's on Hollywood Boulevard, where he would invariably sit for hours on end. He liked to dine at the Hollywood Brown Derby. He met S. J. Perelman and his wife Laura while working at Paramount, and while there he met and became almost as friendly with Arthur Kober, who, an Austrian immigrant, had made a name for himself in New York theatrical circles as a press agent. He was hired by Paramount in 1931 to come to Hollywood to write original screenplays and supervise screen adaptations. In 1925, Kober had married Lillian Hellman, who was working at the New York publishing firm of Boni & Liveright.

Hellman, who has written three books about her life so far and may write one or two more, was a very independent woman from the start. She rapidly grew bored with her life and found most of her days tedious, her nights no less so. She drank heavily. She was convinced at times that it was her destiny to be a writer.

In the Greenwich Village restaurants in the Twenties which Lillian Hellman preferred to visit, young people sat together and talked about Hegel and Kant and Nietzsche and what was wrong with the world. In later years, when she had won acclaim in her own right, Hellman would drag Hammett to get-togethers with the Algonquin Hotel crowd, Dorothy Parker, H. L. Mencken, George Jean Nathan, where the same discussions would take place, only heightened by verbal glitter and witticism. It was a change for Hammett, to say the very least, from sitting with his little girl on his lap in a cheap apartment in San Francisco and reading to her every day from Dostoyevsky's *Crime and Punishment*.

Hammett was plagued by only an occasional cough and a mild sense of disorientation when he met Hellman at a Hollywood restaurant. Lillian had followed Kober to the West Coast. She urged Kober to move out of the small apartment he was renting—he could afford it on $450 a week, she said. Kober was reluctant because he wasn't at all certain that such easy money was going to last. By the time they moved into a large house in the hills above Hollywood Boulevard, Hellman would spend her days in a leather chair reading and her nights drinking. She finally persuaded Kober to help her find a job. She went to work for Metro-Goldwyn-Mayer as a manuscript reader. She was unhappy with her marriage and unhappy with herself. She had never been a particularly attractive woman, but Hammett, who was getting over a five-day drunk, may not have noticed; and he must have been charmed by Hellman's unabashed admiration for him. Possibly, too, he may have found her intellectual conversation stimulating. In Hollywood, during any era, a woman talking the way Hellman writes would make heads turn.

Amid sporadic screen work, Hammett was still on the party circuit. That summer Hammett had gone to Turkey Hill with screenwriters Ben Hecht and Charles MacArthur. It was a wooden castle perched on a Hollywood hill. MacArthur and the agent Leland Howard lived there with Hecht. It got its name from the 250 turkeys which roamed the grounds. The partying was continuous. Around the bar, one could find gathered an assortment which included Jean Harlow, blazing sex to match her blond hair, holding hands with her current fiancé, Paul Bern, who found he couldn't perform adequately after their marriage and killed himself. John Gilbert, whose career was already fading, with three whores he had rented for the night, was glued to the bar. He spent his last years literally passed out. He was married for a brief time to Virginia Bruce, who would bring him along to a party or on a social visit. Gilbert would ask where the nearest bedroom was, if he could speak at all; usually, he just wandered around until he found a bed and then fell into an alcoholic slumber until Virginia would wake him, saying it was time to go. Gilbert insisted on driving everywhere they went. Harpo Marx would be there, playing craps with Ernst Lubitsch. Howard Hawks, sad-eyed, with a drink in his hand, would listen to a scarcely sober George Antheil rendering a melody at the piano. The agent Myron Selznick would drop in to check over any new starlets who might be in need of proper management. He soon delegated most of the work to minions in his talent agency and devoted himself to full-time drinking. He might, however, be called in on urgent business, such as consulting with George Raft whether or not a certain part was right for Raft's career. Raft, you'll recall, like many others, found that Selznick's advice wasn't always sound.

Now Hollywood was passing into its winter, which, back then, without smog, was sunlight and frequent rain. Hammett had recently lost a damage suit filed by Elise de Viane, who alleged that Hammett had taken her to his apartment, ostensibly for a couple of drinks, but had then proceeded to "make violent love to me." Most women were quite willing, as Hammett had reason to know; maybe he liked the challenge of one who wasn't.

Hammett was taken with Lillian's rejection of the Hollywood way of life. She loved to drink, and that they did more and more of the time, drinking and talking. Hellman was soon spending most of her time with Hammett, and very little at home with Kober, to which Kober had no real objection. He liked Hammett and, apparently, was circumspect enough to realize that his union with Lillian held very little for him.

Laura Perelman's brother was Nathaniel West, an extraordinarily gifted writer and satirist. The reader can well imagine the effect on Hammett of an evening with the Perelmans and West, longing for New York and the stability of the East. Hammett was living the life of the Hollywood bachelor. He had a man-servant, Jones, to look after his laundry. He spent most of his money, as George Raft did, on a succession of women; they taught him nothing, but, like alcohol, they did deaden the pain of existence. If his lungs bothered him, he would frequently take his temperature and count the number of times he went to the toilet.

The Perelmans, Nathaniel West, and, on March 4, 1931, Lillian Hellman went back to New York. A few nights after her departure, Hammett wrote to Hellman: "Sweet, Jones rescued the pajamas from the cleaners this evening. I'll dispatch them to you presently. Arthur [Kober] was in for a couple of hours, left just a few minutes ago for an early bed so he could rise early. If I can make it we'll probably do the fights tomorrow night. . . . I've been to the toilet approx-

imately eight times today, with hopes of running it up to around 10 before bed-
time, and I've shut the door each time, and locked it once. . . . I daresay my absence from the Brown Derby, coinciding with your departure, has started a
crop of fresh and juicy rumors. I'll see they don't die from want of feeding."

Perelman and Laura returned to Hollywood. Hammett ran in to them at the
Brown Derby, in the company of Arthur Kober. He pumped them about information on Lillian, suspecting her, in a playful mood, of the loosest conduct.
When Alfred Knopf sent Hammett a telegram to inform him that *The Glass
Key* was getting a good reception, Hammett pressured him into coming across
with a thousand dollars. Hammett went on the wagon and continued writing
The Thin Man, which he had begun in 1930. The original version is currently
in the possession of the E. P. Guyman, Jr., Collection of the Occidental College
in Los Angeles. The detective was named John Guild, a dark, retiring man with
a personality similar to Ned Beaumont's and an attitude toward his work
reminiscent of the Continental Op. The book was the last thing Hammett was
working on before he went to Hollywood to accept Paramount's offer. The
first version ran sixty-five pages and was postponed originally because Knopf
delayed publication on *The Glass Key* for eight months. Hammett was dissatisfied with the book and decided he would have to start it over from the beginning.

When Lillian Hellman returned to Hollywood, she had made up her mind to
divorce Arthur Kober. He was amicable. He had his attorney represent her, another partner in the same firm representing him. At the hearing, Hellman had
difficulty suppressing her laughter when she heard the grounds read as cruelty.
Hammett and Kober remained friends. In future years, Kober held Hellman's
opinion in such high esteem that he had her approve the decorations in an apartment he intended to lease in New York and even asked her to pass judgment on
his fiancée, Margaret Frohnknecht. Lillian was matron of honor at his wedding
in 1941.

After her divorce, Lillian and Hammett moved to New York. The job at Paramount had ended and Hammett needed money. The Perelmans had moved East
also, purchasing a home in Bucks County. Nathaniel West, at the time, secured a
job as the manager of the Sutton Hotel in New York. Hammett got another advance from Knopf out of which he paid his rent on the Diplomat's Suite at the
Sutton. West magnanimously allowed Lillian and Hammett to charge their
meals. The quarters were downright dingy and the food nearly inedible, but the
two of them were obviously very much in love and found it all extremely exciting. In Hollywood, observers noted that when they were together Hammett and
Lillian couldn't keep their hands off each other. Now they were sequestered
from the world and Hammett was working. No drinking and no parties were
the rules of the day. Hammett locked himself in with his typewriter and began
The Thin Man anew. Hellman tried her hand at short stories.

Hammett decided he would update his detective to this new set of circumstances. Nick Charles, who was formerly in the employ of the Trans-American
Detective Agency in San Francisco, is temporarily living in New York. He was
portrayed as a hard-drinking, fun-loving, charming personality. However tough
Nick may once have been, he has mellowed and now is only cocky. He refuses

to take anything seriously, quite in keeping with the frivolous tone Hammett associated with Lillian and her Eastern friends. Nora, who is wealthy, has married Nick. He has retired from his profession to manage her business interests. Together, their life is one of unceasing drinking and partying. Nick doesn't want to work, but Nora gets him into a situation where he has to. The book was populated with a varied group of characters definitely out of the Hammett milieu, starting with Nick's old flame Mimi Jorgensen, who lies as adeptly as Brigid O'Shaughnessy, the wacky Dorothy Wynant, who is Mimi's daughter, Herbert Macauley, a crooked lawyer intent on pretending that the missing Wynant is still alive for his own personal gain, and Shep Morelli, a nervous gangster. "I love you, Nicky," Nora tells him, "because you smell nice and know such fascinating people." Nora's dislike of Nicky's off-color playmates wouldn't emerge until the late Thirties in the screenplays Hammett worked on, showing how Lillian's fascination with his world had undergone an alteration, attendant to her subtle influence on him to upgrade his literary inclinations.

Hammett dedicated the book "To Lillian." Hellman, in her Introduction to *The Big Knockover*, said of the writing of *The Thin Man*: "I had never seen anybody work that way: the care for every word, the pride in the neatness of the typed page itself, the refusal . . . to go out for a walk for fear something would be lost."

After delivering the manuscript to Knopf, the two had happy nights and days of continuous drinking and partying. Lillian introduced Hammett to as many of her New York intellectual friends as she could. The talk about books and writers was endless. The Perelmans invited them down to their home in Bucks County. Hammett discovered a fish in the closet when he went to hang up his coat. "This is fishing country," Perelman informed him. It was here that Hammett shared weekends with not only the Perelmans and Nathaniel West, but Robert Coates, the literary critic, and, occasionally, William Faulkner. Hammett and Faulkner became fast friends. Back in New York, Hammett and Faulkner would meet nightly to drink and to argue. The sessions would run all night. By morning the two men would rejuvenate themselves with or without breakfast, but always with another bottle. Lillian would sleep through most of it. As wide ranging as their debates might be, one recurrent theme was Hammett's supposed disbelief that Faulkner could possibly have written *Sanctuary* (Cape & Smith, 1931) just for the money.

Hammett sent *The Thin Man* to a number of slick magazines for a prepublication sale. It was rejected. Edwin Balmer of *Red Book*, however, liked it and decided to run it. He was shocked, though, at Nora asking Nick after he's tied up with a good-looking woman: "Tell me the truth: when you were wrestling with Mimi, didn't you have an erection?" Nick answers, "Oh, a little." Knopf thought enough of the line to include it as a major part of his promotional campaign, a situation which outraged Balmer sufficiently for him to make a public statement on the matter condemning Knopf. When Hammett received his money from *Red Book*, he went with Lillian to the Florida Keys, where for the spring and summer he lived in splendid isolation surrounded by the wilds. He was happier there than he had been in New York.

Metro-Goldwyn-Mayer negotiated the screen rights for *The Thin Man* with

Alfred Knopf. The book, upon publication, had proved a runaway success, with critical raves in New York and in London. Everyone found the idea of a detective who gets up in the middle of the night and asks his wife, first thing, if she would fix him a whiskey and soda, the perfect antidote to Depression blues.

Before I reintroduce William Powell into this narrative, I should perhaps spend a moment or two on Myrna Loy. She was born Myrna Williams on August 2, 1905, near Helena, Montana. Her family moved to California while she was still in high school. She was intent upon a theatrical career and managed to work in several of the prologues which were customary at Grauman's Chinese Theatre on Hollywood Boulevard. She made an impression on Rudolph Valentino's wife, who undertook to see that she got work in pictures. Loy had a bit part in *Pretty Ladies* (M-G-M, 1925) and continued, for what remained of the silent and part-talkie era, to take character parts in countless films. Her parts varied. In a film I'm sure few have seen, *Rogue of the Rio Grande* (Sono-Art, 1930), she played a Mexican dancer and did very little more than wiggle her 110-pound torso seductively in a costume dress.

She met Arthur Hornblow, Jr., while she was working on *Arrowsmith* (United Artists, 1931), directed by John Ford for Samuel Goldwyn. Hornblow was still Goldwyn's right-hand man. It was love at first sight, according to Loy. She told Hornblow of her tremendous ambitions. He was instrumental in getting her a contract with M-G-M, where her first role was in *Emma* (M-G-M, 1932). Metro used her for all manner of roles, mostly villainous. In *The Mask of Fu Manchu* (M-G-M, 1932) she played Fa Lo Suee opposite Boris Karloff's Fu Manchu. She might have been stuck in villain roles indefinitely had Woody Van Dyke not cast her to play with Warner Baxter in *Penthouse* (M-G-M, 1933). It was a screwball comedy which also included Charles Butterworth and Mae Clarke in the cast.

Van Dyke cast Loy opposite William Powell, as I have already mentioned, in *Manhattan Melodrama* (M-G-M, 1934). The trades announced that Van Dyke was taken off the *Thin Man* project in order to get *Melodrama* out first. Van Dyke thought the rapport between Powell and Loy exactly what he wanted to bring Nick and Nora Charles to the screen. Louis B. Mayer wasn't at all convinced. He thought Loy was best as an Oriental and the studio wanted Powell for *The Casino Murder Case*. Van Dyke, who was accustomed to shooting pictures with a staggering rapidity, assured Mayer that he could have the film in the can in twelve days. Powell was still negotiating his contract with Metro through Myron Selznick. Mayer thought no harm could come of it if Van Dyke could finish it that quickly. Edward Ellis, whom the studio had originally intended for the Nick Charles role, was, oddly enough, retained in the role of Clyde Wynant, the actual "thin man" of the novel. Edward Brophy ineptly was cast as the gangster Joe Morelli (altered from Shep in the novel). Nat Pendleton played Lieutenant John Guild. Porter Hall was the crafty attorney, Macauley, and Minna Gombell was Mimi Wynant. Albert Hackett and Frances Goodrich wrote the screenplay in three weeks.

Van Dyke didn't make it in twelve days, but he did in eighteen. He would have one setup behind the camera and one in front of it. As soon as he finished shooting the scene in front of the camera, he would have the crew turn around and the cast change positions and shoot until that scene was finished while the other stage was being readied for yet the next scene. The picture was brought in for only $231,000. Upon release, it showed a staggering profit of $729,000. Out of some forty pictures for the 1933–34 season, *The Thin Man* (M-G-M, 1934) had 9,911 bookings. *Manhattan Melodrama* had taken twenty-four days to shoot, had cost $355,000, and made a profit of $415,000. Metro knew that it had a winner in the teaming of Powell and Loy.

Following *The Thin Man*, Powell's contract terms with M-G-M were met. It was carried in the trades that his first picture under the contract would be *The Casino Murder Case*, but the continuing critical and popular acclaim of *The*

William Powell and director W. S. "Woody" Van Dyke welcome white-haired Dashiell Hammett (center) to the M-G-M production of *The Thin Man*.

PHOTO COURTESY OF THE NATIONAL FILM ARCHIVE.

Thin Man caused Metro to shelve that idea in favor of putting Powell in another picture with Loy.

Much of the initial success of *The Thin Man* had to do with the fact that Powell really loved the role. For one thing, being a steady drinker (at his home in Palm Springs he was never without a glass in his hand), he could be entirely natural. The dialogue made the film sparkle and brought to life the rather routine plot. When Nora asks Nick if that is her drink, he asks her what she's drinking. She responds rye. He guzzles it and quips, "Yes, yes. It's yours." Nick teases Nora about her financial status.

NORA: I think it's a dirty trick to bring me all the way to New York just to make a widow out of me.

NICK: You wouldn't be a widow long.

NORA: You bet I wouldn't.

NICK: Not with all your money.

Evelyn Prentice (M-G-M, 1934) was next. The plot had Powell married to Loy. Powell is a noted criminal lawyer. On one of his business trips, he has an affair with Rosalind Russell. To get back, Loy takes up with Harvey Stephens. But before long, she realizes that she doesn't want an affair, breaks it off, and reconciles with Powell. They plan a trip to Europe. Stephens spoils Loy's plans. He invites her over to his apartment and tries to blackmail her with a letter she wrote. She picks up a gun and threatens him. He strikes her. She falls against a wall and the gun goes off. Stephens hits the floor. His mistress, Isabel Jewell, is accused. Loy persuades Powell to defend Jewell in court. During the trial, Loy jumps up and confesses to firing the fatal shot. But Powell saves the day when he breaks Jewell down on the stand to admit that Loy's shot missed, while hers didn't.

Metro knew that it had an extremely salable property in the Thin Man series, so it did what no other studio had the wisdom to do. It decided to space out the pictures over the years, limiting exposure and keeping the property current. On November 12, 1934, *Variety* announced that Metro was planning on starring Powell and Loy in *The Casino Murder Case*, which would be their third picture running. The studio met resistance from Powell. He had had enough of Philo Vance, with or without Loy. Instead he was starred in *Reckless* (M-G-M, 1935) with Jean Harlow. He then went on loan-out, permitted by his contract, to make *Star of Midnight* (RKO, 1935).

The property Powell really wanted Metro to prepare for him, rather than Philo Vance, was *The Great Ziegfeld* (M-G-M, 1936). Powell was nominated for an Oscar for Best Actor with *The Thin Man*, losing out to Clark Gable in *It Happened One Night* (Columbia, 1934). He felt that *The Great Ziegfeld* would do it for him. Myrna Loy was naturally cast as Billie Burke. The real Billie Burke said that Powell was apt for the part "not because he looks like Flo, or has Flo's mannerisms, but because he is like Flo in his graciousness toward women, especially beautiful ones." Powell did not win the Oscar, although the picture did.

The second picture on a two-picture deal with RKO was *The Ex-Mrs. Bradford* (RKO, 1936), which cast Powell as a surgeon in Los Angeles who is comically and consistently distracted by his former wife, who wants him back and who manages to embroil him in a race-track murder because of her interest in crime detection. It was played in the Thin Man vein and proved extremely popular with audiences.

Another picture that Powell very much wanted to make was *My Man Godfrey* (Universal, 1936). In it, he was co-starred with his ex-wife, Carole Lombard. Powell, having always been a retiring man, admired Lombard's vivacity. She dragged Powell to every kind of party. This was in violent contrast to the true William Powell, who, although he dressed well, didn't like to dress until the last possible moment. He preferred staying in bed and had an extra-large bed built just to spend his time in it. Powell wasn't the least bitter after the divorce in Carson City, Nevada, and commented about Lombard that "she was ready to spread her wings and marriage enabled her to do it." In *My Man Godfrey*, he played a butler, and all through the picture, knowing how he disliked the reference, Lombard insisted on calling him Philo off screen. The picture was an undisputed success.

Metro was quick to cast Powell again with Loy in *Libeled Lady* (M-G-M, 1936) while his second Thin Man picture was in preproduction. The fan magazines felt the two made such a perfect couple on screen that they should marry in private life. That was highly unlikely. Arthur Hornblow had finally succeeded in getting a divorce so he and Myrna Loy could marry. William Powell fell in love with Jean Harlow.

Albert Hackett and Frances Goodrich again did the screenplay for *After the Thin Man* (M-G-M, 1936). Hunt Stromberg was the producer, Woody Van Dyke the director. Metro had engaged Dashiell Hammett to provide the original story. After their Florida sojourn, Hammett returned to Hollywood and Lillian Hellman went to New York. She finished her first play, *The Children's Hour*, which was published by Knopf. "I'm still surprised at the fuss THE THIN MAN made out here," Hammett wrote to Hellman. "People bring the Joan Crawfords and Gables over to meet me instead of the usual vice versa! Hotcha!" Metro was pleased to have Hammett associated with the new films in the series.

Hellman insisted that Herman Shumlin, a producer, read her play. She knew him through her former husband, Arthur Kober. Shumlin read the play while Lillian flipped through a magazine. When he finished, he said he would produce it. She had only $55 in her bank account. The play would earn her $125,000. In its initial engagement in New York, it ran for 691 performances. The play proved sensational because of its lesbian theme.

"Hammett had held the limelight since the publication of *Red Harvest* in 1929," Richard Moody writes in his book *Lillian Hellman, Playwright* (Pegasus, 1972). "After their meeting in Hollywood, she had shared the mixed pleasures of public adulation. Now the focus was shifting. He was to delight in her success, and she well knew that the rewards that were hers belonged also to him. He taught her to persist, to learn her craft, to scrap whatever did not qualify, to sharpen, to mold, to rework, to temper until they both approved. He started her on her way as a playwright and from then on until his death in 1961, every play had to have his critical stamp before being released to the producers. At least once, for *The Autumn Garden,* he supplied a major speech. At the same time, she recalled long after his death, 'we thought differently and were totally different writers. He frequently objected to my use of violence. He felt that I was far too held up by how to do things, by the technique.'"

Metro was satisfied to have Hammett turn in story outlines. Hellman appreciated Hammett's help and encouragement on her plays. It didn't occur to Hammett to turn *After the Thin Man* into a novel. Since January 1934, Hammett had been supplying copy to Alex Raymond, creator of Buck Rogers, on a comic strip Raymond syndicated under the name *Secret Agent X-9.* It provided Hammett, coupled with his royalties from publishers and film companies, with what he considered a suitable income. Working with Hellman, occasionally living with her, and above all his associations with her friends made him yearn to write something other than what he was adept at writing. His drinking intensified.

In *After the Thin Man* Asta, the wire-haired terrier who ranked almost as a co-star in the series, is the father of pups. Although Nick and Nora are always discreetly pictured sleeping in their twin beds—and much of the bedroom dialogue is the best in the picture—there are two revelations at the end. The mur-

Woody Van Dyke directing William Powell, Myrna Loy, and Sam Levine in *After the Thin Man* (M-G-M, 1936).   PHOTO COURTESY OF THE NATIONAL FILM ARCHIVE.

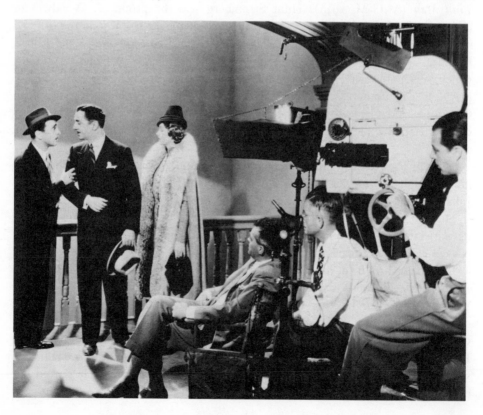

derer is exposed and Nora announces she will have a baby. The rest of the time was spent in banter between Nick and Nora or in a chase around the house pursuing Asta. Detection was secondary.

Another Thin Man (M-G-M, 1939) came nearly three years later. In the interim, Powell and Loy starred in *Double Wedding* (M-G-M, 1937), in which Powell played an artist taking an interest in the stage careers of two young hopefuls. It was a slapstick comedy. That same year, Powell was seen constantly with Jean Harlow. She wore an extraordinarily large sapphire ring from him on the third finger on her left hand. She had been married three times, Powell twice, but they were destined not to marry each other. In the spring of 1937, while working on *Saratoga*, Harlow was stricken with an inflamed gallbladder. Uremic poisoning followed and she died on June 7, 1937, at the age of twenty-six. Powell was overwhelmed by grief. He wept uncontrollably at her funeral. He purchased a crypt at Forest Lawn and endowed the Jean Harlow room, in which there was crypt space for three coffins, Jean's, her mother's, and his own. Fresh flowers were to be set at her grave in perpetuity. After the funeral, Powell spent a month on Ronald Colman's yacht (they had long been close friends). Then he went to Europe. Shortly after he returned, Powell discovered that he had cancer of the rectum. He agreed to undergo a colon bypass operation attended by radium treatments.

Metro announced to the trades that in view of Powell's difficulties the next Thin Man picture would star a new team consisting of Virginia Bruce and Melvyn Douglas. Ever since making *The Casino Murder Case* with Paul Lukas and Rosalind Russell, Metro had been taking out insurance, looking for a new team that clicked like Powell and Loy. Not only were they concerned about Powell's living long enough to make another picture, but Loy herself, who was quite difficult to get along with and anything but the perfect wife off-screen, was constantly after the studio to give her major star buildup like that of Joan Crawford and Greta Garbo.

Fast Company (M-G-M, 1938) was one substitute team attempt. Melvyn Douglas and Florence Rice were cast as a team of bibliophiles who are regularly stumbling into murder. In this case, it was rare book collector George Zucco who gets done in. Edward Buzzell directed, and much was made in the screenplay about the hero getting shot in the posterior, forcing him to wear a pneumatic tube for comfort. Edwin L. Marin directed the second entry, *Fast and Loose* (M-G-M, 1939), this time starring Robert Montgomery and Rosalind Russell as the married bibliophiles. Harry Kurnitz did the screenplay. The plot has the two encounter a series of murders in connection with a rare Shakespeare manuscript. There was so little ingenuity in the script that this time Montgomery gets shot in the posterior and so *he* has to use a pneumatic tube! *Fast and Furious* (M-G-M, 1939) was the last of it. Franchot Tone and Ann Sothern played the couple. Busby Berkeley directed. Harry Kurnitz wrote the screenplay. Murder occurred in connection with a phony beauty contest, but, thankfully, there was no need of a third pneumatic tube.

Columbia sought to compete with *There's Always a Woman* (Columbia, 1938). The picture starred Melvyn Douglas and Joan Blondell as a husband and wife detective team. *There's That Woman Again* (Columbia, 1939) was a follow-up picture. Melvyn Douglas had the same role, but his wife was changed to Virginia Bruce. It wasn't a very good picture, but it convinced Metro that the team of Douglas and Bruce, on loan-out for the film, might be worth trying as Nick and Nora Charles.

Fortunately, Powell recovered. However, beginning with *After the Thin Man*, Loy was growing more and more resentful of being kept in her part of Nora, and she wasn't pleased that Powell got so many more scenes than she did. The press mentioned none of this. The fan magazines carried reams of copy about the marvelous rapport between Powell and Loy on the set. In fact, as early as 1935, in a lawsuit against Metro to get out of her contract, Loy had claimed "the manner in which I have been handled finally led to a near breakdown."

The studio nevertheless tried its best to exploit the alliance. *Love Crazy* (M-G-M, 1941) cast Powell and Loy as Steven and Susan Ireland. Gail Patrick, Jack Carson, and Sidney Blackmer rounded out the leading players, with a plot that found Powell committed to a mental institution in a comic effort to keep his marriage together. This was at least a cut above the previous year's *I Love*

Nick and Nora Charles surprised Louis B. Mayer, who didn't think a successful marriage on the screen could be box office because it would try audience credibility. The Hays office kept them in separate beds.

PHOTO COURTESY OF METRO-GOLDWYN-MAYER.

You Again (M-G-M, 1940), a Powell and Loy takeoff on Metro's *Dr. Jekyll and Mr. Hyde* (M-G-M, 1941), which was then in preproduction with Spencer Tracy in the lead role.

While Hammett was working on *Another Thin Man*, he wrote to Lillian Hellman that his story was little better than a "new fable of how Nick loved Nora and Nora loved Nick." He commented in a sprightly tone that while there might be better writers than he was "nobody ever invented a more insufferably smug pair of characters. They can't take that away from me, even for $40,000."

Hammett was satisfied to have Metro think up its own story for *Shadow of the Thin Man* (M-G-M, 1941). After the success of her play *The Little Foxes*, Lillian Hellman bought a farm some distance from Pleasantville, New York. Hammett stayed there with her, as did other men friends, many of whom presumably looked to her for advice or counsel. Hellman called the farm Hardscrabble, after the road which it bordered. "The Adventures of the Thin Man" began regular broadcasts in 1941 over NBC, with Lester Damon and Claudia Morgan as Nick and Nora. Hammett was amused, and perhaps a bit depressed, that this one property should prove so popular. Warner Brothers was in the process of remaking *The Maltese Falcon*, and Paramount was preparing a new screen treatment of *The Glass Key*. When war was declared, Hammett went for a physical, enlisting in the U. S. Army. Despite the tuberculosis which still showed on his X-rays, he was admitted to the service. He was stationed several places, but for most of the war he was in the Aleutians. He liked the rigor and discipline of military life, working with the younger men, editing the base newspaper, and from all indications was happier than he had ever been in Hollywood or New York.

Harry Kurnitz, who had worked on the Metro husband and wife bibliophile mystery series, worked on the screenplay for *Shadow of the Thin Man* (M-G-M, 1941), along with Irving Brecher, who was credited on screen, and Manfred B. Lee and Frederic Dannay, the duo who wrote the Ellery Queen stories, who were not. Hunt Stromberg produced and Woody Van Dyke directed. Between *Another* and *Shadow*, Powell met Diana Lewis at Chasen's Restaurant. She was a twenty-one-year-old contract player at Metro. When they went upstairs together, Mousie, as she was called, sang from a collection of old songs. "I couldn't believe that a youngster like her knew the oldies. I went for her and knew she was for me." A couple of nights later, William Powell and Diana Lewis eloped and were married.

It was with *Shadow* that Metro decided to make a soap-opera saga out of the Thin Man as the studio was doing with Andy Hardy. By spacing out the pictures, every two or three years the audience could tune in to see how the Charles family was doing. Dickie Hall was cast as Nick, Jr. Most of the film was given over to Nick and Nora going to a wrestling match where Nora becomes far too animated, or to Nick taking little Nick, who is four, to an amusement park. Contract players like Donna Reed and Barry Nelson carried much of the plot line, which was thin to begin with. Nick refuses to become involved in an investigation of a murdered jockey, but when one reporter is killed and another is suspected of having done it, Nick does come out of retirement.

Myrna Loy was ambivalent about being spanked in *The Thin Man Goes Home*
(M-G-M, 1944). PHOTO COURTESY OF METRO-GOLDWYN-MAYER.

William Powell, now that he was married, began spending more and more
time in Palm Springs. Powell's only son, William, Jr., entered the military and had
a brilliant war record. He later turned to screenwriting. Tragically, in his forty-
third year, in 1968, he stabbed himself to death with a paring knife.

Myrna Loy was active. On June 7, 1942, she divorced Arthur Hornblow and
a week later married John Hertz, Jr., an advertising man and heir. She quit pictures and went to New York, disgusted at the treatment she had been given by
Hollywood and the way her talent had been overlooked. Metro released her
from her contract provided she would agree to continue in the Thin Man series,
whenever such a picture was scheduled. On August 21, 1944, at Cuernavaca,
Mexico, she divorced Hertz on the grounds of mental cruelty. She married
Gene Markey, a screenwriter and producer whose star seemed on the rise, on
January 3, 1946. She confided to the press that *this* was love at first sight.

In between, she had time for *The Thin Man Goes Home* (M-G-M, 1944).
Robert Riskin and Harry Kurnitz did the screenplay. Richard Thorpe directed.
Nowhere before had there been any indication that Nick had a family, but here
it was: Harry Davenport as Dr. Charles and Lucile Watson as his mother, living
in Judge Hardy's house on the Metro back lot. In one scene Nick becomes
so exasperated with Nora that he takes her over his knee and paddles her derri-

ère with a newspaper. Myrna Loy objected to it because it was undignified, but not as adamantly as when Columbia Pictures offered her a role in *Murder by Death* (Columbia, 1976), and she turned down the part because she felt it would ruin her image as Nora Charles to have her seventy-one-year-old bottom pinched by David Niven! On the whole, however, *The Thin Man Goes Home* proved superior to the two entries which preceded it—as a comedy vehicle, if nothing else.

Loy commented bitterly to the trades that, while there had once been a give-and-take camaraderie between Nick and Nora, it had now disintegrated into nothing more than a sequence of gagging wisecracks. Treating murder as essentially comic belonged, in her words, to a "cynical, satiated time" which had passed. "I can't blame them" she said of M-G-M, "for not liking it. After all, the men who knew what it was about—Dash Hammett and Hunt Stromberg—have gone elsewhere and our director Woody Van Dyke is dead."

Meanwhile the would-be competitors kept coming. *A Night to Remember* (Columbia, 1943) featured Loretta Young and her author husband Brian Aherne as newlyweds moving into a Greenwich Village basement apartment where they are at once drawn into a murder plot. Gale Sondergaard was in the cast, and it only lacked George Zucco to make the farce complete.

Loretta Young and Brian Aherne appeared in a spin-off of the Thin Man, *A Night to Remember* (Columbia, 1943). It did not become a series.
PHOTO COURTESY OF COLUMBIA PICTURES INDUSTRIES.

Louis B. Mayer loved the "family" atmosphere of the Thin Man films. This, of course, had nothing at all to do with Hammett's original conception, but then, Metro now literally owned the property. When Hammett was released from the military, he went to live again with Lillian Hellman. Ellery Queen was intent on bringing all of Hammett's pulp stories back into print. Lillian Hellman nixed the idea, according to Frederic Dannay, claiming that it would only re-emphasize what she considered to be Hammett's inferior work. Hammett, however, was independent enough to give Queen the go-ahead. It is, therefore, Ellery Queen that we have to thank for preserving at least in some measure the brilliance, purity, and vividness of all Hammett's early prose. In the ensuing years, even though he tried living alone for a time in a cabin he rented in Katonah, New York, Hammett became Lillian Hellman's protectorate. Maybe she felt that he was the prize she should have for all her years of loveless existence; maybe, because after the Government persecuted him he was totally dependent on her just to survive, he didn't mind. But capture him she did; work was out of the question. Dashiell Hammett, according to friends, had become totally dependent on Lillian Hellman's emotional support. She reflects harshly in *Scoundrel Time* (Little, Brown, 1976) on what her attachment to Hammett cost her, but she was nearly as radical in her ideas as he was. She and Hammett both belonged to the period of Roosevelt liberalism in American politics. They were ill-prepared for the swingback which, it would seem, followed with an equal fanaticism.

Song of the Thin Man (M-G-M, 1947) was the swan song. Leon Ames was in the cast, as were Patricia Morison, playing Ames's wife, Dean Stockwell as Nick, Jr., Keenan Wynn, Gloria Grahame, Jayne Meadows, Tom Dugan, and Jimmy Flavin as a cop. Edward Buzzell directed, and Steve Fisher and Nat Perrin, among others, worked on the screenplay. Nat Perrin produced.

"Bill Powell was bored with his role," Ames told me, "but that was nothing. Here was America's happiest couple. For years, the public had believed that. And they never talked. Except when they were in front of the camera. I'm surprised that they talked even then. Some of the time, they talked to the camera alone and the film was edited together later."

Metro's publicity stressed the fact that Asta, who had died in 1946, had been replaced by his son, Asta, Jr., and was doubled by his brother, Zip. Like Metro's other canine star, Lassie, Asta, Jr., was given his own dressing room.

Myrna Loy was clearly fed up with being cast as the perfect wife. Nor was the dialogue anything like what it had been. When Nick finds a razor blade in the murder room, he reflects for a moment, saying, "Somerset Maugham? No, it couldn't have been."

William Bishop played a mobster who is blackmailing Patricia Morison. Nick takes the case and Asta is more of a companion to him than Nora. His wife is busy in their ultramodern apartment being a nondrinking mother. It is so advanced that the Charles family even has a television set! At the finish, Patricia mercilessly drills Leon Ames until her gun is empty.

Myrna Loy did have a brief cameo appearance as Powell's wife in *The Senator Was Indiscreet* (Universal, 1947). In the autumn of 1950, she divorced Gene

Myrna Loy began showing strain by the end of the series in this scene with Leon
Ames and Patricia Morison from *Song of the Thin Man* (M-G-M, 1947).

PHOTO COURTESY OF METRO-GOLDWYN-MAYER.

Markey, in Mexico, although she herself was not present. Her grounds were
mental cruelty. In June 1951, she married Howland H. Sargeant, a Deputy Assistant Secretary of State. They were divorced in 1960.

William Powell spent his declining years on the screen in a series of minor vehicles and character roles, until his permanent retirement in 1955. Increasing
deafness made him disinclined to give interviews, although he liked quiet parties
with friends, golf outings, and sitting in front of the television set he had installed in his bedroom in his Palm Springs home, which, over the years, he kept
adding to until it was of sizable proportions. Powell, when he was younger, used
to comment that people are born with one of two temperaments, happy or melancholy, and that he was somewhere between them. But his final years in Palm

Springs, surrounded by the incessant heat and the seclusion, with his television and Mousie, and the drink in his hand and the occasional cigarette, even hardness of hearing did not interfere with the sense of philosophical tranquillity which surrounded him.

For Dashiell Hammett, it was otherwise. He very much loved the United States. He never once in his life ventured outside its borders except to the Aleutians during the war. Unlike Lillian Hellman, who used her stage success to promote herself into trips to Europe, particularly Russia and Yugoslavia, talks with President Tito and attempted conferences with Marshal Stalin, invariably making a noise in the press about political matters, Hammett's flirtation with Marxism, if more radical, was also more internal. He knew the American system was hopelessly corrupt, but he wasn't certain any other system would be preferable. His alienation was deep-seated, but, again unlike Lillian Hellman, it never turned to scathing hatred.

In April 1951, Hammett was called before Federal Justice Sylvester Ryan. Hammett didn't know the names of the contributors to the bail-bond fund of the Civil Rights Congress, which had permitted several Communist sympathizers to elude the arm of the law. Though Hammett himself was a Marxist, he was not a member of the Communist Party. However, he had contributed to their funding campaigns. He wasn't going to be dictated to by any judge, and so he went to prison for six months, on a charge of contempt of court. He was confined to the Federal House of Detention on West Street in New York and then transferred to the Federal Correctional Institute near Ashland, Kentucky. His duties while in prison consisted of washing out prison latrines.

When Hammett was released, he was called before the House Un-American Activities Committee. Wisconsin Senator Joseph McCarthy was investigating, among other things, Communist infiltration into the books issued by the U. S. Information Service. McCarthy asked him, "Mr. Hammett, if you were spending, as we are, over $100,000,000 a year on an information program allegedly for the purpose of fighting Communism, and if you were in charge of that program to fight Communism, would you purchase the works of some 75 Communist authors and distribute their works throughout the world, placing our official stamp of approval on those works?"

Hammett replied: "Well, I think—of course, I don't know—if I were fighting Communism I don't think I would give people any books at all."

The Federal government decided that any writer who felt that way should be denied any income from his creative works. The McCarthy hearings did nothing to Hammett, but the Internal Revenue Service found him guilty of tax evasion and seized all royalties from his books, radio, and motion picture residuals for the remainder of his life. Lillian Hellman, at one time, had broken off relations with Hammett because of his excessive drinking. When in a state of severe delirium tremens, he gave his word to his physician that he would quit, and he did. Hellman rented a cabin with a tower-like windmill in the upper room of which Hammett lived. He didn't complain when on two different occasions, citizens wanting to take justice in their own hands fired shots at him, hoping for a hit.

"I was insensitive to the real problems of the sick—how to stand up, how to walk down stairs," Lillian Hellman wrote later. "It was a terrible thing to watch, since the last days of emphysema deprive the brain of oxygen, to see a man who had such respect for thinking and intelligence not able to think, and for him to know it."

She took care of him through those enfeebling years. She would not let him enter a veterans' hospital when he was no longer able to take care of himself. She withheld from him the knowledge that he was dying of inoperable lung cancer. Toward the very end of his life, Lillian offered Hammett a second martini. He was by then accustomed to only one drink a day. He refused. She told him that she never thought she would live to see the day when she would offer him a drink and want him to have it. He replied that he had never dreamed that he would turn one down.

He was hospitalized and he died. The funeral eulogy was delivered by Lillian Hellman. Quentin Reynolds, Bennett Cerf, Dorothy Parker, Leonard Bernstein, Arthur Kober, and Lionel Trilling were among those in attendance. Hellman told her listeners that Hammett was "a man of simple honor and great bravery. He didn't always think very well of the society we live in and yet when it punished him he made no complaint against it and had no anger about the punishment."

Lillian Hellman became the executrix of Dashiell Hammett's literary estate. While it was possible, she had been the favorite of those in political power; when national sentiments changed, she sought refuge in the academy and sympathy from readers, particularly deprived peoples with whom she attempted to establish an affinity. New York continued to love her, while Hollywood blacklisted her for a time. When she came back to motion picture work, it was with a screenplay for the film *The Chase* (Columbia, 1966). Most of what she has written has been inspired by hate. But, in a way, you cannot blame her, since she was, perhaps undeservedly, thrust into the political limelight for a time, and then humiliated, without ever really understanding that when an artist becomes a politician he or she ceases to be an artist. She has her reasons for withholding Hammett's legacy from the American public. All of which only means that the final assessment of Dashiell Hammett and his place in American letters must await a future generation.

Columbia stressed the radio tie-in.   PHOTO COURTESY OF COLUMBIA PICTURES INDUSTRIES.

SEVEN:
The Detective in Transition

> "Have a slug of Scotch, Queen. Do you good."
> "Brandy," said Mr. Queen faintly.
> "Brandy!" The Boy Wonder looked pleased.
> "Now there's a man with discriminating
> boozing habits. It gets your ticker after a while,
> but look at all the fun you have waiting for
> coronary thrombosis."
>
> *from* The Four of Hearts
> *by* Ellery Queen

I

I do not know what would have happened to the detective Ellery Queen had he not gone to Hollywood. Two novels which I have enjoyed came out of it, *The Devil to Pay* (Stokes, 1938) and *The Four of Hearts* (Stokes, 1938). I might also add that I am in a minority in liking the series of photoplays Columbia Pictures made based on the Queen characters filmed in the early Forties. Frederic Dannay, the surviving member of the writing team that created Ellery Queen, summed up these cinematic adventures with a laconic suggestion that I should "leave sleeping dogs lie."

In his biography of the Queen phenomenon, Francis M. Nevins, Jr., went so far as to ask his readers, "Is there something about the Queen canon that defies translation into cinematic terms?" This question comes after a rather critical and dissenting survey of the Queen films. Ralph Bellamy, who played Ellery Queen at Columbia, was not much more encouraging than Dannay when first, on the telephone, I mentioned wanting to discuss the pictures with him at length.

"But," he objected, "I didn't know anyone thought they were very good."

I felt like an Ellery Queen mystery that begins with a negative clue and works, for most of the book, in the wrong direction.

There is very little written about the Hollywood novel as a distinct literary genre, but there does exist a wealth of novels about people in Hollywood. Ellery Queen's two novels, which I have mentioned, and his later *The Origin of Evil* (Little, Brown, 1951), would appear to fall into this group. It would further seem, according to most, if not all, novels about Hollywood that it is a place where, if you're lucky, you can become the person that otherwise you can only pretend to be. This is the premise with which an author begins before he shows you the reverse of the fantasy, or the effects of the corruption of the fantasy.

The Hollywood of Ellery Queen's novels found people eating in restaurants in the shape of hats or lighthouses, streetcars rattling down Hollywood Boulevard, and movie studios where it was merely a joke if a writer was paid for six weeks to do nothing and then was offered a new contract at $1,500 a week. Hollywood seemed strange and inexplicable to Ellery because he was born and nurtured in New York, and in truth, although Hollywood changed forever the manner in which the Ellery Queen stories were written, it was to New York that he hurriedly retreated.

Frederic Dannay was born Daniel Nathan in 1905; his cousin Manford Lepofsky was born the same year. Both changed their names early in life. As Manfred B. Lee and Frederic Dannay they chose yet other names under which to write their books, principally Ellery Queen, but also Barnaby Ross for a series of four books in the early Thirties.

Lee's childhood was spent in Brooklyn. Early in his life, he enacted an "inner immigration," turning to books as a refuge from the violence in the streets. Dannay's parents moved from New York City to the upstate town of Elmira, where he could roam through the fields and woods. He longed to be a poet. His family returned to New York City in 1917. It was then, while he was suffering from an abscess of the left ear, that his aunt offered him a book to read: *The Adventures of Sherlock Holmes.* It was only the beginning of a lifetime fascination with detective fiction. Lee, in the meantime, went to Boys High School, in New York City, with his cousin and on to New York University, where Dannay did not go. It was Lee's expressed desire to be the Shakespeare of the twentieth century. In the late Twenties, when both the cousins were out of school, Dannay working as a copywriter for an advertising agency and Lee in publicity for a film company, they would meet for lunch. *McClure's Magazine,* in conjunction with the publishing firm of Frederick A. Stokes, was offering a $7,500 prize in a contest open to the public to see who might produce the best detective story. The cousins worked nights and weekends to produce *The Roman Hat Mystery* (Stokes, 1929).

McClure's let word out that the cousins' submission had won, and then the magazine was bought up by *The Smart Set.* The new owners picked a different entry. The prize money was suddenly forfeit, but Stokes agreed to publish the book anyway. The contest had required that entrants use pseudonyms. The cousins chose Ellery Queen, not only because he was the detective in the book, but because they felt the double identification would be easily remembered by the public. The book was heavily indebted to S. S. Van Dine. Inspector Queen of the New York Police Department shared a Manhattan apartment with his son Ellery, a bookish, pompous young man with a pince-nez, and Djuna, their houseboy. The Queens had a penchant for referring to each other in casual conversation by various names out of Greek mythology or classical literature. This wasn't the only trying thing about the book. The plot was ludicrously involuted and the guilty person is scarcely a character, merely a name that you meet along with a great many other names in the course of the investigation.

Years later, in 1975, when the newest Ellery Queen television series was about to go on the air, Rand Lee, one of Manfred Lee's children from his second marriage, wrote an article for *TV Guide*. "It amazes me now," he remarked, "that Dad and Cousin Fred could have produced so many Queen works. Their writing methods were unorthodox. All the time I was growing up they did their work over the telephone. Cousin Fred plotted all the novels and short stories, creating the characters and providing Dad with detailed skeletons that Dad fleshed out. Their talents determined this arrangement. I'm sure Dad could never have come up with the sort of plots Fred did. Dad's and Fred's differences were not only professional. Often I would pick up the phone, hoping the line was free, and put down the receiver moments later with Dad's and Fred's arguing voices still ringing in my ears. On one occasion, Dad threw down a plot outline and exclaimed, 'He gives me the most ridiculous characters to work with and expects me to make them realistic!' Cousin Fred probably felt the same frustration sometimes with Dad's treatment of his plots."

I may observe at this juncture that in all the Ellery Queen books I have read I find the plots the most disappointing thing about their fiction. Manfred Lee, as the years went past, seemed to improve immensely in his ability to give verisimilitude and substance to the plots, but, do what he might, the plots were still farfetched or absurd. In *The Chinese Orange Mystery* (Stokes, 1934), one of my favorite examples, the mystery is why a man is murdered in a room where all his clothes are put on backwards, all the furniture turned upside down, and all the pictures turned toward the wall. The other clue is that the man's tie is missing. The solution to such a set of circumstances, totally fair and equitable to the reader, or so Queen's supporters assert, is arrived at through logical deduction. And what does Ellery deduce? Why, the man must have been a cleric. The murderer wanted to hide his identity by turning everything around. Wearing a Roman collar, however, the man had *no* tie to lose.

Beyond the early books, which all had geographical titles until the authors wearied of the gimmick, the plots don't improve but they do get more complicated. In *The Four of Hearts*, when two reigning Hollywood stars decide to marry, they are spirited off in an airplane and poisoned. The man who spirited them off in pilot's togs didn't do it. The woman's rich father is dead but being impersonated by a down-and-out actor. Finally, in order to trap the murderer, Ellery has the son and daughter of the couple, also intent on matrimony, get married in the same airplane so this clever murderer can try to put them out of the way in the very same way!

Yet I continue to read Ellery Queen, as many people do. It is due, I suppose, to the quality of characterization which crept into the books in the Forties, especially in *Calamity Town* (Little, Brown, 1942) and *Cat of Many Tails* (Little, Brown, 1949). The plots are, if anything, more topsy-turvy, but the descriptions of the small New England township in *Calamity Town* or of New York City in *Cat* in summer during a heat wave when the city is preyed upon by a psychopathic killer are extremely well written.

The cousins, in the mid Thirties, quit their jobs and devoted themselves to writing detective stories full time. They tried editing a magazine, which failed after the first few issues. They tried writing for the slicks. They went on a lecture tour in which they both wore masks, Dannay as Barnaby Ross, Manfred Lee as Ellery Queen. Their desire was to thoroughly merchandise Ellery Queen by means of adroit promotion so that they could enjoy the success that S. S. Van Dine had fallen into more or less by accident. The cousins were highly conscious of changing trends in detective fiction. When Philo Vance went into eclipse and the hard-boiled operatives began to take his place, Ellery dropped his pince-nez and Inspector Queen gave up their houseboy.

Hollywood first approached the cousins in the form of Nat Levine, who had founded Mascot Pictures in the late Twenties to produce chapter plays. He became so adept at it that he soon branched out into feature production. He was a trail blazer in the low budget field. When Mascot merged in 1935 with Consolidated Film Industries to form Republic, Levine was placed in charge of production. By this time he had introduced science fiction to the Western and he had introduced Gene Autry to motion pictures. He introduced at the same time two detectives to the screen, Dick Tracy and Ellery Queen. Tracy fared the better of the two, and I will have more to say about him in the next chapter.

The Spanish Cape Mystery (Stokes, 1935) was purchased for the screen and filmed the same year it was published. The cousins very much wanted a movie sale, and Levine was their only taker. The nominal producer on the film was M. H. Hoffman, who had started out the Thirties by setting up Allied Pictures to produce and distribute a series of Hoot Gibson specials. Lewis D. Collins, who worked primarily in low budget Westerns and action films, was the director. Donald Cook played Ellery Queen. The same year he would portray the crazy murderer in *The Casino Murder Case* (M-G-M, 1935). Helen Twelvetrees was the heroine and a romantic attraction developed between her and Ellery. The production manager on *The Spanish Cape Mystery* (Republic, 1935) was Rudolph C. Flothow, who would later be involved in detective series at Columbia Pictures.

The screenwriters at Republic cannot really be held to account for the manner in which they dealt with Ellery. The novels themselves at this time had no characterization of Ellery or the inspector on which they could base a treatment. The emphasis in the novels was all on the puzzle and its solution; it was a study in mental gymnastics.

Guy Usher, almost invariably a heavy, was cast as Inspector Queen, but he was in the picture for only the first few scenes. Berton Churchill played Judge Macklin, who accompanies Ellery on a vacation in California to Spanish Cape, a secluded area overlooking the Pacific. Helen Twelvetrees' uncle is kidnaped by

EVEN SHERLOCK HOLMES' HAIR IS UP IN THE AIR OVER THIS ELLERY QUEEN THRILLER!

"SPANISH CAPE *Mystery*"

STARRING
HELEN TWELVETREES
WITH
DONALD COOK

Directed by LEWIS COLLINS
Adaptation and Screen Play by
ALBERT DeMOND
FROM THE NOVEL BY
ELLERY QUEEN
A REPUBLIC PICTURE

REPUBLIC PICTURES

As you can see from this trade ad, *The Spanish Cape Mystery* (Republic, 1935) was supposed to be a thriller. It wasn't quite that.

PHOTO COURTESY OF VIEWS & REVIEWS MAGAZINE.

Richard Cramer, and she is tied up in the cottage Ellery and the judge intend to occupy. From then on, with her discovery, one member after another of her relations is murdered. Harry Stubbs was cast as the loudmouthed, quick-to-act sheriff. One change was made from the novel. The first victim, instead of being nude when he is found, is provided a pair of swimming trunks. The judge in one scene reads *The Adventures of Ellery Queen.* Enough of the original plot was carried over to make the picture somewhat confusing.

The Mandarin Mystery (Republic, 1937) was made the next year and was based on *The Chinese Orange Mystery.* What were the screenwriters to do?

You cannot really film an Ellery Queen plot, and the characters as yet were so undeveloped that a producing company ended up simply buying the title of a book. So it was felt the screenplay should become a comedy of the absurd. Charlotte Henry arrives in New York with a postage stamp worth $50,000. She is implicated in a murder where the victim has his clothes turned backwards. Ellery was portrayed by vaudevillian Eddie Quillan and presented as an idiot. Wade Boteler was Inspector Queen. The picture was so terrible I really would prefer to say no more about it.

Republic chose to purchase no more novels. The cousins turned to radio and worked energetically to get Ellery his own radio series. Their efforts proved successful, especially when they volunteered to write the scripts for next to nothing until a sponsor could be found. "The Adventures of Ellery Queen" was first aired over CBS on June 18, 1939. To engage feminine interest, Ellery was given his secretary/companion, Nikki Porter, portrayed on radio by Marian Shockley, whose short-lived career in films was highlighted by playing opposite Tim McCoy in the chapter play *Heroes of the Flame* (Universal, 1931).

The cousins had collaborated on a stage play with Lowell Brentano titled *Danger, Men Working*. It closed after a few nights in Baltimore and Philadelphia. Paramount Pictures, however, bought the play and Bertram Milhauser adapted it for the screen. It was released as *The Crime Nobody Saw* (Paramount, 1937) and starred Lew Ayres. Their agent got the cousins a short stint in the Paramount writing department which served as the basis for the novels *The Devil to Pay* and *The Four of Hearts* but otherwise led nowhere. Ellery Queen in these two novels still has little if any personality, but in this case it can be justified insofar as the cousins devised these books with the hope of securing a sale to motion pictures and an actor could easily flesh out the character.

Larry Darmour now made his entrance. He had produced the Mickey McGuire shorts with Mickey Rooney before he began producing features for Majestic release. When Majestic Pictures was merged into Republic, Darmour switched releasing to Columbia Pictures and began with a series of Ken Maynard Westerns in the mid Thirties. In 1940 he commenced negotiations with the cousins. He wanted to bring Ellery Queen to the screen in a new series for Columbia release and he wanted the cousins to work on the screenplays. Darmour had been producing a series of Jack Holt pictures for Columbia, and the studio agreed with him that Ellery Queen would be a good substitute. The Gulf Oil Company sponsored the Ellery Queen radio programs and went along with the idea of the cousins doing their Ellery Queen broadcasts on the West Coast while working on scripts for Darmour.

To portray Ellery Queen, Darmour selected Ralph Bellamy, who had just appeared in a hilarious role in Howard Hawks's *His Girl Friday* (Columbia, 1940), released in January. Darmour felt the Queen role would build a new image for him. The cousins were scheduled to begin work in August of 1940. The contract called for Darmour to make three Ellery Queen pictures a year.

Larry Darmour was himself a native of Flushing, New York, where he was born on January 8, 1895. It's kind of an important date because, despite his youth, he didn't live out his contract with Ellery Queen. He was educated at

Princeton University. He was sufficiently successful, especially after he began independent production for Columbia release, to have his own production facilities on Santa Monica Boulevard. Among his projects in the Thirties was the production of Columbia's chapter plays. While he wanted the cousins to work on the screenplays for the Ellery Queen series for at least their name value and their approval of what was being done, he had very little actual work for them to do. Their agent in the meantime arranged for them to do a short stint at Metro-Goldwyn-Mayer in the writing department. Nothing came of their efforts at Darmour's studio or at Metro, nor at Columbia Pictures. The cousins had fought so fiercely when they were at Paramount that others had complained about the battles as a disruption to their work. It was the same other places. Columbia wanted original story ideas from the cousins, as did Metro and Darmour. Instead, there were a great many violent hassles. The upshot of it all was that the cousins were back in New York by November 1940, having done little more than a polish job on *Shadow of the Thin Man* (M-G-M, 1941), for which, as I have noted, they received no screen credit.

Ralph Bellamy was born on June 17, 1904, in Chicago. He was expelled from high school for smoking beneath the auditorium stage. He held various jobs from soda jerk, office clerk, sheep pelt sorter, to fruit picker. When his father fired him from a Chicago advertising company, it was then that Bellamy decided he would enter the theater. He joined a stock company in Madison, Wisconsin. In the ensuing years, he was with nine different stock companies and played over four hundred roles. He was well received in *Town Boy* on Broadway in 1928, but the play opened on a Friday and closed after the Saturday matinee. Joseph Schenck of United Artists brought him to Hollywood in 1931, but the contract proved disagreeable and the two parted company. Bellamy free-lanced for the next several years until he signed with Columbia Pictures. While there, he was on suspension some of the time, but he finally learned how to deal with Harry Cohn, Columbia's production chief.

Bellamy liked to play tennis. In 1934, he and his good friend Charles Farrell went to Palm Springs. Few people lived there, and most of them were tuberculars. Fewer still had ever heard of it. Together the two bought a tract of land from Alva Hicks for $3,500, amounting to some fifty-three acres. A short time later they sold forty acres for $5,000 and on the remaining land hoped to build a tennis court for themselves. They ended up building several, added a swimming pool, and before long the place had so overgrown itself—the debts had mounted to a whopping $78,000—that they determined the best thing they could do would be to open for the public and call it the Palm Springs Raquette Club. Pooling names of their friends and acquaintances, they sent out letters to 173 people, offering single memberships at $50 each, family memberships at $75. The idea was to keep the price low and get everyone to join. No one joined. So they tried the next best thing. They raised the prices. By the time the price had ascended to $650 a year, there was a waiting list.

Bellamy has married four times. His third marriage to organist Ethel Smith made headlines when he sued her for desertion and she cross-filed for half his income. She was accustomed to locking their apartment door from the inside at

11:45 P.M. If he wasn't home by that time, he didn't get in; but she would heap abuse on him from behind the door.

Ralph Bellamy is a gracious man who, as he has aged, has grown more and more distinguished. As Ralph Bellamy is today, he reminds you more of Franklin D. Roosevelt in *Sunrise at Campobello* than Ellery Queen in *Ellery Queen, Master Detective*. He had had a role in *Rosemary's Baby* (Paramount, 1968), and I asked him about Roman Polanski.

"He's a brilliant director," Bellamy replied, "and a perfectionist. You will go through a scene again and again until you hear this chuckle from behind the cameras. Then you know that Polanski liked it, that he got what he wanted. I was offered John Huston's role in *Chinatown* [Paramount, 1974]. I turned it down. I was sent a script that didn't look at all like the picture when Polanski finished with it. It read like a porno film. They had me in an incestuous situation already on the third page."

"I'm aware," I said, "that you can't believe anyone could possibly like the Ellery Queen pictures you made, but, as I told you, I'm one of the few who does."

"I don't know how," he protested. "They were such quickie pictures. We would shoot them in ten days, I guess. They didn't like retakes. It was on those pictures that I learned how to ruin a take when I didn't like how a scene was going."

"You made four of them."

"I didn't know they'd made more than those four until you told me. I was signed to appear in four Ellery Queen pictures at $25,000 a picture. Larry Darmour was the producer, but he wasn't around very much. Rudolph Flothow—his family was associated with the Sells-Floto Circus—was always on the set. I had to go to New York to meet with Lee and Dannay. They took me around to different squad rooms so I would get a feel for what went on in one. Many years later, when I was starring in *Detective Story* on Broadway, I went to squad rooms again to see what they were like. I spent six weeks in squad rooms. When Chester Morris was going to take the show on the road, I took him to squad rooms, the 52nd Precinct, I guess it was. He had never been in one before."

"You'd think he'd have known what they were like, since in every Boston Blackie picture he usually ended up in one."

We laughed.

"A funny thing happened while we were there," Bellamy continued. "There were three blacks lined up along a counter who were being questioned about various things, with cops on the other side typing out reports, with two fingers, you know. The lieutenant had a little office off to one side. The sergeant was moving around between the three blacks. The window was open and a bat flew in through the wire mesh. You wouldn't believe the commotion. The sergeant pulled out his gun and was about to shoot at it. The lieutenant came out of his office and yelled, 'Not in here. You'll hit someone.' So all of them together, the sergeant, the lieutenant, the guy behind the desk, the three blacks, they're like a ballet moving around the squad room in unison, chasing this bat. Finally one of them stuns the bat with a broom. The lieutenant is aware again of where he is. 'All right, you guys,' he yells at the blacks. 'Get back over to the desk.' If you put that into a movie, nobody would believe it, how well they all worked together. When William Wyler was going to film the movie version of *Detective Story*, I took *him* to a squad room. I've got pretty familiar with them."

"What did you dislike about the Ellery Queen films?" I asked. "They had good casts."

"Yes, they did. They had very good casts. The problem was the scripts. I was after Darmour to get better scripts, but he would listen to me and then come back that it wasn't in the budget. There were a lot of setups every day, and some location shooting. But Flothow was always there behind the director, a skinny fellow, what was his name?"

"James Hogan."

"Yes, Hogan. He didn't have a chance to direct. The idea was just to get the picture finished."

"Did you read the Ellery Queen novels before you worked in the pictures, to give you an idea of the character?"

"No," said Bellamy, "not before the series came up. I read a lot of them later. I liked Erle Stanley Gardner. I knew him when he had that place in the desert. He raised horses out there, but he was afraid of them. He might feed them, when he walked up to the corral, but get on top of one, never! He didn't like telephones. He didn't have a phone on the ranch. He didn't want to be disturbed. If you wanted to get hold of Gardner, you had to call a Standard station in Temecula. When one of Gardner's crew drove past the station, the attendant would flag him down and relay the message. If Gardner thought it important, he would come down to the station and make a call from the telephone there."

"You also worked in *Woman in the Dark* [RKO, 1934], based on one of Dashiell Hammett's stories."

"I made that in New York," Bellamy said, nodding.

"Did you meet Hammett? I understand he took quite an interest in the filming of his properties."

"Yes, I did. He was in New York with Lillian Hellman. They were with that Algonquin crowd. Dotty Parker, George Kaufman, that group. He was a nice, intellectual man, with a sharp, witty sense of humor. When I was the head of the Actors Equity, I was responsible for setting up our guidelines concerning membership, you known, when there was the trouble. We were much more liberal than the other guilds. I sent out copies of the guidelines. I remember Bernard Baruch telephoned me. He said I should come out to his home at seven-thirty in the morning. He lived on Long Island. I went out there. He was sitting behind his desk. 'I'm not afraid of many things,' he told me. 'But I'm very much afraid of Communism.' I didn't know what to say. He had been a liberal adviser for so many years. So I said nothing."

Ellery Queen, Master Detective (Columbia, 1940) was directed by Kurt Neumann. It was, in my opinion (as the reader doubtless has already deduced), an excellent film. Bellamy combined the bookishness of the Ellery of the novels with a worldliness that the character needed to appeal to a larger audience. I have recorded how it came late in Philo Vance's film career that he felt the first promptings of the heart. Well, it wasn't so belated in Ellery's. He was flirtatious from the beginning, absurdly so, with Eddie Quillan grinning into his bouquet of posies for a newspaper photograph. But in *Master Detective*, the amorous relationship between Ellery and Nikki Porter was given a dignity, and therefore integrity, that was lacking in the two previous entries from Republic. Charley Grapewin was cast as Inspector Queen. James Burke was the loutish but lovable Sergeant Velie.

According to what information is available, there are three versions, wholly different, as to how Ellery came to meet Nikki: one developed on radio, one in the stories, and the one developed in *Master Detective*, this last growing logically from the plot. Nikki is intent on becoming a mystery writer. She finds herself knee-deep in mayhem when she happens upon a case of villainy that begins with the discovery of the corpse of the head of a health-faddist empire. There is no weapon in the vicinity of the crime. Fred Niblo, that fabulously paid director of the first *Ben Hur* (M-G-M, 1926), was cast as the victim. Inspector Queen and the police, Ellery, and Nikki all head up their own investigations, but even so there's a lot happening, since the murderer is uncommonly enterprising. Michael Whalen, who had been a reporter/detective himself during the Thirties, played Dr. James Rogers. Katherine DeMille, Byron Foulger, and that brassy-voiced heavy Douglas Fowley rounded out the cast. By the fade, Nikki was so impressed by Ellery's detecting skill she agreed to come to work for him, typing his manuscripts.

If you believe everything you read in the trades, *Ellery Queen's Penthouse Mystery* (Columbia, 1941) was better than *Master Detective*. Eric Taylor was credited with the screenplay for *Master Detective*. He stressed comic elements in the plot to give the production a highly humorous tone. He went further in this direction in *Penthouse Mystery*, so much so that at times what was intended as comedy was not funny. James Hogan was the director. The influence of the Thin Man series was apparent in reverse. Ellery and Nikki are unmarried but obviously in love with each other. Taylor, and Hogan with him, must have felt that it was preferable to have them squabbling. Probably the biggest mystery in the film is how Ellery ever gets a book written. Not only is Nikki attractive and perfectly willing to show off her figure—which in the Seventies would have kept them in the bedroom most of the time—but she also likes to write her own stories on Queen's time, and gets carried away doing her own investigations. It is my suspicion that the "you're fired—I quit" state of mind precedes the commitment of the bedroom, so I suppose the relationship has to be accepted on these intolerably adolescent terms. Charley Grapewin and James Burke were back in their respective roles as Inspector Queen and Sergeant Velie.

The plot involved two murders for possession of a fantastically valuable collection of jewels from China brought to the United States to assist, via the proceeds, in the Chinese war effort. The plot was reworked for a Lone Wolf feature a couple of months later. Anna May Wong was around to distract the viewer in one way; Tom Dugan and Mantan Moreland to achieve the same effect in another. Columbia Pictures and the cousins evidently thought enough

One can imagine Ralph Bellamy with such a look in his eye getting a lot of work done.

PHOTO COURTESY OF COLUMBIA PICTURES INDUSTRIES.

of the plots of these entries to fictionalize them in book form. Ellery Queen arranged for their reissue in paperback format in 1968.

There may have been an additional motive for the cousins having done this. In late November 1940, Frederic Dannay suffered an automobile accident which left him in critical condition with several broken ribs, severe internal injuries, and shock. On January 15, 1941, *Variety* announced that Dannay was on his way to Florida for a month's vacation, during which time he hoped to recuperate. The cousins had started work on a new mystery novel and they indicated that they were planning on staying in touch by telephone and wire. The only problem with the novel, as it turned out, was that it used the same basic plot as Agatha Christie's *And Then There Were None* (Dodd, Mead, 1939), so that idea had to be scrapped. The next novel, *Calamity Town* (Little, Brown, 1942),

Charley Grapewin played Inspector Queen, here in the center between James Burke (left) and Ralph Bellamy.   PHOTO COURTESY OF COLUMBIA PICTURES INDUSTRIES.

Nikki Porter smarting off in *Ellery Queen and the Perfect Crime* (Columbia, 1941).
PHOTO COURTESY OF COLUMBIA PICTURES INDUSTRIES.

which most readers consider to be their best, was more than a year away from publication.

The Devil to Pay was made the basis for *Ellery Queen and the Perfect Crime* (Columbia, 1941). Larry Darmour's contract with the cousins permitted him to use any of their published stories as the plot line for a photoplay. It followed the novel rather closely, even to the identity of the murderer. However, it is precisely the plot where every Ellery Queen novel breaks down, in the denouement, the mechanics of the murder. The reviews were nearly unanimous in stressing that it was this element which removed much of the human interest built up in the various characters and their fates. The dialogue ran heavily toward comedy, much of it the result of antics between the police, portrayed by Charley Grapewin and James Burke, and Ellery and Nikki, at it again. The picture, if it had been played straight and another murderer substituted, might have been a compelling drama. It turned out considerably less than that.

Ellery Queen and the Murder Ring (Columbia, 1941) was based on *The Dutch Shoe Mystery* (Stokes, 1931). Leon Ames was cast as the son of the rich Mrs. Stack, who is strangled to death in her own hospital while undergoing an operation. I thought his presence would afford an excellent opportunity to ask him what it was like being on the set of an Ellery Queen movie.

"You know," Ames said, "I'm glad you asked me that. I'll never forget that picture. Do you know why?"

I was about to suggest that perhaps it was due to the high artistic merit of the film or the brilliance of the cast, but the devilish grin on his face made me hesitate.

"No, Leon, why?"

"Because Ralph Bellamy was . . . how old? He was in his mid-thirties at least and he didn't know how to tie a tie. I remember I had to teach him how."

James Hogan directed this entry, as he had the previous two. Gertrude Purcell assisted Eric Taylor on the screenplay. If anything, the picture was played more than ever for comedy, so much so that you find yourself laughing almost all the way through—not exactly the fashion in which you might expect to respond to the serious business of murder. But then, look at the casting. The head of Mrs. Stack's hospital, the chief physician, is none other than George Zucco, and he is maniacally zany with a heart condition that constantly interrupts any conversation he might have by prompting a spasmodic attack. Paul Hurst and Tom Dugan are cast as a pair of incompetent mobsters hired by Leon Ames to get rid of his mother. They fail in their attempt, except that Paul Hurst breaks his leg. So, his leg in a giant cast, Hurst is in the same hospital with his victim, who suffered some injuries when they ran her car off the road. Tom Dugan spends at least a fifth of the picture wheeling Hurst around in an effort to get him out of the hospital after the old lady is killed. Then there is a comic switch in bodies with even more hilarity. Hillary Brooke, not looking at all like herself, was way down in the cast under the screen name Jean Fenwick, playing Leon Ames's sister. In one scene, after doing some investigating, Ellery gets Nikki to his hospital room and tries to give her some dictation on his current novel. Tom Dugan unfortunately proves a disruption, and then the comedy begins anew.

With the departure of Ralph Bellamy, William Gargan seemed a wise choice as a substitute in the role. He had been playing private detectives or police detectives throughout the late Thirties and into the Forties. James Hogan was as firmly situated as director for the series by this time as Eric Taylor was as the series' scenarist. But the emphasis was shifted slightly in the screenplay to accommodate a different characterization of Ellery as both businesslike and professional. Instead of the laughs deriving from screwball characters, the emphasis was now on what is better called "situation" comedy.

Close Call for Ellery Queen (Columbia, 1942) was Gargan's first entry. Ellery is primarily an investigator, secondarily a crime author. He wants Nikki to stay out of the case. Ellery is required to do more detecting than either deducing, as he did in the novels, or creating comic charades, as he did in prior films.

Before *Desperate Chance for Ellery Queen* (Columbia, 1942) could enter production, Larry Darmour died. His widow, Alice Darmour, announced in the trades that she intended to carry on production on the Columbia chapter play then in progress and the two Ellery Queen films scheduled for release that year. The cousins by this time were quite pleased with the series, but they wanted the number of entries to be increased from three a year to four. Columbia Pictures, in contrast, wanted to cut back the number to two. An altercation swiftly evolved. Columbia wanted to commence still another series of detective films coinciding with the new Boston Blackie series. The cousins were adamant.

Desperate Chance was at best a routine picture. *Enemy Agents Meet Ellery Queen* (Columbia, 1942) got Ellery into the war effort, Hogan and Taylor again presiding. The cast was a good one, with Gale Sondergaard, Gilbert Roland, Sig Rumann, and Minor Watson added to Gargan, Margaret Lindsay, Grapewin, and Burke. The plot was possessed of much legitimate humor: the picture was certainly the best entry William Gargan made, and among the finest in the series. Columbia had decided that it would drop the option to renew rather than give in to the cousins' demands for four pictures a year. It was mentioned in the trades that both William Gargan and Margaret Lindsay would be otherwise used to complete their studio contracts.

William Gargan, with Margaret Lindsay smiling at him, was a more sober Ellery Queen.   PHOTO COURTESY OF COLUMBIA PICTURES INDUSTRIES.

Enemy Agents actually marks Ellery Queen's last theatrical appearance. The radio series continued for some years, and every so often Ellery Queen was revived in a series on television, none of which seemed to have staying power. The reason for this may be found, I suspect, in the adolescent limitations of the formula, even if the plots are ignored. A parent-child relationship is not intrinsically as interesting or as capable of variety as relationships based on friendship, be it between two men or a man and a woman.

The French director Claude Chabrol discovered Ellery Queen during the Occupation when he came upon a cache of the Queen novels in an attic. He later tried to bring one of the books to the screen in *Ten Days' Wonder* (Levitt-Pickman, 1972), but Ellery wasn't present and the picture proved a failure both commercially and artistically.

Frederic Dannay, the more scholarly of the cousins, was the impetus behind *Ellery Queen's Mystery Magazine,* which began in the Forties and specialized in detective and crime short stories. He also began the long series of anthologies. Although Ellery became more human in the novels of succeeding decades, the plots never attained a commensurate maturity and sophistication, as I have already pointed out. The last novels and stories in the Queen canon, if Francis Nevins is to be believed (and I must rely on him, since I have not read all of them), were increasingly repetitious, employing plot ingredients from older Queen books. *The Finishing Stroke* (Little, Brown, 1958) was presumably to be the end of the saga, but, despite this intention, the team kept right on writing.

On April 2, 1971, Manfred Lee suffered a fatal heart attack. For years he had lived on his estate in Roxbury, Connecticut, while collaborating over the telephone and occasionally in person with Dannay, who chose to live in Larchmont, New York. Dannay's second wife died in 1972 and there is a possibility he may marry again. The life of neither man was spectacular, as was the case with so many of their contemporaries, but together they constituted a professional writing team that approached their work with a shrewd sense of marketing which accounted for a significant measure of their success.

Ellery Queen, for all that, never really became integrated into the American detective story, if men like Hammett, Chandler, and Gardner are to be considered as its most eloquent practitioners. To an extent, Ellery Queen didn't graduate from the fascination with Philo Vance and the English approach to the detective story, which is only another way of saying that in the Ellery Queen stories, ultimately even in the best of them, situation is still more important than character.

II

Leslie Charteris was born Leslie Charles Bowyer Yin on May 12, 1907, of an English mother and a Chinese father. The latter was a physician, and Charteris is pleased to trace his lineage back to the emperors of the Shang dynasty. The city of his birth was Singapore when it was part of the Federated Malay States and the largest port in the world. According to Charteris, when he was very young he began typing out his own magazine. He wrote everything in it, articles, short stories, poems, editorials, serial installments, and a comic strip. Charteris claims that he wasn't very good as an artist, and rather lazy, so his cartoons consisted of stick figures. He later varied one of these to become the symbol for his only memorable literary creation, Simon Templar alias the Saint.

It was his parents' idea that Leslie should go to England for higher education. He preferred writing. When his first book, written during his freshman year at Cambridge, was accepted, he quit school and embarked on a new career. Charteris was motivated by a desire to be unconventional and to become financially well off by doing what he liked best to do. He continued to write English thriller stories, while he worked at various jobs from shipping out on a freighter to working as a bartender in a country inn. He prospected for gold, fished for pearls, tried employment in a tin mine and on a rubber plantation, toured England with a carnival, and drove a bus. In 1926, when he was just setting out on all this, he legally changed his name to Leslie Charteris, based on an admiration for a certain Colonel Francis Charteris, who was, apparently, a bit of a romantic bounder.

By 1928, he wrote his third novel, *Meet the Tiger*, published by Ward, Lock, in which he introduced the Saint. He didn't have to look very far for a model on which to base this dubious hero, who pursued crime for his own enrichment at the expense of criminals who preyed upon the helpless. Quite naturally, he chose himself. He dabbled with a couple of other books in 1929, but from then on, with one exception, he concerned himself exclusively with recounting the Saint's imaginary adventures. As with many British writers at that time, Charteris felt the best markets were in the United States. He moved there in 1932. Nor was he wrong. He was able to get $400 for his first short story and was soon getting $1,000 a story. He went to Hollywood and was hired in the writing department at Paramount Pictures, where he worked on no important pictures. One of them, *Midnight Club* (Paramount, 1933), starring George Raft, stood out in his memory because he managed to see its premiere in the United Kingdom at a theater in Piccadilly.

Inspector Claude Eustace Teal had been the Saint's major adversary at Scotland Yard. When, like Charteris, the Saint switched his activities to the States, he became the bane of Inspector John Fernack of the New York police. The theory has been advanced by a number of critics that the reason for the Saint's sudden popularity, beginning in the mid Thirties, can be traced to the death of Edgar Wallace. Presumably, the thriller style in which Wallace wrote (Charteris contributed his stories for many years to a British magazine called *The Thriller*) was so popular with readers that they searched about until they could latch upon another who did almost as well at it. Certainly Charteris' stories have always *moved*, but that part of Edgar Wallace's peculiar charm, peopling his books with such a wide assortment of characters and constantly concocting new plot variations, was denied to Charteris. He arrived at a single plot structure: the Saint outfoxing the police and bringing criminals to justice where, by any other means, they would escape. While Wallace anticipated this notion in his novel *Four Just Men*, with Charteris it was the all of his fiction. The Saint did not really take the police seriously, but he was relatively convinced that there was such a concept as justice. In this belief, he was even more romantic than the inevitable plots in which he was involved.

Although Charteris became a naturalized American citizen in 1946, he was thoroughly English in his sympathies. Like his character, he still felt that the British, for all their pomp and obsession with tradition, were capable in their pursuit of life of achieving a grace denied to their American counterparts. It is probably to this circumstance alone that we owe the fact that in all instances where the Saint was brought to the screen, as much as Charteris disapproved of the studio treatments, his character was portrayed by British actors.

Charteris' first novel with an American setting was *The Saint in New York* (Hodder & Stoughton, 1935). It was this book which RKO Radio Pictures purchased and made the basis for their first Saint film. William Sistrom was the producer. Sistrom was born in Lincolnshire, England, on March 19, 1886, and got his start with Carl Laemmle at Universal Pictures. He joined RKO in 1935 and the studio wisely put him in charge of the Saint project. To play Simon Templar, Sistrom cast romantic actor Louis Hayward, who was born in Johannesburg, South Africa, on Sistrom's birthday in 1909. Hayward was a slight man, 154 pounds, a trifle over five feet ten, dark brown hair, blue eyes, a foppish lover at Warner Brothers, an actor whose screen work began in British films, and, to agent and producer Edward Small, at least, the embodiment of Louis XIV and the Count of Monte Cristo. Charteris didn't care at all for him. The screenplay was by Charles Kaufman and Mortimer Offner. Ben Holmes, who had directed *The Plot Thickens* (RKO, 1936) for Sistrom, was the director.

The script followed the novel rather closely. New York is laid low by a crime wave. Right-thinking citizens and the police despair of the judicial system. The Crime Commission, of its own accord and despite his off-color reputation, decides to call in the Saint. If judges won't serve the cause of justice, perhaps the Saint will. Templar is charged with bringing six gangsters to justice, or, barring that, eliminating them. Kay Sutton provided the love interest. The dialogue was good. Disguised as a nun, the Saint shoots a gangster just as he is about to plug a policeman. The mystery is who is the Big Fellow? Most pictures of this ilk during the Thirties were concerned with the Big Fellow. The Saint dispatches all the underlings before he comes, finally and inevitably, to the Big Fellow, who is, just as inevitably, the most upright of all, the man who hired him to start with. Jack Carson was cast, rather effectively, as a gunman.

The Saint in New York (RKO, 1938) was, on the whole, an entertaining film. Jonathan Hale, who was cast as Inspector Fernack, returned for the next picture, *The Saint Strikes Back* (RKO, 1939). Louis Hayward didn't. RKO decided to cast on loan-out from Twentieth Century-Fox character actor George Sanders.

Sanders was born on July 3, 1906, in St. Petersburg, Russia. His parents were of Scottish descent. When the Russian Revolution broke out, the family fled across the icy wastes of Finland, finally settling in England. George thought little of English schools, and his masters, apparently, thought even less of him, for he recalled leaving school "with a sense of utter worthlessness and the conviction that I was too stupid to cope with life." He tried working in a textile factory but ended up moving to Argentina to find employment with a cigarette-manufacturing company. He was put into market research. He enjoyed the position as much as he did the wilds of South America. When he was chucked out, he went to work for a different tobacco company, this time in Chile. According to Sanders, this job was terminated when he found himself in prison for fighting a duel with the fiancé of the woman with whom he was sleeping. He returned to England in relative disgrace. Soon he went to work for an advertising agency where he met Greer Garson, who was head of the market research and information department. She induced him to join her amateur theatrical group and read a part. He worked for varying periods of time, all brief, in several plays before he was cast in a role in a British film. When the British and Dominion studio, where he was under contract, burned down, Sanders went to Hollywood and was contracted by Twentieth Century-Fox to appear in the Tyrone Power vehicle *Lloyds of London* (20th-Fox, 1936). I have already recorded how dissatisfied he was with the parts he had in pictures like *Mr. Moto's Last Warning* (20th-Fox, 1939). He accepted the role of the Saint because it was the lead and might come to something better.

The Saint Strikes Back cast Wendy Barrie, later intimate with mobster Bugsy Siegel, as a gang leader. The script was based on the Charteris novel *Angels of Doom*, published in England as *She Was a Lady* (Hodder & Stoughton, 1931). The screenplay was by John Twist, who set the story in San Francisco. Robert Sisk produced and John Farrow directed. The plot showed the Saint dancing at a New Year's party where one of Wendy's men tries to shoot someone. New York sends Inspector Fernack to help the San Francisco police protect the community from the insidious Saint. Before Fernack can leave, the Saint arrives in New York and accompanies Fernack to the West Coast. The mystery becomes more involved once the Saint begins to search for a master criminal named Waldman. He not only finds him but, at the same time, proves Wendy's deceased father, a policeman, was dishonestly framed.

George Sanders next had to go to England to make a picture. RKO thought the situation presented a ready opportunity for him to do another Saint film, this time on location. *The Saint in London* (RKO, 1939) was produced by William Sistrom. John Paddy Carstairs directed. Lynn Root and Frank Fenton, a writing team who had recently joined RKO and about whom I will have more to say presently, prepared the screenplay, which was based on Charteris' short story "The Million Pound Day." It is probably Sanders' best performance in the role. The script perceived the Saint as a combination of a modern Robin Hood and a British Jesse James.

Charteris didn't like it, no matter what the public enthusiasm or the critical response. He felt Sanders at six foot three inches was better cast physically than Louis Hayward at five feet ten, but that's where his approval stopped and his grousing began. Jack Hively, who was assigned to direct the next entry, *The Saint's Double Trouble* (RKO, 1940), once suggested to me that perhaps most of Charteris' complaining about the casting of the Saint derived from a frustrated desire to enact the role himself. Certainly, Charteris closely identified with the character and had even gone so far as to say that he might readily be considered an inferior brother to the Saint. Hively thought him eccentric.

"My objections to what RKO 'did with' the Saint," Charteris responded to this assertion, "did not arise from a frustrated desire to star in the part myself. Much as I should have enjoyed this, a glance in the mirror was quite enough to show me that it just wasn't in the cards. However, this did not make me any happier about what I considered the gross miscasting of Louis Hayward, George Sanders, and Hugh Sinclair [who would later be cast]. I hardly think that this concern for good casting makes me 'eccentric.' If the adjective is meant to refer to any other of my idiosyncrasies, it rather surprises me. I have always thought that I was regarded, personally, as rather a square.

"Even more than the casting, I objected to RKO's treatment of character and story lines. Here of course I was fighting the well-known 'producer syndrome,' which automatically makes any film executive a genius who knows how much better a character could be portrayed and a plot developed than the stupid original creator. *The Saint Overboard* [Hodder & Stoughton, 1936] was an incidental case in point. It was one of the books which RKO bought, but by the time the studio wizards had got through with it, there was absolutely nothing left of the original except the title, and that was by then totally irrelevant. I therefore prevailed on them to give me back the title, and thus preserved my property intact for possible future use."

I am not about to comment on Charteris' abilities as a storyteller. Obviously, he has for many, many years pleased a wide audience. However, fiction is only one medium, and it is a commonplace that what works in one medium may not in another. Any film based on a book, as Stanley Kramer, among many others, has said, starts out by chopping out three fourths of the narrative plot merely for considerations of time. Charteris had his own ideas of his character, but they were not necessarily cinematic; and, even if they might have been, they were not necessarily commercially viable to moviegoers. RKO had a successful product, and the capable personnel they had making the films did not particularly appreciate Charteris' outspoken and volatile interference.

The Saint's Double Trouble found George Sanders playing a dual role, that of the Saint and that of Duke Plato, a gangster. It was a bit difficult for the viewer to tell the two Sanders portrayals apart, since he was obviously bored with both characters. The look-alike aspect did bring about some amusing routines. In the end, Sanders tricks his alter ego into getting shot. Jack Hively directed. Cliff Reid, who had to his credit producing pictures like *The Lost Patrol* (RKO, 1934), directed by John Ford, *The Informer* (RKO, 1935), also directed by Ford, and Howard Hawks's *Bringing up Baby* (RKO, 1938), took over as producer on the Saint series. Obviously the studio regarded the pictures as important.

None of this phased Charteris, however much it may explain why RKO put up with him for as long as they did. Charteris criticized the studio for what he felt to be George Sanders' sneering attitude and the lack of total and detailed dependence on literal translation of his character and plots to the screen. RKO tried Lee Marcus as executive producer. He had formerly been in distribution and a past president of the RKO subsidiary Pathé Pictures. It was conceded to Charteris that he could tinker with the screenplay for the next entry, *The Saint Takes Over* (RKO, 1940), written by Frank Fenton and Lynn Root. He was credited on publicity as having made script revisions.

For all that, the plot wasn't extensively different. Wendy Barrie was back, this time as the murderess. Jack Hively directed. Organized crime arranges for Jonathan Hale as Inspector Fernack to be kicked off the force. The Saint determines to help his ambivalent friend. One after another, the underworld members to the conspiracy are killed off. Paul Guilfoyle as Purley Gates is the Saint's sidekick. Although Wendy confesses, she is shot at the fade. One interesting alteration is the Saint's insistence in the picture that all he accomplishes must be done by legally acceptable means.

On October 27, 1940, George Sanders gave up his cherished bachelor status for the first time in a completely unpublicized marriage to Elsie M. Poole, who worked in pictures under the professional name of Susan Larson. Even then, George was a somewhat contemplative and retiring man who liked, among other things, to spend his time reading or sleeping. He insisted that he was meant for a life of idleness and that it was the only thing he was good at. When, in 1960, he came to write his autobiography, *Memoirs of a Professional Cad*, he produced a book which had a fascinating beginning but then dropped off, as if, after the first few chapters, he had become bored even with retelling the story of his life. He did manage to quote enough arcane literature, though, to substantiate his far-flung reading. Among others, he quoted Ovid:

> *Till man's last day is come we should not dare,*
> *Of happiness to say what was his share,*
> *For of no man can it be truly said,*
> *That he is happy till he first be dead.*

The Saint in Palm Springs (RKO, 1941) was George Sanders' last appearance as the Saint. Jack Hively directed. Howard Benedict produced. Jerry Cady, who had collaborated at Fox on detective films like *Mr. Moto's Gamble* (20th-Fox, 1938) and *Time Out for Murder* (20th-Fox, 1938), did the screenplay. Leslie Charteris personally provided the story outline. Jonathan Hale as Fernack asks the Saint to protect a friend of his going to Palm Springs with $200,000 in postage stamps on his person. When the friend is shot, Simon holds onto the stamps and intends to turn them over to the friend's niece, played by Wendy Barrie of course. Paul Guilfoyle is back as Purley Gates. Wendy's part builds all through the second half of the picture, as does the emphasis on the Saint's roving eye for feminine pulchritude. By the final scene, the Saint has both exposed the murderer, with a minimum of location shooting, and saved the stamps.

There seemed to be no quieting Charteris. He announced to the trades that he was so unhappy with the series that he was about to undertake producing Saint pictures himself. Nothing came of the plan. Because of the war, RKO decided to spend funds that were frozen in England and produce the films there. *The Saint's Vacation* (RKO, 1941) featured Hugh Sinclair in the role of the Saint and was made with an all-British cast. Sinclair, being a British actor himself, might well keep the appeal of the character for the foreign market and, anyway, taking the Saint back to London might in some measure have a soothing effect on Charteris.

The picture was directed by Leslie Fenton. Leslie Charteris was credited on the screen for the screenplay in collaboration with Jeffrey Dell, based on *The Saint's Getaway* (Hodder & Stoughton, 1932). Monte Hayward is the Saint's sidekick, an obvious parody of Louis Hayward. Sally Gray follows Simon and Monte on vacation. They see a man murdered. All the excitement is over a music box. The same train is employed that Alfred Hitchcock used for *The Lady Vanishes* (Gaumont-British, 1938), and Cecil Parker, who played a stuffy coward in Hitchcock's thriller, is the master villain in *Vacation*. In the music box plans are hidden for a coveted sound detector.

Charteris got his vengeance. Hugh Sinclair was no George Sanders and he wasn't even fair as the Saint. Audiences knew it, and the picture died. Charteris knew it, but then he had been saying all along they should cast Cary Grant in the role.

Louis Hayward, seen here in *The Saint's Girl Friday* (RKO, 1954), both began the series and ended it. PHOTO COURTESY OF THE NATIONAL FILM ARCHIVE.

There is, to be sure, an epilogue of sorts. RKO tried Hugh Sinclair in one more film before dropping the series entirely. In 1954, RKO came back into the scene when they agreed to distribute a British film, *The Saint's Girl Friday* (RKO, 1954), made by Royal Productions in London and produced by Julian Lesser, Sol Lesser's son. Sol Lesser owned, among other properties, the screen rights to Tarzan. Louis Hayward again played the Saint, thus starting and ending the series. Charteris had a percentage in the picture, but it did not inspire a new series. An attempt in France with Felix Marten in the lead so disgusted Charteris that he refused to further license the company to use his character.

In the Forties, Charteris, besides continuing to write Saint stories, scripted the Sherlock Holmes radio series featuring Basil Rathbone and Nigel Bruce. He felt vindicated in 1962 when the British-produced television series of hour-long Saint adventures went into production and played successfully for six years around the world with Roger Moore in the Simon Templar role. In fact, he was so enthusiastic that, having run out of ideas himself, he permitted scripts from the television series to be turned into fictional treatments and published as further adventures of the Saint in printed form. But even here, he hadn't really changed. When the producers altered the locations of his stories, or plot elements, he balked, complained, and took his right of script approval quite seriously, to say the least. What finished the series this time was Roger Moore's resolve not to make any more episodes. "I really mean it," Moore was quoted at the time. "I am becoming lazy in my work because I have a set character. I have been playing the Saint non-stop for six years and have made 120 complete stories, and now I need a change of pace."

Leslie Charteris' readers feel somewhat differently. They have remained loyal to the romantic hero of the books for four decades, and, even now, the stories are issued and reissued. The character has captured the popular imagination, although a new generation saw him otherwise than in the droll, sophisticated, but bored image consummately projected by George Sanders.

III

It was so cool in the courtyard that, for the moment, glancing at the swimming pool, I almost forgot that I was in Palm Springs. Maurice Geraghty had admitted me through the wrought-iron gate and led me through several doors of the sloping house. He told me that he preferred to divide his time between living in England and living here, in the desert. I remarked in return that in writing this book I had spent more time in the desert than anywhere else.

As we entered the living room, Maury showed me a painting done by his sister, Carmelita Geraghty, now deceased, who had been a leading lady in Westerns with Buck Jones and Ken Maynard.

Over glasses of sassafras, I got down to business.

"You know, your records are extraordinary," I said. He had supplied me with budget sheets in great detail on every Falcon picture he had produced. "Howard Benedict started the series, didn't he?"

"He did," Geraghty agreed. "He produced the first three, before he went over to Universal to work on their Sherlock Holmes series."

Howard Benedict was born in Baltimore, Maryland, on June 10, 1902, and was educated at Johns Hopkins University. He worked for the wire services and then in public relations, among others for the late Noel Coward. In March 1935 he joined RKO.

In view of the many problems the studio was having with Leslie Charteris, they pounced upon a new formula for a detective series. George Sanders, of course, would continue to star. The new detective was based on a character from a short story, "Gay Falcon," by Michael Arlen. The character was named Gay Stanhope Falcon, changed to Gay Laurence for the film. Arlen was born in Rustchuk, Bulgaria, in 1895 and christened Dikran Kuyumjian. His parents were Armenian. As a boy he went to England and in 1922 became naturalized as a British subject. He was educated at Malvern College and, in 1928, married Countess Atalanta Mercati. Until the outbreak of the Second World War, the couple lived at Cannes. Arlen made his splash in the literary world writing a novel in English called *The Green Hat* (Doran, 1924). It earned him better than a half million dollars in royalties. But try as he might, Arlen couldn't duplicate his success. The explanation is evident. Arlen concerned himself with a social order that was obsolete even as he wrote about it. Intimates described him as alert, vain, friendly, a man who relished his acclaim and, unabashedly, pursued the acquisition of wealth. Apparently his superficial sophistication concealed an incredible naïveté. Arlen wasn't very ambitious. He worked as a screenwriter for a time and produced exactly nothing. But why should he? His hard-boiled short story, written in a new style, was sold to RKO for $5,490. The picture *The Gay Falcon* upon release proved a success and generated a series. Arlen again collected royalties.

"I was perfectly content," Arlen commented on his stint in the M-G-M story department. "I'm a very indolent man. I'm a loller." More than a bit of Arlen's personality crept into Gay Laurence's screen characterization. George Sanders didn't have to try too hard to project anything differently in the role than he had when he was playing the Saint. The whole situation only further outraged Leslie Charteris.

"RKO's switch to the Falcon was not, in my opinion, due to my discontent," Charteris confided to me, "which I credit them with a completely pachydermatous ability to have survived. Simply and practically, RKO discovered that by attributing their formula to the Michael Arlen character, they were able to save a huge percentage of the price they were paying me. Indeed, their promotion of the Falcon was so shamelessly liable as to allow many dull-witted audiences to think they were still getting the Saint. I brought a suit against them for 'unfair competition.'"

RKO had yet to release *The Saint Meets the Tiger* when this new flare-up with Charteris occurred. Like *The Saint's Vacation*, it had been produced out of funds frozen in England and was part of an attempt to placate Charteris. Hugh Sinclair was again cast as the Saint. It was a very slow and a very dull picture. The plot involved a bank robbery in London of a million pounds. The Tiger is a mystery man, disguising himself as a newspaper photographer. Paul Stein directed. Disgusted with the whole business, RKO settled out of court with Charteris and then sold *The Saint Meets the Tiger* to Republic Pictures for American release. It was a smart deal. RKO received a sum sufficient to pay them back their investment in the picture and what they had to pay Charteris. Eventually distribution rights reverted to RKO.

The Gay Falcon (RKO, 1941) preceded *The Saint Meets the Tiger* into production. It started in preproduction in March 1941, and shooting commenced in June 1941, lasting into July. *The Saint Meets the Tiger* began in production at RKO British studios in late June 1941. The studio was relieved to be rid of Charteris, but probably no more so than he was to be quit of them. The working title for *The Gay Falcon* was *Meet the Viking*, possibly as a result of an attempt to keep it a secret.

In all fairness to RKO, the studio felt what it had to sell was George Sanders personality and not the Saint. The closer they got to Charteris' character in the stories, the less popular the pictures proved. *The Gay Falcon* for a plot presented Gay Laurence as a rich playboy engaged to Anne Hunter, who insists that, if he is to marry her, he must give up his interest in crime and other women. Neither is easy, especially since Wendy Barrie is back as a girl in distress who inveigles the Falcon to help her. An adept notion of casting made Allen Jenkins the Falcon's assistant. He played very well opposite Sanders, particularly when you remember how rueful he was in the Paul Drake role in the Warner Brothers Perry Mason films. His advice to Barrie, when she first approaches Gay, is to "try Ellery Queen." But Barrie succeeds and the Falcon ends up exposing a ring of high-class jewel thieves. Arthur Shields was the police captain, Ed Brophy and Eddie Dunn teaming up as a dumb duo assigned to keep tabs on the Falcon. Hans Conried was given a comic role as a police artist. The studio liked the picture. Irving Reis directed. A follow-up picture went into production in late August 1941, titled *A Date with the Falcon*.

Lynn Root and Frank Fenton did the screenplay for the second Falcon entry. Root and Fenton, when they had worked together in the story department at Twentieth Century-Fox, authored the screenplay for *While New York Sleeps* (20th-Fox, 1939). This was the second entry in a new detective series that Fox thought held promise. The first picture was *Time Out For Murder* (20th-Fox, 1938). In the pictures Michael Whalen played a roving reporter with Chick Chandler as a news photographer and comic support. Cliff Clark was a dumb cop in *Time Out*. Root and Fenton made the dumb cop idea a duo for *While New York Sleeps*. Lucky Humberstone directed both pictures and stressed the comic elements in the inevitable conflict between Whalen and the police. Edward Gargan, the elder brother of William Gargan, was teamed with Clark for the second entry.

When Root and Fenton prepared the screenplay for *A Date with the Falcon*, they brought the idea of the dumb duo along with them. Michael Arlen received $2,250 for the use of his characters and the budget charged off $7,000 to Root and Fenton for the script. James Gleason replaced Arthur Shields in the role of Captain Mike O'Hara and Edward Gargan played Mike's assistant, Bates.

Here is some typical dialogue. Bates is sent by O'Hara to pick up Waldo Sampson, a noted scientist working on a formula to manufacture synthetic diamonds inexpensively. Bates finds Sampson gone and calls his chief.

GARGAN: This is Bates, Chief. Sampson ain't here. —How do I know where he went? Well, after making a thorough examination, I deduced the following facts. First, he must have forgotten the combination to his safe. —What do you mean, how do I know? A guy don't blow his safe open if he remembers the numbers.

O'HARA: That's great!

GARGAN: He must have forgotten where he put something 'cause he wrecked the place trying to find it before he left. But I come right over and he ain't here. Yuh got nothing to worry about, Chief. I'll get right on his trail.

O'HARA: (yelling) And when it runs out, meet me in front of the employment office on Sixth Avenue.

Of course, O'Hara is forced, under the circumstances, to involve his friend the Falcon. Sanders, if anything, is even more sardonic than when he was playing the Saint. At one point, he is kidnaped by the gang of thugs after the diamond formula. In a car stopped at an intersection, Sanders sticks out his tongue at two patrolmen in a police car. They make an issue of it. Sanders pretends he's drunk and even slaps one of the officers. That does it. He's arrested and thus eludes his captors. Sanders especially enjoyed scenes like this, since it permitted him to act naturally.

A Date with the Falcon was first released in January 1942. *The Falcon Takes Over* (RKO, 1942) was the third entry. Wendy Barrie, who had been in the first two pictures, was dropped, being replaced by Lynn Bari, only one of the girls Sanders finds infinitely charming. Much of the comedy went to Allen Jenkins as Goldy and his jousts with Moose Malloy, six foot five of retired wrestler, and heated interrogations by the police, Gleason and Gargan back but none the wiser. This was the final Falcon film Howard Benedict produced. Irving Reis directed it, as he had other entries, but the plot wasn't quite up to standard. Arlen was paid his $2,250, and Root and Fenton got their $7,000, but the screenplay was based on *Farewell, My Lovely* (Knopf, 1942), a novel by Raymond Chandler. Sanders had his moments, however. After he finishes questioning Anne Revere, who plays Jessie Florian, an old alcoholic widow of a deceased tavern keeper, she throws a whiskey bottle at him and it smashes against the door. Sanders sticks his head around the corner and shakes his head disparagingly.

"Tch, tch, now you won't get your deposit back."

Sanders still had a split contract between Twentieth Century-Fox and RKO Radio. He felt he was getting typecast in the Falcon series and didn't want to make anymore. Opportunities that he got, such as playing Charles Stickland in David L. Loew's splendid adaptation of Somerset Maugham's classic South Sea tale *The Moon and Sixpence* (United Artists, 1942), only reaffirmed his obdurate refusal.

"RKO was very anxious to have Sanders continue in the Falcon series," Geraghty explained. "But their pleading fell on deaf ears. Then one of the

George Sanders preferred to think of himself as a debonair and romantic scoundrel, warming up here to Lynn Bari. PHOTO COURTESY OF VIEWS & REVIEWS MAGAZINE.

bright front-office executives got the idea of offering to co-star George's brother, Tom Conway, just to get another picture out of George. They gave George a glowing picture of how it would make a star of his brother, but, actually, they had no such intentions. They just wanted another picture from George. So it was astonishing to them when Tom Conway caught on right away and carried the series on, even outgrossing the pictures George had made."

Sanders had long ago wearied of supporting his family. He had been instrumental in securing Tom a job as a contract player at RKO. He thought the idea a noble one. Besides, it would make Tom self-sufficient. Although Tom also had been born in St. Petersburg, and had gone to Brighton with George, in fact had once got them expelled from a school by holding a loaded gun on a master, he was more withdrawn than George, more saturnine, with a quiet suavity nourished by heavy drinking. George had seen to it that Tom changed his last name from Sanders to Conway before he was signed at M-G-M. Tom had begun acting in 1933 in Manchester, slightly before George had, and was first signed by M-G-M when Sanders refused to attend a luncheon with Louis B. Mayer. George was disgusted with the role, so obviously Tom should have it.

George Sanders with his usual girl in both Saint and Falcon entries, Wendy Barrie, and his sidekick Allen Jenkins.   PHOTO COURTESY OF MAURICE GERAGHTY.

Basil Rathbone used to tell the story of how he went to New York for a year to appear on Broadway. When he returned to Hollywood, he ran into George Sanders.

"Dear boy," Sanders expostulated, "I thought you were dead. It's been so nice, because I've been getting all of your parts."

Sanders agreed to make *The Falcon's Brother* (RKO, 1942). It cost only $114,965.73 to make, compared to $140,315.70 for *The Falcon Takes Over*. It was shot in fourteen days, compared to twenty days required for *Takes Over*. The reason was that Maurice Geraghty was promoted to producer of the series by RKO.

Maurice Geraghty was born in Rushville, Indiana, on September 29, 1908, two years after his brother Gerald. The brothers attended Princeton. Gerald early began contributing fiction to pulp magazines. He turned to screenwriting and went to work for Mascot Pictures. The company, still specializing in serials, had its offices located above a cement factory across the street on Santa Monica Boulevard from the Hollywood Cemetery. Maury joined Gerald at Mascot. The first picture the two collaborated on was the feature version of the twelve-chapter serial *The Phantom Empire* (Mascot, 1935), which was released as *Radio Ranch*. They stayed together when Mascot was merged into Republic Pictures, working on numerous Republic Westerns with Gene Autry or the Three Mesquiteers. Both also worked for Harry Sherman on the screenplays for the Hopalong Cassidy series released by Paramount. Maury signed with M-G-M for a short stint in the writing department. Then he joined RKO.

"Michael Arlen got his usual fee for *The Falcon's Brother*, I suppose," I said to Geraghty.

"Yes," Maury replied. "We paid him for the story on each picture. But he had nothing to do with them. He would send in a paragraph or so every time, a suggestion, but nothing I got seemed fertile. Arlen was happy, and so was RKO."

Production began on June 25, 1942. The writing chores were somewhat dispersed. Earl Fenton, Frank Fenton's brother, was paid $1,400, working until June 1. Frank Fenton and Lynn Root each got $500 working to completion. Craig Rice was paid $875, working until June 6. Stuart Palmer got $1,750, working until June 13. Craig Rice and Stuart Palmer got screen credit.

"The picture was made in the days when studios had total control of screen credits," Geraghty commented, "and arbitrarily decided who got credit. Thus, for example, when I started writing screenplays I was left off of credit and naturally objected. I was told it was not studio policy to give credit to a writer on his first few screenplays. After I had written a few more, they said, I would get credit. The Writers Guild now determines credits, which is more fair, but not entirely. I inherited Fenton and Root, who had written all the previous scripts before I was hired to take over. It seems that someone had promised them they would be the producers of the Falcon series after Benedict left. I came in with no knowledge of this and found there was a certain lack of communication between Fenton and Root and myself. I thought they had done a fine job on the series and wanted them, but couldn't get anywhere. So they left and I got other

Tom Conway and George Sanders face to face in *The Falcon's Brother* (RKO, 1942).   PHOTO COURTESY OF MAURICE GERAGHTY.

writers. Their charges on the budget do not necessarily reflect what they were paid on *The Falcon's Brother*. Craig Rice and Stuart Palmer were both top mystery-detective writers. The accountants juggled around the charges since Palmer and Rice were writing on other scripts, and their charges were no doubt all plunked into *Brother* because the studio expected the series to fold."

George Sanders was paid $14,000 for his last entry. Tom Conway only got his contracted salary.

"What were they like?"

"Oh," Maury responded, "George had personality. He was extravagant. He loved parties on yachts. He had a certain giggle."

"George once said he sold his yacht because he preferred being a guest to being a host."

"That was George," Maury agreed. "Tom was different. He was one-dimensional, but full of overtones and undertones. He was self-conscious, shy. But when the series became more and more popular, it went to his head. He thought *he* was the series and the only reason for its success."

The dumb cop duo of Cliff Clark and Edward Gargan that traveled between studios and ended up hassling the Falcon. PHOTO COURTESY OF MAURICE GERAGHTY.

Conway and all the other stock RKO players combined cost only $2,500. The spelling of the Falcon's last name was altered from Laurence to Lawrence.

Consistent with the war themes of the time, both Gay and Tom Lawrence are battling Nazi spies who use magazine covers to relay messages. The plot is to assassinate Dr. DeSola. Cliff Clark replaced James Gleason opposite Edward Gargan, so now the team from the Twentieth Century-Fox pictures was together again. In a gallant act, George sacrifices his life, taking the bullet intended for DeSola. Tom swears to carry on in his memory.

Throughout the picture Sanders was humdrum. He had none of the wit and amusement he had had earlier. It probably wasn't deliberate, but it did tend to accentuate Tom Conway's performance.

Edward Dmytryk was signed to direct the next picture, Tom Conway's first starring vehicle, *The Falcon Strikes Back* (RKO, 1943). Dmytryk and Maurice Geraghty had gone to Hollywood High together and were both on the football team, Maury right end, Eddie left end.

I had asked Dmytryk about George Sanders.

"He was a lot like Warren William," Dmytryk recalled. "You know, a do-it-yourselfer. He built a telescope. He loved math. We would exchange difficult math problems when we were both at RKO. But he was a very unhappy man, very insecure. Like Warren William, too, George began early in his career to make poor pictures. He was always being forced to make pictures he didn't want to make. A man has to adjust to this sort of thing, and it isn't easy. Men become so vain, worried about how they look. Women actually dominate them because they are so worried about getting old and not being attractive to them. Sanders was like a rebelling teen-ager.

"You have to understand actors. They need a lot of encouragement. I always try to build up their confidence. I take time to try and figure them out. George would be rude one day and the next day he would apologize. But he would compound his problem, because he would become even more rude when he was apologizing."

"Tom Conway wasn't at all like that," I said.

"No, he wasn't. He took a nice walk through a picture. He couldn't really give anything to a part."

Just prior to *The Falcon Strikes Back*, Dmytryk had directed *Hitler's Children* (RKO, 1943) with Tim Holt and Bonita Granville. It cost $178,000 to make and grossed $3,250,000 upon release.

"Was it because you had used Harriet Hilliard in *Confessions of Boston Blackie* [Columbia, 1941] and, of course, in *Sweetheart of the Campus* [Columbia, 1941] that you used her in the Falcon picture?" I asked.

"Yes," Dmytryk replied. "But I must tell you, Jon, that for some reason I simply don't remember much about that particular picture."

Later I mentioned this circumstance to Geraghty as we talked. The house was silent in the desert heat.

"Eddie was one of the finest directors who ever worked in pictures. I didn't know then anything about his being a Marxist, and, if I had, I wouldn't have cared."

I nodded. But I remembered Dmytryk with his graying hair and his lined, solemn face, sitting across from me, his eyes unfathomable.

"People used to come to Hollywood with such enthusiasm," he said. "Some became rich and famous, only to find themselves not any the happier for it."

"And you?" I prompted.

"I was an idealist. When you're young, you think you're doing something so important. You think you can change everything. You really believe in what you're doing."

"You believed enough in what you thought to go to prison for it."

Eddie gazed at me in silence for a long time. Then he sighed.

"Yes, and, all of a sudden, you look around. And you're an old man. Don't forget that. You're just an old man. And you've wasted a lot of your life believing you could change things, only to learn that all that's changed is yourself, you're older."

The plot of *The Falcon Strikes Back* was light years away from us.

Barbara Hale and Tom Conway on the set of *The Falcon out West* (RKO, 1944).
PHOTO COURTESY OF BARBARA HALE WILLIAMS.

Dmytryk was paid $500 a week for five weeks' work. Tom Conway got his stock company salary. The screenplay was the combined result of Edward Dein and Gerald Geraghty, who received credit, and Craig Rice, Stuart Palmer, and Maurice Geraghty, who did not. Craig Rice, who was born Georgiana Ann Randolph in Chicago in 1908, took some time off to ghost a detective novel called *Crime on My Hands*, which was published in 1944 with George Sanders credited as the author. Sanders played himself by name and went about solving a series of murders at a film studio. It was Sanders' swan song to the detective genre. Earlier in the Forties, Craig Rice had similarly ghosted two detective novels for the stripper Gypsy Rose Lee.

Edgar Kennedy, who was starring in a series of short comedies for RKO, was given the part of a crazed puppeteer. He was paid $1,500 a week and guaranteed two weeks' work. But the biggest surprise was Wynne Gibson, perhaps best known for her role of Iris Dawn in *Night After Night* (Paramount, 1932) with George Raft and Mae West. She received $500 a week for two weeks' work. She was thirty-five but looked fifty. Her life hadn't been kind to her, and that's how Dmytryk played it in the picture.

Cliff Clark's character name was Donovan, to distinguish him from the two previous Mike O'Haras. He was back with Edward Gargan again for the sixth entry, with Eddie Dunn as Grimes to consummate the dumbness of the police. *The Falcon in Danger* went into production on April 13, 1943, and took twenty-two days to complete. Three Falcon pictures a year, in release, would earn RKO over a million dollars.

William Clemens, born in Saginaw, Michigan, in 1905, directed the next picture and one of the best in the series, *The Falcon and the Co-eds* (RKO, 1943). It was Clemens who had directed the Nancy Drew pictures at Warner Brothers in the Thirties, starring Bonita Granville, and he had one Torchy Blane to his credit. He had also directed *Calling Philo Vance* for Warner's in 1940. He did such a fine job on *The Falcon in Danger* that Geraghty used him for three of the eight Falcon films he produced.

The Falcon out West was shot in just over three weeks. Both Joan Barclay and Barbara Hale were among the pretty girls the Falcon met during the course of his investigation. The working title was *The Falcon in Texas*. Thurston Hall was originally cast as Dave Colby but, at the last minute, was replaced by Minor Watson. Watson had played exactly the same character, even to having the identical name, in *Hidden Gold* (Paramount, 1939), an entry in the Hopalong Cassidy series the Geraghtys had worked on. William Clemens was the director.

Barbara Hale was an RKO contract player who had previously appeared with Tom Conway in Val Lewton's film *The Seventh Victim* (RKO, 1943). Barbara was born in De Kalb, Illinois, on April 18, 1921, and was signed by an RKO talent scout as a result of her work as a model in Chicago.

When Barbara Hale and I breakfasted together once, I told her that I wanted to know whatever she could remember of making *The Falcon out West* and, later, *The Falcon in Hollywood* with Tom Conway.

"You know, Barbara," I said, "the only thing of any substance that has been written about you is the career study to be found in *The RKO Gals* [Arlington House, 1974]."

She knew the book. The biography of her in it had stressed presumable discord in her marriage and how she had always downgraded her career opportunities to preserve the continuity of her role as a wife and mother.

"The author of that book never even talked to me," Barbara commented. "How can he say those things about me when he doesn't even know me?"

"That's the easiest way to be able to say them."

"I wept when I read what he wrote."

She had tears in her eyes.

"Listen, you've played Della Street, the consummate professional secretary, for too many years to take anything so seriously. I know what we should do. Let's watch *The Falcon out West* together."

"But I was so young when I made that picture. I so much want to help you, but I don't know if I can remember anything. I know that Tom Conway was just as charming to me on the set as he was in the pictures he made. He helped new actors. He had a real feeling for their problems. I remember once in *Out West* we had a scene where I was on top of a horse. I forgot to take the reins. He didn't stop the take. He picked up the reins and handed them to me, and said, 'Haven't you forgotten something?' I had to laugh because I had. I had forgotten my reins. But they left it in like that and no one noticed."

The Falcon in Mexico (RKO, 1944) saw Conway graduating from stock. He was paid $3,262 for his work on the picture, better for him but a long way from the $14,000 George had received. William Berke was the director.

Emory Parnell, the murderer in *Mexico*, was back as a police officer in *The Falcon in Hollywood*. Frank Jenks was his dumb assistant. Sheldon Leonard played a mobster, in love with rising young star Barbara Hale. Conway was paid $5,500 for walking through the picture and solving the series of murders, a facile task in the face of police stupidity (Parnell and Jenks are arresting various characters in nearly every scene).

The Falcon in San Francisco (RKO, 1945) was the last entry in the series produced by Maurice Geraghty. Sid Rogell, brother of director Albert Rogell, was now in charge of studio operations. RKO's fortunes were flagging. Only the Falcon series and the Tim Holt program Westerns were supporting it. Rogell immediately involved himself in all studio operations. When the director George Sherman was being considered for a contract, Rogell called him to his office.

"I can't believe that you used to be only a second assistant director at Republic," Rogell snapped.

"And I can't believe you once held Ken Maynard's horse," Sherman shot back.

Nothing came of their negotiations. Tom Conway was paid $7,333.34 for *San Francisco*. It was a strong picture, with location shooting, but Rogell agreed with Conway that what the pictures had to offer was Conway as the Falcon.

The budgets should be cut. Production values could be sacrificed. The films were being overproduced.

Geraghty left. William Berke, the director on *Mexico*, was made the new producer. Ray McCarey directed *The Falcon's Alibi* (RKO, 1946), the first picture with the Rogell economy measures. It was all done on indoor sets. Rogell started chopping contract players. No care was taken with the script and the identity of the murderer is nearly transparent from the beginning.

There was a suggestion in *The Falcon's Alibi* that the plot from *The Gay Falcon* had been adroitly reworked. The suggestion became a certainty in *The Falcon's Adventure*, which was a weak remake of *A Date with the Falcon*. William Berke was assigned the direction and Rogell personally took credit as the executive producer.

The Geraghty Falcon films were accustomed to having as many as 15,000 bookings. The series fell way off after Geraghty left. Rogell attributed this to a change in public taste. He offered the Falcon property for sale. It was purchased by Philip N. Krasne, who was the producer among the independents who, the reader will recall, acquired both the Charlie Chan and Cisco Kid properties from Twentieth Century-Fox when that studio dropped production of them.

The new Falcon films were based on the radio series which had been on the air for some time. The Falcon's name was changed to Michael Waring, as it was on the radio. John Calvert was given the role. *Devil's Cargo* (Film Classics, 1948) was the first entry. It was filmed in ten days and looked it. So the budget was cut for the next picture, *Appointment with Murder*, coming in at eight days. *Search for Danger* (Film Classics, 1949) was the end of it. The notion of continuing the series was scrapped.

Tom Conway's contract at RKO was not renewed. He took to free-lancing. What lay ahead for RKO was a gradual diminishing of efforts on all fronts, a closing down of facilities, and finally the sale of all assets to the General Tire and Rubber Company. Howard Hughes, who had seized management of the company in the Forties, lost any interest he might ever have had in filmmaking. Sid Rogell went on to a successful career in finance.

Conway's second marriage, like his first, ended in divorce in 1962. He played Bulldog Drummond in two pictures produced by Edward Small for Fox release and, briefly, had a television series in which he played a detective, "Mark Sabre." His last role was in a Perry Mason episode in 1963. How different it was to look across a desk at Raymond Burr and Barbara Hale, both of whom he had known at RKO.

On September 14, 1965, Conway celebrated his sixty-first birthday. He was living in a two-dollar-a-day room at the Charles Hotel at 23½ Winward Avenue in Venice, California. Gene Youngblood of the Los Angeles *Herald-Examiner* interviewed him. An operation for cataracts had left him nearly blind. He had been the Saint and Sherlock Holmes on radio, but no one remembered. He told Youngblood, as he reclined in the glare of a naked bulb taped to the headboard of the bed, that he had lost his last $15,000 in a lumber swindle. His features were worn, his hands trembled from years of alcoholism. A welfare worker had

On the set of *The Falcon in Hollywood* (RKO, 1944). Veda Ann Borg is off to the right, Rita Corday to the left, and the dumb cop duo of Emory Parnell and Frank Jenks next to Tom Conway.   PHOTO COURTESY OF BARBARA HALE WILLIAMS.

rejected his application for relief and he was refused bus fare for transportation to a camp for the indigent.

The interview gained him a certain notoriety. He was telephoned by many who had seen him as the Falcon, wishing him well. An offer of free room and board in West Hollywood fell through. His physical condition was such that he could not work. Soon after he entered a hospital and underwent intensive treatment until he died on April 22, 1967, of cirrhosis of the liver. His brother, with whom he hadn't spoken for years, made arrangements for the body to be shipped back to England.

George Sanders, younger by two years, fared much better. His marriage to Zsa Zsa Gabor on April 2, 1949, ended in divorce in 1954, after he had wearied of being a paying guest in her Bel Air home and had moved into his own house. Sanders had consulted a number of psychoanalysts before trying Zsa Zsa's. The psychiatrist cured him, he said later, of his compulsion to be self-destructive, and above all the self-punishment of his marriage to Zsa Zsa. Good fortune led Sanders to find happiness and success at last in his marriage to Benita Hume, Ronald Colman's widow, on February 10, 1959. To many it seemed a strange, even an inexplicable combination. But for George Sanders it worked. Prudently, he had concentrated on playing character roles. Sanders' career prospered. He got into trouble through an investment in a food-processing factory in Scotland which, after consuming better than a quarter of a million of his savings, led him to declare bankruptcy rather than to continue to remain the dupe of court injustice and creditors' malice.

Yet happiness, once you find it, outside of the movies, seldom lasts. Benita died in 1967. It was over for Sanders then, and he knew it. He had once said of Tyrone Power, "He spent his money freely. He had a yacht, a private airplane, and gave lavish parties. And women, who are usually more expensive than yachts and airplanes, found ways of spending his money when he ran out of ideas. Ty didn't seem to mind. Perhaps he had some premonition that he did not need to save for his old age." That was in 1960. When in an interview in 1969 Rex Reed accused him of liking Tyrone Power, Sanders objected. "Who told you that? He died on the set of *Solomon and Sheba* [United Artists, 1959]. But he was just someone I knew. One knew lots of people. Every film is like an ocean voyage, a transatlantic crossing. You swear you will meet each other again. But you never do. I have no friends. No relatives. No family. Everyone is dead. Now I am going to die, too."

George Sanders had one relative, his sister in England. One day he left a note in Spanish instructing that his body should be sent to her care. The $1,500 in cash in his hotel room in the resort town of Castelldeféls, near Barcelona, would be enough to get him there. The note he left in English said something else.

"Dear world, I am leaving because I am bored. I feel I have lived enough. I am leaving you with your worries in this sweet cesspool. Good luck."

With that, Sanders committed suicide.

"The nadir of my career," George had once remarked, "was the period when I was lent out to RKO by Fox to appear as a whimsical amateur detective called the Saint, who employed barely legal methods to apprehend crooks and murderers. I've looked it up, and nadir means 'the time of greatest depression or degradation.' "

George Sanders' last role was as a transvestite in the picture *The Kremlin Letter* (20th-Fox, 1970). He had been signed to play a homosexual in his next picture. He had reached a new nadir. He had sold his home to Charles Boyer. He didn't know where he wanted to live. He had lived in so many places and found them wanting. He was a romantic, incurably so. Few knew it. Commander W. G. Ogden, a friend of Sanders, did, "Below the sneer illusion," he said, "George was a kind and emotional person, strangely enough in truth, more like a somewhat lost and overgrown schoolboy than the cad he pretended to be. He took great care of his family for years and did many little known good turns to others. I believe Benita's death really shook him for at long last he had found happiness with her, and from then until the end he became more lost than ever, but had she lived, he would never have been 'bored.' "

Unlike Charles Strickland, whom he had portrayed so well in the movie, it was not, Sanders felt, his lot in life to leave behind any work of art that justified his existence. But there was his life. He had that. And he knew how perfectly to end it, before old age, before palsy, before he lost everything save the obstinate but instinctual will to go on. No one survives old age. Edward Dmytryk understood George Sanders, as he has understood so many of the players he has directed. An actor needs constant encouragement. When the world no longer had that to offer George Sanders, he wisely saw that he no longer had anything to offer the world.

EIGHT:

Detective Series in the Forties

I

The Ellery Queen series had come to a close and Columbia Pictures was forced to find a new series for the next season. Ralph Cohn was put in charge of the project. One property seemed apt for cinema treatment. Since 1940 a half-hour radio program known as "Crime Doctor" had had eleven million faithful listeners who tuned in every Tuesday night on CBS. The program was created and scripted by the German-American playwright Max Marcin, who was born in Posen, Germany (now Poland), in 1879 and who came to the United States when he was a child. The psychiatrist-detective was Dr. Benjamin Ordway. Ray Collins was the first to be featured in the role on radio.

Warner Baxter, who was born in Columbus, Ohio, on March 29, 1893, entered films in 1922. He had not had an easy childhood. When he was nine, he moved to San Francisco with his widowed mother, and later the family was wiped out by the disastrous earthquake. "For two weeks," Baxter later recalled, "we lived in a tent, in mortal terror of the fire. I can remember a young woman, almost naked, hysterically rubbing her head into the ground. And the countless thousands frantically searching for their kin."

Baxter began in vaudeville in 1910. Except for brief periods where he worked in sales to tide him over, he kept to the stage with touring companies and then, finally, Broadway. The picture which established him in starring roles was the first talking Western, *In Old Arizona* (Fox, 1929), in which he played the Cisco Kid. His career in the Thirties was varied. "I was a failure and a success three times in Hollywood," Baxter was subsequently quoted. "I have even had trouble paying my rent . . . My three depressions were suddenly ended by three pictures, each of which boosted me higher than I had ever been. *In Old Arizona* ended a two-year slump. *The Cisco Kid* [Fox, 1931] brought me back into popular favor after a series of bad stories. And *42nd Street* [Warner's, 1933] revived me after *The Cisco Kid* had worn off. Like most actors, I wanted to cling to

Jack Barrymore being handcuffed by his brother Lionel in *Arsène Lupin* (M-G-M, 1932). PHOTO COURTESY OF METRO-GOLDWYN-MAYER.

juvenility to the bitter end. But after I repeated *42nd Street* several times, it occurred to me that actors, drugged by pride, can make first-class asses of themselves."

The Return of the Cisco Kid (20th-Fox, 1939) marked Warner Baxter's third time in the role. He made the fewest of all the screen's Cisco Kids in number of features, but surprisingly he seems to be better remembered in the role than anyone else. Baxter's contract with Fox was about to expire when he suffered a nervous breakdown and underwent psychoanalysis. He was in his late forties and the Cisco Kid couldn't do it for him a third time. He had to resign himself, it would appear, to playing character roles.

If this was the case, then, Columbia Pictures had the perfect vehicle for him. Columbia wasn't at all certain that a series would result, so they hedged their bet and gave Margaret Lindsay to Baxter as a love interest in *Crime Doctor* (Columbia, 1943). If it proved a success, it was reasoned, Baxter and Lindsay could take over where Gargan and Lindsay had left off in the Ellery Queen series. The picture was a success and a series followed, but it didn't work out as planned. Margaret Lindsay's contract came up for renewal and it was decided to drop her. She worked in some programmers for Monogram and Producers Releasing Corporation before turning to character roles. Warner Baxter, on the other hand, for what was left of the Forties had found a home.

Graham Baker and Louis Lantz did the screenplay for *Crime Doctor* as adapted by Jerome Odlum from the radio program. Michael Gordon directed. Ray Collins was cast in the picture as a physician who takes in Baxter after an automobile crash has left him a helpless amnesiac. While questing to find out his real identity, Baxter assumes the name of the man who has founded the hospital where he is staying, Dr. Robert Ordway (changing the first name of the character from Benjamin), and takes up the study of medicine. Once he is graduated, Ordway goes to work for an insane asylum. In his capacity as a psychiatrist, Ordway meets Margaret Lindsay, who is on the parole board. A touching love affair, one of Margaret Lindsay's best performances, develops.

Leon Ames plays a hardened criminal in *Crime Doctor*. I asked him about Warner Baxter.

"Nervous breakdown?" he inquired. "You couldn't prove it by me. He looked perfectly all right. He was always a pleasant man, very charming when we were on the set. He had lots of outside interests. While we were making that picture, I remember I was invited to a party at his home. It was held on the tennis court. Baxter was sponsoring a new comedian and he wanted everyone in Hollywood to see the man perform. It was Sid Caesar. We had a good time, I can tell you that. Caesar had everyone in stitches."

The subplot of *Crime Doctor* is that, in his former life, Baxter was a criminal. John Litel and Harold Huber, trying very hard to be tough hoodlums, haunt Ordway, thinking his amnesia is a pretense and that he can really lead them to a stash of money. They end up getting jailed. Ordway brings his case before a jury. He is acquitted.

The idea at the fade is that now Baxter and Lindsay can put the past behind them and settle down to nuptial bliss. *The Crime Doctor's Strangest Case* (Co-

HIS GREATEST MYSTERY WAS HIS OWN AMAZING LIFE STORY!

WARNER BAXTER in CRIME DOCTOR

WITH MARGARET LINDSAY

JOHN LITEL · RAY COLLINS · HAROLD HUBER · DON COSTELLO · LEON AMES

SCREEN PLAY BY GRAHAM BAKER AND LOUIS LANTZ

Directed by MICHAEL GORDON · Produced by RALPH COHN · A COLUMBIA PICTURE

Publicity for *Crime Doctor* (Columbia, 1943) still stressed romance.

PHOTO COURTESY OF COLUMBIA PICTURES INDUSTRIES.

lumbia, 1943) went immediately into production, but, alas, Ordway was a bachelor, and such he remained throughout the rest of the pictures. All of which gave young love a chance to blossom into a full-blown subplot. Constance Worth played Ordway's nurse in the picture, and at times the role almost seemed to be that of another Nikki Porter without Margaret Lindsay, but the notion didn't last.

In *Strangest Case*, Lloyd Bridges and Lynn Merrick portrayed a young couple very much in love. They come to Dr. Ordway to seek his advice. They want to marry. However, Bridges has been acquitted of poisoning his former employer only after a new trial arranged by Ordway. When his present employer is poisoned, the police leap on him as the obviously guilty culprit. He escapes. Barton MacLane plays the lead detective. The solution to the crime entails explanation of a murder thirty years old, which Ordway's investigation uncovers.

It was an adroitly plotted mystery, with the screenplay by Eric Taylor and directed by Eugene Forde. With this picture, Rudolph C. Flothow became producer of the series. Flothow was born in Frankfurt, Germany, on November 23, 1895. He entered the industry at twenty by going to work for Paramount. He had charge, at Columbia, of the Crime Doctor series and the Whistler films. Baxter's contract with Columbia only called upon him to appear in two pictures a year. This was consistent with what Columbia wanted from the Crime Doctor series, and what, of course, they had been unable to get from Ellery Queen in making the Queen pictures.

Baxter only made one Crime Doctor film in 1944 because he was given a strong supporting role in the lavish production based on Kurt Weill's music *Lady in the Dark* (Paramount, 1944), which dealt heavily with psychoanalytic themes. The title song for the picture gained some stature when Leopold Stokowski recorded it with the Hollywood Bowl Symphony the next year.

Shadows in the Night (Columbia, 1944) was by far the best entry in the Crime Doctor series. Opening to an appropriately stormy night, a youthful Nina Foch shows up at Ordway's home. She is being troubled by recurring suicidal nightmares. When Ordway learns their conversation has been overheard (by that lovable subcriminal Ben Weldon), he decides to accept Nina's invitation to come for the weekend to her oceanside home. George Zucco, in a typical role, plays Nina's slightly unbalanced uncle who is engaged in chemical experiments to create a wholly new synthetic fabric. He becomes a suspect when Ordway discovers that Nina's nightmares are induced by a hypnotic gas piped into her bedroom. Minor Watson as an attorney is another likely red herring. Eugene Forde again directed, and Eric Taylor once more provided the original screenplay.

George Sherman joined the Flothow-Taylor team for *Crime Doctor's Courage*

Warner Baxter in conversation with that delightful heavy Ben Welden, from *Shadows in the Night* (Columbia, 1944).

PHOTO COURTESY OF COLUMBIA PICTURES INDUSTRIES.

(Columbia, 1945). His direction was competent if not particularly imaginative. Stephen Crane has been married twice and on both occasions his new bride has come to a tragic death on their honeymoon. Now it's Hillary Brooke's turn. Consistent with the kind of casting Hillary got at Columbia (she confided to me that it was because she wouldn't permit Harry Cohn to pat her bottom), she's marrying Crane only for his money. Dr. Ordway is on vacation at the Beverly Hills Hotel, retitled for the picture the Hotel Royale. Hillary manages to gain Ordway's sympathy. He isn't involved in the case very long before Crane is shot, an apparent suicide which Ordway reveals as really murder. Anthony Caruso and Lupita Tovar are the obvious suspects, since their lives are surrounded by mystery. They live in Bela Lugosi's actual estate (which Lugosi had trouble keeping up when times got lean) and, since they're never seen in the daylight, it's thought they may be vampires. This is all a publicity build-up for the dance team concocted by Jerome Cowan. Ordway finally cracks the case, without much help from the police, personified in the characterization of Emory Parnell.

When you stop to consider that Eric Taylor did the original screenplay and William Castle directed *Crime Doctor's Warning* (Columbia, 1945), the year's second entry, you might feel, aptly, that it should have been a better picture than it was. John Litel returned, this time as an inspector asking Ordway for assistance. A model is murdered and the artist painting her, who has lapses of memory, is the ready suspect. But there is more to it than that, as Ordway soon discovers.

Leigh Brackett, who had worked so effectively on Howard Hawks's productions of *To Have and Have Not* (Warner's, 1944) and *The Big Sleep* (Warner's, 1946), did the screenplay for *Crime Doctor's Man Hunt* (Columbia, 1946), and William Castle directed. Like *Warning*, it should have been a very good picture but wasn't, in part perhaps because of Castle's basic indifference. Ellen Drew had the very taxing role of playing a schizophrenic in both her personality manifestations. William Frawley as the inspector introduced the only humor in a picture that, otherwise, might have consisted of wrenching suspense, as William Castle's best Whistler films could and did, but which in this case settled instead for slow pacing.

Just Before Dawn (Columbia, 1946) also had about it elements for a more extraordinary picture than it turned out to be. Eric Taylor did the screenplay with William Castle directing. Martin Kosleck and Marvin Miller devise a phony insulin kit. Ordway accidentally injects a victim with the solution. When he dies, the police ask Ordway to participate in the investigation. The gang is headquartered in a mortuary, made even more eerie by Castle's experimental lighting. Ordway pretends that he is blinded by a bullet and resorts to a disguise in order to expose the gang.

George Archainbaud, who was directing Gene Autry Westerns at Columbia, took over for *The Millerson Case* (Columbia, 1947), with most of the action, not altogether unexpectedly, taking place in a rural community using the Columbia ranch Western set as a background. Ordway is on vacation when he runs smack into a typhoid epidemic. In all the confusion, Trevor Bardette is poisoned and Ordway heads up the investigation. The charm of the film is created by the

Miles Mander is at it again in *The Crime Doctor's Warning* (Columbia, 1945).

PHOTO COURTESY OF COLUMBIA PICTURES INDUSTRIES.

excellent character actors who comprise the town's more notable citizens, namely Clem Bevans as the sheriff, Addison Richards as a county doctor, James Bell, and Paul Guilfoyle. An amusing subplot is the boredom of most of the town's housewives, which prompts them to carry on clandestine affairs with Bardette, the town barber. His amorous inclinations prove to be his nemesis. Ordway, after much trial and error, arrives at the identity of the murderer.

William Castle returned to the series to direct *Crime Doctor's Gamble* (Columbia, 1947), but his enthusiasm had reached an even lower ebb than it had in *Just Before Dawn*. Ordway, on a visit to Paris, is invited by the police to assist them in determining who murdered a noted art dealer. The picture was so bad that the trades began to warn Columbia that it had better do something to save the series from becoming poison at the box office.

The problem may have been due partly to Warner Baxter's arthritis, which was becoming increasingly crippling. His condition became so serious that in 1948 no entries were made in the series. When he returned for *Crime Doctor's*

Diary (Columbia, 1949), the last film in the series, he was off the screen most of the time. Seymour Friedman directed.

Baxter's last role was as a prisoner trying to escape in *State Penitentiary* (Columbia, 1950). Lew Landers directed the picture. Off-screen, Baxter agreed to submit to a partial lobotomy in an effort to ease the pain of his arthritic condition. I doubt if he had read any of the psychoanalytic literature which suggests that severe arthritis may be the result of a psychosomatic disorder. It didn't matter, as the case turned out. He did not survive the operation.

Yet, Warner Baxter was a suave and gentle man, whatever the encroaching brittleness of his portrayals, and in the best of the Crime Doctor films lent an ease and charm to his characterization that occasionally belied the very limited budgets with which Rudolph Flothow had to work. And, even if he didn't mean it, Baxter not only said it but went on to typify his words. "Most actors object to typing," he once commented. "I don't. In the first place, it is the public who types an actor, not the studio. If an actor is good in a certain character, he can afford to submerge his urge to portray many parts in favor of a neat financial return." Baxter made no further attempt to fight his lot, but instead bore it all with a shrug of the shoulders and a stoical smile.

II

Brett Halliday was born Davis Dresser in Chicago in 1904. He spent his childhood in Texas, until he ran away at the age of fourteen and jointed the U. S. Army, serving at Fort Bliss in El Paso on the Mexican border. He was discovered eventually and was discharged at sixteen for being underage. He returned to finish high school and then, as he somewhat romantically puts it, set out again in quest of adventure. He worked as a roughneck in the oil fields from Burkburnett in Texas to Signal Hill in California. He next shipped out on an oil tanker which put into port at Tampico, Mexico.

His second night in port he went ashore with a group of sailors. They ended up in a tough waterfront bar filled with Mexicans who didn't like gringos. The only other American in the bar was a redheaded Irishman who was sitting alone at a table in the rear, a bottle of tequila and a glass of ice water in front of him. A fight inevitably broke out, and Halliday was slugged and fell to the floor. The Mexicans were armed with knives. The Irishman, surveying the odds, rose from his table in the rear and, fists swinging, entered the fracas. He had the glint of battle in his eyes. He knocked the natives this way and that, clearing a path to the doorway through which the sailors expeditiously could make their hurried retreat.

Halliday attended Tri-State College, in Indiana, long enough to get a certificate in civil engineering. He then resumed his wandering, seeking jobs as an engineer or a surveyor. In 1927, he began writing stories and submitting them to the pulp magazines of the day. He wrote all kinds of stories under a variety of names with only a modest success. When the Depresssion prostrated the country, he wrote more and more.

Halliday found himself in New Orleans. In another of those incredible coincidences with which life, in its infinite arbitrariness, occasionally confronts us, he strolled into a Rampart Street bar one evening looking for story material and once more saw the redheaded Irishman. He was again sitting alone at a table, a bottle of cognac in front of him this time, and a glass of ice water. Halliday went over and introduced himself. The man smiled when Halliday recounted how he had first seen him in Tampico. He confided that he was a private detective in New Orleans on a case.

Halliday was sitting with his back to the door. He saw the Irishman stiffen in his chair, his eyes narrowing to bleak gray slits. Scarcely moving his lips, the man told Halliday to get out of the saloon fast and to forget he'd ever seen him. Halliday got to his feet slowly. The man's eyes commanded the situation. Two men had come through the entrance. As Halliday headed out the door, he saw the men approaching the Irishman's table. Lingering outside, the redhead emerged after a time with the two men, one on either side with bulging pockets. It was that night that Halliday decided he would write a mystery novel featuring a redheaded, two-fisted, cognac-drinking Irish detective as his hero.

Dividend on Death (Holt, 1939) was the novel, Michael Shayne the detective. If the reader is asking at this point why it took Halliday so long to get the book into print, that's because it was all of four years getting rejected by publisher after publisher. The series proved successful and, easily, twenty-five million copies of Halliday's Mike Shayne stories have been sold to date. *The Private Practice of Michael Shayne* (Holt, 1940) followed.

Twentieth Century-Fox Film Corporation was looking for a detective series character to replace Mr. Moto. Lloyd Nolan was signed to portray Shayne. It was a one picture deal, but when the film clicked at the box office, Nolan was put under contract to Fox. When the Shayne series began, Halliday was in the process of publishing his fourth Shayne novel, so, after the first entry, the studio used other story ideas on which to base the photoplays. Perhaps for this reason, coupled with Nolan's excellent, albeit idiosyncratic, approach to the role, the character on screen appeared more substantial than he was in the novels. Moreover, with the exception of the Falcon at RKO, the Mike Shayne films were probably the finest detective series in the early Forties.

Michael Shayne, Private Detective (20th-Fox, 1940) was directed by Eugene Forde. Clarence Kolb hires Nolan as Shayne to keep an eye on his erstwhile daughter, played by Marjorie Weaver. Douglas Dumbrille portrayed a gambling casino owner. Walter Abel, the owner of a racehorse, commits, as part of the mystery, a substitution at the track which brings him a lot of money on a long shot. Donald MacBride, whom Lloyd Nolan once described to me as "a bottle baby," played Captain Painter, Shayne's protagonist in the stories, with Adrian Morris (Chester Morris' brother) filling in as his assistant to make for the dumb cop team which was a requisite of detective films in the Forties.

The unique element in the picture was Elizabeth Patterson as Marjorie Weaver's aunt. She is fascinated by detective stories and tells Shayne at one

Lloyd Nolan as Mike Shayne in his office.

PHOTO COURTESY OF TWENTIETH CENTURY-FOX FILM CORPORATION.

point that she has read and solved most of the Ellery Queen novels. She is constantly relating complex and artificial detective story plots to Mike, expecting him to solve them. It was sort of a backhand slap at the kind of detective fiction Ellery Queen was writing and the more realistic fiction which Hammett in *The Maltese Falcon* had come to represent. Halliday himself was heavily indebted to Hammett for much of the setting into which he placed his detective. Charles Coleman played Ponsley, the butler, and he and Auntie keep elaborate files on their detective fiction reading, much in the fashion of the later Miss Marple movies.

Lloyd Nolan now lives in Brentwood, a suburb of Los Angeles. The last role I had seen him in was as the murderer in an Ellery Queen television episode with Jim Hutton as Ellery. Lloyd has always had a bad memory. Once, years ago, he got into a car with some friends and gave them lengthy instructions on how to find his home when they were only half a block away. One of the things Lloyd forgot for all of his career, since it can be found virtually nowhere, is his age; but he was born on August 11, 1902. He is a voracious reader of books on art and history.

Lloyd Nolan and Marjorie Weaver, one of the regulars in the Shayne series.
PHOTO COURTESY OF TWENTIETH CENTURY-FOX FILM CORPORATION.

He was born and raised in San Francisco, where his father owned a shoe factory. Lloyd wanted no part of the family business. For five years, he attended the Santa Clara Academy and went out for theatricals. He entered Stanford University but was so busy with the university players that he flunked out after the first year. With a fraternity brother, he shipped out on a freighter for twenty-five cents a month, or so it seemed to him at the time. The ship burned up in New York Harbor and Lloyd had to send home for money in order to return. By 1927, he was working at the Pasadena Playhouse, for nothing, supporting himself out of the money his father left him. He went to New York after a year, while he still had the fare to get him there. He worked in New York, on Cape Cod, and in stock. In 1933 he married Mel Efird while they were appearing together in minor roles in a play called *Sweet Stranger*. His break on the stage didn't come until he won the part of Biff Grimes in *One Sunday Afternoon*, which had a forty-three-week run on Broadway. He was tested by Paramount in 1934 and decided to accept the contract they offered him. After sitting around in Hollywood doing nothing for six months, he was cast in *Stolen Harmony* (Paramount, 1935). The star of the picture was George Raft.

We bypassed Lloyd's German shepherd and went upstairs to his study, in the back of the house.

"I'm really worried about this memory business," I told him.

"Well," he said, pulling out a red folder with a number of pages of typescript inside of it, "maybe this will help. It's a list of all my film appearances that a fan made up and sent to me. Those with the stars after them are titles of pictures he has prints of."

I accepted the folder and opened it to the first page.

"He's got you starting in *Stolen Harmony*. So far so good."

"That was a George Raft picture. George was a bad actor. He always wanted his lines shortened. He didn't like dialogue. But, for playing such a hard guy all the time, he didn't drink and was a very devout Catholic."

"You've always played both heavies *and* good guys."

"About fifty-fifty. My first break came because Chester Morris only wanted to play heroes and leads. He was offered the part of the main heavy in *Texas Rangers* [Paramount, 1936] and he turned it down. I took the part."

"You knew Morris?"

"Oh yeah. And I knew him when he was playing Boston Blackie. How he hated that role. I thought about that myself when I told them I didn't want to play Mike Shayne anymore. I didn't want to get channeled into playing only one character. I was getting to be another king of the 'B' pictures, and I didn't like it."

"Can you remember anything that happened on the set during the seven Mike Shayne pictures you did make?"

Lloyd laughed, that infectious laughter of his which comes across so well on screen.

"Now you're asking me to remember."

Lloyd stopped to think.

"No," he said finally, "nothing really. Except I liked the role. I liked the Mike Shayne character, the kind of guy he was."

"Do you remember anything about the first picture, *Michael Shayne, Private Detective?*"

"I don't even remember the part I had in the Ellery Queen television episode," Lloyd confessed.

"Nothing? Nothing at all about the first Shayne?"

"Only that it must have been popular, because Fox signed me after it was released."

"Lloyd!"

He knitted his forehead for some moments.

"No. Nothing."

"But Lloyd, how can you remember all your lines?"

"That's a funny thing. I can remember lines for a week or two when I'm working, but once I forget them, I forget everything."

"Lloyd. Can you remember which picture is your favorite of the many you've made?"

"Oh, that's easy," Lloyd responded. *"The Man Who Wouldn't Talk* [20th-Fox, 1940]."

We couldn't help grinning at each other.

Sleepers West (20th-Fox, 1941) was the second entry in the series. Lou Breslow and Stanley Rauh did the screenplay. It was based on a novel by *Black Mask* writer Frederick Nebel which had originally been filmed by Fox as *Sleepers East* (Fox, 1933) with Preston Foster in the lead role. Eugene Forde directed the Mike Shayne version. Mike meets an old flame, played by Lynn Bari, at a train depot. Shayne is trying to get Mary Beth Hughes, a surprise witness in a murder trial, back to San Francisco to testify. Ed Brophy was cast as a railroad detective. Much of the action took place aboard the train.

Dressed to Kill (20th-Fox, 1941) had Mary Beth Hughes back, this time cast as Shayne's fiancée. Eugene Forde again directed. Banning O'Connor and Stanley Rauh did the screenplay, an adaptation of an original story by Richard Burke. Just as Mike is leaving the marriage licensing bureau with Hughes, he hears a shot and a scream. A hotel is adjacent to a theater and it turns out there were actually two guns fired simultaneously. Mike successfully solves the case, but not without enduring Hughes's rancor; she jilts him.

Shayne got involved with the war effort in *Blue, White and Perfect* (20th-Fox, 1941) which was based on a story by Borden Chase. Detective Lieutenant Frank L. James was credited on this film and others in the series as a technical adviser. Herbert I. Leeds directed. Mary Beth Hughes is about to marry a phony Russian. Mike puts a stop to it by calling in the police, represented by Cliff Clark as the police inspector. Hughes agrees to marry Mike provided he gives up detective work. He finds a job as a riveter in an airplane factory; actually it's detective work, undercover. A smuggling ring is at work stealing industrial diamonds, transferring them to Honolulu in dress buttons, and selling them to the Axis powers.

The series up to this point had been more or less consistent, with the first two pictures perhaps a cut above the second two. It began to improve with *The Man Who Wouldn't Die* (20th-Fox, 1942), based on the novel *The Footprints on the Ceiling* (Putnam's, 1939), by Clayton Rawson. The book featured his detective, Merlini the Great (a previous Merlini novel had been filmed by Metro, *Miracles for Sale* [M-G-M, 1939], based on *Death from a Top Hat* [Putnam's, 1938]). Merlini has only a cameo in *The Man Who Wouldn't Die*, when Shayne consults him about magicians who are able to practice the art of shallow breathing. Herbert I. Leeds directed. The picture opened to the now familiar Baskerville Hall set.

Just off Broadway (20th-Fox, 1942) came next and was even better, Herbert I.

Leeds again directing. Arnaud d'Usseau did the screenplay. Phil Silvers was splendidly cast as a free-lance photographer who makes a lot of trouble for Mike. Shayne is on jury duty at a murder trial. Janis Carter is being tried for the crime. Marjorie Weaver is a reporter. When a key witness is knifed while on the stand, Mike slips out of his guarded hotel room and undertakes to solve the case. Weaver accompanies him once she finds that he is out detecting when he isn't supposed to be. All through the picture Silvers is constantly trying to photograph Mike, and much of it is quite comical. Mike cracks the case and, in a wholly unorthodox fashion (and rather incredibly, I should add) manages to enlist the co-operation of the district attorney's office, cross-examines witnesses, and explains the mechanics of the murder without a single objection from anyone in the crowded courtroom. He does pull a sixty-day sentence for his activities.

Lloyd Nolan in a scene from *Time to Kill* (20th-Fox, 1942), the best film version of Raymond Chandler's *The High Window*, with Heather Angel.
PHOTO COURTESY OF TWENTIETH CENTURY-FOX FILM CORPORATION.

Time to Kill (20th-Fox, 1942) was Lloyd Nolan's last Mike Shayne picture, and, in my opinion, his best. It was based on *The High Window* (Knopf, 1942), by Raymond Chandler. The film, directed by Herbert I. Leeds, is in every way superior to the later remake, *The Brasher Doubloon* (20th-Fox, 1947), wherein George Montgomery portrayed a colorless Philip Marlowe. The plot is better presented in *Time to Kill*, and only the apprehension of Mrs. Murdock is somewhat hokey (in fact, she isn't apprehended; she chokes on a T-bone steak). The comedy is better than in any other Shayne entry, and the scenes, the characters, and the plot constitute the strongest in the series. Whereas in *The Brasher Doubloon*, Montgomery produced a 16-mm. film of the first murder at the denouement, the plot here is simpler and more believable. One of the characters, an amateur photographer, has a photograph of the crime, as in the novel. Clarence Upson Young did the faithful adaptation. It is as much a pleasure to watch the plot unroll in *Time to Kill* as it is tedious in the later Marlowe entry where everything is wrong.

With Sol Wurtzel gone, Twentieth Century-Fox cut back "B" production. The Charlie Chan series, the Laurel and Hardy comedies, and the Mike Shayne pictures all fell by the wayside. Production rights to Mike Shayne were acquired in 1946 by Sig Neufeld. Neufeld had been in independent production since the mid Thirties. He had been responsible for signing Tim McCoy to a series of ten Puritan Westerns released via the states' rights market. McCoy later made an additional seven Westerns for Neufeld issued by Producers Releasing Corporation. Probably as bad as Monogram was among the small independents, PRC was worse. Most of Neufeld's productions were directed by his brother Sam Newfield.

In the novels, by the time Neufeld took over, Shayne had married Phyllis Brighton, one of his clients. (Somewhat removed, she had been the basis for the Marjorie Weaver character in *Michael Shayne, Private Detective*.) Phyllis dies young, in 1943, after which Shayne moves to New Orleans for a time, hiring Lucy Hamilton as his secretary. His office is very much like Sam Spade's, and the characters he meets are only a further testament of Halliday's debt to Hammett. Eventually Mike and secretary Lucy make their way back to Miami, where the saga had its beginning. Halliday by this time had learned that an author does not marry off his detective, although it is perfectly acceptable for the detective to sleep with his secretary. Phyllis, who succumbed while in the throes of childbirth, had threatened Shayne with the total personal annihilation of domesticity, a fate holding more terrors than any external force Shayne again meets in the course of his work. To date, the saga has come to include some sixty novels and countless short stories.

The majority of the PRC films, made hurriedly over a two-year period, were worse than awful. Not only was the dialogue wretched, but scene after scene was so dull, incompetent, and soporific that the only emotion you are capable of is mounting boredom. Hugh Beaumont was cast as Shayne. Beaumont was born on February 16, 1909, in Lawrence, Kansas. He attended the University of Chattanooga and the University of California. The screenplays gave him the obnoxious habit of continuously eating peanuts all through the films and throwing

Hugh Beaumont was Mike Shayne at Producers Releasing Corporation and Cheryl Walker was the girl who "wanted to be more than a secretary." Lyle Talbot in hat.

PHOTO COURTESY OF VIEWS & REVIEWS MAGAZINE.

away the shells on the floor or street, wherever he was. Probably excessive peanut eating was considered more virtuous than the fictional character's original proclivity for cognac.

In the first several entries, Cheryl Walker, an attractive actress who somehow never managed to graduate trom "B" minus films, played Shayne's secretary, Phyllis Hamilton, a combination evidently of Phyllis Brighton and Lucy Hamilton in the stories. She established her self-appointed role in Mike Shayne's life early in the series with the line, "But Mike, I want to be more than a secretary." The "more" was a shrewish, jealous, interfering snoop who resented it every time Shayne had a pretty female client. Because of this characterization, she proved more a drag to the series than a benefit.

Just off Broadway, with Lloyd Nolan, had been bad enough, but at PRC, Shayne went even further, tampering with evidence, withholding information during an investigation of a murder, removing evidence from the scene of a crime, and a half-dozen other activities which, had they occurred in actual practice, would have led to Shayne's getting his license revoked long ago.

Murder is My Business (PRC, 1946) was the first picture in the series, but other than the title it bore no relationship to the novel of the same title published by Dodd, Mead in 1945. The screenplay was by Fred Myton.

Larceny in Her Heart (PRC, 1946) credited Raymond L. Schrock with the screenplay. It is possibly the best Mike Shayne picture PRC made, which still isn't saying very much. The next installment was *Blonde for a Day* (PRC, 1946), in which Kathryn Adams replaced Cheryl Walker as Shayne's secretary. Shayne has moved to San Francisco, but his friend's cry for help leads to his returning to Los Angeles (the films were always set in New York or Los Angeles, never New Orleans or Miami). Shayne buys information from a Negro doorman who tells him, "Yuh came to the rahight mahrket, duh black mahrket." Fred Myton did the screenplay; this was the height of his attempts to be funny.

Three on a Ticket (PRC, 1947) credited Fred Myton's screenplay to a Mike Shayne novel, but it wasn't *Tickets for Death* (Holt, 1941); that was used for the next and last entry, *Too Many Winners* (PRC, 1947). Cheryl Walker is back as Phyllis, but the peroxide splotches in her hair only detract from her appearance. By now Producers Releasing Corporation was in its death spasm, but way too late, since it had inflicted so many bad pictures on the public. William Beaudine directed *Too Many Winners*, but he was no better than Newfield, and in some ways worse. The picture dealt with too many winning race tickets, about as entrancing a subject as the baggage claim ticket cut into thirds had been in the previous *Three on a Ticket*.

Hugh Beaumont went on to play a more savory, if squarish, father figure on television's "Leave It to Beaver." After the film series ended, Jeff Chandler bombed out with a Mike Shayne radio series, and Richard Denning seconded him on the small screen after playing Mike Shayne in thirty-two hour shows.

I like to remember Shayne the way Lloyd Nolan played him. The Fox films were slick, polished, and entertaining. Perhaps Erle Stanley Gardner was right: when your characters are dealt with foully by the movies, the distaste lasts far too long, hurting you more than the money can ever assuage.

III

What possibly inspired Louis Joseph Vance most as an author of popular fiction was the suspense of being in debt. It isn't the same thing as poverty. No one particularly cares about the poor (save in an election year); those in debt never have a moment's peace from the importunities of creditors.

Vance was born in New York on September 19, 1879, the son of Wilson Vance, a newspaperman and novelist. He attended the Polytechnic Institute of Brooklyn. At nineteen, Vance married Elizabeth Hodges. He was already in debt at that tender age, and marriage only added to his financial woes. Vance attended the Art Students League in hopes of becoming a commercial illustrator. It didn't work out. He worked at various jobs during the day and wrote six hours every night. The first story he wrote was universally rejected. His second story sold for twenty-five dollars.

Thus reassured, Vance continued to write prolifically, turning out every type of hack prose he could sell anywhere. When *The Brass Bowl* (Bobbs-Merrill, 1907) became a best-seller, his career took a turn for the better. Vance followed it with one popular novel after another.

Eventually all he did was write, exclusively at night. It was his custom to plot out his books to the last detail before committing anything to paper. He typed his manuscripts and could turn out a 100,000-word book in two months. He did a lot of rewriting. Some chapters he would rework up to forty times.

Vance's novel *The Lone Wolf* (Little, Brown, 1914) was scarcely a new idea. E. W. Hornung, a son-in-law to Sir Arthur Conan Doyle, created an expert cracksman named Raffles in a series of short stories published in 1899. Raffles began life impoverished and desperate in Australia. Although, according to Hornung, he might have succeeded at any number of professions, he chose a life of crime. Raffles was an excellent cricket player who moved easily in the best social circles in English society. Thanks to this circumstance, Raffles found it close at hand to make a fine living stealing from the rich, motivated by his own greed and the desire to live well. But even if it were not for these obvious benefits of his occupation, he was exhilarated by his sport, the constant danger of exposure. He relished the uncertainty and had the admirable ability to remain cool and detached under the most stressful conditions.

Hornung followed his first collection of short stories about Raffles with two more collections and then a novel, *Mr. Justice Raffles*, published in 1905. Joined by Eugene Presbrey, Hornung collaborated on a successful stage drama entitled *Raffles, the Amateur Cracksman: A Play in Four Acts*. It was first produced in London with Sir Gerald du Maurier in the role of Raffles. In 1903, Kyrle Bellew, a matinee idol of the day, took the lead in the United States.

None other than G. M. Anderson, later famous as Western player Broncho Billy, brought Raffles to the screen for the first time in a two-reeler for Vitagraph in 1904, based upon the stage play. In 1911, a silent serial was produced in Italy featuring the character. But after *Mr. Justice Raffles*, Hornung wrote no more stories about him, turning to other kinds of crime fiction.

The market was therefore ripe for a successor to Raffles and the Lone Wolf was it. Vance's character, born a virtual slave and raised as Michael Troyon, comes under the influence of a professional thief from whom he attempts to steal while the man, Bourke, is staying at a Paris hotel. Bourke apprentices Michael and teaches him all the skills he will need to be a master criminal. Michael changes his last name to Lanyard and goes forth into the world armed with Bourke's wisdom, summarized in the first book in three basic principles: "know your ground thoroughly before venturing upon it; strike and retreat with the swift precision of a hawk; be friendless. And the last of these is the greatest."

Some years ago the Lone Wolf books were reprinted, and it was then that I had the occasion to read them. They are very romantic, and probably the first is the best. Jewel theft is organized by a group called "The Pack." They find out

Lanyard's identity as the Lone Wolf by night, rich man-about-town by day. They threaten to expose him to the police unless he agrees to throw in with them and pay them a percentage of his take. This the Lone Wolf refuses to do.

His rule to remain friendless is destroyed by Lucy Shannon, who is in the power of an evil master criminal. The tension mounts as The Pack cuts off the Lone Wolf's outlets for his stolen wares, discovers his hideout, and closes its net around him. Between times, Lucy and Michael fall in love, and one wonders if they will ever be permitted to bask in the warmth of wholly requited love.

No doubt independently of Vance, Maurice Leblanc in France created Arsène Lupin, who made his debut in 1907 in the book *Arsène Lupin: The Gentleman-Cambrioleur*. Leblanc was not a young man when he embarked on his tales about Lupin. He was born in Rouen in 1864. He studied law before he turned to hack writing and police reporting for French periodicals. When Leblanc published his first Lupin short story, he won an immediate following that increased with each new story.

Lupin was not like Raffles or the Lone Wolf in that he in no way tried to keep his profession a secret. In fact, he spurned the police and delighted in the notoriety his exploits gained for him. Leblanc was in a better position to write about a professional thief in that he at least had an opportunity to meet many of them in the course of his journalistic activities. But his stories are in many ways no more realistic than the imaginative fantasies of either Hornung or Vance. While all three tell their stories from the protagonist's point of view, Leblanc alone tends to let the reader puzzle out how Lupin is going to bring off his daring robberies.

Leblanc lived a relatively long time, until 1941. Hornung died in 1921, but his creation proved more indestructible. In 1933, by arrangement with the E. W. Hornung estate, Philip Atkey, under the pseudonym Barry Perowne, revived Raffles and wrote a new series of adventures which began appearing in Great Britain in *The Thriller*. The reader will recall that Leslie Charteris was also writing for *The Thriller* at the same time, and the Saint is not so far away from any of these nefarious characters, save that he goes after bigger stakes and robs the robbers rather than the rich.

The Second World War interrupted Perowne's Raffles stories. But he started writing them again in 1950, this time for *Ellery Queen's Mystery Magazine*. He gave these later stories a turn-of-the-century background, and most critics feel they are superior to even the original tales by Hornung.

After *The Lone Wolf*, every few years Vance would add another novel to the saga, marrying off the Lone Wolf and telling of his children. He kept switching publishers. *Alias the Lone Wolf* was published by Doubleday in 1921. Dutton published *The Lone Wolf Returns* in 1923; the book went through nine printings and was Vance's most popular book to that time. By the Thirties, Lippincott was his publisher, with entries like *Encore the Lone Wolf* in 1933 and *The Lone Wolf's Last Prowl* in 1934.

This last title appeared posthumously. On December 16, 1933, Vance died in his apartment, ostensibly as a result of falling asleep while smoking a cigar. He was found lying on the floor of the apartment, his head and right shoulder resting on the seat of a blazing upholstered armchair. The unclothed upper part of his body was severely burned.

The cinema escapades of this trio of gentleman thieves are a more complex matter. Louis Joseph Vance's first Lone Wolf novel was purchased and brought to the screen by Lewis J. Selznick, David O. Selznick's father, in 1917. Bert Lytell was given the role, largely on the basis of his good looks and dashing mien. Paramount next cast Henry B. Walthall in the role in *The False Faces* in 1919, a year after the second Lone Wolf novel by the same title was published. In the novel, Michael Lanyard's now motherless daughter was introduced, although Vance waited until *Red Masquerade* (Doubleday, 1921) to tell her complete story. This element was made the basis for *The Lone Wolf's Daughter* (Hodkinson, 1919), also released through the Paramount circuit.

Jack Holt, a Universal serial player and Paramount action star, was given the role for *The Lone Wolf* (Associated Exhibitors, 1924), a remake of the Selznick picture. The plot followed closely that of the first book. Dorothy Dalton played Lucy Shannon, actually a Secret Service agent intent upon regaining plans for a stolen defense apparatus. The Lone Wolf agrees to help her provided he is given asylum from The Pack in the United States. The thrilling escape in an airplane was too good to pass up, and the picture made good use of it as well as the confusing array of master criminals with whom the Lone Wolf had to battle in the novel.

Columbia Pictures then purchased screen rights to the property and for the next two decades kept resurrecting the Lone Wolf. *The Lone Wolf Returns* (Columbia, 1926), based on the 1923 novel of the same title, was the first entry in the new series. Ralph Ince directed. He had been under contract to Selznick when Bert Lytell made his screen debut as Michael Lanyard in 1917, and so, naturally, Lytell was cast as the Lone Wolf.

In all of these early pictures, while Lanyard does commit a burglary or two, he is definitely on the way to reform. The Hays office perhaps most of all was to blame for making it impossible to depict a criminal sympathetically on the screen, but more of that later.

Alias the Lone Wolf (Columbia, 1927) came next. Bert Lytell, who in real life was born in New York in 1885 and began on the stage at the age of three, managed to surprise everyone, and no one more so than the heroine, Lois Wilson, by revealing himself to be a Secret Service agent. E. H. Griffith directed. His pacing was so sure and his scenes so well conceived that the film won critical endorsement at the same time as it proved popular with audiences. Louella Parsons in her column singled out the picture as a prime example of how Columbia had capably upgraded its feature photoplay product from the quickie films for which the studio had formerly been known.

For their next entry, Columbia decided to remake *The Lone Wolf's Daughter* (Columbia, 1929). The novelty wasn't the plot; it was the addition of sound in the first reel. The sound wasn't very good. Reviewers hastened to remind their readers that simultaneously with the release of the picture Bert Lytell was appearing on stage in New York in the play *Brothers*. This was because Lytell, as the Lone Wolf, in the employ of Scotland Yard to catch a band of thieves, seemed to lisp on screen. He says "Inthpector" and talks of "vithiting" and "tho forth."

Bert Lytell's final appearance as the Lone Wolf in *Last of the Lone Wolf* (Columbia, 1930) was the first all-talking film in the series. It was also Lytell's worst picture. His voice was all right, due to improved recording techniques, but the plot was farfetched and the picture dragged.

The Lone Wolf was off the screen for a couple of years. When he came back, it was in *Cheaters at Play* (Fox, 1932), the only non-Columbia entry during the sound era. Thomas Meighan starred as Michael Lanyard, who, according to the screenplay, had once been known as "Lone" Lanyard.

The Lone Wolf Returns (Columbia, 1936), while a remake of the Bert Lytell picture of a decade earlier, remains, to my mind, the best of the Lone Wolf films. Melvyn Douglas, born in Macon, Georgia on April 5, 1901, played Michael Lanyard and gave the role both the romance and sophistication it required, much as he did later when he played Arsène Lupin. Gail Patrick played the heroine, Marcia Stewart, whose aunt has a prized emerald collection. Joseph Drumgold, Bruce Manning, and Robert O'Connell did the screenplay. Roy William Neill, who directed most of the Universal Sherlock Holmes entries with Basil Rathbone, was the director. Thurston Hall made his first appearance in the role of Crane, a retired detective called back into service from his farm in upper New York State to match wits with the Lone Wolf.

The picture opens with Lanyard cracking a safe and hiding in his cigarette case the pearls he finds. To escape the police, he crashes Gail's party. The two fall in love. The romance is adroitly handled and the acting of both Douglas and Gail is splendid for its understatement. The screenplay delved deeply into the characters of Lanyard, Marcia, and Crane, so that the emphasis was shifted from the rapid pacing of events to human concerns. Raymond Walburn performed aptly as Lanyard's valet, Jenkins, who joins the Lone Wolf in all of his escapades.

Lanyard decides to change his ways because of his love for Marcia. Douglas Dumbrille, appropriately nasty and self-contained as the mastermind of a jewel theft ring, is a convincing and credible adversary. Lanyard is framed, but he exonerates himself by the end. The script is so adept, the direction so sensitive, that the viewer can tolerate Lanyard's indiscretions with equanimity and even sympathy while, at the same time, condemning the more vulgar and determined chicanery of Dumbrille and his gang. The lighting invests the whole picture with that romantic sheen of the Thirties, the glamour, polish, and sparkle of the best sophisticated comedies. Nor was comedy neglected in *The Lone Wolf Returns*. It isn't heavy-handed as in so many subsequent entries, but subtle, as delicate in its way as Crane's worry over his precious flowers which he raises, Lanyard's gentle embarrassment about his past life, Gail Patrick's caution about loving anyone so completely. Dumbrille, who paid a lot of money for two of his minions to go to Europe to prepare the heist, complains as Crane is carting him off to jail, "Every time I get ready to go to Europe, I end up going to jail."

The Lone Wolf in Paris (Columbia, 1938) wasn't a good picture, although it should have been. Lucien Ballard, who has done such exceptional work, was the

Melvyn Douglas and Gail Patrick at the close of *The Lone Wolf Returns* (Columbia, 1936). PHOTO COURTESY OF COLUMBIA PICTURES INDUSTRIES.

cinematographer. Albert Rogell was the director. Francis Lederer as Michael Lanyard and Frances Drake as the Princess Thania may have, according to the screenplay by Arthur T. Horman, tried to re-create the spectacle of a combination of *The Lone Wolf Returns* and *The Prisoner of Zenda* (United Artists, 1937), but they didn't. Michael gets his hotel room in Paris only because he can produce letters from detective bureaus in all the major capitals testifying to his reformation. He sets about to help out the princess by retrieving the crown jewels to her vest-pocket kingdom in Austria in the possession of three unsavory nobles. The butler Jenkins was portrayed by Olaf Hytten. Perhaps it was merely another instance of a high budget idea victimized by too much "B" picture corner-cutting.

Columbia Pictures came back in earnest the next year with the concept for a series. Joseph Sistrom, brother to William Sistrom, then at RKO and instrumental in the Saint films, was made associate producer on the first entry. Warren William, who had bought up his Warner Brothers contract before it expired so he could free-lance in films like *The Gracie Allen Murder Case* (Paramount, 1939), was signed to play the lead and became a Columbia contract player. If casting for *The Lone Wolf Spy Hunt* (Columbia, 1939) was weak, with Don Beddoe as Inspector Thomas and Leonard Carey as Lanyard's valet, it more than compensated for it with Ida Lupino as the outspoken, aggressive girl friend Val Carson, and Rita Hayworth as Karen, consort to principal heavy Ralph Morgan.

The Lone Wolf Spy Hunt started with the old script for *The Lone Wolf's Daughter*. Fortunately, Jonathan Latimer, who later worked on *The Glass Key*

Ida Lupino as a temptress in *The Lone Wolf Spy Hunt* (Columbia, 1939).
PHOTO COURTESY OF COLUMBIA PICTURE INDUSTRIES.

(Paramount, 1942) and who was one of Raymond Chandler's few close friends in La Jolla, was assigned to the screenplay.

The script used as the basis for *Spy Hunt* did hinder Latimer somewhat, but he managed to overcome the limitations of the plot through adroit characterizations, particularly with the women. Ida Lupino's role of a tempestuous, flagrantly aggressive female was off-beat for her, compared to the moody, neurotic parts she was more accustomed to getting, and she obviously relished it. The complexity of Karen's role was such that it proved a considerable challenge to Rita Hayworth, who had at once to appear seductive and, variously, hard as the occasion demanded. Jack Norton, whose career consisted of playing drunks, got a strong part in the screenplay. Thanks in large measure to Latimer, after the success of *Spy Hunt*, Columbia was able to settle down to the comfortable formula of a popular series. The screen name of Lanyard's valet was changed from Jenkins to Jameson in *Spy Hunt*. In the next entry, *The Lone Wolf Strikes* (Columbia, 1940), the spelling was altered to Jamison, but a fine stroke of casting led to Eric Blore's being assigned the role. Blore had been Philo Vance's valet in *The Casino Murder Case* (M-G-M, 1935). He brought to his characterization of Jamison an outlandish sense of humor combined with British understatement, which played exceptionally well opposite Warren William's rather sober and sophisticated Lone Wolf.

Joan Perry, who later married Columbia production chief Harry Cohn, had the feminine lead in *The Lone Wolf Strikes* and comedy player Fred Kelsey was cast as Sergeant Dickens. The screenplay was by Dalton Trumbo, who would become one of the Hollywood Ten during the McCarthy era. Lanyard, who has retired to a New York apartment, now collects tropical fish, an enthusiasm that the reader may recall was also a central preoccupation in William's *The Dragon Murder Case* (First National, 1934). Addison Richards involves Lanyard in trying to regain possession of a pearl necklace robbed from his business partner and which, supposedly, brought about the partner's death through foul play. The police naturally suspect Lanyard to such an extent that they close their minds to any other possible interpretation of the evidence.

This, then, became a leitmotiv in the series. Thurston Hall returned as Inspector Crane in *The Lone Wolf Meets a Lady* with Fred Kelsey as his assistant. From this point on, the plots became standardized so that while the Lone Wolf customarily would help someone in distress, the police invariably blamed him and he was constantly being either handcuffed by Kelsey or arrested for the particular crime. From year to year I don't suppose this mattered much, but were you to watch the pictures one after another it is repetitious and irritating.

The Lone Wolf Meets a Lady (Columbia, 1940) was highly entertaining, with some very good scenes in Lanyard's New York apartment and in the sequence where Kelsey trails Lanyard. *The Lone Wolf Takes a Chance* (Columbia, 1941) was only slightly less so. Evalyn Knapp, a heroine of Westerns in the Thirties, played one of the gang of thieves. This wouldn't be notable except that the footage of the Lone Wolf overtaking a speeding train with the safe car attached to it was lifted directly from *Speed Wings* (Columbia, 1934), a film in which Evalyn Knapp played the heroine opposite Tim McCoy.

Addison Richards, Eric Blore in his role as Jamison, Warren William, and behind them the Lone Wolf's collection of tropical fish.

PHOTO COURTESY OF COLUMBIA PICTURES INDUSTRIES.

Ralph Cohn became the producer on *The Lone Wolf Takes a Chance*, as he was for the next entry, *The Lone Wolf Keeps a Date* (Columbia, 1941). Don Beddoe, who had been playing cops so far in the series, was miscast as a mobster and at the bottom of a kidnaping attempt foiled by the Lone Wolf. The setting was Florida, but that didn't matter; Hall and Kelsey were called in to assist the Florida police and, at once, pinned the whole thing on Lanyard.

Edward Dmytryk, whose early career in the Thirties had found him the film editor on several Bulldog Drummond pictures, was signed to direct *Secrets of the Lone Wolf* (Columbia, 1941), following it with *Counter-Espionage* (Columbia, 1942). *Secrets* opened to Hall and Kelsey asking the Lone Wolf's advice as to how best to protect the newly arrived Napoleon jewel collection and then, when the collection is stolen, accusing him of having done it. Like *Confessions of Boston Blackie* (Columbia, 1941), which Dmytryk directed at the same time, he stressed comic elements in the script. There is a hilarious episode when a ring of organized jewel thieves mistake Jamison for Lanyard and seek to make him their leader. *Counter-Espionage* was a transition film, as the Lone Wolf, joined by other Columbia characters like Boston Blackie and Ellery Queen, entered the war effort on the side of the Allies. The setting was London during the height of the Battle of Britain. Dmytryk vividly re-created the atmosphere of an air raid shelter, and sound effects during a blitz were ghastly in their drama. Hillary Brooke was in the cast as a worker in the shelter. Forrest Tucker played a Nazi spy. The Lone Wolf's mission is to hinder Tucker's success. Unfortunately, neither Scotland Yard nor the American police are aware of the patriotic sympathies inspiring Lanyard's activities.

Hillary Brooke thought Warren William splendid to work with and she noted how much he liked the comic aspects of the screenplay. Eddie Dmytryk felt otherwise.

"Warren William was a nice guy," Dmytryk told me, "not at all like the sophisticated role he was playing. He had a Shakespearean manner, though, and, of course, a Barrymore profile. I couldn't get to him, Jon. Mostly it was because Warren had such a negative attitude toward making cheap pictures, and the Lone Wolf pictures were minimum budget films. He had fixed up a truck into a mobile dressing room. He parked it near the sound stage where we were shoot-

Warren Hull holding a gun on the dumb cop duo of Fred Kelsey and Thurston Hall, with a young Bruce Bennett in uniform.
PHOTO COURTESY OF COLUMBIA PICTURES INDUSTRIES.

ing. He never hung around the set. He always hid out in his dressing room. He never had a twinkle in his eye . . . unless a broad walked past. But he loved to do his own stunts. All that running around on steam pipes in *Secrets of the Lone Wolf* he did himself."

William's weariness with the role, and perhaps his boredom with the low-budget pictures to which his career now seemed permanently condemned after it had once held such promise in the early Thirties, began to tell on his characterization in *One Dangerous Night*. He had become so dissatisfied in the role by the time he had made his ninth film in the series, *Passport to Suez* (Columbia, 1943), I doubt if it would have even amused him had he known that today's villain Gerald Mohr would succeed him as tomorrow's Lone Wolf. John Stone, who had contributed so many fine ideas to the Charlie Chan series, wrote the screenplay and Andre de Toth directed. But the picture couldn't be saved. Sheldon Leonard had an offbeat role as a cafe owner in Constantinople, much like Humphrey Bogart's Rick in *Casablanca* (Warner's, 1942). Lanyard is working for the British Government in an attempt to prevent a Nazi take-over of the Suez Canal. Perhaps the effects of William's terminal illness were already beginning to be felt. *Passport to Suez* was William's last Lone Wolf. He died on September 24, 1948, of multiple myeloma, a rare bone disease. Eric Blore and Thurston Hall, who had become close friends, were at the funeral. William's ashes were scattered in Long Island Sound. His wife, Helen Nelson William, who had developed a heart ailment, did not survive him by very long.

A hiatus in production ensued. When Columbia resurrected the series with *The Notorious Lone Wolf* (Columbia, 1946), Gerald Mohr was in the lead. Only Eric Blore's Jamison gave this new entry any life. William Davidson played Crane. The dialogue was less than scintillating. Mohr at one point observes, "If you find the ice cubes fuzzy, it's because these modern rugs are constantly linting." Lanyard's absence from the screen is explained by the fact that he has been in the military service. D. Ross Lederman directed the film in a workmanlike and sluggish fashion. When a sapphire is stolen, Lanyard is suspected; true to form, he eventually solves the case.

The Lone Wolf in Mexico (Columbia, 1947) was also directed by Lederman. Nothing improved. The Mexican casino milieu was strictly indoor sets. Lanyard, as usual, is the most likely suspect to the police, if not to the audience.

It got even worse in *The Lone Wolf in London* (Columbia, 1947), with Lanyard now in the British capital doing research for a book he is writing on famous gems. When a gem collector asks Lanyard's assistance in disposing of his collection, the matter gets momentarily complicated when the most priceless jewels are stolen. *The Lone Wolf and His Lady* (Columbia, 1949) finished the theatrical series. It had a new Michael Lanyard in Ron Randell, number nine to be exact. Alan Mowbray was Jamison. William Frawley was cast as Inspector Crane. Lanyard now works for a newspaper, covering a gem exhibit. When the third-largest diamond in the world is stolen from the exhibit, Frawley arrests Lanyard.

It was an entertaining idea, especially when you recall pictures like *The Lone Wolf Returns* (Columbia, 1936). But low budgets, bad acting, poor stories all took their toll. Louis Hayward, in the Fifties, starred as Michael Lanyard in a television series, but by then the idea had been exhausted through overexposure. On the whole, although he was featured in fewer pictures, Arsène Lupin fared better.

As early as *Raffles, The Amateur Cracksman* (Hiller-Wilk, 1917), a feature-length remake of the two-reeler Broncho Billy produced, John Barrymore was playing the lead in this type of role. Barrymore was the first and best of the Arsène Lupin characterizations in the sound era. Preceded by silent American entries like *Arsène Lupin* (Greater Film Company, 1917), *The Teeth of the Tiger* (Paramount, 1919), with David Powell as Lupin, and *813* (Robertson-Cole, 1920) starring Wedgewood Newell, *Arsène Lupin* (M-G-M, 1932) was directed by Jack Conway. The screenplay by Carey Wilson was based on the short story "Arsène Lupin in Prison," which appeared in 1907. Lionel Barry-more was cast as the prefect of police. The picture served as a showcase for the brothers to try to outdo each other in stealing scenes. It opens to a house being robbed. Lionel arrests Jack but has to let him go. Jack Barrymore's Lupin is a duke, but one without money, much the kind of sympathetic rogue he would be in *Grand Hotel* (M-G-M, 1932). The rest of the story has to do with Lupin's stated intention to make off with all the valuable *objets d'art* of a nobleman, his attempt at it only to be foiled by the police, leading to his suc-cessful purloining of the *Mona Lisa*. Lionel lets Jack go free in an act of gratuitous flamboyance at the fade.

Nothing was done with the property again until *Arsène Lupin Returns* (M-G-M, 1938). The notion for the film was inspired by Columbia's *The Lone Wolf Returns*. Melvyn Douglas was now under contract to Metro, and so the studio, having screen rights to the Lupin stories, immediately starred him as the French thief. The famous director George Fitzmaurice had charge of the pro-duction, with the screenplay by James Kevin McGuinness and detective story writer George Harmon Coxe, among others. Franz Waxman did the musical score. In this photoplay, Lupin has retired, thought by the world to be dead. He has secluded himself at an estate in the country where he raises pigs and terriers while carrying on a romance with Virginia Bruce. E. E. Clive, an English crook, and Nat Pendleton, a bumptious American, are Lupin's confederates and are re-sponsible for much of the comedy in the film. Warren William, who was about to become the Lone Wolf, was cast as an American detective in search of a necklace stolen in New York. George Zucco was on hand to play the prefect of police, which he handled about as adroitly as Bela Lugosi the next year was to play a Soviet commissar in *Ninotchka* (M-G-M, 1939)—which is saying that it was, for Zucco, one of his best performances. Monte Woolley is one of a group also after the emerald neckpiece.

With a cast like this, the picture couldn't miss. Douglas and William vie with each other for Virginia Bruce's attentions. If anything, the polish and sheen of Douglas' appearance since the Lone Wolf had heightened. At times, the action could be described as elegant. Jonathan Hale, that staple from the Saint films, played a special agent for the FBI. Suspicion as to who is back of it all is better handled than in most detective films, and the suspicion which shrouds Lupin is far more effective than the clumsy use this ploy was given in the Lone Wolf pictures.

Enter Arsène Lupin (Universal, 1944) was the last feature film about Lupin. It was originally intended as a budget effort to gain additional exposure for Ella Raines, Howard Hawks's discovery whom Universal was in the process of building into a star. Ford Beebe, that venerable Universal serial director, was at the helm. Charles Korvin played Lupin, again a thief, stealing an emerald from Ella Raines but regretting his action at once when he perceives how beautiful she is and that she is also in danger of being murdered for her estate by an unscrupulous aunt and uncle. J. Carrol Naish, Miles Mander, and Gale Sondergaard, staples in Universal thriller pictures of this sort, rounded out the cast.

While Lupin and Lanyard were engaged in these various adventures, the original gentleman thief was far from inactive. *Raffles* (United Artists, 1930) was one of a complement of pictures Samuel Goldwyn was producing for United Artists release. Harry D'Abbadie D'Arrast started out directing it, but he had problems. Lucky Humberstone was assistant director on the picture. Goldwyn screened D'Arrast's rushes and told him bluntly he didn't like the way he was making the picture. "You and I don't speak the same language, Mr. Goldwyn," D'Arrast responded. "I'm sorry, Mr. D'Arrast," Goldwyn snapped, "but it's my money that's buying the language."

Ronald Colman was cast as Raffles, because of the success he'd had as Bulldog Drummond. A screen test was run of Bette Davis for the part of Lady Gwen, the woman with whom Raffles falls in love and who succeeds in reforming him. Goldwyn, when he saw the test, jumped out of his chair in outrage. "What are you guys trying to do to me?" he shouted. His response to Davis was certainly as negative as had been that of Carl Laemmle at Universal. Goldwyn couldn't see her protuberant eyes and clipped speech as becoming in a heroine. George Fitzmaurice was assigned to the picture. He had previously directed Ronald Colman seven times. He understood Goldwyn and, while they argued, they never fought. Colman himself was pleased by the change.

Raffles, The Amateur Cracksman (Universal, 1925) had been directed by King Baggott with a screenplay by Harvey Thew. House Peters played Raffles, and Hedda Hopper had a role. Goldwyn's production used the same plot, but Goldwyn wanted more glamour and sophistication, and Fitzmaurice gave this to the film. Above all, Goldwyn wanted a love story, and Ronald Colman and Kay Francis as Lady Gwen provided it. Alison Skipworth was cast as Lady Melrose, whose diamond necklace Raffles intends to steal to save his friend Bunny, played by Bramwell Fletcher, from suicide over financial ruin. Colman is successful, but the police are after him. Lady Gwen helps him elude the police. The hope is that the two will rendezvous presently in Paris.

In 1940, Goldwyn decided he wanted to remake the picture. Nothing had been done with the property since the Colman film, save for *The Return of Raffles*, a British film of 1932 starring George Barraud. Goldwyn cast David Niven as the lead in *Raffles* (United Artists, 1940), and Olivia De Havilland played opposite him. Sam Wood, who in his long career in Hollywood had directed the Marx Brothers in some of their best pictures, was selected to direct. The plot was altered slightly. This time it is Raffles' prospective brother-in-law who needs help, and Raffles attempts to steal a necklace at a weekend house party. Unfortunately a gang beats him to it, so, in spite of his intentions, he ends up working on the right side.

With the original George Fitzmaurice had unquestionably directed a better film, although his later Arsène Lupin entry for Metro holds up better as a sound vehicle. Surveying the entire crew of international thieves (in terms of his fictional exploits the Saint should certainly be included), it was one of the quirks of the late Thirties that, increasingly, bad men, if they were to be heroes, had to be portrayed as either retired or essentially good. This quirk was in large measure the doing of the Hays office, which had early in the talking era undertaken to legislate the morality depicted on the screen and see to it that American audiences were permitted to witness an image of society and crime that was, to put it charitably, a lie. Nurtured in such a never-never land, the next generation —when suddenly it found itself relentlessly confronted by the harsh truth of crime—was totally ill-prepared either to react to it sensibly or to understand what it was all about. The movies helped make reality, when at last it penetrated, a devastating surprise. Crime cannot be shown to pay, the Hays office insisted. But when it was learned irrefutably that crime *did* pay, the result unhappily wasn't anger, only apathy.

Melvyn Douglas as Lupin is cracking a safe while Virginia Bruce and Warren William watch him in *Arsène Lupin Returns* (M-G-M, 1938).

PHOTO COURTESY OF METRO-GOLDWYN-MAYER.

Here's how Dick Tracy looked when he came to the screen.

PHOTO COURTESY OF UNITED FILMS.

*I decided that if the police couldn't catch the
gangsters, I'd create a fellow who would.*

—*Chester Gould*

IV

Chester Gould was born in 1900 in Oklahoma. He moved to Chicago to complete his education at Northwestern University. After graduation, he found employment as a commercial artist. In the years 1921–31, he submitted many ideas
for a comic strip to Captain Joseph Medill Patterson of the Chicago *Tribune*
syndicate. They were rejected. The idea which did win acceptance was a strip
about a plainclothes detective who was willing and able to fight criminals on
their own terms, using fists and guns where necessary. Gould originally wanted
to call his detective Plainclothes Tracy. Patterson suggested his first name be abbreviated to the common slang word for detective. Dick Tracy made his initial
appearance for the Chicago *Tribune* syndicate on October 4, 1931.

The public craved such a hero because law enforcement agencies seemed helpless in the face of organized crime and, with the acquisition of considerable wealth and paid political influence, the court system became a protector of the criminal. Both judges and police commissioners were hasty to point out how thoroughly the indigent lawbreaker was dealt with; traffic offenders and first-time violators were severely punished. It was an effective propaganda campaign to obfuscate the fact that crime itself was a major American industry.

Dick Tracy set himself in opposition to this trend. His popularity grew till he was carried in over 800 newspapers around the world and had a readership of 100 million. If organized crime in real life reaped rich and enduring rewards, at least in fantasy, in a comic strip, the results of crime were not so favorable.

I have mentioned Nat Levine at Republic Pictures with respect to his two entries in an Ellery Queen series. His most successful detective venture by far, however, was *Dick Tracy* (Republic, 1937), a fifteen-chapter serial he brought to the screen the same year Universal did its version of Dashiell Hammett's *Secret Agent X-9*.

In the comic strip, Tracy had lean lines, a sharp nose, and a square jaw, a hard-boiled rendition of Sherlock Holmes, but with the emphasis clearly on action. The villains Tracy confronted were highly colorful, their physical deformities lending them nicknames rather after the fashion of underworld parlance: Flattop, Pruneface, the Mole (who lives underground), Mumbles, and Pear Shape. Tracy's love life is occupied by Tess Trueheart, his girl friend for eighteen years and then his wife. His assistants include Junior, Tracy's adopted son who is a police artist, his sidekick, Sam Catchem, and Chief of Police Pat Patton. Diet Smith, the millionaire, is saved by Tracy and, out of gratitude, makes available to Tracy over the years the fruits of his inventive genius, gadgets which once were science fiction but now are commonplace, such as two-way wrist radios and closed-circuit television.

To play Tracy in the serial, Levine signed Ralph Byrd and placed him under contract to Republic. Byrd was born in 1909 in Dayton, Ohio. At a very early age he joined the Albright Players and toured the Middle West. He also sang on the radio. He studied at the Hollywood Little Theatre and it was there that a talent scout from Columbia Pictures saw him. Byrd was signed to play in *Hell Ship Morgan* (Columbia, 1936) before joining Republic. He was a pipe collector who ended up with some 350 pipes. He enjoyed riding horses, playing tennis, and cooking. But his main hobby was music and he had a collection of several thousand symphonic albums, accumulated during the course of his career. It must have been inspired casting because the public so liked Ralph Byrd that he continued to play Tracy on and off for the next twenty years.

For the serial "Dick Tracy" Tracy was transformed from a policeman to a G-man. Kay Hughes played Gwen, the equivalent of Tess, and Smiley Burnette, Gene Autry's stooge, was Mike McGurk, a character probably based on nothing more than Levine's casting instinct for stooge comedy. Tracy is assigned to bring to justice a mysterious arch-criminal named The Spider and to smash his gang. The identity of The Spider remains unknown until the fifteenth episode. Tracy is even given a brother: Dr. Mulloch, played by John Picorri, operates on him and, thus enslaved, he becomes one of The Spider's followers. Lee Van Atta portrayed Junior. Ray Taylor and Alan James, both veteran action directors, shared directorial credit. The initial chapter was by far the best, with Tracy confronted by a futuristic airplane called the Flying Wing, with which The Spider can destroy a suspension bridge as a show of his power.

The chapter play was so successful that it was followed by a second serial, *Dick Tracy Returns* (Republic, 1938). Byrd was Tracy. Lee Ford took over for Smiley Burnette as Mike McGurk, but his intelligence was still so wanting that he perhaps made viewers wonder how he ever made the FBI. Jerry Tucker played Junior. Lynn Roberts was Gwen. Tracy is assigned to bring to justice the notorious Stark gang, headed by Charles Middleton and consisting of Middleton's five screen sons, some of the nastiest heavies you might want to meet.

The fabulously effective serial director team of William Witney and John English directed *Dick Tracy Returns*, as they did the next two serials featuring Tracy. *Dick Tracy's G-Men* (Republic, 1939) had Jennifer Jones in one of her early screen appearances playing Gwen, billed under her real name of Phylis Isley. Junior and McGurk were both absent. But the highlight of the serial was its villain, Zarnoff, played by Irving Pichel, who was also a director, including in his credits *She* (RKO, 1935), Merian C. Cooper's production of the H. Rider Haggard novel.

Herbert J. Yates was now the head of Republic Pictures, having bought out Nat Levine. He had a deal with Chris-Craft whereby he received a number of free speedboats every year provided he featured them in various productions. *Dick Tracy's G-Men*, as a result, had a lot of speedboat action.

Dick Tracy vs. Crime, Inc. (Republic, 1941) was fourth and last of the Republic chapter plays. It was, in my opinion, the best. It utilized some of the best footage from the previous Tracy serials—in case you hadn't seen them— and with its mystery villain, The Ghost, who could make himself invisible by means of a gadget he wore similar to a cartouche, the special effects were quite the equal of those in the film based on H. G. Wells's 1897 novel *The Invisible Man* (Universal, 1933), which inspired its own series.

Jan Wiley was cast as Tracy's girl friend, June Chandler. Nothing else in the serial, except Tracy's name, had the slightest relation to the comic strip, but for all that the pacing was frantic, the stunting exhilarating as only Republic could do it, and the action continuous.

Dick Tracy was off the screen until RKO revived the idea in 1946. Morgan Conway was cast as Tracy in the first entry of the new series, *Dick Tracy* (RKO, 1945). William Berke directed and, in his lighting and mood effects, paid an unacknowledged tribute to Edward Dmytryk, even to casting Mike Mazurki as a vicious slasher called Splitface, because of an ugly scar on his somewhat haunting, if expressionless, countenance. Anne Jeffreys, a former heroine from "B" Westerns at Republic, was cast as Tess. Lyle Latell played Pat Patton, but the character on screen was in the role occupied by Sam Catchem in the strip. Junior was portrayed by Mickey Kuhn.

Chester Gould himself was asked to review the film by his paper, the Chicago *Tribune*. Gould seemed to like the picture. "The gentleman with whom I had shared sweat, blood, and tears for almost 15 years—Dick Tracy in the flesh—Morgan Conway's flesh, to be exact—right on the screen at the Palace. And for once he did the talking and I listened. I felt pretty helpless, too, because I couldn't use a piece of art gum to change his face or hat, and what he said came from a script and not from a stubby old lead pencil held by yours truly."

Herman Schlom, who produced the Tim Holt Westerns for RKO, was the producer on the series. *Dick Tracy*, since retitled *Dick Tracy, Detective*, was well paced and never flagged in its unrolling of the plot. Eric Taylor, so intimately associated with nearly all the Columbia detective series, did the screenplay. Morgan Conway as Tracy, a virtual unknown at the time, incited generally good reviews for his portrayal. There is no mystery for the audience, really, as to Mazurki's identity as the savage killer, but his relationship with Trevor Bardette isn't quite apparent, and Tracy acts the part of a professional policeman rather than a government super-sleuth.

Gordon Douglas, a director who would excel at detective films in the Sixties, directed the next entry, *Dick Tracy vs. Cueball* (RKO, 1946). The screenplay, by Dane Lussier and Robert E. Kent, strove to keep more of the original flavor of the comic strip, and Cueball is an appropriately fantastic villain. Anne Jeffreys again played Tess opposite Morgan Conway's Tracy. Jimmy Crane was Junior and Ian Keith played the preposterous Vitamin Flintheart. Cueball, who is involved in a diamond theft, ends up murdering several people out of simple animal brutality; he even turns on his cronies. He is about to put Tess out of the way when Tracy rescues her.

Ralph Byrd replaced Morgan Conway in an effort to improve the Tracy series and because Morgan Conway's option was not renewed by studio management. *Dick Tracy's Dilemma* (RKO, 1947) was directed by John Rawlins. Kay Christopher replaced Anne Jeffreys as Tess. Ian Keith returned as Vitamin and Lyle Latell stayed on as Pat Patton. But the alterations in casting couldn't save the picture. In an effort to duplicate the zany quality of the comic strip, the plot ingredients lacked any sense whatsoever. William B. Davidson played an insurance man named Peter Premium. Schlom apparently felt that the more divorced the Tracy pictures became from reality the more acceptance they would receive. The villain was The Claw, a man with a hook for a hand who commits four murders before he is finally finished off.

This tendency toward hokum became even more pronounced in the final entry, *Dick Tracy Meets Gruesome* (RKO, 1947). Boris Karloff was signed to play Gruesome and handed in a totally predictable performance. John Rawlins again directed and Eric Taylor worked on the screenplay. The dialogue was so uninspired that at one point Pat Patton, still played by Lyle Latell, remarks of Gruesome, "If I didn't know better, I'd think he was Boris Karloff." In another scene, Tracy, in the course of his investigations, goes to visit Dr. A. Tomic and instead meets the scientist's assistant, I. M. Learned, played by June Clayworth. When a mysterious fluid is spilled, thought to be a dangerous poison, Tracy stoops down and tastes some of it, commenting, "It tastes like water to me." The gadget used by the villains is a gas which freezes everyone in the vicinity for several minutes, allowing banks to be robbed and other such.

RKO decided, after *Dick Tracy Meets Gruesome*, to drop the series, just as it had with the Falcon pictures, for reasons of economy. No one thought to purchase production rights for theatrical films. But in 1950, a new series of thirty-nine half hours starring Ralph Byrd was produced for television. This series went even further in the *outré* plot treatments of the last RKO photoplays and introduced new characters from the comic strip, like Diet Smith, played by Thurston Hall, Inspector Crane in the Columbia Lone Wolf films. When Byrd completed the television series, he was quoted in the trades as saying, "I'm proud of that series and I think we did a good job of them." A few weeks later, while on vacation, Byrd died of a heart attack. When Dick Tracy returned again to the television screen, it was in the medium of a five-minute cartoon series.

Dr. Mulloch and the Spider are just about to perform a lobotomy on Ralph Byrd as Tracy.   PHOTO COURTESY OF UNITED FILMS.

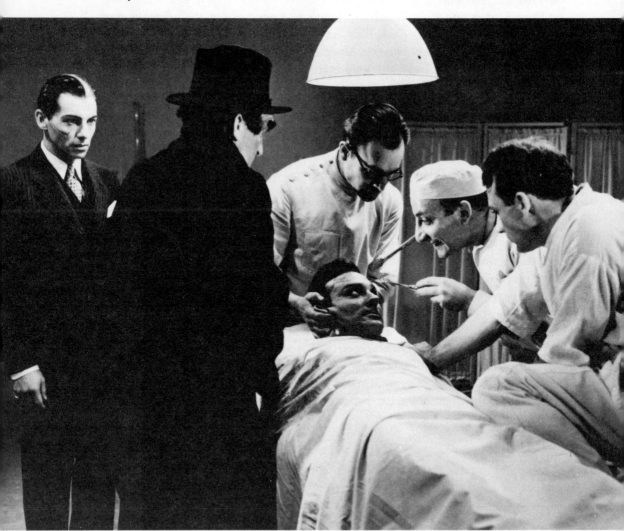

V

Although I will mention William Castle on several occasions in this narrative, it is in connection with The Whistler films at Columbia that he made his initial impact as a director of highly special gifts. *Chance of a Lifetime* (Columbia, 1943), about which I will say more, was his first solo credit as a director. Shortly after the Boston Blackie picture was released to unfavorable critical notices, Harry Cohn summoned Castle to his office on the Columbia lot. He handed Castle the script for his next picture. It was titled *The Whistler* and was based on the popular radio program originating on the Columbia Broadcasting System. The screenplay was by Eric Taylor and was based on a story idea by J. Donald Wilson, who scripted the radio series.

"I tried every effect I could dream up to create a mood of terror: low-key lighting, wide-angle lenses to give an eerie feeling, and a hand-held camera in many of the important scenes to give a sense of reality to the horror," Castle recalls in his book *Step Right Up!* (Putnam's, 1976). "To achieve a mood of desperation, I insisted that [Richard] Dix give up smoking and go on a diet. This made him nervous and irritable, particularly when I gave him early-morning calls and kept him waiting on the set—sometimes for an entire day before using him in a scene. He was constantly off-center, restless, fidgety, and nervous as a cat. When I finally used him in a scene, I'd make him do it over and over until he was ready to explode. It achieved the desired effect—that of a man haunted by fear and trying to keep from being murdered."

The plot concerned a small industrialist, Richard Dix, who is so distraught by the loss of his wife, for which he feels partially to blame, that he hires an assassin to murder him. The go-between whom Dix contacts, Don Costello, is killed by the police soon after he talks to Dix. The contract makes its way to J. Carrol Naish, the man whose business it is to kill Dix. When Dix learns that his wife is not dead after all, but held prisoner in a Japanese internment camp, he attempts to stop the terrible machinery he has started. He cannot. The suspense mounts as Naish decides, before actually shooting Dix, that he will try to frighten him to death. Gloria Stuart was cast as Dix's secretary, who finally comes to his rescue. *The Whistler* (Columbia, 1944) won rave reviews from the principal New York papers and even inspired enthusiasm from some of the usually contrary Los Angeles critics.

Richard Dix's career as a popular leading man up to this time had been the result primarily of appearing in Westerns. On April 4, 1944, it was announced by Columbia Pictures that Dix had been signed on a contract to appear in the Whistler series. Rudolph C. Flothow was the producer. *The Whistler* was filmed at the Darmour lot on Santa Monica Boulevard. Dix's reason for agreeing to the series had mostly to do with his health. In the early Forties, he was generally red of face and short of breath. "Blood pressure," he explained in an interview. "I've had to cut down on the booze, and no more big action stuff for yours truly. But the industry's been very good to me, and I'll keep going as long as they want me."

In truth, Dix had long been a heavy drinker, and he never really eased off as much as he wanted to. Even in the Thirties, he would usually show up on the set with a hangover. Of itself, that wasn't so much of a problem. But Dix was subject during his morning-after recuperation to fits of hiccups. You never knew when the hiccups might begin, so whoever the director was at the time would rush him before the camera. Then the hiccups would start, right in the middle of the scene. The other actors might try to cover them, but nothing could be done. Dix would have to rest until noon, by which time the hiccups had generally subsided. Thanks to Castle's sensitive direction, even though the

Richard Dix looking grizzled in *The Whistler* (Columbia, 1944).
PHOTO COURTESY OF COLUMBIA PICTURES INDUSTRIES.

Dix doesn't know it, but Paul Guilfoyle (far left) is the man whose money he has claimed. PHOTO COURTESY OF COLUMBIA PICTURES INDUSTRIES.

pictures were to be budgeted between $65,000 and $75,000, they won critical acclaim combined with enthusiastic audience patronage.

Both Dix and Flothow wanted William Castle to direct the next entry, *The Mark of the Whistler* (Columbia, 1944). If anything, it was even better than the first picture. The original story was by Cornell Woolrich, whose tales of suspense were having, and would continue to have, a tremendous effect on *film noir* in the Forties. In the picture, Dix was cast as a down-and-out hobo sitting on a park bench. He sees a notice in a newspaper that a bank is seeking to locate heirs for various accounts it is holding and which are unclaimed. Dix determines that he can successfully pretend to be one of the account holders. He manages, after much anxious worry, to get the money, $99,010. Instead of leaving town, he checks into a high-class hotel. He learns to his dismay that there is a man set on killing him, believing Dix to be the man whose identity he has assumed. Paul Guilfoyle is cast as Limpy, a begger selling pencils, who befriends Dix, as does Janis Carter, a reporter. Dix finally liberates himself from his difficulties, but not without having to confess the fraud.

The Whistler radio program was broadcast exclusively to the West Coast. As one reviewer put it, "Director William Castle has made another exciting picture based on the adventures of The Whistler. The latter is a radio character known only on the West Coast and I, for one, am grateful to Columbia Pictures for selecting the mysterious Whistler for a series of thrilling adventure films and thus introducing him to the country at large. The Whistler may be Fate, or he may be the voice of conscience signaling a warning to a person about to take his first plunge into crime. We see him in *The Mark of the Whistler* . . . merely as a shadow accompanied by an eerily whistled refrain." That was Kate Cameron in the New York *Daily News*. She gave the picture three stars.

When *The Power of the Whistler* (Columbia, 1945) was released, Dorothy Masters, reviewing it for the same paper, gave it only two and one half stars. "It was director William Castle," she wrote, "who produced a 'sleeper' (low budget film of exceptional merit and appeal) in *The Whistler*, and while Lew Landers maintains considerable suspense and some control over the players, his picture doesn't quite rate a three-star par." Aubrey Wisberg did the original screenplay. It was a film that Alfred Hitchcock or William Castle might have done much better. Richard Dix is hit a glancing blow by an automobile and suffers temporary amnesia. He meets Janis Carter, who tries to help him find out his real identity from certain objects he finds in his pockets. The emphasis is strictly on detection in the first two thirds of the film, as Dix, Carter, and Carter's sister, played by Jeff Donnell, follow out the various clues. But then, of a sudden, Dix becomes aware of his identity and that he has escaped from an asylum with one objective before him, to murder the administrator of the asylum and the judge who placed him there. This is foreshadowed by the death of various creatures with which Dix comes in contact, a canary in the girls' apartment, a kitten being played with by a child, a squirrel in a park. Janis Carter, when she learns who he is, is also in danger of her life.

William Castle was back to direct *The Voice of the Whistler* (Columbia, 1945). Lynn Merrick, perhaps the best *femme fatale* working in the Columbia "B" unit, renders a performance which nearly qualifies the picture to be considered as *film noir*. Richard Dix is cast as an ailing industrialist, lonely, dissatisfied, who is given only a short time to live. He takes a vacation and hopes to lose his identity. Fortunately, he is befriended by Rhys Williams, a prizefighter turned taxi driver in Chicago. The friendship theme generates an uncommon degree of sympathy. Before leaving to live on the ocean in an isolated lighthouse, Dix proposes to Lynn Merrick, a nurse engaged to a young intern. He offers her all of his wealth when he dies if she will marry him. After some soul-searching, turning hard against the prospect of poverty and struggle facing her, Lynn agrees. When, sometime later, Dix does not die but instead falls in love with Lynn, and the fiance arrives for a visit, both rivals plot murder. Dix succeeds but he loses his freedom. And Lynn, who wanted wealth and loved people, is seen at the end, living quite alone in the lighthouse.

Mysterious Intruder (Columbia, 1946), directed by William Castle, with story and screenplay by Eric Taylor, may well be the best entry in the series. Nor am I alone in my affection for the picture. Don Miller, in an engaging essay titled "Private Eyes" for the English film magazine *Focus on Film*, Autumn 1975, observed that "the Eric Taylor original had a fine gimmick, the quest for some rare Jenny Lind recordings, and some unforgettable characters, such as Mike Mazurki's brutish killer without a word of dialogue. Most haunting of all was the sleuth, Don Gale, as played by Richard Dix. 'I'm an unusual kind of detective,' says Dix early in the film, which is pure understatement. Dix had played a madman in a Val Lewton film a few years previously, but compared to the maniacal intensity of his Don Gale, it was a performance of placid calm. . . . There is always the possibility that part of this characterization is attributable to Dix rather than the script, but in either case the effect is unsettling yet fascinating."

William Castle in his treament of the story had certainly been influenced by what Eddie Dmytryk had achieved in *Murder, My Sweet* (RKO, 1944). The settings are musty old shops and a dilapidated house where Mazurki is sleeping off a drunk. All the important action takes place in fitful lighting and heavy shadows. Dix's private detective is motivated by greed, as are most of the other

Lynn Merrick and her boy friend, James Cardwell (right), are just about to have their engagement broken by Richard Dix.
PHOTO COURTESY OF COLUMBIA PICTURES INDUSTRIES.

characters. He proves himself smarter than the others but, ironically, in his haste makes a fatal mistake. I would go so far as to suggest that *Mysterious Intruder* is the best film Castle made at Columbia.

Unquestionably, *The Secret of the Whistler* (Columbia, 1947) was a letdown. None of the characters were sympathetic and there was no imagination in either the acting or the direction. George Sherman directed. Dix is an artist who has to depend on his sick wife for his bounty. When his wife, played by Mary Carrier, overhears him making love to his model, portrayed by Leslie Brooks, herself a spiteful gold digger, his wife tells Dix she intends to disinherit him. Dix tries to poison her. She makes a note of the occurrence in her diary. Then she dies of a heart attack. Dix, thinking he has murdered her, cremates the body. He marries the model. To get her hands on Dix's fortune, the model plots to get evidence against him. She finds the diary. Before she can show it to the police, Dix strangles her. The police arrive with proof that Dix hadn't murdered his wife, but by this time it's too late to save him from a murder charge.

The Thirteenth Hour (Columbia, 1947) wasn't any improvement. It had Karen Morley as Dix's girl friend. The two of them carried the picture, but it simply wasn't enough. William Clemens directed. The plot had Dix running a trucking company. He stops to see Karen Morley and has a drink. When he is involved in an accident, the liquor on his breath leads to the suspension of his license. During the six months he cannot drive, he attempts a run. He is ambushed by a mysterious figure and a highway patrolman is murdered. Dix is suspected and hounded by the police. By the end, he manages to expose the culprit. But the story by that time had become tedious.

Dix's health began seriously to fail. *The Thirteenth Hour* proved to be his final film. In October 1948 he suffered a massive heart attack and was placed for a time in a sanitarium. He sold his Santa Monica ranch and set sail with his wife for Europe. In August 1949 he had a fatal heart attack while aboard ship at Cherbourg. He was kept alive until he made it back to California, with lengthy stays in hospitals in New York and Chicago. He died on September 20, 1949, at the Presbyterian Hospital in Hollywood.

Columbia thought it might save the series by completely revamping it. Instead of using a continuing single star like Richard Dix, the new series would concentrate on stories alone. *Return of the Whistler* (Columbia, 1948) was the only entry without Dix. It was directed by that indifferent veteran D. Ross Lederman. The original story was by Cornell Woolrich. A man intends to marry a French girl he has known for only a few weeks. His state of being in love is rather trying on the patience. When the girl unaccountably disappears, the man, played by Michael Duane, searches frantically for her. Richard Lane plays a private detective much in the fashion of his portrayals of Inspector Farraday in the Boston Blackie series. The denouement is in an insane asylum where the girl, played by Lenore Aubert, is being held against her will. The Woolrich story had stressed the impossible, crushing autocracy of asylum administration and its bending medical practice to serve whoever is paying the bill. None of this was in the film, save in the most fleeting insinuations. Reviewers almost unanimously lamented the loss of William Castle to the series, and so, with this picture, the Whistler took his last bow.

Publicity for *Boston Blackie Goes Hollywood* (Columbia, 1942).

PHOTO COURTESY OF COLUMBIA PICTURES INDUSTRIES.

VI

When I lived in Milwaukee, Wisconsin, I was frequently asked in the course of my travels, why. The answer was that I was born there. But it wasn't a very good reason for staying, and so as soon as I could I did something about it. Milwaukee is a provincial version of Chicago, with cloudy weather, drab buildings, and unfriendly people. It is dominated by a single newspaper syndicate which publishes both the most widely read morning paper and evening paper. Politics is a career opportunity and, once elected, officials usually retire from their posts at advanced ages. The judges are the circumspect instruments of Establishment viewpoints. When a traffic court justice was exposed by an attorney for sentencing female traffic violators, pregnant or not, to sexual intercourse with him before they were freed, the judge shot himself in a lavatory in the Gothic courthouse which is situated as a castle guarding the city's financial district; the attorney was disbarred for his efforts. I once parked in a taxi stand near a tobacconist who was about to close up for the night. I wanted to purchase some cigarettes. Before I knew it, I was yanked from my car, frisked for a gun, told I was attempting to make an escape, and summarily informed that if I so much as twitched I would find four lead slugs in my brain. I was carted off in a paddy wagon, fingerprinted, photographed, and placed in a cell, prohibited from making so much as a phone call for six hours. Once I was released on bond, I called the local newspaper. The incident was reported in the morning edition. A reporter from the evening paper phoned me the next day to tell me that the arresting officer had committed both his mother and brother to an asylum for the criminally insane, but that I would be pleased to learn that the chief of police had agreed to place the officer on the second shift patrolling hippies on the East Side provided the paper didn't publish the account. The city attorney advised me that all charges would be dropped if I would sign a release for false arrest.

It was into this thoroughly well-policed and politically fortified metropolis that Chester Morris came to appear at the local Pabst Theatre, a landmark built by a beer baron, starring in the Broadway success based on Allen Drury's novel *Advise and Consent*. Had I talked to him prior to the performance, I could have told him that it was a mistake to announce to reporters that "politics is a dirty business." Political leaders had been given free tickets for the play. One of them called a press conference. He claimed that it would be unthinkable for him to attend the play after a person of Chester Morris' standing in the theater had so calumniously indicted politicians without taking into account the careers of so many men totally devoted to public service and who thanklessly pursue these ends all their lives without unjust enrichment.

"Maybe you took the Boston Blackie character too seriously," I suggested.

"Maybe I take America *too* seriously," he snapped back.

We were in the star dressing room backstage. The first article I had ever written was propaganda to save the Pabst Theatre from demolition. In this dressing room, I had first interviewed Leopold Stokowski. He was a guest conductor of the Chicago Symphony that year. There had been a great snowstorm and the orchestra members were forty-five minutes late and without their tuxedos. Stokowski had announced to the audience that he would conduct the entire concert as scheduled in spite of the weather. He was applauded. But half the audience left at the intermission because they wanted to get home before weather conditions worsened.

"This is a cold city," Morris remarked, lighting a cigarette. He looked much as he had in the Blackie films at Columbia, his straight black hair slicked back from the temples, his ready grin, his harsh-toned voice. "And I don't mean the temperature outside."

I recalled that Sir Thomas Beecham, when he had come to conduct the Chicago Symphony in Milwaukee, had told me that the city "was more bleak than Berlin." Pierre Monteux had been more laconic. "*Je vais maintenant à Chicago. Comme on dit en anglais?*: 'Whew!'"

"I wanted to talk to you about the Boston Blackie series at Columbia?" I said to Morris.

"What about them?"

"That's what I want to know. What about them?"

Morris chuckled.

"I was signed by Columbia to make those pictures. At the time, I thought it was a great contract. But those pictures nearly ruined my career. I did thirty-six of them, four a year for nine years. We could shoot one in twelve days. And then it would be four or five months before we'd start another. The studio wouldn't let me do anything else. I nearly went to pieces just finding something to occupy my time. All the Blackie pictures were 'B' films. They didn't do a thing for my career."

"Why didn't you star in the television series?"

Morris inhaled from his cigarette.

"I didn't want to. I had been Boston Blackie on the radio, you know. And I was in all the movies. They were always playing on television in those days. How typecast can an actor get? I wanted to do something else."

The something else in 1951 was *Detective Story* at the Ivar Theatre in Hollywood. Morris starred with Allen Jenkins and Marvin Miller in support. That began nearly two decades of Broadway and road work in theatrical productions.

"Didn't you think Blackie's relationship to the Runt was peculiar?" I asked. "In the television series with Kent Taylor, the Runt was replaced by a dog."

Morris threw his head back and laughed.

"No, not really," he replied. "Georgie Stone. I won't ever forget. He was the delay on those pictures. He could never remember his lines. Everyone was held up by him. But he was perfect for the role. And a real sweet guy. Besides, the Runt was in a story by Jack Boyle on which the whole thing was based. He was as important to the pictures as Farraday."

"I've got another question," I said.

"What's that?" Morris asked, lighting another cigarette.

"It has to do with your remarks about politics."

Chester Morris' return to the stage after Boston Blackie began with *Detective Story*, shown here as it appeared in Hollywood with Marvin Miller and Allen Jenkins.
PHOTO COURTESY OF THE NATIONAL FILM ARCHIVE.

"What about them?"

"What's wrong?"

"Now that's a very good question." He leaned back in his chair. "It isn't so much what's wrong with politics. Everything's wrong with politics in this country. What's really wrong is that we hide from it. We don't like to admit that it's a dirty game played by dirty men for their advantage. That's what's wrong, and I wonder how long it's going to be before we have the backbone to wake up and see it. I'll tell you this. We'd better wake up soon, because if we don't, it'll be too late. Then it won't much matter, will it?"

It was nearly a decade later that Chester Morris was staying at a motel in New Hope, Pennsylvania. He was starring at the Bucks County Playhouse in *The Caine Mutiny Court-Martial.* He was sixty-nine. He talked to cast members and seemed happy the morning of September 11, 1970. He had a luncheon appointment he had said on the telephone that he intended to keep. Barbara Britton's son, who had been Chester Morris' valet for a time in stock, had recorded, some years later, of how sick and frail the actor had appeared, of how he missed smoking when, at the twilight of his life, he had to give it up. Those closest to him knew that Morris was suffering from an extremely rare and incurable ailment that reduced his weight to under a hundred pounds, prevented him from drinking and eating most foods. His memory was so shattered by the malady that he lived in perpetual terror of forgetting his lines. His weakened and hopeless condition brought him frequently into a state of despair. The coroner refused to inform the press whether or not the overdose of Seconal was accidental, but it hadn't been.

Boston Blackie had a start in fiction with a background similar to that of the Lone Wolf, which is to say as a reformed cracksman. Jack Boyle published a story collection titled *Boston Blackie* (H. K. Fly, 1919), bringing together magazine tales he had published earlier. It was to be Blackie's only appearance in book form. In the stories, Blackie is a resourceful man who has declared war on society. His best pal and confidante is his wife, Mary, who joins him in his exploits.

Boston Blackie's Little Pal (Metro, 1918) was the first cinematic presentation. It was followed the next year by *Blackie's Redemption* (Metro, 1919). Bert Lytell, who played the Lone Wolf, starred as Boston Blackie. These pictures had an orientation inspired by William S. Hart's Westerns, of the good bad man who is redeemed through the kind office of a devout heroine. Most of the drama centered on Blackie's wrestling with himself to do the right thing. Lionel Barrymore played the character in *The Face in the Fog* (Paramount, 1922). Blackie here came to the rescue of a Russian princess, retrieving her jewels from the Bolsheviks and assisting her in a romance with a crown prince.

Missing Millions (Realart, 1922), made the same year, had David Powell playing Blackie. This time he joins forces to help Alice Brady rob a ship's safe in an act of vengeance against an unscrupulous stockbroker who framed her father. *Boston Blackie* (Fox, 1923) was next with William Russell in the title role. Fox decided to rework the original story line from the Boyle book, and the photoplay depicts Blackie as a convict who goes straight following a prison term so he can expose an inhuman warden. *Through the Dark* (Goldwyn, 1924) went the whole route with Forrest Stanley as Blackie, this time escaping from prison because of the inhuman warden, being converted to reform by Colleen Moore, and winning a pardon through a good deed. It is interesting to contrast the social representations of films like *Through the Dark*, and they were legion, where criminals earned their pardons by performing heroic actions. Today, it would seem, when a criminal begs to die, he is then given a stay of execution; or when, as in the case of Charles Manson, when he once pleaded to be kept in prison, according to *Helter-Skelter* (Norton, 1974), he was paroled. *The Return of Boston Blackie* (First Division, 1927) closed out the silent era with Raymond Glenn in the role. In this picture, Blackie undertakes to reform Corliss Palmer, a pretty blonde, who has stolen a necklace.

The property remained dormant until *Meet Boston Blackie* (Columbia, 1941). Chester Morris, who was born February 16, 1901, in New York City, had been a

Charles Wagenheim played the Runt only in *Meet Boston Blackie* (Columbia, 1941).
PHOTO COURTESY OF COLUMBIA PICTURES INDUSTRIES.

contract player with Columbia Pictures since 1936. He came from a theatrical family. After several years on the stage, he became a motion picture star with *Alibi* (United Artists, 1929), for which he was nominated for an Oscar. He didn't make thirty-six Blackie films, as he said, but only fourteen. In 1926 he married actress Suzanne Kilbourne; they were divorced in 1938. In 1940, Morris married Lillian Kenton Barker, the original Chesterfield girl from the "They Satisfy" advertisements.

Ralph Cohn served as the producer on *Meet Boston Blackie*. Robert Florey directed. The plot found Blackie returning from a trip to Europe. He is met while still on the boat by Inspector Farraday, played by Richard Lane in all the films. Farraday jumps to the obvious conclusion when a corpse is found in Blackie's stateroom. Blackie has to escape in order to clear himself. This became the formula for all the entries. The films, however, were played for comedy and Chester Morris was perfectly suited to the role with his brash, airy manner. Blackie's sidekick in the series was the Runt, played in the first film by Charles Wagenheim. Blackie, with Rochelle Hudson's assistance, finally discovers the murder to be the work of a spy ring that is after government secrets and is using an oceanside carnival as a blind.

Confessions of Boston Blackie (Columbia, 1941) was the best film in the series. It was directed by Edward Dmytryk. It was for him a transitional film before exceptional pictures like *Murder, My Sweet*. George E. Stone was ably cast as the Runt, and he was retained in that role. The Runt was Blackie's gnome-like companion, living and traveling with him, cooking for him, and trying to keep him out of trouble with the police. Lloyd Corrigan was cast as Blackie's wealthy, if featherbrained, friend, Arthur Manleder. Walter Sande, who had played a uniformed cop in *Meet Boston Blackie*, was promoted to the role of Sergeant Matthews, Farraday's dim-witted assistant. Harriet Hilliard played the feminine lead. A gang of swindlers is selling phony art objects. When Harriet gets too close to the truth, she is shot by one of the gang. Blackie is suspected. Joan Woodbury played Blackie's girl friend, who, in a fit of jealous rage, smashes up Blackie's apartment. Corrigan got most of the laughs for his portrayal of Manleder, but it was all played against an excellent cast.

I asked Dmytryk about the picture.

"Of course, it was easy to work with Chester Morris," he said, "even though he didn't particularly like the role. He did what he had to do. But he didn't like stunt work and refused to do anything strenuous, even so much as stand on a box. Chet was an amateur magician and he was always carrying a deck of cards around with him doing tricks. I knew it was a comedy, but I tried to introduce a sort of gallows humor into it. It was so well liked that I was rewarded with two Lone Wolf pictures."

Alias Boston Blackie (Columbia, 1942) kept the same basic cast. Cy Kendall was added to the roster as Jumbo Madigan, a pawnbroker who comes to Blackie's assistance. Larry Parks, later famous for his portrayal of Al Jolson at Columbia, played Joe Trilby, who escapes from prison while Blackie is putting on a magic show for the inmates. Lew Landers was the director.

Boston Blackie Goes Hollywood (Columbia, 1942) is quite possibly the funniest film in the series after *Confessions*. Arthur Manleder, played by Corrigan, gets himself into trouble with a gang of hoodlums led by Blackie's old cellmate, William Wright. In *Meet Boston Blackie*, Farraday made quite a to-do about getting Blackie's fingerprints, but by this time it was established that Blackie has a prison record, so the character was undergoing *some* changes. Jumbo Madigan provides Blackie and the Runt with disguises, the Runt decked out in junior togs and playing Blackie's child! The height of hilarity is to be found when Blackie infests Farraday and Matthews with an ant colony which he dumps on them while they are trying to do an undercover tail job. Michael Gordon directed.

Lew Landers was back to direct *After Midnight with Boston Blackie* (Columbia, 1943). The country and Western singer Johnny Bond was on the set at Columbia when this film was being made. He had his hand-operated camera along

Harriet Hilliard, Chester Morris, Richard Lane, and heavy Kenneth MacDonald in the best film in the series, *Confessions of Boston Blackie* (Columbia, 1941). MacDonald, like Morris Ankrum, went on to become one of the usual judges on television's "Perry Mason." PHOTO COURTESY OF COLUMBIA PICTURES INDUSTRIES.

and recently showed me the footage he had shot when the stunt of Blackie jumping from the top of a building was in production. Chester Morris was on the sidelines in a powder blue suit, smoking and laughing. It made me regret that at least one of the Blackie films hadn't been made in color.

William Castle was assigned to the Boston Blackie series for *The Chance of a Lifetime* (Columbia, 1943). "Chester Morris, a fine actor, played the lead," he recalled. "He tried to breathe some life into a part that had died at birth. Jeanne Bates hopelessly tried to play the *femme fatale*. Every day I viewed the rushes, and my assistants told me what a great job I was doing. Irving Briskin remained silent as long as I didn't change a word of dialogue. Finally I started to believe I was getting a good picture, and I plowed ahead, completing the picture in twelve days. I saw the final cut with Irving Briskin. When the lights came up he turned to me and uttered the not unexpected. 'It's a piece of shit!'"

This was Castle's first directorial effort. Irving Briskin was in charge of Columbia's "B" department. Rather despairingly, Castle observed that "to help me

Lloyd Corrigan was superb as Arthur Manleder, while George E. Stone (center) made an excellent Runt. Stone would later become the bailiff on television's "Perry Mason." PHOTO COURTESY OF COLUMBIA PICTURES INDUSTRIES.

correct the 'piece of shit,' Briskin took the end of the picture and put it at the beginning, then spliced a section of Reel Four into Reel Two, a section of Two into Four, and some of Five into Six. Reel Seven he took out entirely. Eight he trimmed, and Nine he left alone. After his glowing contribution, *Chance of a Lifetime* became even more muddled and screwed up than it had been originally, if that was possible."

The reviews were unanimously bad. Not having seen the original script, I cannot verify what changes Briskin made, but the picture's beginning could in no way come at the end. The story concerned Blackie's scheme to get a group of convicts released from prison to work in Arthur Manleder's machine shop making war materials. One of them has the loot of a robbery, and Douglas Fowley and his partner want it. Blackie is in hot water. But the other convicts, staying at Blackie's apartment, make Fowley confess and all ends well, with Blackie getting yet another batch of convicts for his rehabilitation program.

Boston Blackie Booked on Suspicion (Columbia, 1945) marked Lloyd Cor-

Chester Morris and George E. Stone had fun donning disguises.

PHOTO COURTESY OF COLUMBIA PICTURES INDUSTRIES.

This is the intercut after Blackie's jump in *After Midnight with Boston Blackie* (Columbia, 1943). The man between George E. Stone and Richard Lane is Walter Sande, who played Sergeant Matthews.

PHOTO COURTESY OF COLUMBIA PICTURES INDUSTRIES.

rigan's last portrayal of Manleder. Walter Sande was replaced by Frank Sully in the Sergeant Matthews role. Arthur Dreifuss directed. Manleder purchases a rare-book shop. When the manager falls ill, Blackie agrees to impersonate him at the forthcoming auction. Lynn Merrick works in the shop. She is the common-place hard-driving, ambitious, ruthless blonde of the Forties, keeping Steve Cochran, her escaped convict husband, in her apartment. She plots a fraud, a phony original edition of Dickens' *The Pickwick Papers*, and then shoots her accomplice. Blackie is the one Farraday suspects, but Merrick is caught by the fade.

Nina Foch was given the female lead in *Boston Blackie's Rendezvous* (Columbia, 1945). Harry Hayden played Manleder, and then after this entry the character was wisely dropped. At one point, running from Farraday, Chester Morris and George E. Stone get themselves up in blackface and play a couple of colored chambermaids. When questioned by a passing cop about Boston Blackie, they reply, "No. We'se from Adaho."

John Stone, still living on his reputation from the Charlie Chan entries at Fox, took over as the producer on *A Close Call for Boston Blackie* (Columbia, 1946). Lew Landers directed. It was followed by *The Phantom Thief* (Columbia, 1946), directed by D. Ross Lederman, a director at Columbia who seemed to approach every assignment with no enthusiasm whatsoever.

Boston Blackie and the Law (Columbia, 1946) gave Chester Morris ample opportunity to perform magic tricks, although the script was a reworking of *Alias Boston Blackie*. The film depended on stock footage such as the face of a giant clock from *Sherlock Holmes Faces Death* (Universal, 1943) and the interior of a bank from Frank Capra's *You Can't Take It with You* (Columbia, 1938).

Unlike nearly every other screen detective series, the Blackie films did not wind down to a slow-paced, bitter finish. The next entry, *Trapped by Boston Blackie* (Columbia, 1948), came after a year's hiatus. Perhaps it was a stronger picture than many of its predecessors because Rudolph C. Flothow took over as associate producer on the Blackie series. Flothow was free because Warner Baxter's poor health had caused a delay in the Crime Doctor films Flothow had been producing. Seymour Friedman directed *Trapped*.

Boston Blackie's Chinese Venture (Columbia, 1949), which has never been released to television, was the final entry. George E. Stone regrettably was replaced by Sid Tomack. Flothow produced and Friedman directed.

"Friend to those who have no friends; enemy to those who make him an enemy" is the way Boston Blackie was introduced on radio. All in all, it was a characterization that, over the air at least, brought out Chester Morris' personality. I would not do the man justice were I not to say of him, in parting, that he was a most committed actor. He might be so sick he could hardly function, as he was near the end; he might miss his lines because he couldn't remember due to illness. But he invariably gave of himself, and he kept trying long after most men would have given up.

NINE:

A Conference with Raymond Chandler

*I thought . . . but thinking got me nowhere. I
remembered the half-bottle of Scotch I had left
and went into executive session with it. An
hour and a half later I felt fine, but I still didn't
have any ideas. I just felt sleepy.*

from "Trouble Is My Business"
by Raymond Chandler

I

Raymond Chandler was a solitary man all his life. When, in the second half of
his life, he began writing detective stories, he took to sending lengthy letters to
friends, associates, publishers, editors, even strangers. This correspondence was
carefully preserved. In one letter or another, he recorded his reactions to most
things going on around him or narrated the events of his life. We have this fact
to thank for the uncommonly detailed and articulate biography of Chandler
written by Frank MacShane, *The Life of Raymond Chandler* (Dutton, 1976).

As secretive as Chandler may have been, as socially reticent, as shy with anyone but a few intimates, in his letters he became expansive, confidential, uninhibited. The image you have of Chandler is a man sitting alone in his study at night,
the same room where he wrote in the mornings, where he slept, where he revised his work, where he proofread his galleys, where, you might well say, the
best and truest part of him lived. Here he could be himself. He talks to you
through his letters in a way he could never have spoken to you had you known
him.

MacShane concludes that Chandler was an extremely lonely man. This is no
cause for sentiment. It was a self-imposed loneliness, and I think Chandler liked

Raymond Chandler out in the street of his Los Angeles.

PHOTO COURTESY OF THE UCLA ARCHIVE.

it. No one I have spoken with who knew Chandler has the foggiest notion of what he wanted out of life. He was quite outspoken as to what he disliked about the world, and, in particular, Southern California.

Perhaps it would surprise him to learn that he is generally considered to have been the most important author of detective fiction in the history of the genre. Then, again, maybe it wouldn't. When you consider how viciously he was denigrated by John Dickson Carr or Anthony Boucher, who reviewed his books as they appeared, it is certainly a curious, even ironic, turn of events. His excellence, as he himself would admit, came about because he tried to overcome the restrictions of the form in which he worked. To the extent that he succeeded, he wrote not detective stories at all, but parables of his time, fantasies, romances; and he dwelt upon a singular creation, his detective, who, as he gained depth and dimension, became more human and probing than the conventions of his formula would reasonably permit.

The two American writers who probably influenced Chandler the most were Dashiell Hammett and Ernest Hemingway. He never equaled the incredible hardness of Hammett, nor did he penetrate so deeply into the confused darkness of the soul as Hemingway did. Despair was ineffable in Hammett. Hemingway became a citizen of the world. Chandler never experienced, as Hemingway did, the rubbery feel of an animal's beating heart, or the plunging of the knife, and the hot blood spilling over his fingers. Life was never so tenuous for Chandler because he did not live his life so fully conscious of the terrible immediacy of death. But he knew the attendant emptiness. *The Long Goodbye* (Houghton-Mifflin, 1953) became his epiphany and, at the same time, his masterpiece, his consummate withdrawal not from struggle but from life.

All of his years as a writer Chandler lived in California, where nearly all his stories are set. He shared Hammett's insularity. I suspect it was this, even more than the form in which he chose to write, that unnecessarily limited him in his scope as a novelist. From what we know of him, travel wouldn't have mattered; it wouldn't have changed anything. California bound him as the South did William Faulkner, and he never seemed aware that life might have a different tempo, existence an alternate throb or sunlight a variant glare.

Raymond Chandler was born on July 23, 1888, in Chicago, of an American father and an Irish immigrant mother. His parents were divorced when he was eight and his mother took him with her to England. Chandler was educated in English public schools and attributed to them much of his subsequent moral code. He attended Dulwich College for a time in 1905. After trying out for the Civil Service, which entailed a stay in Paris, he quit and attempted to write poetry. His poems are no credit to him, then or those he wrote after he was an established author. He finally decided to sail to the United States. Because he returned within three years of attaining his majority, he retained his American citizenship.

Landing in New York, he made his way West, spending a few weeks in St. Louis, arriving at last in Los Angeles. Chandler took what jobs he could, from picking apricots to stringing tennis rackets. At the beginning of the Great War in 1914, Chandler left California to enlist in the Canadian Armed Forces at Victoria, British Columbia. Curiously, he falsely declared himself a naturalized British subject. His battalion went first to England and then to France. Upon discharge in 1919, he was thirty-one years old and without a job. He had been shaken by the scenes of carnage he had witnessed in the trenches. He went to work for an English bank in San Francisco. The duties bored him so he moved back to Los Angeles, where, at the top of the steps known as Angels' Flight, he lived with his mother, who had joined him, caring for her in her dying years. He determined on a career in the oil business and started with the Dabney Oil Syndicate.

A few weeks after his mother died, Chandler married Pearl Cecily Hurlburt, or Cissy, as she was called. He had met and fallen in love with her while she was still married. He had even sat and discussed the whole business with Cissy and her husband before Cissy was divorced. Cissy was eighteen years his senior. It was a strange relationship, to say the least. I won't be so conventionally Freudian as to suggest that Chandler was merely acting out an aspect of the Oedipus complex. The French have a better expression for the attraction that apparently brought these two together: *psychose à deux*. One parallel which comes to mind is the darkly dramatic and passionate marriage of Nathaniel Hawthorne and Sophia Peabody. Their love fed on the same reclusiveness and emotional symbiosis as did that between Chandler and Cissy. Biographer MacShane goes to great pains to warrant how Chandler's marriage added to his stability and gave him the inner confidence he needed in order to persevere through the ordeal of becoming a writer, but his honesty and objectivity as a biographer do not allow him to overlook the embarrassment Chandler suffered in later years being married to such an old woman, whose frailty and sickliness caused him untold anguish; how he had to remain reclusive because of Cissy and his sensitivity over their relationship; or how, when Cissy died, Chandler went completely to pieces and could never pull himself together again.

The impression you get of Chandler is not so much of a man struggling with his own obstinate creativity, nor with artistic problems of any kind, but rather trying constantly to free himself from a keenly neurotic romanticism and an undue dependence on Cissy, and then on the memory of Cissy, trying desperately to fill the void which her loss occasioned.

As he became more successful as an oil company executive, Chandler endeavored to save himself, to separate himself from Cissy. He courted his secretary and took to weekending with another girl from the office when his original overtures were rebuffed. He drank. His father had been an alcoholic, but Chandler had grown up without any notion of his divorced father. Chandler was, as I imagine he had been with his mother, totally dependent upon Cissy in a very unpleasant manner and yet nevertheless desirous of breaking the bondage which held him to her. Cissy stayed with him. MacShane provides her with the best of all motives. She was quite simply too old to easily find another man.

Had Chandler been able to resolve this division in his own soul, he might never have taken to writing at all, or, if he had, he would almost certainly have been a different kind of writer. Instead, he put his frustration, his dissatisfaction, his distress into his fiction, and he conjured what for him seemed the embodiment of the only alternate acceptable to him. Philip Marlowe lived alone, worked alone, and, however lonely his life, it was enough for him.

By 1929, Chandler was an executive in several oil companies organized into the Dabney Oil Syndicate. The constant drinking, the womanizing, the inability after a time of being able to function at all led to his being terminated. He made no effort to find other employment. Chandler had read *Black Mask* magazine. He decided he wanted to write. He made an extremely detailed synopsis of one of Erle Stanley Gardner's short stories and attempted to rewrite it several times after his own fashion. "I found out that the trickiest part of your technique," he once confessed to Gardner, "was the ability to put over situations which verged on the implausible but which in the reading seemed quite real."

If Chandler admired Gardner's gift for adroit plotting, it was Hammett's style and world view which had the deepest effect on him. "Hammett wrote at first (and almost to the end) for people with a sharp, aggressive attitude toward life," Chandler once said. "They were not afraid of the seamy side of things; they lived there. Violence did not dismay them; it was right down their street. . . . He had style, but his audience didn't know it, because it was a language not supposed to be capable of such refinements. . . . He was spare, frugal, hard-boiled, but he did over and over again what only the best writers can ever do at all. He wrote scenes that seemed never to have been written before."

Chandler thought there was truth in the pulps. He wanted to write detective stories where the people one meets are more important than the puzzle. He liked the detective formula because it permitted him to include people from all strata of society. He wanted a hero unlike Hammett's, who were all hard men lacking, as Hammett did, any kind of sentiment. Chandler's hero was a different kind of fantasy, an honest man, a lonely man, a protector of women and the helpless, a lousy businessman, adolescent maybe, but outside his milieu by choice and temperament, and liberated from all binding human relationships. After all, Chandler could face his detective's bleak world with equanimity and make it stunningly vivid because he himself was not alone. He had Cissy. Because he had her, and couldn't shake himself loose of his need for her, in more than one sense we have Cissy to thank for Chandler's having given us Philip Marlowe.

Chandler submitted his first short story, "Blackmailers Don't Shoot," to *Black Mask*. Captain Shaw couldn't decide whether the eighteen-thousand-word story was remarkably good or cleverly fraudulent. He sent it to one of his established writers, W. T. Ballard, for an opinion. Ballard responded that it was remarkably good. Shaw published it in the December 1933 number and paid Chandler one cent a word. In 1934, Erle Stanley Gardner published his first Perry Mason novel, Hammett published his last novel, and Raymond Chandler was forty-five years old.

Chandler wasn't prolific. He found it extremely difficult to devise stories. "Killer in the Rain" was one of three for 1935. He published five in 1936, only two in 1937, three in 1938, five in 1939, and then not another one until 1941. Chandler's earnings were meager. In 1938, his stories netted him $1,275. Later, when he was a screenwriter at Paramount, he would confide to the various women with whom he hoped to enter into a liaison that one of the reasons he felt an obligation to his aged wife was that her money helped them survive those lean years.

Whiskey was the fuel of Chandler's detective. In the early tales, every time a corpse is discovered, the detective has to have a drink to get him through it. The atmosphere is always heavy with the tension antecedent to a storm of violence, a violence that once it cuts loose destroys all sense of order. The detective alone defends against the darkness and chaos of human malaise. Characters are dispatched with relentless regularity, although at no point does this methodology reach the bloody extravagance of Hammett's *Red Harvest*.

When Chandler liked a simile, he was no more above using it again than when he integrated several of these early stories to make up certain of his subsequent novels. In "Trouble Is My Business," at one point the detective comments: "I felt terrible. I felt like an amputated leg." In *Farewell, My Lovely* (Knopf, 1940), Marlowe tells the reader, "I got up on one foot, then on both feet, straightened up, wobbling a little. I felt like an amputated leg."

Chandler wanted to exceed Dashiell Hammett. "I thought," he wrote, "that perhaps I could go a bit further, be a bit more humane, get a bit more interested in people than in violent death." Like Hemingway, whom he very much admired, Chandler conceived of a novel as an extended short story. If he was to make a living as a writer, he felt it must be as a novelist. He had served his apprenticeship. He was ready. He took the plunge. And he was right. As a novelist, he gained international prominence and even several credits as a screenwriter. He once criticized John Dickson Carr for saying that he disliked the process of writing, but Chandler could and did say: "Everything a writer learns about the art or craft of fiction takes just a little away from his need or desire to write at all. In the end he knows all the tricks and has nothing to say." I do not know if he truly meant that.

When Captain Shaw was released from *Black Mask*, he went to work for a literary agent, Sydney Sanders. Chandler rewove "Killer in the Rain," "The Curtain," and fragments of two other stories, with much new material, into his first novel, *The Big Sleep* (Knopf, 1939). Sanders became Chandler's agent and placed the novel with Alfred A. Knopf, a tragic blunder. Knopf was a haughty man who ran an extremely cold publishing company. He preferred to publish what he considered quality fiction, which usually, because it was chosen according to his own whim, left him in the red. Therefore he had a line of detective thrillers which helped pay the bills. Hammett's books had been published by Knopf, as had the novels of James M. Cain. It was an easy matter for Sanders to place Chandler with Knopf because the firm was a ready market for hard-boiled detective fiction, but, given Chandler's ambitions, it was a bad place to be. He was only another name on the Knopf list. Knopf did virtually nothing to promote Chandler, nor did Knopf see in Chandler anything but a continuation of the successful formula Hammett had devised. Chandler's correspondence with the publisher appears in retrospect to be a constant and pitiful effort to elicit some sort of understanding from Knopf as to what Chandler was doing. It was wasted. Eventually, Chandler had to break with Knopf, which caused a split in continuity. Once a new connection was established with Houghton-Mifflin,

Knopf did nothing, and the new publisher, naturally, had no control over the previous books and thus no capacity to pursue a policy of perpetual reissue or stress Chandler's development as a writer. Because of Knopf's indifference, Chandler's first four novels had nowhere near the backing they needed to put them across, and Chandler with them, to the American reading public. (Just how important a publisher can be is perhaps best illustrated in the instance of William Faulkner, who worked on the screenplay for *The Big Sleep* [Warner's, 1946]. By staying with Random House for most of his years, and because of the sympathy his editors had for his work despite the lack of real commercial appeal in his fiction, in his later years all of the consistent plugging away for two decades finally achieved results and, for a time at any rate, Faulkner did enjoy a certain vogue. All Chandler could say at the end of his ten years with Knopf was, "It's a cold show. I have never been able to deal with people at arm's length.")

Of all Chandler's short stories, I prefer "Red Wind." Next would be "Try the Girl," published in 1937. Chandler reworked "Try the Girl" with "The Man Who Liked Dogs" and "Mandarin's Jade," into the complex plot of his second novel, *Farewell, My Lovely.* Los Angeles was the city in which nearly all his stories had been set. The impact of his first two novels brought Chandler himself to Hollywood.

Farewell, My Lovely was purchased by RKO Radio Pictures in 1942 for $2,000 and used as the basic story line for *The Falcon Takes Over.* Knopf's contract with Chandler called for more than the usual apportionment to Knopf for sale of performing rights, so even here, at this low asking price, Chandler received less than he would have had he been with another publisher. The picture was also an upsetting experience for Chandler. The Falcon films, as I have had occasion to comment elsewhere in this book, had their own splendid formula for crime detection with a high comic tone. The only thing that prevented *The Falcon Takes Over* from being a complete cinematic success was Chandler's plot. The characters belonged to Chandler's stark view of California and seemed out of place in New York being investigated by debonair George Sanders. The police, represented by James Gleason and Edward Gargan, were buffoons compared to the brutal and secure men Chandler had drawn. Chandler's third novel, *The High Window* (Knopf, 1942) was sold to Twentieth Century-Fox for $3,500 and was used, as I have mentioned, to form the basis for *Time to Kill* (20th-Fox, 1942) in that studio's Mike Shayne series.

Whatever Chandler's reaction to these films, the sale of the performing rights, combined with the fact that Joseph Sistrom, who was at Paramount and a detective story enthusiast who liked Chandler's books, led to his landing a writing job at Paramount, working first with Billy Wilder in preparing *Double Indemnity* (Paramount, 1944). Dick Powell, principally known as a singer and dancer, wanted the role of Walter Neff, the co-conspirator in the James M. Cain story. Wilder scoffed at the idea, and Fred MacMurray was cast instead. Chandler's colorful and concise prose style and his vision of crime were beginning to have their impact on Hollywood. Around this time RKO decided to remake *Farewell, My Lovely,* this time as a Philip Marlowe story—actually Marlowe's first screen appearance. Dick Powell was able to convince the film's director, Edward Dmytryk, that he should be cast in the lead.

"Dick Powell was a hog farmer from Missouri," Eddie Dmytryk told me. "He fit the character, as far as I could see. After all, what is Marlowe? He's no Sam Spade. He's an eagle scout among the tough guys. He's a moral, ethical man, with a strong sense of responsibility. I only met Chandler once. He was unusual, not at all what you'd think a detective story writer would be like. He had an off-beat way of looking at things. He hated corruption. Putting Chandler on film, I knew I couldn't improve on his dialogue. I tried my best to keep faithful to the spirit of the book."

Eddie paused to light his pipe and reflected for a few moments.

"I had looked at the Falcon picture," he resumed. "I thought it was a great story, but it had been butchered by attempting to make it fit the Falcon formula. As you know, I directed a Falcon myself, although I can't remember it. The whole tone and feel was different. In putting Chandler on the screen, you have to use a lot of shadows. Lenses and lighting were all important. I worked

Mike Mazurki hires Dick Powell in *Murder, My Sweet* (RKO, 1944).
PHOTO COURTESY OF EDWARD DMYTRYK.

out the camera positions I wanted and I picked the lenses carefully. I employed low-key lighting throughout the picture, getting rid of fills and making more contrasts. The picture was budgeted at $450,000 and we shot it in forty-four days."

Another problem confronting the screenwriter in transposing Chandler's prose to film was the imagistic expressiveness of his first-person narrative form. Dmytryk solved the difficulty by doing the picture as a series of flashbacks narrated by Marlowe himself. This permitted Powell to tell the audience that he felt awful, he felt like an amputated leg; that Moose Malloy, one of the characters, "looked about as inconspicuous as a tarantula on a slice of angel food." Malloy had been played by Ward Bond in a padded suit in *The Falcon Takes Over;* Mike Mazurki was given the role in *Murder, My Sweet* (RKO, 1944). (RKO had reservations about Chandler's original title for the novel. Knopf had objected to it because he thought it made the book seem like a love story. RKO was afraid that the title might make the public think it was getting another Dick Powell musical. They prevailed where Knopf hadn't. The sale had been outright, so Chandler received no more money, just a credit.)

The claustrophobic milieu of Chandler's world comes across in *Murder, My Sweet* as in almost no other film. Critics at the time felt that Dick Powell was ideally cast with just the right balance of adolescent banter and brash toughness. His manner was flippant. In comparison, Humphrey Bogart was probably at his best as a Chandler-like character in *Dead Reckoning* (Columbia, 1947), a film with which Chandler had nothing to do but which was highly influenced by him. Howard Hawks, who directed *The Big Sleep* subsequently at Warner's in 1946, with Bogart as Marlowe, had Bogart act out the role in the third person, whereas Powell is the constant interpreter of the action, as is Marlowe in the novels. Yet, frankly, I doubt if Marlowe was ever adequately translated to the screen. Like Nero Wolfe and Philo Vance, he cannot really exist outside the romance of his fictional setting.

One of the most stunning scenes in *The Big Sleep* is Bob Steele's poisoning of Elisha Cook, Jr., with Bogart as a silent witness. What *Murder, My Sweet* lacked in this kind of restrained brutality it compensated for in its penchant for night scenes, its close rooms, narrow hallways, and its highlight photography. At one point, Marlowe is gazing out his window, and every time a neon sign flashes off Mike Mazurki's image is seen reflected in the glass pane.

"That's where my training in science and mathematics at Cal Tech really helped me out," Dmytryk went on. "I had Dick sit at his desk. When light is reflected in glass, the image becomes smaller, not larger. I wanted the effect of it being larger. So I had a sheet of plate glass placed directly in front of the camera, with Powell sitting way beyond it. As the light goes on and off, Mazurki's image is reflected in the glass, but because it was closer to the camera than Powell is he looked gigantic in comparison. I used glass again in the final scene when I had to have a gun go off near Powell's face. The glass was between Powell and the gun. But on the screen you couldn't tell it."

"How did you get the spider web effect in the scene where Powell wakes up in the sanitarium?" I asked.

Edward Dmytryk directing Claire Trevor in *Murder, My Sweet* (RKO, 1944).
PHOTO COURTESY OF EDWARD DMYTRYK.

"I managed the effect by means of a superimposition," Dmytryk explained. "I had stills of cigarette smoke blown up in size and magnified them over the image of Powell returning to consciousness. I used a variant of the falling sequence in *Mirage* [Universal, 1965], where I had a similar scene. I put an actor on a black platform and shot him with a revolving lens, zooming the camera away. A body falling will accelerate as it falls, and there is an amount of air resistance. I then crossed the piece of revolving film with another shot with a camera zooming away faster and faster.

"To get natural effects effectively, you have to do it unnaturally. When *Murder, My Sweet* came out and Selznick was producing *Spellbound* [United Artists, 1945], he called me to ask my advice on handling a dream sequence in his picture."

"How much advice did you give him?"

"Not too much." Dmytryk smiled. "It wasn't my picture."

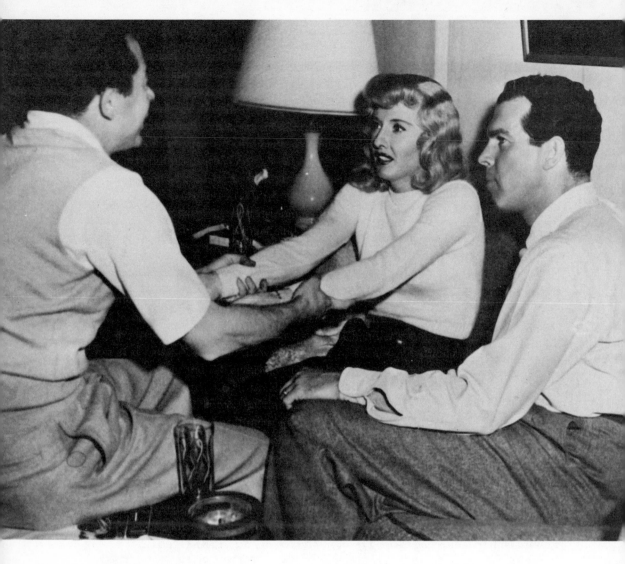

Billy Wilder directing Barbara Stanwyck and Fred MacMurray in *Double Indemnity* (Paramount, 1944).   PHOTO COURTESY OF THE NATIONAL FILM ARCHIVE.

Dmytryk didn't have Salvador Dali to work on his dream sequence in *Murder, My Sweet*, as Alfred Hitchcock did in *Spellbound*, but the effects nonetheless are nearly as impressive in a different way.

The plot of *Murder, My Sweet* is surprisingly near Chandler's makeshift original. Dmytryk managed a remarkable achievement in so designing the visuals that they lent support to Marlowe's intense subjectivity. But what I miss most in the film—and in Dick Richards' third make of it, with Robert Mitchum—is that hilarious scene Chandler wrote in which Marlowe and Mrs. Gayle proceed to get pie-eyed and fall to necking when Marlowe is supposed to be interrogating her. There is an element of comedy and satire in Chandler that none of the film versions has ever succeeded adequately in capturing.

Claire Trevor was cast by Dmytryk to play Mrs. Grayle. It was a wise choice. At one point all that indicated her presence in a room was the exhalation of cigarette smoke from where she lay reclining on a sofa. Her appearance added weight to that Chandleresque fantasy of the Forties that blondes are trouble and, where there's a murder at issue, probably at the bottom of it.

When I met with Billy Wilder in the office of his bungalow on the Universal lot in the summer of 1975, it was morning and there was bright sunlight in the room. I glanced at the golden Oscars on one of the library shelves. Billy directed me to a chair alongside his desk, which faced windows overlooking a studio street.

"You worked with Raymond Chandler on *Double Indemnity* [Paramount, 1944]," I said after a few preliminary remarks, "and the only thing you've been quoted as saying about that collaboration is that Chandler was a 'kook.'"

"Well, he was," Billy said, sitting down in his desk chair. He leaned over in my direction. "Joe Sistrom thought he would be very helpful with the dialogue. A meeting was eventually set up between us. I was to direct the picture."

Billy bounced up from his chair and began to pace about, slapping his leg with a short, silver-topped cane.

"Ray was a naïve, sweet, warm man," he said. "He had never worked in this medium before and he didn't know how to collaborate with others. He thought he was supposed to write the whole screenplay. He came back in a few days with an eighty-page screenplay we couldn't use because it consisted mostly of unfilmable descriptions."

He stopped abruptly in his pacing.

"You think that's funny?" he accused in his pleasing Viennese accent. "I had to teach him movie techniques. We started really working together."

Their association lasted ten weeks. I reminded Billy that Chandler had described the whole business as "an agonizing experience" and claimed it had probably shortened his life.

Billy was pacing again.

"He had a wonderful flair for description. We tried to find some way to use it. That's why we decided to let MacMurray open the picture confessing to the murder plot he was in with Barbara Stanwyck. That way he could describe everything. I really thought we were getting on together when one day it was nine-thirty and no Chandler. I found out later he had gone to the front office to quit. He had drawn up a long list of complaints against me."

I recalled the list: "Item—Mr. Wilder is at no time to swish under Mr. Chandler's nose or to point in his direction the thin, leather-handled malacca cane which Mr. Wilder is in the habit of waving around while they work. Item —Mr. Wilder is not to give Mr. Chandler orders of an arbitrary nature, such as 'Ray, will you open that window?' or 'Ray, will you shut that door, please?'

"He even complained that I talked to some broad for thirty-six minutes on the phone," Billy went on, pacing and slapping his leg with the cane. "He was a reformed alcoholic, as you know, and I think a little peculiar, but still a totally unique man."

Billy cast the picture. Besides Fred MacMurray and Barbara Stanwyck as the conspirators in the murder, Edward G. Robinson was chosen to play the insurance investigator who finally arrives at the truth. The film proved in tone and lighting to be a pacesetter in the cinematic style that has come to be known as *film noir*.

"Whose idea was it to change the ending and cut out the scene of MacMurray in the gas chamber?" I asked.

"Mine," Billy said. "It was anticlimactic. That's why I deleted the scene. But by that time Ray was already off the picture."

I recall reading a letter by James M. Cain, quoted in *Film Heritage*, relating how Wilder tried to convince Chandler to use Cain's original dialogue. Billy even went so far as to hire some actors to recite the book. It didn't work. Chandler told Billy that Cain's dialogue was written for the eye. They should try to duplicate only its spirit. Billy called in Cain himself. Cain agreed with Chandler. "Chandler," Cain remarked, "an older man a bit irked by Wilder's omniscience, had this odd little smile on his face as the talk went on."

II

While *Double Indemnity* was in production, Chandler contributed to the script of *And Now Tomorrow* (Paramount, 1944) and did a polish job on *The Unseen* (Paramount, 1945). After the release of *Murder, My Sweet* and when *Double Indemnity* was nominated for an Academy Award for its screenplay, Chandler's stock as a screenwriter rose. The option on Chandler's Paramount contract was up in November 1944. By January 1945 a new contract was negotiated. Chandler had hoped to return to writing fiction, but he couldn't turn down the money he was being offered. He was to be paid $1,000 a week.

Alan Ladd was going into the service in three months and Paramount wanted another picture from him. In conversation with John Houseman, producer on *The Unseen*, Chandler mentioned that he had an unfinished novel of about 120 typescript pages which he felt might work better as a motion picture. Houseman suggested the property be turned into the Ladd vehicle the studio wanted. Chandler agreed.

The screenplay which Chandler subsequently wrote, *The Blue Dahlia* (Paramount, 1946), was published by Southern Illinois University Press in 1976, prefaced by a reminiscence by John Houseman. He and Chandler became friends because they had both attended English public schools. Houseman couldn't help commenting on Chandler's curious marriage. "In Hollywood, where the selection of wives was frequently confused with the casting of motion pictures," he wrote, "Cissy was an anomaly and a phenomenon. Ray's life had been hard; he looked ten years older than his age. His wife looked twenty years older than he did and dressed thirty years younger." Houseman imagined that it was Chandler's sexual inhibitions, in addition no doubt to his problematical marriage, which prompted him to become such a skirt chaser while working in the Paramount story department.

Alan Ladd and his good friend William Bendix in a scene from *The Blue Dahlia*
(Paramount, 1946).   PHOTO COURTESY OF MCA-UNIVERSAL.

Chandler set to work at once on the screenplay, after collecting a sizable fee
above his salary for selling the property to the studio. He was able to turn in
about half the screenplay in three weeks. Shooting under director George
Marshall commenced at once. Then Chandler hit a snag. He couldn't finish it.
Studio brass, naturally concerned, tried to bribe him with an extra $5,000 bonus
if he completed the script on time. This threw Chandler into emotional apo-
plexy; he felt that his honor was at stake. He made a shocking proposal to
Houseman. Although he hadn't been drinking for some years, since he had become a writer in fact, he was convinced that he could finish the screenplay
while drunk. When Chandler drank, he didn't eat. He didn't suffer from hang-
overs, he explained, and malnutrition could be avoided through injections; just
coming off a drunk was such a physical ordeal.

After some consideration, Houseman conceded. Chandler was provided two limousines with drivers, night and day, to run errands. He had a direct line to the studio switchboard. Six secretaries in teams of two were constantly available. Chandler concluded the script and shooting ended with six days to spare. "During those last eight days of shooting," Houseman recalled, "Chandler did not draw one sober breath, nor did one speck of food pass his lips. He was polite and cheerful when I appeared and his doctor came twice a day to give him intravenous injections. The rest of the time, except when he was asleep . . . Ray was never without a glass in his hand. . . ." Chandler didn't overdo it. He drank only enough to keep himself in a perpetual state of euphoria. It required a month for his nervous system to recover from the shock when it was all over.

The Blue Dahlia, when it was released, grossed in excess of $2,700,000, and Chandler received his second nomination for best screenplay.

Chandler stayed on good terms with Houseman for many years, but he reacted violently to an article Houseman wrote for *Vogue* in which Houseman revealed his growing disappointment in what had happened to the Marlowe character over the years, becoming "a drab, melancholy man of limited intelligence and mediocre aspiration, who is satisfied to work for ten bucks a day and who, between drinks, gets beaten up regularly and laid occasionally." Yet Chandler could and did write to Houseman shortly before he died that "I never really thought of what I wrote as anything more than a fire for Cissy to warm her hands at. She didn't even much like what I wrote."

The High Window (Knopf, 1942), Chandler's next novel, wasn't based on old pulp stories. It is one of his less popular. Apparently he thought so little of it that he could sum it up to his publisher as having "no action, no likeable characters, no nothing. The detective does nothing." Chandler's books still weren't selling as well as he hoped, but no one in Hollywood knew that. Warner Brothers paid $10,000 for screen rights to *The Big Sleep*.

It was hot in Palm Springs when I went there to visit with Howard Hawks. The heat rose from the city streets in silent eddies. Howard was used to it. He walked very slowly. His legs were blistered from cactus poison.

"I've been in the hospital for the last three days," he remarked, lowering himself into a leather chair and propping up his legs. He was careful. "I was out motorcycling with my son. I made the mistake of riding through a clump of poisonous cactus. I'll be laid up at least another week, maybe ten days."

"You knew William Faulkner," I began.

"Yes, I did," Hawks responded. "I was in New York working on *Scarface*. I read Faulkner. He was employed as a clerk in Macy's bookstore. I later bought his short story 'Turnabout' and made it the basis for the picture *Today We Live* [M-G-M, 1933]. Faulkner was by then living back in Mississippi. I sent him a check and invited him to come to Hollywood to M-G-M, where I was under contract, to assist on the screenplay.

"He came to my office. 'I'm Howard Hawks,' I told him. 'I know,' he said. 'I saw your name on a check.' He sat there and smoked his pipe while I took a couple of hours to explain what I wanted. He said nothing until I finished. Then he stood up. 'Where are you going?' I asked him. 'I'm going to write your screenplay,' he said. 'It should take me no more than a week.' He didn't know anything about screenwriting. 'Wait a minute,' I said. 'I want to know something about you.' He hesitated. 'Have you got a drink?' he asked. I pulled out a bottle and we began to talk. When we finished that, we went out and visited a few saloons. By three in the morning, when the last cigarette was drowned in a whiskey glass, it was the beginning of a relationship. We were friends from that day until his death."

I remembered, as I sat in an easy chair, a letter Faulkner had sent to Howard once he returned to Oxford, Mississippi, after his stint at Metro. "I'm sitting on the porch with the rain dripping off the eaves, drinking bourbon, and I hear a wonderful sound—the toilet, and it's due to you."

"He worked for you again when you were at Warner Brothers, didn't he?" I asked. "On *The Big Sleep*."

"Yes. On that and other pictures. We both liked detective stories and we agreed that Dashiell Hammett and Raymond Chandler were the best. I also hired Leigh Brackett to work on *The Big Sleep*. I thought she was a man: she wrote like one. There was no logic in Chandler's story, but the picture proved you didn't need logic. It was a matter of scenes and pacing. It took Jules Furthman, Leigh, and Bill eight days to prepare the screenplay."

I recalled that Leigh Brackett had told me how she and Faulkner had split up the novel by chapters. Furthman did the polishing.

"Why did you cast Bogart in the Marlowe role?" I asked.

"He was the best of his kind for what I needed," Howard replied. "His first day on the picture, Bogie had five or six cocktails at lunch. He went off the lot to do it. I threw him up against a wall and told him we were going to Jack Warner's office and either he was going to get a new director or I was getting a new star. Bogie wasn't really tough; I had no more trouble with him after that. He was allowed one beer while shooting."

"And Lauren Bacall?" I inquired.

Howard looked at me for a moment. His eyes were distant. So often in his films, he has ignored dialogue and concentrated on eyes.

"I will tell you a story I have never told anyone," he said. The air in the room yawned and fell to dozing. "Her coming to Hollywood was a mistake on my secretary's part. I only wanted to find out about her and my secretary sent her an airplane ticket instead. She showed up in a sweater and gabardine skirt, very excited, with a high nasal voice. I couldn't use her. I told her it was her voice. She asked me what she could do about lowering it. I repeated what I had heard from other people. For two weeks I didn't see her. She went back to the apartment where she was staying and worked on it. When she saw me again, I was amazed. Her voice had become deep, husky.

"I began to invite her to my home for the Saturday night parties I gave. I always ended up having to drive her home.

"'Betty,' as we all called her, 'this isn't going to work. I don't always want to take you home. Can't you interest one of the others in escorting you?'

"'I've never been very good with men,' she said.

"'Why not try being insolent?' I suggested.

A script conference on *The Big Sleep* (Warner's, 1946) with (left to right) Howard Hawks, Sonia Darwin, Margaret Cunningham, Howard's secretary, Lauren Bacall, Humphrey Bogart, and Louis Jean Heydt.

PHOTO COURTESY OF THE NATIONAL FILM ARCHIVE.

"The next Saturday night she comes to me and says she has found a ride home.

" 'How'd you do it?' I asked.

"She said, 'I just walked up to him and asked him where he bought his tie. He asked me why I wanted to know. I told him so I could tell people not to go there. He laughed, and now he's driving me home.'

"It was Clark Gable.

"I got to so like her insolent style that I went to Jules Furthman when I was back on the lot. We were preparing *To Have and Have Not* [Warner's, 1944]. Furthman and Bill Faulkner were doing the screenplay. I asked Jules if he could write a part in for an insolent girl. He didn't see why not. I gave Betty a screen test with the purse scene from the picture, opposite Bogart. She was great."

The famous greenhouse scene.   PHOTO COURTESY OF UNITED ARTISTS TELEVISION.

"They fell in love," I said. "Did you try to capture that in the picture, or later, in *The Big Sleep?*"

"No. I tried to keep it out. Of course, Bogie being in love with her helped Betty. He played all his scenes for her."

Howard grew quiet. Outside the sun blazed mutely.

"Did it occur to you that Bogart was falling in love with someone who was to a certain extent your creation?" I asked.

Howard nodded.

"I even took Betty aside and warned her. 'Bogie is falling in love with you, Betty. He doesn't know it's just a role.'"

He smiled at me.

"But there is a sequel to this story, Jon. This last year when I was invited by the Academy to receive a special award, Betty was there. She came up behind me and kissed me. She said, 'I'm still playing the same role.'"

Chandler was pleased with Bogart as Philip Marlowe. "Bogart can be tough without a gun," he wrote after the picture was released. "Also, he has a sense of humor that contains that grating undertone of contempt. Alan Ladd is hard, bitter, and occasionally charming, but he is after all a small boy's idea of a tough guy. Bogart is the genuine article. Like Edward G. Robinson, all he has to do to dominate a scene is to enter it." Chandler thought Alan Ladd's touchiness about height, in view of his short stature, a defect. The romance between Ladd and Moronica Lake, as Chandler called Veronica, in *The Blue Dahlia* didn't bother Chandler especially, because of his own contemptuous attitude toward Hollywood. It's what he thought was expected. But even he could see the difference between Bogart's scenes with Bacall and those in *The Blue Dahlia.*

Leigh Brackett, when we talked about *The Big Sleep*, hastened to point out to me that Bogart projected an inner power into the Marlowe character which he didn't have in the novels. It was her second picture with Howard Hawks and she knew beforehand that he intended to cast Bogart in it. She had had him in mind while she worked on her part of the scenario.

"Bill Faulkner was good at construction," she told me. "But he was too reclusive to ever get to know very well. Then he would just disappear for two or three days at a time."

"He was supposedly drinking," I said.

"He was a very hard worker and always courteous, but I don't suppose he really liked Hollywood."

Chandler was invited to the Warner Brothers lot while *The Big Sleep* was in production. He met Leigh Brackett, William Faulkner, Humphrey Bogart, and Howard Hawks. He told them that he was happy with the screenplay and liked the ending Leigh had devised. Howard had to shorten the ending, however, because Jack Warner wanted the Bogart-Bacall romance stressed. It was becoming one of the most popular romances in the gossip magazines. The way Leigh wanted the film to conclude was that Carmen Sternwood, played by Martha Vickers, would be machine-gunned by accident. Instead it is John Ridgely playing the gangster Eddie Mars who is accidentally shot down in the final scene.

When they were filming the sequence where Owen Taylor's car is pulled out of the water on Warner's tank sound stage, Bogie asked Howard who had murdered him. After all, as the detective he felt he should know. Howard confessed he wasn't sure, but he'd ask Faulkner. Faulkner said he didn't know. So Howard wired Chandler. Chandler replied facetiously that the butler had done it. In the novel it is Brody, played in the film by Louis Jean Heydt, who murders him. But Howard couldn't find out and it was filmed without any resolution. Jack Warner did comment on the telegram to Chandler, however; he suggested that Howard not waste money on such nonsense.

There is a most memorable scene in the novel. Marlowe is taken out to a greenhouse to meet General Sternwood, who brings him into the case. In one of the source stories, "The Curtain," the scene runs approximately 1,100 words, whereas Chandler expanded it to 2,500 words in *The Big Sleep*. Chandler made tangible the physical reality of the humid heat and the decay, but it took Howard Hawks's sensitivity to human relationships to get the characters in the film off talking tough and revealing a momentary affection for one another, such as between Bogie's Marlowe and Charles Waldron's General Sternwood. Throughout the picture Marlowe is able to relate to people in a way he never can in the novels. The loneliness in which Marlowe perpetually dwells is lifted. *The Big Sleep* on the screen is not haunted by that heavy emotional oppression which the book establishes in the greenhouse and never relinquishes.

In 1943, Chandler put together two of his finest short stories and added a wealth of new material to create the detective novel which I feel to be his most engaging, *The Lady in the Lake*. Metro-Goldwyn-Mayer bought screen rights to it in 1946 and paid $35,000.

Chandler, who in *The High Window*, in a thinly veiled characterization, described Alfred Knopf as "a big burly Jew with a Hitler moustache, pop eyes, and the calmness of a glacier," finally had enough and began seeking a new publisher. But he had no new novel. Paramount had thrown a party for him at which *The Blue Dahlia* was screened. Chandler was becoming increasingly difficult to deal with. After turning down a number of books recommended by the studio, he worked for a time on adapting a novel called *The Innocent Mrs. Duff*, but his contract expired before he finished. The project was shelved.

George Haight, who was the producer on *Lady in the Lake*, hired Chandler to work on the screenplay. Chandler complained about everything at the Culver City lot, starting off with the fact that writers weren't allowed couches on which to lie down while cogitating. He was eventually allowed to work at home. Haight was displeased with the results because Chandler kept rewriting the book. He told Haight it was his story and he was sick of it, so why not create a new story? Haight's comeback that the studio had bought the book because they wanted the story fell on deaf ears. After thirteen weeks, all his contract called for, Chandler quit and was replaced by Steve Fisher. Fisher did the screenplay but got in a hassle over screen credit with Chandler, a hassle which almost brought Chandler to blows with Frank Gruber, a friend of Fisher's, at the *Blue Dahlia* party. Fisher got the credit.

Chandler's next assignment was for Universal, where Joseph Sistrom went after leaving Paramount. Chandler was paid $4,000 a week for two years, producing one original screenplay entitled *Playback*. It was never filmed. Chandler later made it the basis for his last, and worst, novel, published with the same title by Houghton-Mifflin in 1958.

Chandler's final screen collaboration was for Alfred Hitchcock, adapting Patricia Highsmith's novel *Strangers on a Train* (Warner's, 1951). He didn't get along much better with Hitchcock than he had with Billy Wilder. He was guaranteed $2,500 a week for five weeks' work. He was living now in a large house in La Jolla. Hitchcock drove down for a story conference. Chandler was antagonistic from the start. "Look at that fat bastard trying to get out of his car!" he remarked so loudly to his secretary that Hitchcock overheard it.

Hitchcock found his meetings with Chandler difficult, not only because of Chandler's customary rudeness, but because Chandler couldn't seem to get the idea of a co-operative enterprise through his head.

"We'd sit together and I would say, 'Why not do it this way?' and he'd answer, 'Well, if you can puzzle it out, what do you need me for?'"

Hitchcock looked steadily at me as he recalled working with Chandler.

"A cobbler should stick to his last," he summed it up.

Chandler proved Hitchcock right when he complained morosely that the director was "full of little suggestions and ideas, which have a cramping effect on a writer's initiative. . . . This is very hard on a writer, especially on a writer who has any ideas of his own, because the writer not only has to make sense out of a foolish plot, if he can, but he has to do that and at the same time do it in such a way that any kind of camera shot or background shot that comes into Hitchcock's mind can be incorporated into it."

Chandler was forced to share a credit for the screenplay with Czenzi Ormonde, a woman writer who worked as one of Ben Hecht's assistants. He didn't like it and he didn't like the fact that the picture proved such a success upon its release. "I don't know why it's a success," he wrote to his English publisher, Hamish Hamilton; "perhaps because Hitchcock succeeded in removing almost every trace of my writing from it."

Matthew J. Bruccoli put it rather aptly in his Afterword to the published version of the screenplay from *The Blue Dahlia.* "But blame also attaches to Chandler," he wrote, after weighing both sides, "whose contempt for the professionals rendered him incapable of collaborating with them comfortably, even when he was assigned to work with the best in the business. Indeed, this contempt was hardly distinguishable from self-contempt. When he was in the position to write *The Blue Dahlia* alone, he had to anesthetize himself."

III

Robert Montgomery, who took over direction of *They Were Expendable* (M-G-M, 1945) when John Ford broke his leg, wanted to direct films rather than act in them. He urged the studio to let him make a film based on John Galsworthy's *Escape,* about the effect an escaped convict has on the people around him. His idea was to do it using the first-person camera technique: no one had ever done a film using this technique throughout. The studio responded by offering him *Lady in the Lake.* Montgomery countered that he then would want to portray Marlowe through the new technique. Louis B. Mayer, still in charge of production, not only nixed the idea but went so far as to say it was absolutely impossible to sustain audience interest with such idiocy.

Montgomery got Eddie Mannix, the studio's general manager and Mayer's assistant, to agree to make a test of the new technique. The way Montgomery had it done was to employ a series of fast pans until the camera came to the person or object it was to focus on, very much like natural eye movement. Mannix, once he saw the test, told Montgomery to proceed despite Mayer's hostility to the notion.

I arranged to visit with Montgomery in New York. He had not changed very much in the years since he had been off the screen. He was a bit heavier; his glasses were set in lighter colored frames than when he was the host on early television's "Robert Montgomery Presents." The gentleness which had characterized him all through his career was still evident along with that quiet but firm sense of artistic integrity which had forced him to retire from television production rather than accept network domination.

"Once Mannix gave me the go-ahead," Montgomery recalled, "I started preparing the script at once and casting the picture. Preparing the script was easy."

"Is there any particular reason you can think of that Steve Fisher changed the time in the film to Christmas?" I asked.

"None I can think of. The real challenge was the filming itself. We had to do a lot of rehearsing. Actors are trained *not* to look at the camera. I had to overcome all that training. I had a basket installed under the camera and sat there, so that at least the actors could respond to me even if they couldn't look directly at me. Jayne Meadows, who played the landlady, had a very difficult scene with a half page of dialogue delivered to the camera without being able to look away once. The head of the camera department had to mount the camera on a boom to get me standing up from a sitting position. But the most complicated scene, as I remember, was that where Marlowe crawls to the telephone booth. It took four people just to handle the action. We had to remove all the walls of the booth after Marlowe gets inside."

Montgomery smiled.

"But every day we were ahead of schedule. We averaged three minutes of finished film a day. We were nineteen days ahead when the last scene was shot.

"It was an inexpensive film to make. Mannix liked it a lot. So, too, in the end did Mayer. When it turned out that *Lady in the Lake* was M-G-M's third top grossing film for that year, Mayer even had an article run in the trades with the heading 'Mayer Does It Again.'"

After films like Dmytryk's *Murder, My Sweet* and Hawks's *The Big Sleep*, it cerned about the project?"

"Not at all. I had total control on the picture because no one really knew *what* was going on. The real trick of the whole thing was to always keep in mind that the audience would actually be playing a part in the picture."

After films like Dmytryk's *Murder, My Sweet* and Hawks's *The Big Sleep*, it may seem heretical on my part to suggest that *Lady in the Lake* was the best of the Marlowe films, but I cannot help it. Montgomery's conception of the role comes closest to the way I have pictured Marlowe in the novels. Steve Fisher's screenplay sparkles with wisecracks. At one point, Audrey Totter, playing with consummate adeptness the role of Adrienne Fromsett, is discussing Marlowe's manuscript of a detective story with Leon Ames as Derace Kingsby, head of Kingsby Publications. She relates how full it is of vividness and excitement, and then, at a loss for a word, turns to Marlowe and sweetly asks, "What would you say it was full of, Marlowe?" Marlowe gets his chance later on when he is describing Adrienne's conduct. He makes a few superlative suggestions and then turns to Adrienne, "What would *you* say you're full of, Miss Fromsett?" When

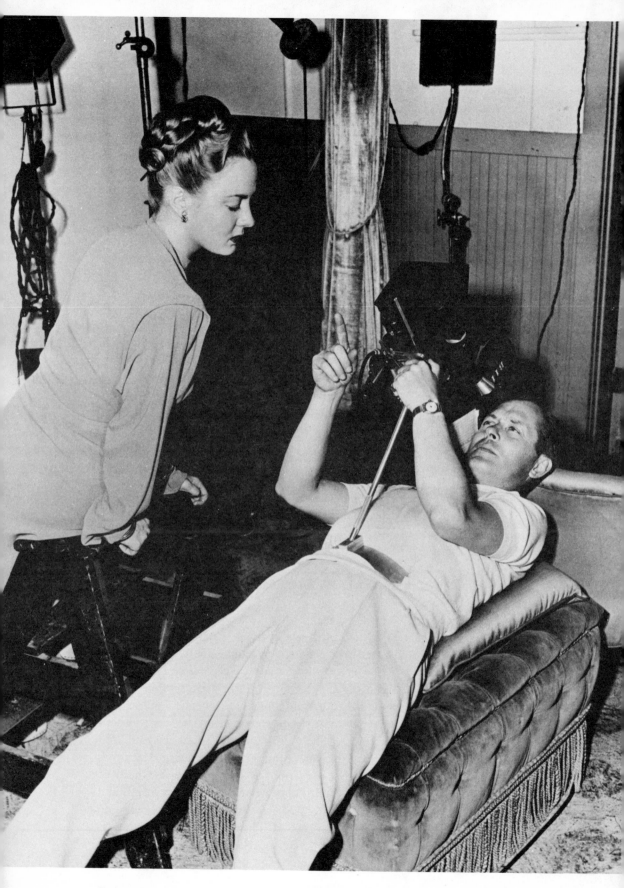

Robert Montgomery himself photographing the scene where Audrey Totter bends over him to talk sweet. PHOTO COURTESY OF THE NATIONAL FILM ARCHIVE.

Adrienne tries to prompt Marlowe as to how he should express himself in describing her, Marlowe returns bluntly, "I was thinking of a shorter word."

From the very outset, Montgomery involves us in the story and with Marlowe. The pictures opens in Marlowe's office and Montgomery talks directly into the camera, explaining how he got into the case to begin with. On and off throughout the film, in addition to engaging the suspects in conversation or in making observations to the audience, Marlowe also builds his own personality, ruminating, as when he says to himself more than to the audience, "Quit wondering, Marlowe. Get out of it."

In no other Marlowe film do you find quite the same degree of alienation between Marlowe and the world in which he lives, so true in the novels, as here. You feel almost physically that sense of suspicion and separation which the detective must always maintain. There are brilliant effects, such as when Marlowe talks to Jayne Meadows, both of them standing in front of a store window, and

Lloyd Nolan when he belts Marlowe, acting into the camera.
PHOTO COURTESY OF THE NATIONAL FILM ARCHIVE.

Audrey Totter and Leon Ames acting into the camera.

PHOTO COURTESY OF THE NATIONAL FILM ARCHIVE.

Lloyd Nolan and Jayne Meadows at the end, facing Marlowe as the camera.

PHOTO COURTESY OF THE NATIONAL FILM ARCHIVE.

you see her face only in reflection. Or when Lloyd Nolan, such an uncommonly lovable guy off screen, constantly threatens or menaces you, grimacing in his frustration, or viciously pouring whiskey over you, as the camera's eye, trapped in an overturned car while in a semicomatose state. Or the headlights of Nolan's pursuing car, seen only through the rear-view mirror, gaining on you. For me, the technique works.

"I nearly lost an eye in that picture," Lloyd Nolan told me. "In the final scene, I'm supposed to be shot by a gun fired from outside the window on the fire escape. They had to physically shoot a gun pellet through the glass to get the splintering effect. The pellet ricocheted at a ninety-degree angle."

Lloyd motioned with his hand.

"One piece flew into my eye, actually curving around the cornea. They rushed me to a hospital where a female doctor carefully removed it."

Chandler's most significant contribution to the cinema of the Forties was his dialogue. Perhaps many of his problems as a screenwriter, other than the obvious fact that he was a very difficult and fussy man, stemmed from the circumstance that he wasn't visual in the way a film director has to be visual. Chandler was word-bound. Billy Wilder liked his descriptions, but of people, not places. Chandler's style was distilled in Marlowe's contempt, his verbal isolation, his cracking wise.

The novelty of Chandler's prose was completely lost when Twentieth Century-Fox undertook to remake *The High Window* in 1947, as *The Brasher Doubloon*. George Montgomery was utterly lifeless and routine. The picture was actually no more than a "B" unit effort, the first Marlowe picture per se to be that. It was also the last Marlowe picture filmed during Chandler's lifetime.

Chandler condemned Hollywood screenwriters as unimaginative hacks in a nasty article for *The Atlantic*. His bitterness didn't help him with Hollywood producers, nor did his decision to turn down what scripts *were* offered to him. After *The Brasher Doubloon* Hollywood gave up on Chandler. Movies, of course, had accepted his idiom, the reliance on slang and hyperbole and tough talk and the wisecrack. Increasingly American society was depicted as afflicted with an intrinsic corruption. But Philip Marlowe, Chandler's balance, his shining knight, vanished. The screen detective took on yet other characteristics.

There was a long hiatus between books. *The Little Sister* (Houghton-Mifflin, 1949) appeared a full six years after *The Lady in the Lake*. *The Long Goodbye* was published in 1954. *Playback* came in 1958.

When Marlowe was again revived on screen in 1969, it was probably inevitable that he should come out looking like a James Garner. Chandler's world view no longer held the same currency because, like the California climate, which had altered from clear skies to smog-filled clouds, the world had changed and the social milieu with it. The dialogue style had to change because the way Americans talked and acted on screen had undergone a dramatic transition. The basis for *Marlowe* (M-G-M, 1969) was *The Little Sister*, which was ostensibly Chandler's Hollywood novel. It wasn't that in large measure because Chandler never quite understood how Hollywood during the period he wrote actually altered a person's entire perspective; Chandler settled for Hollywood types he had

Sharon Farrell as the "little sister" hiring James Garner's Marlowe.
PHOTO COURTESY OF METRO-GOLDWYN-MAYER.

known. It's not the same thing and, by 1969, even the types of characters he had known had little basis in contemporary reality. Marlowe was the prudish detective who, in *The Big Sleep*, had torn up the sheets on his bed rather than fornicate with a female suspect and contaminate his apartment with sexuality; now Garner had to be given a girl friend and idled away his spare time watching the girls in a modeling school across an areaway go through their exercises. The toughness, the loneliness, the sense of claustrophobic isolation gave quarter to only a superficial wittiness.

In the final years of Cissy's life, as she died by inches of fibrosis, Chandler dried out sufficiently to write what critics generally concede to be his finest novel. The reader already knows that I do not think it his best detective story, but I willingly admit the claim that *The Long Goodbye* has to being considered as literature rather than in any way a thriller. Having been unsuccessful in his efforts to overcome his total dependency on Cissy, Chandler became sentimental, telling all what a happy marriage it had always been and how much it had enriched his life. I do not doubt that he actually persuaded himself that it had been so.

The Long Goodbye was Chandler's creative thrust in one direction while his emotions were agonizingly being torn apart in the opposite. Marlowe's isolation, his alienation are more acute, more bitter than ever before.

When Robert Altman came to direct *The Long Goodbye* (United Artists, 1973), he felt very strongly about the Marlowe character: Adolescence in the United States had come now to extend to at least twenty-five years of age. Marlowe, well over thirty, has refused to grow up and his attitude toward women is prepubescent. Therefore, Marlowe is a loser; he is a mumbler and a bumbler. Altman told Leigh Brackett, who worked on the screenplay, "I see Marlowe the way Chandler saw him, a loser. But a *real* loser, not the fake winner that Chandler made out of him. A loser all the way."

One cold day in the winter of 1972, I was sitting in Bart Farber's office at United Artists on Seventh Avenue in New York. Bart is legal counsel and vice president of television for the firm. He was in the process of renegotiating television rights for United Artists to continue to distribute *The Falcon Takes Over* and *Murder, My Sweet* from the current owner of performing rights on the Chandler literary properties.

"Who's going to direct *The Long Goodbye* for you?" I asked him.

"Robert Altman."

"He's the best we have. But the picture can't work."

"Why not?"

"Because if you do it as a period piece, it will be too dated for much audience empathy. If you update it, why buy a dated novel?"

He shrugged his shoulders.

"I just negotiate the rights," he said. "I don't decide what pictures to make."

After the picture was released to a disappointing box office, I talked to Leigh Brackett about it. Her reaction was similar to what mine had been.

"The problems for me," she responded, "began with the plot. It broke down. You couldn't really translate it to the screen. It was hackneyed even when

Robert Altman directing Nina van Pallandt and Elliott Gould in *The Long Goodbye*
(United Artists, 1969). PHOTO COURTESY OF THE NATIONAL FILM ARCHIVE.

Chandler wrote it, riddled with clichés. The big decision we had was whether it should be done as a period piece or if we could update it. I felt we should update it. The Los Angeles Chandler wrote about was long gone; in a sense it never really existed outside of his imagination. Nor do people, even in the movies, talk anymore the way they talk in a Chandler novel. Brian Hutton was supposed to be the director, but he got offered another picture. Bob Altman took over. Hutton had wanted Elliott Gould for the part of Marlowe. Elliott Kastner, our producer, went to United Artists and made the deal so Hutton could have Gould. Bob is a good director. But when he got on the picture, he had Elliott Gould and *The Long Goodbye*."

"I don't think they really go together," I said.

"It's what we had, though," Leigh said. "Bob and I spent a lot of time talking over the plot, who'd done it, who lost what. I wrote one script, and then had to change the construction later. Bob wanted Marlowe to be a loser. I had to agree with him that all Chandler ever wrote had about it the feeling of a loser."

"I more than half suspect," I said, "that for Chandler life appeared that way. He felt he had lost at everything he ever tried. He romanticized Marlowe's barren life about as much as he romanticized his marriage."

"I met Chandler only once," Leigh returned. "I know he wanted Marlowe to be depicted as an honest man, and somebody who was his own man. I wanted to get that in my screenplay. But I also had to show Marlowe the way he looks to us now in the Seventies. The first script I had was too long. I shortened it. But the ending was inconclusive. I had Marlowe shooting Terry Lennox at the end. It was the only way I could think to handle it. The alternative would be for him to just be a louse, to walk away from it. I didn't think that a moral ending. Hutton had wanted to end it this way."

"How did Bob Altman look at it?" I asked.

"He wasn't so concerned about the ending as how we got there. He conceived of the film as a satire. Bob changed a lot of things. Nina Van Pallandt was his idea as Mrs. Wade. So was Sterling Hayden as Wade. Bob didn't have too much choice. I wrote the part for Dan Blocker, but he died. So when Hayden was cast, the whole plot was thrown off base. The Malibu location was Bob's idea. So was Wade's suicide, walking into the ocean. I had written Blocker in as a large, cowardly type who would strike his wife. A big man with nothing inside. When Bob came to do the scenes between Marlowe and Wade, he had Gould and Hayden ad lib most of the dialogue."

"Whose idea was the scene where Mark Rydell rams the Coke bottle into his girl friend's face?"

"Bob Altman's. That's pure Altman. So, really, is the Gould-Marlowe character. Bob built up his character from the bar and cat scenes. Gould isn't tough at all. He looks vulnerable. You have to work with what you have. Marlowe isn't what he was in *The Big Sleep*, but Elliott Gould isn't Humphrey Bogart."

"But," I interposed, "when you've changed a character that much, what was the good of basing him on Marlowe at all?"

Leigh sighed. "Because Marlowe, as Chandler saw him, would be unthinkable in the Seventies."

Robert Altman was working on a picture titled *Three Women* when I visited him on location in Palm Springs. The idea for the picture had come to him in a dream. As fate had it, the bus terminal scene was being filmed. Ruth Nelson was cast as an old woman in the film, and Bob Altman, out of homage, had talked her husband, director John Cromwell, into taking a part as well. During a break, I thought it an excellent opportunity to talk with Cromwell about a film of his —which both Altman and I greatly admired—*Dead Reckoning*. Cromwell was ninety. He had let the stubble of his beard grow for the part.

"I don't suppose anyone has told you lately that *Dead Reckoning* was a good picture," I said.

"What was that?" he asked, stepping closer.

"*Dead Reckoning?* It was a good picture."

He screwed up his face in a look of disgust and made a downward motion with his thumb.

"He doesn't like any of the pictures he made," Ruth Nelson explained.

Altman was dressed casually, wearing khaki shorts and a golf cap. His hair and beard were shot with gray. He would track all the shots with the camera himself before he decided on a take.

"Was it your idea to cast Elliott Gould in *The Long Goodbye?*" I asked once we had a chance to talk informally.

"No. David Picker, who was then president of United Artists, had the idea. Jerry Bick, one of the producers, came over to my house one night and asked me what I thought of Gould as Marlowe. United Artists saw in it a way to get Gould through with his contract with them and Bick, if he could get the picture together, had a deal. I thought Elliott was a great idea. I went on for two hours telling Bick why. That was my mistake, I guess. The picture had been offered to Howard Hawks and then Peter Bogdanovich. They had both turned it down. In telling Bick that he should cast Elliott, I just talked myself into doing it."

"Did you really think of Marlowe as Gould?"

Altman smiled.

"There's no reality in the Marlowe character. Marlowe can only exist in the minds of the readers or in an audience. He's an anticharacter. I tried to play him as if he had been asleep for thirty years. There was a line they cut out which summed him up. Marlowe's friend, Terry Lennox, sees some girls in the next apartment bathing without their tops on. He says to Marlowe, 'I'll bet you have a lot of fun here.' Marlowe replies, 'It's no fun anymore, unless I can take off their brassieres.'"

"Did you agree with Leigh Brackett's ending?"

"I wouldn't have done the picture if it had a different ending. Marlowe's biggest mistake was depending on friendships. Lennox was his friend. Friendship was all Marlowe had. When his friend betrayed him, he had to kill him."

Altman was called back to the set. Once the scene was completed, the entire company was to return to the motel set. Altman climbed into the car with me.

"Now tell me about this book you're writing," he said.

I explained to him that what I was concerned with was the detective genre.

"Well," he said, "that's what *The Long Goodbye* was about. It was about a private detective. It's not a very honorable profession, you know. It's never had anything to do with digging up the truth. A private eye turns over what he finds to whoever hires him and his employer can put it to whatever use he chooses."

We drove out of the parking lot. Altman glanced back at the bus terminal.

"Whew," he said, "I'm glad that's finished. I feel like such an idiot making a movie in public places. Everyone always stares at you as if you're crazy, or something."

"Leigh told me that you improvised a lot at the Malibu setting, especially the dialogue between Marlowe and Sterling Hayden."

"Just the scenes where they were drinking were improvised," Altman replied.

Robert Mitchum's older, wearier Marlowe.

PHOTO COURTESY OF SWANK MOTION PICTURES.

"I wanted the Hayden character to represent Chandler. I love Chandler. He didn't think plot was very important, and neither do I. A plot for him was just an excuse to hang onto it a hundred little thumbnail essays. I tried to put myself into Chandler's position, if he was alive in 1973 and doing a movie. I never finished *The Long Goodbye*. I read the end of the book, and the beginning, but I didn't read it all the way through. I used *Raymond Chandler Speaking*. I had everyone read it. I wanted to put more of Chandler in the movie than Marlowe. I thought the philosophy of the picture was summed up with the notion of live and let live. That's why I ended it with the theme 'Hooray for Hollywood.' I wanted to say to the audience, 'It's just a movie, folks.' "

"That's one of the things that bother me," I said. "If it was your intention to do *The Long Goodbye* as a satire, why have the scene where Mark Rydell, as the hoodlum, smashes a Coke bottle in his girl friend's face?"

Altman gave me a knowing grin.

"That was a calculating device," he returned. "The audience of today has trouble dealing with drama and humor. They won't allow you to do both to-gether. The Coke bottle sequence brought violence into the film. It was sup-posed to get the attention of the audience and remind them that, in spite of Marlowe, there is a real world out there, and it is a violent world. It was the same with Hayden's suicide. In the novel, it's faked. It's really murder. But be-cause Hayden was based on Chandler, I put all of Chandler's suicide notions into the character and made the suicide real. It was right out of *A Star Is Born.*"

After parking the car outside the motel set, Altman went inside. The rest of the cast and crew was arriving.

"I just don't feel like working today," he confessed to an assistant. "How about a little pool," he suggested, looking at me. He racked the balls and began to play. He scratched. Then he scratched again. "I'm good at sinking the white ball," he said.

"I know the critics have read a great deal of symbolism into the scene at Malibu where Elliott Gould is reflected in the glass doors while Hayden is hav-ing an argument with Nina Van Pallandt," I said.

"That's what symbolism is, isn't it?" Altman asked, preparing his next shot. "Something critics read into a picture that wasn't intended? It works for them. All I wanted to do in that scene was to avoid violating Marlowe's point of view. I didn't want the audience to see anything Marlowe didn't. That's why I super-imposed his image over the scene."

"Chandler's fans didn't like the picture," I said.

"I know," Altman said. "It surprised me. It still surprises me. But you know, people will accept anything as all right in their own lives, but they make strong demands on their heroes. People like to continue to believe in what they once believed in. Even if they feel differently than they once did, they don't want to feel differently about their heroes."

"I have reason to know that's true," I interjected.

"It's no different with detectives than cowboys," Altman went on. "But if I had the picture to do over, I wouldn't change a thing. People were disappointed because they expected to see Bogart, not Marlowe. But Bogart, when he died, marked the end of a certain style. It doesn't exist anymore. When I was doing *Nashville,* I had to figure out everything very carefully so as not to offend any-one. We picked out the wardrobe so that our actors weren't all that gaudily dressed. The people on the street, who weren't the actors, were dressed far more extremely. We couldn't do that with the actors. That's the way it is in a film. People won't accept the truth. If you give it to them, you'll be condemned for it. My concern in *The Long Goodbye* was with Chandler and Marlowe as they would have been in 1973, not with Bogart, or with anything from the Forties. That's why Marlowe drives an old car. He's the only character who smokes in the picture, and he does so incessantly. Elliott wore only one suit and one tie. The only thing he changed was his shirt."

"Apparently," I said, "producers had been having trouble with Gould. That wasn't your experience."

"No. I had made three pictures with him and found Elliott to be very professional. He's quiet on the set and doesn't talk much to anyone. But he knew what we were doing and he went along with it completely."

Altman laid down his cue stick and faced me.

"You might say I have a distorted view of things. But it's my view. And I cherish it."

What *The Long Goodbye* lost most of all in its translation to the screen was the Chandler dialogue. Instead of Marlowe remarking, "I reacted to that just the way a stuffed fish reacts to cut bait," Elliott Gould says the cops have the case "all zippered up like a big bag of shit." Chandler used to keep notebooks where he jotted down similes and metaphors he liked. He would consult these notes when he sat down to write.

Chandler had said originally of *The Long Goodbye*, "I cared about the people, about this strange corrupt world we live in, and how any man who tried to be honest looks in the end either sentimental or plain foolish." In the Altman film, Marlowe is neither: he has surrendered to unmotivated and, consequently, meaningless rage against the world and all that is in it.

Elliott Kastner, who produced *The Long Goodbye*, was also the producer on *Farewell, My Lovely* (Avco Embassy, 1975). After their $959,000 gross with *The Long Goodbye*, United Artists had no desire to distribute the third film adaptation of Chandler's second novel. In this, they were mistaken. The picture was surprisingly successful, both in the United States and in Europe. It was directed by Dick Richards. I thought highly of his Western *The Culpepper Cattle Company* (20th-Fox, 1972) and told him so as we sat in his office at the Goldwyn Studios on Santa Monica Boulevard.

"I have visited several times with Howard Hawks," I said. "I have on at least two occasions talked extensively with Eddie Dmytryk about *Murder, My Sweet*. Both Robert Montgomery and Bob Altman have spoken with me at length. I am amazed that you can find so many different interpretations of the Marlowe character. I have several tape recordings made from transcriptions of the Marlowe radio shows in the late Forties, those with Gerald Mohr, who played the Lone Wolf in the movies, not Van Heflin, who was the first radio Marlowe. Marlowe comes off almost better in the Mohr broadcasts than in any of the films, except for perhaps *Lady in the Lake*. I think Marlowe is time-bound, I guess. But Bob Altman updated the character. Why didn't you?"

Richards sat poised behind his desk, his blue-green eyes attentive.

"I was given an updated script when I was offered the picture," he replied. "I turned it down. I thought it was sacrilegious to screw around with that book."

"What happened then?"

"It was the same producer, Elliot Kastner, as on *The Long Goodbye*. Jerry Bick, the other executive producer, had also been on *The Long Goodbye*. They told me to make any changes in the script I wanted to make. David Goodman and I rewrote the whole thing, making it a period piece."

"Well," I said, "I have to admit that the way you did it, it worked. When *The Long Goodbye* was in preproduction, I didn't think it was possible for it to be brought off as a period piece."

"*The Long Goodbye* is very late Chandler," Richards said. "*Farewell, My*

Lovely is from Chandler's early period. I think he wrote well in that period. His dialogue is sharper. Everything was better. I tried to stay true to Chandler. The dialogue is what makes Chandler tick. That I wanted to keep. There was a lot about the book that was unbelievable. But not the dialogue."

"You changed the plot. You substituted a cathouse for the asylum and a madam for the psychic, Jules Amthor."

"I didn't like Amthor as a villain. That's one of the things I found unbelievable in the novel. It played better, I thought, the way we changed it. And we created a subplot. We gave Marlowe a friend. In the novels, he has no one."

"In the novels," I said, "he doesn't trust anyone enough to make him a friend." I thought of Marlowe's relationship with Anne Riordan in *Farewell*, but her part was written out of Richards' screen treatment.

"Well, that's where Bob Mitchum came in," Richards went on. "He played Marlowe like a man of his age. He's tired. Marlowe is tough, smart, but fallible. He can say, almost at the end, 'Now, I get it.' It's nearly too late. But he knows how to get information."

"How did Mitchum take to the role?"

"Oh, he liked the role. But he was worried about how he would be accepted, playing Marlowe. Bob Mitchum is a great sardonic character. That's the way I wanted him to play Marlowe. And, of course, he had always wanted to play Marlowe. We talked over the role quite a bit. But we agreed what kind of guy Marlowe was."

"Did you look at *Murder, My Sweet?*"

"I looked at *Murder, My Sweet* and at the Falcon picture. I wanted Los Angeles to be seedy in my film, the way it had been when Chandler described it. We shot the whole picture right here. I used an old boat for the gambling ship."

"Chandler based Bay City on Santa Monica," I said. "Eddie Dmytryk told me that they used to lock up Santa Monica at night. Chandler drew his cops as corrupted men. You didn't."

"No. For me, the picture was about Marlowe. In *The Culpepper Cattle Company*, there are no heroes. Marlowe is a hero. We debated for months how to handle the last scene, where Marlowe gives money to the widow. I wasn't so concerned with corruption. There's plenty of that in the picture. I wanted to stress Marlowe's honesty."

IV

After the death of Cissy in December, 1954, Chandler had a chance to travel and spent as much time as he could in England. He was given an opportunity to meet both Somerset Maugham and Noel Coward at a party. Once the party was in progress, as Chandler did so often, he telephoned to beg off. He used to claim Cissy was his excuse. When he could no longer do that, he still avoided meeting people. If this strikes the reader as rather curious, in view of how most writers, even when they're introverted, go out of their way to meet new people for the sake of variety in their fiction, it is less common among detective story writers than anywhere else. Perhaps this is one of the reasons that characters in detective fiction so infrequently come to life. Chandler's early stories and novels were drawn from the people he was forced to encounter as an oil company executive. His later novels resulted from acquaintances while he was a screenwriter. Once he gained the seclusion he wanted, he didn't have anything more to write about.

Those who knew Chandler at all attributed his reclusiveness to Cissy, embarrassment about his marriage, or to an innate shyness. He rarely looked at the person he was talking to. A skin irritation made him disinclined to shake hands. When an admirer at the Paramount commissary once came over to his table and asked merely to shake his hand, Chandler refused curtly. It was an old man. When the old man turned away, Chandler remarked loudly, "Who's that old bastard? Imagine coming around here and making a nuisance of himself."

While he lived in La Jolla, and when he was writing, it was Chandler's custom to type out his fiction in the mornings from nine to twelve or one o'clock. He used half sheets of yellow paper to save on the amount of retyping he might have to do should he decide to add something. Often the night before he would sit for some time and work out in his head what he intended to type the next morning. When a manuscript was completed, Chandler would start the story all over again, many times not even consulting the previous manuscript. When, at last, he felt the book was ready, he would have a secretary type it.

When Cissy died, there were all of eight people at the funeral. Chandler had her cremated and placed in a vault in the Cyprus View Mausoleum in San Diego. "For thirty years, ten months, and four days," Chandler wrote later, "she was the light of my life, my whole ambition." Freed of her, he set out to find another woman to replace her in his life. He failed. For a long time he courted Natasha Spender, who was married to English literary critic Stephen Spender. As might be imagined, Spender was not altogether pleased with the attentions Chandler paid his wife, nor the intentions he had, but was surprisingly tolerant all the same.

Chandler's books and subsidiary rights earned him between $15,000 and $25,000 a year. He spent most of it foolishly on potential candidates for marriage. He made over his will to at least two other women before he finally settled it on Helga Greene, his literary agent who lived in London. She had agreed to marry him. Chandler got as far as New York on his way to consummate this new love match, when the urgent letters from another woman he had adopted while in La Jolla summoned him back to California. He had been drinking incessantly for years, especially since Cissy's death. On March 23, 1959, he was submitted to the La Jolla Convalescent Hospital with pneumonia. He died three days later.

The woman in La Jolla was outraged that Chandler had deflected his estate of $60,000, plus his copyrights. Helga Greene was in England, too ill to come to the States. So Chandler's corpse lay alone in the funeral parlor, a sort of testament to the indirections of his life. Although the same minister who had performed the burial service for Cissy presided at the proceedings, no one thought to have Chandler's remains cremated, as had been his wish, nor was he even buried in the same cemetery with Cissy.

For me, Raymond Chandler's fiction is a protracted study in loneliness and, like so many of the films based on it, a representation of the greed, malice, and predatory nature of many human relationships. Life found Chandler "a lonely old eagle." He could solve the problem of loneliness only through excessive drinking or a sentimental attachment to a woman in whom sexuality was not the decisive factor. For Marlowe, Chandler could find no solution at all. He tried, not very successfully, to marry off Marlowe in a novel he left unfinished.

Robert Altman may not have been too wide of the mark by reacting to Chandler's vision of the world with hostility. Marlowe lives in the cruelest isolation. But, taken on his own terms, as one of the dubious heroes of American fiction, he nonetheless does have his own unshakable integrity. Raymond Chandler should have been so fortunate.

TEN:
Interlude: Film Noir

*"Some day fate, or some mysterious force, can
put the finger on you or me for no reason at all."*
Tom Neal in Detour (PRC, *1946*)

I

Dashiell Hammett was fond of using dreams and fables in his fiction. In *Red
Harvest,* the Continental Op has two dreams, both dealing with pursuit and both
ending in capture. The dreams, occurring at different points in the narrative, are
intended to externalize for the reader internal changes which are taking place in
the Op. In the second dream, the Op takes a plunging fall with his enemy. In his
attempt to fight corruption, he has embraced it. In *The Glass Key*, Janet Henry
dreams that she and Ned Beaumont are lost in a forest. They come upon a
house. They are starving. Inside the house are many good things to eat, but the
key to the door is made of glass. It breaks in the old lock. The door, once
opened, cannot be shut again. The house is full of snakes. They pour out on top
of them. The snakes hadn't been visible when they had looked through the windows.

The first time she relates this dream to Ned Beaumont, the Henry girl doesn't
tell him the right ending. We find it out later. In trying to get at the good
things in life, we expose ourselves to mortal danger. But we're starving, so we
really have no choice.

In *The Maltese Falcon*, Sam Spade tells a story to Brigid O'Shaughnessy.
When he was an operative in an agency, a woman retained the agency to find her
husband, who some five or six years before had disappeared. She believes she
saw him in Spokane. She wants him traced and Spade is assigned to the case. He
finds the husband all right, a man named Flitcraft. The man tells Spade why he

Humphrey Bogart just about to find out the truth in *Dead Reckoning* (Columbia,
1947) with Lizabeth Scott.　PHOTO COURTESY OF COLUMBIA PICTURES INDUSTRIES.

left his wife. He had been a model husband, a good father, a provider, a hard worker. Then one day he was walking down a street and a beam came within inches of smashing the life out of him. It knocked a piece of cement from the sidewalk which hit him on the cheek, drawing blood. The man ran away. Now he has re-established himself. He runs a successful auto dealership. He has remarried.

Like most people, Flitcraft is a creature of habit. When the tenuous quality of existence suddenly penetrated into his consciousness, he became painfully aware of the caprice by which we all live and die and that nothing means anything. After acting in accord with the irrational and purposeless nature of life for a couple of years, the man's mind slowly deadened the shock of awareness. He crept back into his comfortable pattern again.

Life *is* caprice. The basis of human existence is irrational. Logic is a projection. Order is an illusion. Men are too busy getting and spending to reflect on reality; they hide their anxieties in a quest for wealth, or security, or power. C. G. Jung found that even our theology is an elaborate structure erected to safely remove our fearful and easily unbalanced psyches from the immediacy of religious, which is to say irrational, experience.

Hammett was part of the heightened consciousness of his time in championing distrust over belief, skepticism over faith, cynicism over hope. It is the truly capable man who can sustain these mental postures and go on as confidently as the man who relies on all manner of comforting fantasies to get him through.

The *film noir* trend of the Forties and Fifties, surfacing primarily in detective and crime films, was the closest the American cinema to that time had dared come in re-creating in the collective consciousness of the audience the emotional traumas and sensations men experience when the key breaks and the door cannot be shut again. Freud suggested, near the end of his life, that the light of reason was very dim and ever threatening to flicker out. The misdirection psychoanalysis may have taken was in its effort to be therapeutically functional. Ludwig Binswanger, a student of both Freud and Jung, once commented to me: What can the analyst do with a life that has been wasted, with a psyche that lives in a body that has been shot up in war, imprisoned in concentration camps, a psyche that cannot deal competently with deception, exploitation, frustration, and failure? And what of impotence, old age, physical exhaustion, death? What is the therapy for these? Not religion. Not politics. Not hard work so as to pay taxes and tithes so others need not work so hard. What then?

For the first time, really, in any consistent fashion the detective and crime films of the Forties and Fifties began to ask these questions. If they came up with no adequate answers, they nonetheless did attempt to expand our consciousness to encompass the deceitfulness of human nature, the improbabilities of existence, while demonstrating repeatedly the ingenuity with which human beings lie to each other and to themselves.

But for the fact that John Huston was forced to make a hero of Sam Spade, *film noir* might have received one of its strongest initial thrusts from *The Maltese Falcon* (Warner's, 1941). But the Bogart character, to which Huston contributed so much in terms of its screen projection in the films he directed with

Bogart in the Forties and Fifties, prevented him from concentrating on the culpability of *all* the characters, the detective included. The cinema still had its patriotic films, its family films, its Westerns with superhuman heroes, its musicals with happy endings, its soap-opera dramas, and its serials with master criminals dispatched in the final episode. But in the detective and crime film, those which eschewed being a series or part of the conventional milieu embodied in the notion of the "master" detective, a new spirit was ingested into the cinema, an unsettling, critical, pervasive, pessimistic representation of life closer to reality than, previously, the cinema had thought commercially feasible.

What has come to be termed *film noir* commenced in earnest with a trio of films: Boris Ingster's *Stranger on the Third Floor* (RKO, 1940), Orson Welles's *Citizen Kane* (RKO, 1941), and Lucky Humberstone's *I Wake Up Screaming* (20th-Fox, 1941).

"Sometimes I wake up in the middle of the night," George Raft told me. "I'm gasping for breath. I turn on the respirator and I breathe, as deeply as I can. I do that for a half hour, maybe an hour. I can breathe a little better then. But I can't get back to sleep." André Gide claimed that his unreserved admiration for Dashiell Hammett was based on the fact that Hammett never drew moral conclusions. William Barrett wrote in his book on the philosophy of existentialism, *Irrational Man* (Doubleday, 1962), that "the American has not yet assimilated the disappearance of his own geographical frontier, his spiritual horizon is still the limitless play of human possibilities, and as yet he has not lived through the crucial experience of human finitude."

All of these themes come together in *film noir*. It is a gasping for breath, a struggling to hang onto life; it is an essay in personal martyrdom, much in the sense of the highly personal philosophies of Friedrich Nietzsche and Søren Kierkegaard, although their names would not be familiar, perhaps, to anyone either making such films or viewing them; it is a depiction of the American *mise en scène* that draws no moral conclusions. Its narrative form is frequently a *temps perdu*, whether narrated by a character in the story to tell the viewer how he got into his predicament, or a reconstruction of a man's past through one kind of investigation or another. Before *film noir* could come into its own, American literature had to undergo the atmosphere of distrust which informed Hammett's fiction, the recognition that the real story isn't the story everyone is telling and that the real story, when it comes out finally, isn't any more pleasant; indeed, it is by all accounts far worse; and that the detective is often the hired agent of men as evil as those he's supposed to find. America finally shared Raymond Chandler's consciousness that looming in the streets are forces darker than the night—but, and this is the essential difference, there is no Chandleresque shining knight to brave the evils of the world for us.

The term *film noir* was coined in 1946 by a cineaste, Nino Frank, who derived it from Marcel Duhamel's *Série Noire* books. And while Orson Welles's *Citizen Kane* was one of the founding pictures, it wasn't until *The Lady from Shanghai* (Columbia, 1948) that Welles perfected a contribution to the form which may well stand as the classic example of *film noir* at its most searching.

Nearly all of the detective films of the Forties and the Fifties were in some way or another affected by the impact of *film noir*. Nor can the movement even be said to have begun without forerunners in the Thirties. But without *film noir*, the new realism in detective films in the Sixties and, above all, in the Seventies would probably not have been quite so pronounced, nor half so confident of audience comprehension.

II

The reader may feel at this point, and not without some justification, that I have neglected detective films which cannot be grouped as part of a series or which do not feature a series detective figure. But there has been a reason for this. If nonseries detective films belong anywhere, it is here, as part of the milieu which created *film noir*.

While those I have chosen to mention constitute by no means an exhaustive catalogue, they can readily serve a dual function. First, they can demonstrate, even more readily than series detective films, the fantasy elements which were so much a part of the genre before *film noir* began to emerge; and, second, and more important, it was in several of these isolated entries from the Thirties that the basic themes so fundamental to *film noir* made their first tentative appearances.

Willard Mack played a police detective in *The Voice of the City* (M-G-M, 1929). He also wrote not so good dialogue for the other players and directed the film himself. It was an after-the-fact story, with Robert Ames sentenced to prison for twenty years for a murder he didn't commit. He makes good an escape, finally, and remains in hiding while Mack traps the real murderer and exonerates him. In *Thru Different Eyes* (Fox, 1929) Edmund Lowe is being tried for murdering his friend, Warner Baxter. The defense attorney sums up the case for the jury via flashbacks, telling one story from the facts; the prosecuting attorney sums it up, via a flashback, from a different angle. The third and last summation proves Lowe innocent but also demonstrates how easily circumstantial evidence can be made to lie. Although both films dealt with the failure of the police to accurately collect data capable of leading to a conviction of the actual culprit and the inability of due process to find out the truth from circumstantial evidence, it had not yet occurred to filmmakers to go the next step and force the audience more completely to identify with the wronged man. Alfred Hitchcock, who was still directing films in Great Britain, is the only one I can call to mind who, even this early, was raising serious doubts as to the efficacy of the judicial process.

Americans were too enamored of the fanciful notion of the amateur sleuth who in the guise of a Philo Vance imitator would surely be able to correctly identify the murderer and guide the police and the district attorney in discharging their offices. Typical of films of this kind was *The Thirteenth Guest* (Monogram, 1933), in which Lyle Talbot was cast as the amateur detective and J. Farrell MacDonald and Paul Hurst formed the official police duo. Ginger

Rogers was the name star, but her role wasn't substantial. *Murder in the Museum* (Progressive, 1934) found Henry B. Walthall suspected of murdering the town's vice crusader when his corpse was found at a freak museum. John Harron, playing a reporter, solved the crime, which had so baffled the police.

Columbia Pictures brought Anthony Abbot's detective Thatcher Colt to the screen, a police commissioner who saves for himself the more complex cases. Adolphe Menjou portrayed Colt. In *The Night Club Lady* (Columbia, 1932) Colt tries to save a female night club owner who receives a threatening letter that she will die one minute after midnight. Despite all the police around her, that's exactly what she does. *The Circus Queen Murder* (Columbia, 1933) was Colt's second case. He has to discover why a trapeze artist was murdered with a poison dart while she was doing her act. The entries were certainly superior to Producers Releasing Corporation's attempt to revive the series in 1942 with *The Panther's Claw*, in which traditional heavy Sidney Blackmer was cast as Colt. It was a one and only!

Yet, simultaneously, John Cromwell, who in the Forties would contribute significantly to *film noir*, was opposing these trends in detective films. His *Street of Chance* (Paramount, 1930) dealt realistically with social issues, based on the life of Arnold Rothstein, New York bootlegger and mobster associate of Owney Madden. Cromwell followed it with *Scandal Sheet* (Paramount, 1931), which was an exposé of how ruthless newspaperman George Bancroft could get in pursuit of a story. He ends up editor of a prison paper. *Street of Chance* was so successful that Paramount resurrected it for remake in 1942. *Scandal Sheet* was remade by Paramount in 1938, and the property was then sold to Columbia Pictures for a *third* make in 1942. But none of the remakes captured the same behind-the-scenes urgency of Cromwell's original films.

In many ways, for audiences of the Thirties, Edmund Lowe symbolized the detective hero. After three years with the Los Angeles stock company, he began appearing in films in 1923 for Fox. He starred in *Scotland Yard* (Fox, 1930), in which he had a dual role as a crook whose face is destroyed by an explosion and who is made to look like a London banker by an unscrupulous surgeon. Joan Bennett falls in love with this new version of her dead husband and assists him in the ruse. Donald Crisp, as a vicious blackmailer, threatens their happiness for a time, but by the fade, incredibly, Scotland Yard, having learned the truth, permits Lowe to continue in his new identity, thinking Bennett will exert a salutary effect on his character. Sol Wurtzel remade the picture under the same title in 1941, with John Loder in the Lowe role; it was Norman Foster's final directorial effort at the Fox studio.

Through parts like this, Lowe quickly established himself in the Thirties as a leading player. Edwin L. Marin, who later cast Lowe as Philo Vance at M-G-M, cast him in *Bombay Mail* (Universal, 1934) as a Scotland Yard inspector on a train en route to Bombay. There are two murders, and Lowe goes back and forth questioning passengers before he arrives at the truth.

Because of the overt caricature of the official police in the Philo Vance stories and so much popular detective fiction, it wasn't until the Forties that producers with any regularity could cast American police investigators as central characters in detective films. Lowe was a Scotland Yard official in *Bombay Mail*. Nigel Bruce acted in a similar capacity in *Murder in Trinidad* (Fox, 1934), which was based on a John W. Vandercook novel of the same title later used as the basis for a Mr. Moto picture. Bruce was a detective sent from London to get to the bottom of a diamond smuggling ring. Louis King directed. Unfortunately in this trend, British detective films could scarcely be used as models for Hollywood in its treatment of Yard investigators. Gerald du Maurier, who produced Agatha Christie's play *Alibi* on the London stage in 1928, got a chance to play a Yard detective in *The Scotland Yard Mystery* (British Alliance, 1935). The master villain in the picture is George Curzon, playing a Yard pathologist. When Frederick Peisley is about to expose Curzon, seated in a chair in du Maurier's office, Curzon enters and offers Peisley a drink out of the bottle on du Maurier's desk. Peisley dies. Curzon knocks the glass out of du Maurier's hand before he can have it analyzed. And still du Maurier isn't sure whom to suspect!

Chester Morris, after playing a villain in Roland West's *Alibi* (United Artists, 1929), was cast as a detective by West in *The Bat Whispers* (United Artists, 1931). It was an old dark house mystery, based on a Mary Roberts Rinehart stage play. Morris had his moment at the end, when he stepped out of character and asked the audience not to reveal the identity of "The Bat" to others who hadn't seen the film. This is similar to the practice today from the stage in London after a performance of Agatha Christie's *The Mouse Trap*.

Miss Pinkerton (First National, 1932) was another Rinehart adaptation. Joan Blondell played a nurse, Miss Adams, who helps detective George Brent solve a murder in an old mansion with the killer running around in a cloak. Brent was cast again as a detective in *The Keyhole* (Warner's, 1933), doing what detectives in real life do most of the time, and almost never in movies, not then and not now: spying on Kay Francis in connection with a divorce case. Other than their regular detective series, Warner's also specialized in semi-detective stories featuring Department of Justice investigators, James Cagney in *G-Men* (Warner's, 1935) and George Brent in *Special Agent* (Warner's 1935), which found Brent on the trail of rackets boss Ricardo Cortez, a role which seemed to fit Cortez better than playing detectives.

The greatest piece of screen deduction I've seen occurs in a G-Man picture, *Let 'Em Have It* (United Artists, 1935) with Richard Arlen in the lead role. A crime expert picks up a glove dropped by a bandit and from just looking at it can tell that its owner is a man, six feet tall, weighing 180 pounds, thirty-two years old, with black hair and dark brown eyes, enjoying vigorous health, who drives a tractor, owns a horse, and has a brace of Belgian hares!

Dore Schary, later David O. Selznick's story editor and Louis B. Mayer's successor at the helm of M-G-M, wrote the screenplay for a detective story, *Chinatown Squad* (Universal, 1935). Lyle Talbot starred as the unofficial investigator who tries to solve a series of knifings in Chinatown while falling in love with Valerie Hobson.

More entertaining was *The Preview Murder Mystery* (Paramount, 1936), which actually had an official detective, played by Thomas Jackson, with the whole of Paramount's Marathon Street studio used as a set, with Reginald

Andy Devine, Bradley Page, Valerie Hobson, and Lyle Talbot in the back of a
paddy wagon in *Chinatown Squad* (Universal, 1935).

PHOTO COURTESY OF MCA-UNIVERSAL.

Denny and Gail Patrick in terror for their lives confronted with a murderer
prowling about the studio. Giving a strong performance as a matinee idol was
Rod La Rocque. The next year he was starred in *The Shadow Strikes* (Grand
National, 1937), based on the long-running—and I mean long-running!—radio
series translated into pulp stories by Street & Smith Publications. Lamont Cranston, as he was eventually called, knows the evil lurking in men's hearts. He
started out in his first picture by being called Granston with an old dark house
mystery on his hands, somehow befitting his usual apparel of a cape and a low-
brim hat. *International Crime* (Grand National, 1938) kept La Rocque as the
star but dispensed with all this hokum, casting him as a crime reporter. Victor
Jory got a chance to play the role in a fifteen-episode serial for Columbia in

1940 before Monogram made a trio of pictures in 1946 with Kane Richmond as Cranston, now joined by his faithful girl friend Margot and taxi driver Shrevvie. *Bourbon Street Shadows* (Republic, 1958) was the last film featuring Cranston, and it went all the way, with him becoming invisible through the use of hypnosis.

When, in the Thirties, on rare occasion a studio did try making a straight police procedural picture, it came out like *This Is My Affair* (20th-Fox, 1937), which cast Robert Taylor as Lieutenant Perry. It is Taylor's job to find out how safe combinations to the nation's banks are falling into criminal hands. Barbara Stanwyck was cast as the love interest—she was very much in love with Taylor off-screen. Taylor's investigation gets him convicted as a bank robber and Stanwyck has to appeal to President Roosevelt—played by Sidney Blackmer due to Republican sentiments at Fox—to grant him a pardon. In 1939, in an effort to replace the Moto series inexpensively, Twentieth Century-Fox tried importing two Inspector Hornleigh films from Great Britain, shot on location out of frozen funds and featuring the popular BBC detective portrayed by Gordon Harker with Alastair Sim as his assistant. The series failed to catch on with American audiences and, after the second entry, *Inspector Hornleigh on Holiday* (20th-Fox, 1940), no more were forthcoming.

Metro made a one-time effort to bring Dorothy L. Sayers' supercilous detective Lord Peter Wimsey to the screen in *Haunted Honeymoon* (M-G-M, 1940), with Robert Montgomery in the lead. It was a variation of the Thin Man formula, with attractive Constance Cummings as Montgomery's mystery-writing bride who involves her husband in a murder investigation while they are honeymooning in a sleepy village. Sayers had tried it as a stage play, but it had bombed in that form also. Not to be outdone, Paramount borrowed Chester Morris from Columbia and cast him as a private detective in *No Hands on the Clock* (Paramount, 1941). Morris is married to Jean Parker, who insists on involving herself in the first case that comes her husband's way during their Reno honeymoon.

Into this happy and glibly carefree world came *Stranger on the Third Floor* (RKO, 1940). The protagonist is the familiar newspaper hero of so many Thirties whodunits. He discovers a murder in an all-night beanery. He tags an ex-con, played by Elisha Cook, Jr., with the crime. The feature story gets him a raise, which he needs to afford marriage, and his testimony gets Cook convicted. All the phony court scenes of the past and the future are chucked in favor of showing what due process is really like: the American legal system is impervious in its prosecution of Cook, the soporific judge has to wake up a juror, the gullible jury itself nodding at the triumphant assertions of the insistent police witnesses and the prosecutor.

At this point, according to Depression era tradition, the film is over. Now the reporter can settle down to domestic bliss and a free conscience. But the tables are turned. John McGuire, the reporter has a dream while in his room, a dream seething with passions and repressions in which Peter Lorre (playing an escaped lunatic in the film) passes through as a fleeting shadow. The man in the room next to the reporter is murdered. Now McGuire is confronted with the same stern, inexorable legal machinery which doomed Elisha Cook, Jr. McGuire's fiancée, played by Margaret Tallichet (who was married to director William Wyler), sets out on her own to find Lorre, the man with the long scarf who committed both murders. McGuire narrates some of the film in the Chandler playback style which became part of the initial *film noir mise en scène*, although the subgenre, if I can call it that, subsequently arrived at a number of variations of this device before dispensing with it.

Citizen Kane, of the next year, brought to the fore not only the reconstruction of the past, which managed to do little more than create a doubtful, lingering "presence" extending into the future; it marked the beginnings, in the American cinema, of questioning the heroes that the Establishment sets up for the populace to enshrine. Welles used a number of narrative recall techniques which, in the manner of a detective story, reconstructed past events. The completed pattern exposed the nerves and tremors of personality, rather than merely the surprise of discovering a culprit. Good and evil were no longer so certain that characters could be broken down into heroes and villains.

The classical detective story nearly always begins after a character's death and presents the reader with a reconstruction. *Film noir*, at the outset, modified this by altering the emphasis; the viewer is more interested in who is dead and what he or she was like alive than in why he or she is dead and who is responsible for it. This is only a progression from Hammett and Chandler and their concentration on character and milieu rather than on the denouement. Alfred Hitchcock at the very beginning of the Forties in *Rebecca* (United Artists, 1940) demonstrated how effectively such a formula could work. Rebecca is dead. The viewer does not know if Laurence Olivier murdered her, or if the housekeeper did it. Using Joan Fontaine as the point of view character, bit by bit we learn about Rebecca, what kind of person she was, how she lived, what she said, what she did. Little happens in the film, yet the viewer is never aware of it; because what is happening is the slow but constant imparting of more information. From admiring a lovely woman at the start, the viewer finds, as the film unwinds, that Rebecca was a human monster, that she was hated by her husband; a ghost literally is vitalized into a living creature, even though she is never seen.

I Wake Up Screaming (20th-Fox, 1941) followed a similar exposition. It was based on a story outline by Steve Fisher which was later turned into a novel. Carole Landis is murdered. Victor Mature is taken to police headquarters and grilled. Laird Cregar in his role as the cop Cornell (a specific reference to suspense writer Cornell Woolrich) tries to frame Mature for Landis' murder because he was in love with Landis and Mature's successful efforts to promote Landis into a personality removed forever any possibility for Cregar to realize his fantasy. Betty Grable played Mature's love interest in the film, although she, too, comes to suspect his guilt. Humberstone in the direction develops the parallel plot ingredients of learning more and more about Landis through flashbacks while keeping the viewer in suspense as to the identity of the murderer. Mature, like the central character in any *noir* picture, is a man imprisoned by circumstances.

Lucky Humberstone (behind camera) directing Victor Mature and Betty Grable in *I Wake Up Screaming* (20th-Fox, 1941).   PHOTO COURTESY OF LUCKY HUMBERSTONE.

There is one scene in particular in the film to which critics have attached great significance. Cregar, on a visit to Betty Grable's apartment, studies a cheap picture hanging on the wall titled *The Garden of Hope*. Grable remarks that it would be difficult to live without hope. "It can be done," Cregar responds, his voice dull and lifeless in despair. It is a foreshadowing of Cregar's subsequent suicide in the film, when his attempt to frame Mature has been made known to William Gargan, a fellow police detective, and Betty Grable, accompanying Mature to Cregar's apartment. Originally, this final death scene wasn't even in the picture. Humberstone had a work print screened for Darryl F. Zanuck.

"Humberstone," Zanuck said, "there are only two things wrong with this picture, as it stands. One: it is a Betty Grable picture in black and white. That's bad enough. But second: the exhibitors will never sit still for a Grable picture where she doesn't sing one song!"

"But, Darryl," Humberstone objected, "you yourself said this was a psychological murder mystery. She can't sing. It wouldn't be consistent with the whole thrust of the picture."

"Listen," said Zanuck, sweeping all that aside with a wave of his cigar, "I've got the perfect ending. The camera, in the last scene, pans into the basement of a busy department store, with dozens of extras running around, buying things, and so on. It tracks in to a close shot of Grable, sitting at a piano, singing a number. She works there, see, and this is the happy ending: her singing a song for the customers."

Lucky went out and shot the scene as Zanuck wanted it. It was spliced into the work print and screened again. Zanuck in those days at Fox customarily had his wife sit in on his screening sessions. After he returned from taking her to her car, he gloomily shook his head.

"Humberstone, Virginia agrees with me," he said gravely. "You've got to be crazy to have Grable singing at the end of a picture like this. It's a psychological picture. It doesn't fit. Get a new ending."

Lucky didn't bother with remonstrance. He went home and thought and thought about how to end the picture. Near dawn, he fell asleep. And he had a dream. The next morning he rushed into Zanuck's office.

"I've got the ending," he announced.

"What is it?" Zanuck asked.

Lucky began: "Laird Cregar is a screwy cop. He has photos and ads of Carole Landis all over his apartment. Mature goes there, to the apartment, at the end of the picture, and he sees this. He meets Cregar, who's coming home with some flowers to put beneath his shrine to Landis. Mature tells him that they've caught Elisha Cook, Jr., and that he's confessed everything, including how Cregar had him cover up. Cregar takes poison and dies. That's how the picture ends, with Cregar dying, a suicide, surrounded by all the pictures of Landis. He was in love with her, but afraid to say anything once she became a celebrity."

"That's great!" Zanuck exclaimed. "Why didn't you think of it before this? You've held up production for weeks on this picture."

"Because I just dreamed it," Lucky said.

"You dreamed it!" Zanuck said in disbelief.

Laird Cregar also appeared in another film usually classed as *film noir*, John Brahm's *The Lodger* (20th-Fox, 1944), a remake of Alfred Hitchcock's outstanding silent film of 1926 in which suspicion, not certitude, is the dominant theme. Cregar went on a violent diet to lose weight in 1946 and wound up hospitalized. It was his battle with weight and despair over his own ugliness which drove him to suicide. Carole Landis committed suicide two years later, in 1948. The "trapped" feeling of *film noir* was, for them, more than a part they had to play.

III

Laura (20th-Fox, 1944), directed by Otto Preminger, featured Gene Tierney as the murder victim. Dana Andrews played the detective who tries to reconstruct her life in order to find out who killed her. Like so many *noir* entries, *Double Indemnity* (Paramount, 1944), *Dead Reckoning* (Columbia, 1947), *The Postman Always Rings Twice* (M-G-M, 1946), *Murder, My Sweet* (RKO, 1944), *The Lady From Shanghai* (Columbia, 1948), and *Out of the Past* (RKO, 1947), the first-person narration was an intrinsic part of setting the mood and providing an interpretation of events. Here most of all, Raymond Chandler's direct influence was most manifest.

Raymond Burr, who was born on May 21, 1917, in New Westminster, British Columbia, studied at Stanford, the University of California, Columbia University, and even the University of Chungking and worked briefly for the Forestry Service before he became a director at the Pasadena Community Playhouse in 1943. He modeled many of his early screen performances on Laird Cregar, whom he very much admired. He was first placed under contract by RKO, but all he did was put on weight while he waited for even a small part. His chance came as the overweight villain in *Pitfall* (United Artists, 1948) and in a similar role in *Red Light* (United Artists, 1949). The idea, in *Pitfall*, of the gargantuan Burr (he weighed three hundred pounds and wore balloon double-breasted suits to further accentuate his obesity) smothering the petite Liz Scott (under five and a half feet and weighing 112 pounds) was a grotesque idea, but *film noir*, with increasing bitterness as the Forties progressed, turned its back on the romantic clichés of former days.

Although we later became good friends, it was in connection with *film noir* that I first had occasion to talk with Lizabeth Scott, in the summer of 1976.

"I really didn't think you would make it," I said.

We were at the Scandia, on Sunset Boulevard.

"I said I would," she said in a husky, breathless voice. "When I say I will keep an appointment, I always do."

She brushed her long, streaked blond hair from her face in a nervous gesture. She wasn't wearing a support garment. Her white blouse plunged between her browned breasts, still firm; her whole body was brown beneath her white clothing.

"I love this place. I come here often."

I pulled out her chair for her and she slid into it with a hurried grace.

The pupils of her deep blue eyes were dilated, seeming more to take you inside them than to look out at you.

"Would you like a drink?" I asked.

"No, I don't drink." Her voice was huskier. "I only had one drink in my whole life." She pulled out a box of long, thin, brown Sherman cigarettes. "But I smoke."

I lit her cigarette.

"Have another drink," she said, looking at my glass. "It's all right. This is on me."

"It isn't that."

She looked at me again, deeply, brushing aside her hair.

"I like to see a man drink," she said, and smiled.

"You're one of the most difficult people to see in all of Los Angeles."

"I don't know why," she said. "But I wanted to see you. I knew this wouldn't be an interview. I hate interviews. I like to talk to people face to face. Just us, you know? About both of us. You have to try to really talk to each other, to say something."

The waiter brought my drink. Liz continued.

"I was just at UCLA. They had a Lizabeth Scott day. It was a film course. They showed *Pitfall*. Afterwards, the students asked me questions. They all wanted to know about *film noir*."

Laird Cregar, with a portrait of Carole Landis between them, haunting Victor Mature.   PHOTO COURTESY OF TWENTIETH CENTURY-FOX FILM CORPORATION.

"So would I . . . frankly."

Liz smiled again.

"They said almost all my films were examples of *film noir*."

"Yes. But what is it . . . for you?"

"There's got to be a woman. She can't have a husband. She's smothering inside. She's driven to do the things she does, driven to it by other people, and by something inside herself."

I remembered talking to Jane Wyatt about *Pitfall*. Jane played Dick Powell's wife. Samuel Bischoff was the producer. Andre de Toth directed from Jay Dratler's screenplay.

"I loved Liz Scott," Jane told me. "You couldn't help but love her. She was so completely neurotic. She always got on the set early so she could be made up. It always took her so long. And she was always by herself."

Raymond Burr was the detective working for Dick Powell's insurance company. He's taken with Liz. Powell is also attracted to her when he visits Liz at her apartment. They sleep together (although this is handled in an incredibly cowardly fashion). Liz has been the recipient of stolen property from a man

Raymond Burr, with his back to the camera, hounding Dick Powell and Lizabeth Scott in *Pitfall* (United Artists, 1948). Burr imitated Laird Cregar in his early acting.
PHOTO COURTESY OF NATIONAL TELEFILM ASSOCIATES.

Edward Dmytryk directing Dick Powell in *Cornered* (RKO, 1945), an early example of *film noir*.   PHOTO COURTESY OF THE MUSEUM OF MODERN ART.

now imprisoned. Powell wants it back. Burr resents Powell's intrusion. Liz hates Burr always hanging around. Burr visits Liz's lover in prison and tells him about Powell and Liz. Powell tries to break it off to keep his marriage together; he had withheld from Liz any knowledge that he was married. Jane Wyatt becomes suspicious and shrewish. When Liz's lover is released, Burr picks him up, gets him drunk, and drives him out to Powell's house. Powell shoots the man, ostensibly in self-defense. He tries to cover it up. Jane agrees to help him, but she reminds Powell that he had best not cross her again by taking up with another woman. It doesn't work. Burr wants Liz to leave town with him. Terrified, she shoots Burr. Powell confesses everything to John Litel, the district attorney. Litel cannot hold Powell, even though he is morally culpable. But they can, and do, prosecute Liz Scott.

"Whenever I worked on a picture like *Pitfall*, I would set up the character I was playing in my mind. I wrote down in a notebook how I felt such a character would act in various circumstances. I had to reason out the person I was portraying."

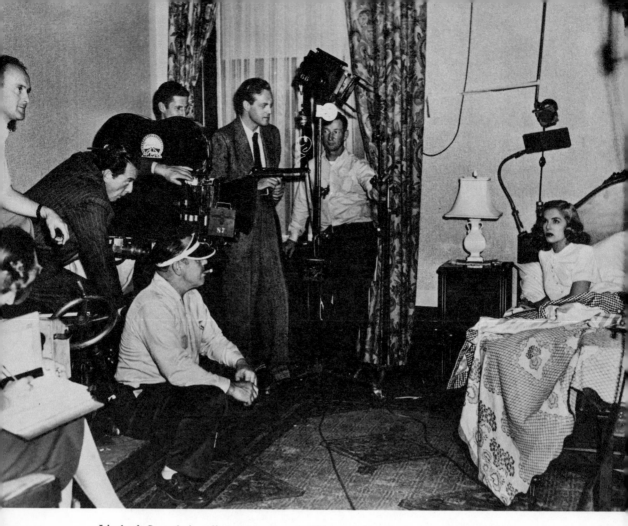

Lizabeth Scott being directed by Lewis Milestone (leaning on the camera), Van Heflin behind the strobe light, in *The Strange Love of Martha Ivers* (Paramount, 1946).   PHOTO COURTESY OF VIEWS & REVIEWS MAGAZINE.

"You played a good girl in *The Strange Love of Martha Ivers* [Paramount, 1946]. Barbara Stanwyck was the murderer. There's an unforgettable scene at the end when Kirk Douglas wants to shoot her and can't, so she puts her thumb over his finger on the trigger and pulls it. Then the camera drops back to see Douglas shoot himself in a double suicide."

"Lewis Milestone directed that film," Liz said, tipping her head, expelling cigarette smoke, and then brushing back her hair. "He was wonderful to work with. But John Cromwell told me he didn't like the picture when I went to work in *Dead Reckoning* [Columbia, 1947]."

The identity of the murderer was concealed until the very end in *Dead Reckoning*, which wasn't always the case in *film noir*. Bogart portrayed a paratrooper returning to the States after the war. He finds a society dominated by hoodlums who have made huge profits during the conflict. His buddy flees from the press when it is announced that, through Bogart's recommendation, he is to receive the Congressional Medal of Honor. Bogart traces him to Gulf City, where he finds him dead. He learns that his buddy was involved in a murder and that he

Director John Cromwell visiting with Lauren Bacall and Humphrey Bogart during the shooting of *Dead Reckoning* (Columbia, 1947).

PHOTO COURTESY OF THE NATIONAL FILM ARCHIVE.

was in love with Liz Scott. The dialogue is crisp and refreshing, filled with Chandleresque similes. Liz plays up to Bogart, but, as had become tradition now, first in *The Maltese Falcon*, then in films like *Murder, My Sweet*, when the heroine proves to be the guilty one, the hero has to turn her in. Speeding down a highway with Bogart, Liz pulls a gun on him. He increases the speed. He warns her that if she pulls the trigger they'll both go. The camera is mounted in the back seat. Liz, facing Bogart in profile, tightens her muscles and pulls the trigger.

"What was Bogart like to work with?"

"I remember that he never prepared his lines ahead of time. He would always do that in the morning. That way, in the whole picture I only did one take with him before noon. He worked his own way. And he wouldn't work after five. He seemed to find working fun. But one day he said to me, 'I hate coming to work. It's really hard for a male to do this kind of work.'"

"And when you shot him?"

"I had to. The character I was playing had to. He was going to stand in her way. More and more between them would stand in the way. She had to shoot him."

"Personally, I like you best in *Too Late for Tears* [United Artists, 1949], when you cold-bloodedly tell Dan Duryea that if he wants the insurance money he's going to have to bump your husband, Arthur Kennedy, or at least help you do it. Up to that point, Duryea thinks he has you scared. But when he hears your plan, he gets scared for himself. And of course, his face is nothing but sheer astonishment and rage when he discovers you've poisoned him, once Kennedy is bumped."

"I had my greatest problem in that picture. In the telephone scene. I had to do all my acting to a telephone. I found that very hard. It took at least six takes before it was right."

Hal B. Wallis brought Lizabeth Scott to Hollywood in 1946 to work for him in the productions he was doing for Paramount. They became very close. Wallis invested Liz's money wisely so that now she lives in comfort. She lives alone. We talked about her efforts to redecorate her home.

"You have to come over when it's done," she urged. "For a drink. In January?"

"I liked Mary Astor playing your mother in *Desert Fury* [Paramount, 1947]. She wanted to stop you from taking up with John Hodiak. But you did anyway. It destroyed him, and almost everybody else in the picture, to a certain extent."

"Whatever happened to Mary, I wonder?"

"She's living out at the Motion Picture Home."

"No? Really. I have to go out to see her."

Liz brushed her hair to one side, and then turned her face toward me once more.

"You know, a picture is so much like a trip to Europe, on a boat. You get to be so close with everyone while you're working on a picture. You all promise that you will see each other constantly when the picture is over. But once it's over, you never see each other at all. Or, if you do, you're kind of embarrassed, because of all the things you said, and . . . I guess, nobody means what they say, ever . . . do they?"

"They may not mean what they say," I said, finishing my whiskey, "but they definitely mean to get the things they want badly enough for which they said them in the first place."

"I know what you mean. It's like telling someone you love him to get something from him. Or her."

"Have you ever known anyone to say 'I love you' who didn't want something?"

Liz smiled demurely. She knew what I meant.

The major influence *film noir* exerted on future detective films was shifting the emphasis from the plot and placing it more firmly than ever on character. In view of the routine and repetitious plots of series detective films, this was a needed contrast. But more than that, the effect of *film noir*, initially, was that crime was taken more seriously; the amateur detective virtually disappeared from the screen and even the private eye, who flourished in the Forties, was seldom seen in the Fifties.

Quiet Please, Murder (20th-Fox, 1942), directed by John Larkin, cast George Sanders as the mastermind of a counterfeit rare-book racket. Richard Denning was the private detective, but his role was strictly secondary to the multiple duplicities which grew out of Sanders' ambivalent relationship with his accomplice in criminality, Gail Patrick. It was a role that Sanders found more to his liking than the Falcon.

Frequently during the Thirties, detective films had been major productions. In the Forties, increasingly, they were relegated to "B" units and shared the bottom half of the bill. Typical of this lower budget type detective film were James Dunn's efforts at Monogram. In *The Living Ghost* (Monogram, 1942) Dunn was cast as Nick Trayne and Joan Woodbury was his female assistant, trying to solve the riddle of who was responsible for giving Gus Glassmire brain paralysis. In *Leave It to the Irish* (Monogram, 1944) Dunn played Terry Moran, this time assisted by Wanda McKay, solving three murders and capturing a gang of fur thieves. *The Caribbean Mystery* (20th-Fox, 1945) was a third remake of *Murder in Trinidad*, with Dunn hiding in the hospital waiting for Reed Hadley, afraid the dead man might talk, to plunge his knife into a corpse.

Preston Foster played a private detective in *Bermuda Mystery* (20th-Fox, 1944), where he is hired by Ann Rutherford to find out who killed her uncle by sending him a poisoned cigarette. William Gargan and Margaret Lindsay finished out their Columbia contracts with *No Place for a Lady* (Columbia, 1943), directed by James Hogan, with a screenplay by Eric Taylor. James Burke was in the cast, so an unwitting viewer might almost think it was another Ellery Queen picture. Gargan went on then to play in a formula Thin Man variation picture, *Follow That Woman* (Paramount, 1945), where he and his wife, played by Nancy Kelly, and his brother, Ed Gargan, cast as Butch, get involved in the murder of a night club singer.

Jerome Cowan, in between playing murder suspects, got his chance, doubtless

George Sanders and Gail Patrick have a "love-hate" partnership in *Quiet Please, Murder* (20th-Fox, 1942).

PHOTO COURTESY OF TWENTIETH CENTURY-FOX FILM CORPORATION.

as a result of his appearance as Sam Spade's partner in John Huston's *The Maltese Falcon*, to play a dapper detective in two minor films, both for Warner Brothers. In *Find the Blackmailer* (Warner's, 1943) Cowan is hired by Gene Lockhart to find a talking crow owned by an ex-convict. *Crime by Night* (Warner's, 1944) found Cowan, assisted by his secretary, Jane Wyman, searching for the murderer of an inventor. Worst of all, perhaps, was *Accomplice* (Producers Releasing Corporation, 1946) with Richard Arlen as Frank Gruber's detective, Simon Lash, and Tom Dugan as his assistant, hired by Veda Ann Borg to find her husband. The wretched acting wasn't helped by the wall-to-wall music track, which only occasionally reflected what was happening on the screen.

Film noir offered directors an opportunity to reflect more accurately social conditions as they perceived them, and it was this as much as anything which acted as an impetus to the *noir* trend. Traditional detective films simply couldn't withstand the increased consciousness of more sophisticated audiences and, like budget Westerns, were a dying breed.

Kiss of Death (20th-Fox, 1947), directed by Henry Hathaway, cast Victor Mature as a small-time crook who makes a deal with Assistant District Attorney Brain Donlevy to inform on his underworld contacts in trade for a parole. Mature wants to care for his two children, who are left alone when their mother commits suicide while he's serving his term. The picture marked not only one of Mature's finest performances, but it contained a chilling portrayal of a killer, played by Richard Widmark. *Film noir*, paraphrasing Chandler, was giving murder back to those who *were* really good at it.

Robert Montgomery's *Ride the Pink Horse* (Universal, 1947) was another exceptional variation on the returning veteran who finds anything but the idealistic America he was taught he was fighting for in countless war propaganda films. Jacques Tourneur directed *Out of the Past* (RKO, 1947), which starred Robert Mitchum as an agent hired by Kirk Douglas to get $40,000 back from Jane Greer, who stole it from Douglas. When Mitchum catches up with Greer, he falls for her line and ends up the victim of a double cross between Douglas and Greer. Mitchum and Greer are gunned by pursuing police.

In this context, Orson Welles's *The Lady from Shanghai* (Columbia, 1948) stands as a remarkable achievement among many excellent films. Welles was married to Rita Hayworth when it was made and he cut her hair short for the role she had in the picture, much to the consternation of Harry Cohn. Welles actually began production on this film in 1946 with a $2,300,000 budget, but he took forever to finish the picture and went far over budget. For the Mexican footage, he leased Errol Flynn's yacht and, perfectionist that he was, worked and worked until he got precisely the effects he wanted. I do not know how many takes it cost him, but even a small sequence like the conversation he has with Rita and her husband in the film, Everett Sloane, terminates with Welles turning away and walking down the beach, an ocean breaker crashing at exactly the moment he turns, giving to the scene a magnificent sense of rhythm which came to characterize the entire film.

Welles narrates the film in character, using an Irish brogue. Rita is attracted to him and has her husband hire him as a hand on their yacht. Sloane is a famous trial lawyer. He frames Welles on a murder charge, acts as his legal representative, and, in an unforgettable courtroom scene, manages expertly to ensure Welles's conviction. The murderer turns out, in *noir* tradition, to be Rita. She and Sloane shoot each other in a house of mirrors at the conclusion. While Rita is dying, she has an exchange with Welles which was indigenous to the subgenre.

RITA: You can fight, but what good is it?
WELLES: You mean we can't win?
RITA: No, we can't win. Goodbye. Give my love to . . .
WELLES: We can't lose, either. Only if we quit.
RITA: And you're not going to do that.
WELLES: Not again!

As he walks away, out of the dark fun house into the light of dawn, Welles narrates to himself and the viewer that now he will be proven innocent. "Innocent," he reflects, "but that's a big word—innocence. Stupid's more like it. I guess I'll concentrate on getting old. Maybe I'll live so long I'll just forget her."

Disillusionment with government, with existence in the United States, disillusionment with love and domesticity brought to the fore a more ambivalent attitude than ever before with regard to women, conceived regularly as castrating bitches, predatory gold diggers, and scheming adventuresses. John Garfield narrated the murderous anguish that his love affair with Lana Turner brought him in *The Postman Always Rings Twice* (M-G-M, 1946), itself another James M. Cain story with a motif similar to Cain's *Double Indemnity*. *Noir* entries like *T-Men* (Eagle-Lion, 1947) and *Canon City* (Eagle-Lion, 1948), used location shooting, which contributed so much to the strange power of these films and others like *He Walked by Night* (Eagle-Lion, 1949).

Call Northside 777 (20th-Fox, 1948), with James Stewart, directed by Henry Hathaway, furthered the critical posture of *noir* films toward Establishment politics. It resembled Elia Kazan's entry, *Boomerang* (20th-Fox, 1947), which reversed the formula and had a state's attorney prove the innocence of a man society and the Establishment wanted him to convict. In *Northside*, a reporter proves the innocence of a man already serving a prison term. Edmund O'Brien in *noir* films like *D.O.A.* (United Artists, 1949), where he became a murder victim through a wholly gratuitous act, or *Two of a Kind* (Columbia, 1951), where he played opposite Lizabeth Scott, set forth the new image of the *noir* protagonist, a man who dominates the action but is in no way related to traditional heroes.

By the late Forties, this new realism rehabilitated the police from the nitwits and comedy teams which had come to typify them through all the previous decades in film. In a picture like *Rogue Cop* (M-G-M, 1954), Robert Taylor played a cop on the take from gangster George Raft. When Steve Forrest, Taylor's rookie brother, is rubbed out by Raft's mob, Taylor reforms and does a cleanup.

Nicholas Ray, in one outstanding *noir* film, furthered this humanization process of the police. For *In a Lonely Place* (Columbia, 1950), with its touching love story between Humphrey Bogart and Gloria Grahame, Ray cast Frank Lovejoy as a sympathetic cop. One is never certain, until the end, whether or not Bogart is the murderer—itself a considerable feat—but Ray goes beyond that in demonstrating the effects of officialdom's lack of imagination and its poisonous suspicions which destroy people's lives during the course of a murder investigation.

Gloria Grahame may well be the most ill-used "discovery" of the early Fifties. Possessed of an admirable talent, a shapely figure, and an uncommon projective ability, she was seldom given sufficient opportunity. Her performance in Fritz Lang's *The Big Heat* (Columbia, 1953) was almost the equal of her role opposite Bogart in *In A Lonely Place*. In the film, Glenn Ford is a cop bumped from the force because he would go up against organized crime, which dominates the city. Although his wife is murdered by Lee Marvin, although he is exposed to and then cheated of Gloria's lush figure (she has her face scarred by scalding coffee flung at her by Marvin in retaliation), Ford does triumph in the end.

Which brings me to the most significant aspect of all about *film noir*. While these films did incorporate a posture critical of the fantasies propelling American society, the hero still does manage to survive most of the time. *Film noir* did make way for the nearly total realism of the Seventies, but it was not itself more than a halfway mark, a dissident voice, but not sufficient by itself of jarring the smug complacency of audiences. Since detective films were uniquely imbued with the *noir* spirit, they nearly vanished from the screen in the decade following *The Big Heat* until the mid Sixties. The era of McCarthyism finished it off, reminding everyone, and middle-class America in particular, that this was no time to criticize the United States when the Russians and the Chinese were attacking us on every front and wanted to rob us of our newly won suburban homes, our two cars, our two kids, our dog or cat, our television set (to which the "B" detectives ably and quickly moved), TV dinners, and the jerry-built swimming pools in back yards. Would anyone in his right mind sacrifice all this to sleep with Lizabeth Scott on a permanent basis?—Dick Powell wouldn't—or Gloria Grahame?—Glenn Ford didn't. *Film noir* teased audiences with unhappy endings, but even if the hero didn't get the girl, justice was still done and the American way of life remained essentially undisturbed.

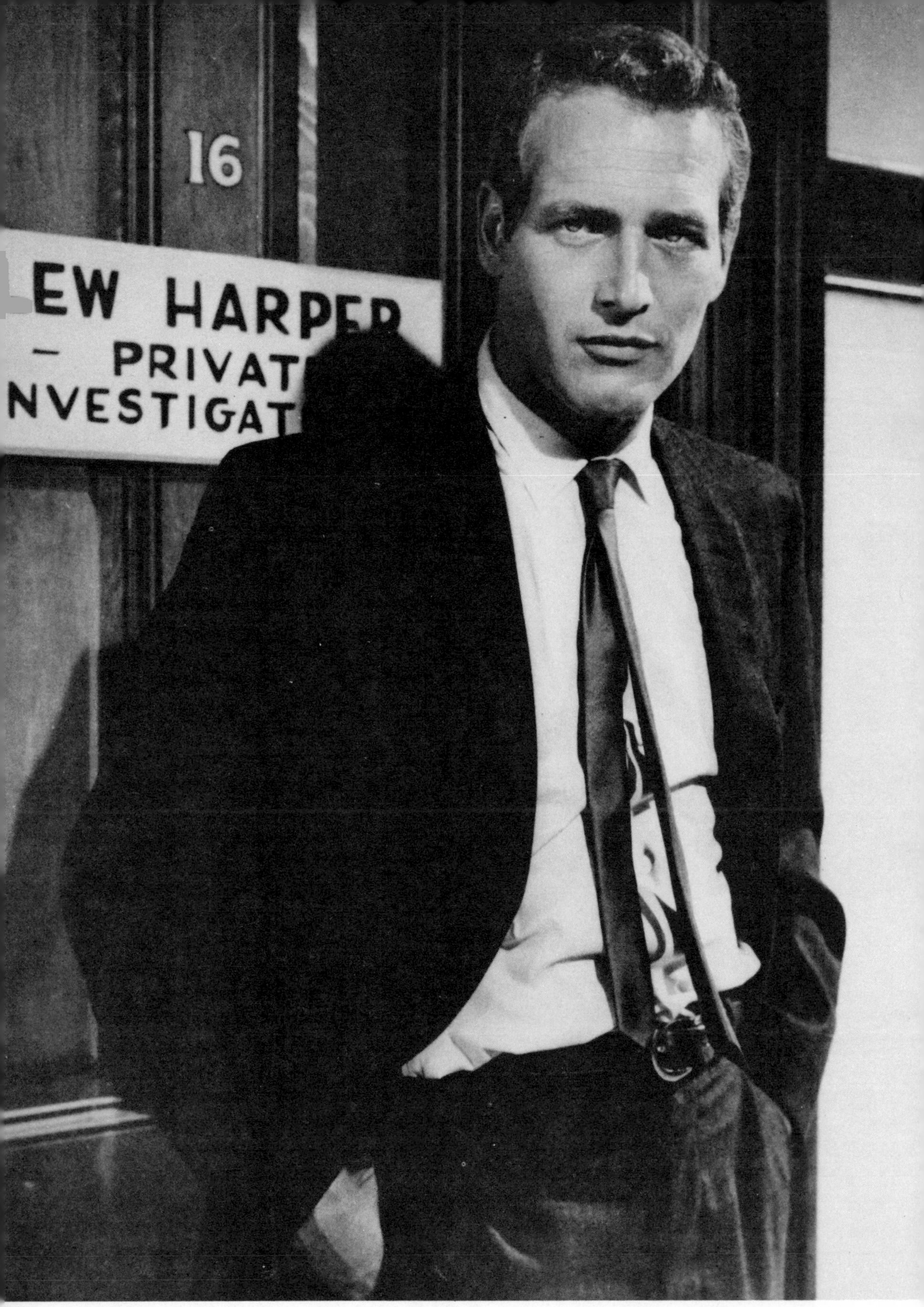
16
EW HARPER
— PRIVAT
NVESTIGAT

ELEVEN:
The Contemporary Scene

> *She's a whore, a pusher, an addict. And she's
> only 19. This town is full of kids all goin' in the
> same direction. It's all part of the Great Society.*
> —*Frank Sinatra in* The Detective

I

William K. Everson, in *The Detective in Film* (Citadel, 1972), writes: "The private eye, in trying to find a new and commercial identity, has used extensively all of the screen's new permissiveness—sex, nudity, extreme brutality, perversion, the coarsest gutter language. The route via the initially objectionable *The Detective* and *Tony Rome* (quickly rendered tame and relatively inoffensive by the excesses which followed) is a violent and ugly one."

This sentiment is occasioned by his preference for *The Maltese Falcon* (Warner's, 1941) as the finest detective film ever made and presumably as a model against which to judge all other pictures in the genre. The error, I suspect, in this line of reasoning goes beyond the fact that *The Maltese Falcon* was not intended to be taken as reality, but rather as a parable of reality; Everson, as possibly for a great many people attached to university film study, seems to have missed the fundamental principle that, increasingly, the motion picture now attempts to depict reality. Even should a filmmaker have to depend on parable or fantasy to embody his visions, he has in his mind the whole time a very clear definition of reality; without such a conscious definition, a parable or fantasy would have no point. Everson makes the fatal mistake of what might be termed "nostalgia" buffs: his romance with the past has caused him to lose his sensitivity for the present.

The changes which occurred in the conception of the detective in the Sixties

Paul Newman as Ross Macdonald's compassionate detective.
PHOTO COURTESY OF VIEWS & REVIEWS MAGAZINE.

had to do with more than the depth of portrayal of the detective himself; the milieu in which he had to work was removed from the mists of the dream and restored to the world in which we all live. Those who approach detective fiction with the same desire to escape from reality as though it were a fairy tale are the first to object to the experiments and forays in the genre attempted by Hammett in stories like "Death on Pine Street" or novels like *The Glass Key* or Raymond Chandler's *The Long Goodbye*. Hammett and Chandler, however much they may have fallen short of their goal, in the tradition they represented sought to penetrate beyond the mask of fantasy and grapple with the reality.

The three films which, more than any others, signify the alteration in tone of the Sixties were all directed by Gordon Douglas, and all of them starred Frank Sinatra: *Tony Rome*, *The Detective*, and *Lady in Cement*. The decade wasn't particularly prolific in the production of detective story films, as in actuality the Seventies haven't been either. But what there was, was remarkable, and I believe praiseworthy.

For me, the tradition of the Sixties began with production of William Wyler's *Detective Story* (Paramount, 1951), ten years earlier. I have already mentioned the association of Ralph Bellamy and Chester Morris with the play, Bellamy and Morris variously portraying the desperate and driven McCloud, a police detective who makes himself judge and jury and feels he alone can arbitrate right and wrong. Wyler wanted Dashiell Hammett to make the screen adaptation. He paid him a large advance, rented a suite of rooms for him at the Beverly-Wilshire, and arranged for Hammett to come back to California from where he was living on Martha's Vineyard in the East to work on the screenplay. It was a powerful vote of confidence in Hammett, considering all his political problems at the time. Hammett accepted the offer.

Wyler would visit him at the Beverly-Wilshire every two or three days to see how the script was coming. Hammett would meet him and they would talk, but Hammett was evasive about his progress. He had been at it three weeks when, one day, he met Wyler at the door to his suite. He had a cashier's check in the amount of the advance. He handed it to Wyler, who was stunned.

"I can't do it," he said simply. "I just can't do it anymore." He paused for a moment. "I'm sorry."

I do not know how *Detective Story* would have looked had Hammett been able to do it. As it was, Philip Yordan and Robert Wyler worked on the screenplay. It was considerably toned down from the stage version, making the picture more an average day at a precinct station in New York City rather than the drama of a man embodying the values of the Forties confronted by the widening scope of reality which the Fifties, at least in the arts, began to press upon the American consciousness.

On the other hand, the picture was well cast, with George Macready as the abortion doctor hated by Kirk Douglas as McCloud, and Eleanor Parker as McCloud's wife. William Bendix was also on hand as McCloud's fellow officer who has a streak of humanity running through his performance of a routine and institutionalized job. Lee Grant was properly offbeat as a first-time offender.

Frank Sinatra and Sue Lyon on Frank's houseboat in *Tony Rome* (20th-Fox, 1967).
PHOTO COURTESY OF TWENTIETH CENTURY-FOX FILM CORPORATION.

The strongest scene in the film is certainly when Eleanor Parker does her about-face. Her marriage to Douglas seems on the surface to be perfect; they are obviously much in love. She can turn it off in an instant, and so can McCloud. They were, each of them, in love with a fantasy; their relationship could not tolerate the stress of reality. And it is reality which finally brings down the curtain on McCloud.

Tony Rome (20th-Fox, 1967) was based on a novel by Marvin H. Albert with the screenplay by Richard Breen, and produced by Aaron Rosenberg. Tony Rome is a detective who lives on his houseboat, harbored in Miami. The notion is rather suggestive of John D. MacDonald's character Travis McGee. So far McGee, a hard-boiled detective who also lives on a houseboat on the Miami coast, has made his only cinematic appearance in *Darker than Amber* (National

General, 1970). Since this film bears certain significant thematic similarities to *Lady in Cement* (20th-Fox, 1968), the second Tony Rome picture, I had best leave off saying more about it until then.

Richard Conte was cast as Lieutenant Santini in *Tony Rome.* He is a cop who takes his job seriously, with a wife and child to support, and is a personal friend of Rome's. In fact Rome is often over at Santini's house visiting with the family. When a hotel dick, who was once Rome's partner, asks his help in taking a girl home, and Rome agrees, for a price, trouble starts. Rome meets Jill St. John at the girl's home, and he takes *her* home. It develops that the first girl Rome took home had possession of a pin wanted by unscrupulous men. This leads to Rome getting sapped, the hotel dick shot, and Rome being hired by the father of Sue Lyon, the girl. Rome sees that the girl's father juices the law to lay off while he searches after the pin.

Rome is a better than average detective. He is relatively honest. But he has a passion for betting on the horses. When Sue Lyon's stepmother also wants to hire him, Rome responds, "I've had to turn down two offers to go to bed since this thing started. I don't ever want to work that hard again." Particularly graphic is the presentation of the various characters Rome meets in the course of his investigation and the realistic re-creation of the American way of life.

The Detective (20th-Fox, 1968), of the next year, had the same producer, Aaron Rosenberg, as well as the same director. Abby Mann's screenplay was based on the novel by Roderick Thorp. In many ways, this is the best detective film, and possibly the best film, Frank Sinatra ever made. It further humanizes the detective, makes him believable, at the same time as the milieu in which he generally works is vividly reproduced. Through flashbacks, we see how Sinatra, on the New York police force, came to fall in love with Lee Remick, and how her neurotic promiscuity caused the breakdown of their marriage.

"There's no question it's a jungle out there," Gordon Douglas told me, "and that's the way we wanted to show it. We did the picture on location in New York. Frank liked the part. We had him fighting cops on the take. But that was only half the battle. He had to fight the system, too. Because the system demanded he make arrests and get evidence for convictions if he wanted promotions. We shot the electrocution in a garage right near the 57th Precinct, where we filmed the picture. The electric chair was the same model they still were using at Sing Sing. Our art director saw to that. The toughest part was when Frank and Lee have it out about her sexuality. I had the whole thing done in close-ups, you know, the way it would be in life. When a man and a woman talk about that sort of thing, when whatever it is they've had has gone to hell and they can't make it go anymore, the way they look at each other, right in the face. That's what I wanted. And I wanted their eyes."

The film is unique. I wouldn't be surprised if, in time, it will be regarded as the most outstanding detective film produced in the Sixties. It goes farther than *film noir* in giving crime back to those who commit it—in this case a man who becomes psychopathic in his attempt to cover up his homosexuality. Even with the enticing Jacqueline Bisset, it doesn't matter; a female isn't enough. So the murderer commits his sexual indiscretion and then, haunted by his action and fear of exposure, because he's on the take in a housing project that's sheer graft, he kills his lover, cuts off his penis, and mutilates his fingers.

"I was glad we were ahead of our time in that picture," Douglas remarked. Then he grinned. "It's better to be ahead of your time than behind it."

Lady in Cement couldn't duplicate either *Tony Rome* or, more importantly, *The Detective*, because the screenplay by Marvin H. Albert and Jack Guss went back to Raymond Chandler, and the world had outgrown Chandler. Dan Blocker was Gronsky, a figure much the same as Moose Malloy, who hires Tony Rome much the same as Malloy hired Marlowe. The picture opens with Frank Sinatra, as Rome, discovering a lady with her feet in cement at the bottom of the bay off Key Biscayne. In this it resembles *Lady in the Lake*. The ending of the picture, with Blocker confronting the setup of a gangster's son and finding his lost love, Raquel Welch, is right out of *Farewell, My Lovely*.

Some of the dialogue is good, better than the plot. Tony tells the gangster boss who has sent his son to college to become legitimate, "You aren't ashamed, with all those other kids burning their draft cards, that your son makes All-American?" One bit of inside humor has Blocker watching "Bonanza" on television while he's hiding out in a massage parlor. Richard Conte was again in the role of Lieutenant Santini.

The film, as I said, had similarities to the McGee picture, *Darker than Amber*, which starts off with McGee on his houseboat discovering a girl tied to an anchor. He saves her life, but the next attempt on it is successful. Rod Taylor played McGee. Robert Clouse directed.

"The shark was real," Douglas told me about *Lady in Cement*. "We shot that sequence in a tank. We had Frank go down in his diving outfit, with the shark swimming around him. The problem we had with the picture was that there was too much back-telling. You used to be able to do that, but not so much anymore."

The lifting of censorship also permitted the detective to have reasonable sexual urges. When Tony is out on the water with Raquel Welch and she bends over, he, looking at her derrière, can come up with something better to do with their time together than go diving for sunken treasure.

As if in recognition of the newly won freedom of the cinema to narrate events as they are rather than how some people might like to have them be, these films of the Sixties made way for *Klute* (Warner's, 1971) in the Seventies. Here, again, the audience was confronted with a sex killer. His prey was call girls. Jane Fonda portrayed the next marked victim, Donald Sutherland the cop assigned to protect her. He eventually falls in love with her, and she with him. The tracking down of the murderer is handled in a realistic fashion, and even his capture is possible, since he is not a man who has bought the protection of either the police or the courts. Jane Fonda won an Academy Award for her performance as Bree, imprisoned by the murderer in the small office of a garment factory after hours. She is forced to listen to a tape recording of the horrible screams of one of the murderer's previous victims in her death throes. Not a word is spoken, nor does Jane emit a sound; but the tears begin to run down her cheeks; they drip from her nose; they become more plentiful; she is struck dumb by agony, a sorrow that is beyond words. The frightful tension of this scene can be relieved only by the brutal action of attempted murder.

At last, with the beginning of the Seventies, the detective film had found itself. Crime can better be understood by the audience if portrayed as it really happens. And Jane Fonda deserved recognition for her portrait of the victim of crime, that combination of despair, frenzy, loneliness, and desperation which has come to characterize the lives of so many in the contemporary world. For that moment, in *Klute*, Jane Fonda was their witness.

II

More nonsense has been written about Alfred Hitchcock than about almost any other film director. This isn't merely because so much has been written about Hitchcock and the "meaning" of his films. His films, almost all of them, focus on the commission of crime, guilt, and the desperate moments in people's lives. With such an orientation, it was perhaps inevitable that critics, drawn to his cinematic *oeuvre*, should seek to find in his productions some sort of hidden moral message or an attempt at ethical philosophy.

It has never been Hitchcock's custom to grant many interviews. Over the last five years, I doubt if he has been interviewed by anyone, save in connection with promoting a picture of his about to go into release. So during our visit, which I have already mentioned, I asked him if this reticence on his part might not be responsible, at least to some extent, for the poor quality of the commentaries about his films which have appeared during the last decade.

"No," he drawled, folding his hands together in his lap as he sat comfortably in a Charles chair. "Of course, I haven't seen all the books that have been published about my films. But of the ones I have seen, I cannot even remember their authors trying to interview me. Their ideas seem pretty well fixed in their minds," a mischievous smile was creeping across his lips, "so why spoil it by interviewing me?"

Hitchcock's objection to the classical format of a detective story is the undue emphasis that has to be placed on the identity of the murderer. Hence the entire thrust of such a film is toward the explanation at the end. Moreover, had Hitchcock felt differently, I doubt if his career would have been quite as successful. Only a very limited number of innovative devices are allowable within the boundaries of the formula.

Yet, because of the character of Hitchcock's films, he has made a significant contribution over the years to the way in which traditional detective films have been treated on the screen. As early as *The Lodger* (Gainsborough, 1926) he showed the maddening power of suspicion and the dire consequences which can come of a blind acceptance of the flimsiest circumstantial evidence. In this case, an innocent man is suspected by everyone of being a notorious murderer. In *Blackmail* (British International, 1929) Hitchcock showed how, even though a homicide might be justified, guilt over the crime was capable of disintegrating the wrongdoer, in this case Anny Ondra, paralleling the growing malice of the Yard detective, John Longden, one of her suitors, whose investigation seems to be motivated by more than a desire to solve the mystery.

Murder (British International, 1930), with Beethoven's *Fifth Symphony* played beneath the opening credits, was Hitchcock's only formula detective story. It was Herbert Marshall's first all-talking picture. Marshall was cast as a member of a jury present at the murder trial of a girl he knew in the theater. He is begrudgingly convinced of her guilt, but then regrets his haste and sets out to investigate the crime on his own. The police are depicted as both unimaginative and lazy. The screenplay raises grave doubts about the efficacy of due process and the British court system, on which model the American system is based. Everson was complaining about the homosexuality theme in *The Detective*, but already here, twenty-eight years before it, the murder was inspired by this very impulse, an effort to keep the murdered woman quiet.

Number 17 (British International, 1932) dealt with the old dark house setting. While it was largely a melodrama, the detective turns out not to be a detective at all, and the stranger turns out to be the detective. Even though the picture served as a preparation for Hitchcock's later concentration on varieties of a climactic chase, Hitchcock himself admits that he allowed himself to become needlessly careless in its direction.

In *The 39 Steps* (Gaumont-British, 1935) the idea of the pursuit was varied. This time the innocent man, played by Robert Donat, is wanted for a crime he did not commit. He is thrown together with Madeleine Carroll, by virtue of being handcuffed to her by the villains. She becomes, as a result, his unwilling accomplice in solving the murder and exposing the real culprit. The arm of the law is portrayed here, as so often in Hitchcock's films, as merciless, unrelenting, and inexorable. Similarly, *The Secret Agent* (Gaumont-British, 1936), based on the Ashenden stories by Somerset Maugham, varies the theme of the least suspicious character, played by an ingenuous Robert Young, who is far more sinister than the obvious blackguard portrayed by Peter Lorre.

Sabotage (Gaumont-British, 1936), while exposing Oscar Homolka almost from the start as the villain, manages to generate, if not sympathy, at least ambivalence for his plight.

Young and Innocent (Gainsborough, 1937), based on a novel by Josephine Tey, returned to the theme of an innocent man being chased for a crime he did not commit, joined in his flight by the woman he loves; but, more importantly, it attacks the stupidity of circumstantial evidence, the unreliable quality of testimony by supposed eyewitnesses, and terrifyingly reveals exactly how the unimaginative approach of the police is literally no match when confronted by a clever murderer. The police are perfectly willing to satisfy themselves with the most obvious suspect, which is to say the suspect against whom the best possible case can be built to bring a conviction in court.

In *The Lady Vanishes* (Gainsborough, 1938) Hitchcock made not only one of his classic films but also a masterful variation on the theme of a person, whom everyone has seen, suddenly removed from the scene. Margaret Lockwood was teamed—again an unwilling alliance at the beginning turning into love—with a

Peter Lorre talking to Alfred Hitchcock during filming of *The Man Who Knew Too Much* (Gaumont-British, 1932). PHOTO COURTESY OF THE NATIONAL FILM ARCHIVE.

traveling musicologist played by Michael Redgrave. *Foreign Correspondent* (United Artists, 1940) found Joel McCrea, an American reporter sent to Europe, falling in love with Herbert Marshall's daughter, played by Laraine Day. At one point McCrea joins forces with fellow journalist George Sanders to expose the culprit. Herbert Marshall's valiant role in *Murder* was reversed.

Suspicion (RKO, 1941) was a very sophisticated treatment of a theme which preoccupied Agatha Christie's "Philomel Cottage," although here the book on which the film was based was *Before the Fact*, by Francis Iles. Joan Fontaine marries Cary Grant, only to suspect Grant of trying to murder her for her inheritance. From this point forward, in fact, a gradual recognition of the truth in all its unpleasantness, often leaving the hero or heroine helpless rather than in command of the situation, or a dissecting of the monstrous motives which lead to a compulsion to commit premeditated murder, and the commission of the planned crime itself, became Hitchcock's most dominant themes: *Shadow of a Doubt* (Universal, 1943), with Teresa Wright falling in love with Joseph Cotten while simultaneously learning of his murderous intentions; or the discovery by his fellow passengers that Walter Slezak in *Lifeboat* (20th-Fox, 1943), far from being a captive, is very nearly their captor. This theme of discovery becomes one of self-discovery as well in *Spellbound* (United Artists, 1945), where Gregory Peck reconstructs a part of his experience that his mind has blotted out after which he identifies the real murderer.

Hitchcock's criticism of the judicial system reached its pinnacle in *The Paradine Case* (Selznick, 1948), with Charles Laughton as a lecherous judge who has the power to twist the law to suit himself, and knows it. *Dial M for Murder* (Warner's, 1954), like the less successful *Strangers on a Train* (Warner's, 1951), almost makes the viewer, because of a certain sympathy with Ray Milland, a party to the commission of the crime. John Williams excels as the Scotland Yard detective, universally suspicious and deadly in his somewhat

Hitchcock reviewing the script with Margaret Lockwood for *The Lady Vanishes* (Gainsborough, 1938). PHOTO COURTESY OF THE NATIONAL FILM ARCHIVE.

bored but persistent pursuit. Hitchcock's Yard detectives, no matter how the effects of their investigations might be portrayed, are always models of efficiency compared to the rather seedy and, as it develops, foolhardy private investigator in *Psycho* (Paramount, 1960).

I realize I am in a minority in liking *Marnie* (Universal, 1964), but here, it would seem, Hitchcock only intensified the psychological milieu of guilt, repression, and misconstruction which, for so long, had been worked and reworked in his films. I think he achieved a perfection in grappling with these particular themes in *Marnie*, which had heretofore eluded him.

With *Frenzy* (Universal, 1972) Hitchcock made a detective, a Yard man of course, a central character, human, harassed, but dogged. Played by Alec McCowen, even the harshness with which the British constabulary had been presented by Hitchcock in so many of his films was mitigated; the arm of the law is flawed, but in *Frenzy* it has sufficient character and self-possession to admit a mistake and make every effort to correct the damage which came as a consequence. But in the end, as *Family Plot* (Universal, 1976) only reconfirms, for Hitchcock film is only make-believe, no matter how serious its subject matter. All of his moralistic commentators to one side, as Hitchcock put it to Francois Truffaut, "My love of film is far more important to me than any considerations of morality." If his films have done nothing else, over the past forty-odd years they have made audiences—and other filmmakers—more cognizant of the mechanics of murder, the emotions involved, the fixations, desperations, anxieties, and the omnipotence of guilt even in the innocent. He may possibly be quite right in believing it is more effective cinema to narrate a story of murder before the event, rather than to tediously try to reconstruct the crime after its commission.

III

There seems to be a very animated dispute among commentators on the detective story whether Agatha Christie or Erle Stanley Gardner is the leader in terms of sales volume. I can shed no light on the debate. Gardner was the more prolific, but Christie certainly rivaled him in every way, and she was at it longer.

Agatha Christie was always a very reclusive person. Before she died, she was at work on her autobiography, but I suspect little more will be found in it—if and when it is published—than can be obtained by reading Derrick Murdoch's *The Agatha Christie Mystery* (Pagurian Press, 1976). As is frequently the case with writers, and with many actors and directors I have met, their private lives hold none of the melodrama and color which might be expected by viewing their work. Agatha Christie was born on September 15, 1890, Agatha Miller at Torquay, in Devonshire, England. Her father, an American, died when she was very young and she was raised together with an older sister by her widowed mother. She had no formal schooling but was educated at home.

When she was sixteen, her mother sent her to Paris for vocal training, hoping she would become an opera singer. Alas, her voice proved too weak and she herself too shy to make it a career. She did, however, retain a lifelong love of the piano. Her mother was of independent if modest means, and entertained the possibility for a time that her youngest daughter might marry well. In 1912 she became engaged to Colonel Archibald Christie of the Royal Flying Corps. It wasn't exactly the marriage her mother had in mind, but presumably the two were in love; they were married on Christmas Eve in 1914.

On a challenge from her sister, Agatha Christie undertook to write a detective story. She had been very imaginative as a child and her mother had constantly encouraged her to write. During the Great War, Mrs. Christie worked as a dispenser for the Red Cross at Torquay and between times addressed herself to her novel. When it was finished, she called it *The Mysterious Affair at Styles*. It was sent to several publishers and rejected by all of them. Collins, after sitting on the manuscript for a year, finally offered her a flat twenty-five pounds for all rights, or the equivalent of $125 in U.S. currency then. She accepted their offer. Both Conan Doyle and Somerset Maugham had settled for similar amounts for their first novels for outright sale, and, as in the case of *A Study in Scarlet*, by Conan Doyle, and *Liza of Lambeth*, by Maugham. *The Mysterious Affair at Styles* is still in print today and will likely remain so.

Styles introduced to the world Agatha Christie's most famous sleuth, Hercule Poirot, a retired Belgian police inspector. I get the impression from some critics that Poirot in this book is more fully developed than he was later to be in most of his adventures, although I do not concur. The character simply is not one about whom I find myself insatiably curious, nor am I charmed by his Gallic phrases and his wholly intuitive reasoning, the "little gray cells," as he refers to his mental processes. Murdoch in his book has endeavored to trace Poirot's origins in the works of earlier writers. The later British detective story writer Eden Phillpotts ostensibly acted as a catalyst while Agatha Christie was at work on the book. The mechanism of murder depended on very specialized information which the author had gained during her tenure with the Red Cross, and doubtless she took little further interest in the technical side of crime, since, as she herself declared, she preferred dealing with murder by poison because she knew something about chemistry and pharmacopoeia. The book was a sufficient success that she followed it with six more novels, some featuring Poirot, some more in the thriller category.

Her marriage to Colonel Christie did not turn out happily. His exemplary war record was duplicated in civilian life by his activities as a stockbroker and, later, director of several companies. But in 1926 he wanted a divorce and his wife refused to give him one. Agatha Christie's mother died. She published *The Murder of Roger Ackroyd* (Collins, 1926), wherein her customary narrator, a Captain Hastings even more dense than Dr. Watson, is replaced by a country doctor who keeps a journal of Poirot's exploits. The book caused quite an uproar, since it was to this narrator that Poirot finally traces the murder. Instead of being warmly welcomed, the book excited disdain and condemnation. Getting into her Morris two-seater on the afternoon of December 3, 1926, Mrs. Christie left her Berkshire home and disappeared. The car was found abandoned in a field, after having been pushed down a hill. The ignition and lights were on. Her coat was on the seat. At first the event was regarded as a publicity stunt, but when she was not found after several days and a national search was mounted, it became newsworthy.

She was located eventually at a resort in Yorkshire registered under an assumed name. I supposed readers were fearing the worst. But, confronted by this situation, they seemed resentful. Agatha Christie claimed temporary amnesia. Archibald Christie was granted his wish for a divorce. He remarried and this time remained married until his wife's death in 1959. His ex-wife continued to write books and traveled as much as she could, especially to the Near Fast. Two years after her divorce, her wanderings brought her to southern Iraq, where C. Leonard Woolley, the noted archaeologist, was head of a joint expedition organized by the British Museum and the Museum of the University of Pennsylvania, engaged in historic excavations at the site of the prehistoric city of Ur.

Agatha Christie had a letter of introduction to Professor Woolley. He entertained her and she was introduced to his assistant, a man of twenty-six years, Max Mallowan. The two of them, in one of those unpredictable occurrences, fell in love, or at least found their personalities sufficiently complementary that they were married in September 1930, when Mrs. Christie was forty. The difference in age mattered little. It seems to be a problem, as in Chandler's case, only when one or another of the two parties is overly sensitive about it. Mallowan was deeply involved in his archaeological work and quite content to encourage his wife to pursue her vocation as—to use her word—an authoress. This second marriage survived.

Agatha Christie herself obviously wearied of Poirot. It was during the Second World War that she wrote *Curtain* (Dodd, Mead, 1975), in which she recounts his death. Many Poirot books came after, so enthusiastic was the public clamor for him, that the book cannot truly be regarded as an end to the saga; the setting itself is slightly before the intensification of the war. *Curtain* originally wasn't to be published until after her death. But in 1975, plagued by ill health, she ordered her London publishers to release the book so the tradition of "a Christie for Christmas" could be maintained.

Agatha Christie's second novel, directly following *Styles*, was *The Secret Adversary* (Collins, 1922), in which she introduced the married couple of Tommy Beresford and Tuppence Cowley. The Fox Film Corporation in Germany produced a film based on it titled *Das Abenteuer G.m.b.H.* None of the European archives have it, including the excellent collection in Prague, Czechoslovakia.

The Passing of Mr. Quin (Strand, 1928) was based on the short story "The Coming of Mr. Quin," eventually contained in the 1930 collection (the picture perhaps inspired the story anthology) *The Mysterious Mr. Quin*, published by Collins. Leslie Hiscott directed, and the film featured Stewart Rome, Trilby Clark, and Ursula Jeans. The plot had to do with the innocence or guilt of a tramp suspected of having murdered a woman's first husband. The story may have had autobiographical overtones, but the picture met with an unexciting box office.

The first Hercule Poirot film was *Alibi* (Twickenham, 1931). After the scandalous reception accorded *Ackroyd*, and the broadsides fired at it by such eminent leaders in the genre as S. S. Van Dine, what more appropriate novel could there be to bring to the screen? Austin Trevor, a British actor who scarcely looked the part of Poirot, was cast in the lead. The fact that Michael Morton dramatized the novel for the stage in 1928 certainly helped inspire the cinematic project. The play, similarly retitled *Alibi* by Morton, opened at the Prince of Wales on May 15, 1928, with Charles Laughton in the role of Poirot. It was then brought to New York in 1932, under the title *Fatal Alibi*, with Laughton in the lead, supported by a young Jane Wyatt. It closed after only twenty-four performances. But on the London stage, it was both a critical and commercial success. Charles Higham, in his biography of Charles Laughton published by Doubleday in 1976, writes: "Given the difficult challenge of making a real human being out of Miss Christie's pasteboard figure of Poirot, Charles gave an excitingly detailed performance, his Belgian accent flawless, his cross-examination of the various witnesses quite deadly, his final pointing at the killer electrifying in its impact on an audience."

Leslie Hiscott directed the film version, at an estimated cost of $50,000. Austin Trevor could not do with the role of Poirot what Laughton did—all the reviewers were agreed on this point—and the film suffered from those traits so common in the British cinema during that era of lethargy and lack of solid, engaging characterization. Franklin Dyall played Ackroyd and J. H. Roberts was the culprit.

Agatha Christie, hard on the success of the stage adaptation of *The Murder of Roger Ackroyd*, wrote an original Poirot play titled *Black Coffee*, which opened at the Embassy in London on December 8, 1930, with Francis L. Sullivan as Hercule Poirot. Twickenham, which had decided to alternate their Sherlock Holmes releases with Hercule Poirot films, followed *Alibi* with *Black Coffee* (Twickenham, 1931) with Austin Trevor again as Poirot, Richard Cooper as Captain Hastings, Melville Cooper as Inspector Japp, and Elizabeth Allan, who had also been a suspect in *Alibi*. The budget was slightly increased. Leslie Hiscott once more directed.

The two pictures did well enough, particularly in the American market, that an original adaptation of *13 at Dinne*r under its British title, *Lord Edgware Dies*, was made in England by Real Art in 1934. Trevor was retained as Poirot, although John Turnbull played Inspector Japp. *Black Coffee* had concerned a scientist who was murdered at a house party after his papers were stolen. *Lord Edgware Dies* followed the plot of the novel and Poirot is beset with the murder of an English lord and the attempted murder of an actress. The film did poorly and so Poirot was off the screen until *The Alphabet Murders* (M-G-M, 1966). Metro-Goldwyn-Mayer, with Jean Hersholt in mind, did buy rights to *The ABC Murders* (Dodd, Mead, 1936) the year the novel was published, thinking that they might enjoy some of the success the British had had with Hercule Poirot; but nothing came of the notion.

Frank Vosper adapted "Philomel Cottage" for the stage, the play opening at Wyndhams in London on February 2, 1936, with Vosper in the lead and titled

Austin Trevor as Hercule Poirot questioning Elizabeth Allan in *Black Coffee*
(Twickenham, 1931).   PHOTO COURTESY OF THE NATIONAL FILM ARCHIVE.

Love from a Stranger. I believe it to be Agatha Christie's best short story. While
the play had a short New York run, the motion picture United Artists made
based on it in 1937 with Ann Harding and Basil Rathbone, filmed in England
and directed by Rowland V. Lee, was not only superior to the remake by Eagle-
Lion by the same title, *Love from a Stranger*, in 1947 with Sylvia Sydney, John
Hodiak, and John Howard, but incorporated a splendid use of suspense only
hinted at in the Christie original.

Mrs. Christie wrote and published *And Then There Were None* in 1939. She
did the stage adaptation herself in 1943, opening at the St. James in London. She
altered the novel for the play, including some desperation detective work by a
man who has stumbled into the murder scheme purely by accident. It was the
stage adaptation which René Clair employed for his stunning film for Twentieth

The gathering of the victims in René Clair's classic *And Then There Were None* (20th-Fox, 1945). From left to right: Walter Huston, Barry Fitzgerald, Roland Young, June Duprez, Louis Hayward, C. Aubrey Smith, Judith Anderson.

PHOTO COURTESY OF TWENTIETH CENTURY-FOX FILM CORPORATION.

Century-Fox release in 1945. Barry Fitzgerald played the judge and Walter Huston was the drunken doctor. Roland Young, C. Aubrey Smith, Judith Anderson, Mischa Auer, and Louis Hayward were also in the cast.

The plot was forthright. A mysterious person has summoned ten people to an isolated island. A phonograph recording identifies each of them as having been guilty of a serious crime from which he or she has escaped unpunished. One by one, each of the terrified party is found murdered, until only Louis Hayward, the man there by mistake, June Duprez, and the murderer are left.

George Pollock, who directed all the Miss Marple pictures, directed *Ten Little Indians* (Seven Arts, 1965), financed abroad and filmed in Ireland with a setting elaborated by uncredited second unit work supposedly shot in the Austrian

Alps. This version in no way could compare to Clair's masterpiece—in many ways the only excellent film based on any of Agatha Christie's works—but it was a workmanlike job with its own moments of suspense. Shirley Eaton, who had her body covered with gold paint in *Goldfinger* (United Artists, 1964), played the love interest for Hugh O'Brian. Fabian, the pop singer, got killed off with a poisoned cocktail early in the action. Wilfrid Hyde-White, the onetime British Philo Vance, was given the role Barry Fitzgerald had in René Clair's film. The remake was lessened in its impact by a gimmick of the type that William Castle was inclined to use in his horror pictures; the film is interrupted near the end to ask the audience to guess at the identity of the man behind the murders.

However disappointing the Pollock film may have been, it was nowhere near the disaster of *Ten Little Indians* (Avco Embassy, 1975) directed by Peter Collinson. It had an international cast with much dubbing, the setting now changed to an isolated hotel on the Iranian desert because the financing was international with Iran as a participant. The film was, to say the least, shoddier than any Christie-based motion picture to date.

To Billy Wilder we owe the only film which approaches *And Then There Were None*, namely his treatment of *Witness for the Prosecution* (United Artists, 1957). The story, as Agatha Christie wrote it, is improbable; her stage adaptation was certainly better, opening in London's West End on October 28, 1953, with Patricia Jessel and David Horne. Patricia Jessel came to New York for the American production, joined by Francis L. Sullivan. It was voted the Best Foreign Play of the season and ran for 645 performances.

"Arthur Hornblow was the producer on the film," Billy Wilder told me. "He had given me my first chance to direct. We both agreed that we wanted Marlene Dietrich and Charles Laughton for the film version. Laughton was very easy for me to work with. He was, in fact, the best single actor I have ever worked with. You can see from the picture how deeply involved he became with the part. We only changed a few things from the original, such as Elsa Lanchester's role as the barrister's nurse."

On his bulletin board, after all the years, Wilder still had a clipping of the London review of the picture's premiere.

Laughton's performance during the trial sequence made the critics ecstatic, and it is still one of his most powerful deliveries, starting at a whisper, rising to a shaking accusation that Dietrich is "a liar," the word reverberating for several seconds.

Neither *The Spider's Web* (Danziger, 1960), based on an original play Agatha Christie wrote and in which Margaret Lockwood starred, nor *Endless Night* (British-Lion, 1971), based on the 1967 novel, was very good. Much better was *The Alphabet Murders* (M-G-M-British, 1966) with its screenplay by David Pursall and Jack Seddon, who worked on all the Miss Marple adaptations, and directed by Frank Tashlin, although treatment of Hercule Poirot still proved a problem; consequently it was done in camp humor style. Tony Randall, with a complicated hairpiece, played the aging Poirot, who has given up smoking and who is followed by Robert Morley, who is connected with the

Home Office and is assigned to Poirot's safety. The plot was complex, involuted, and perhaps to some incomprehensible, done in the Continental manner of Fellini and Bergman, where, if you lose the story line, it really shouldn't matter because the story isn't important anyway. There's good comedy in it; and in one scene, where Poirot is being released from jail, Margaret Rutherford as Miss Marple and Stringer Davis as Mr. Stringer make a cameo appearance. Some of the effects are enterprising, such as the use of mirrors when Morley and Randall first talk to one another. But the novel itself was absurd and the picture was, in part, reflective of its original source.

In that seminal essay for which he is justly famous, "The Simple Art of Murder," Raymond Chandler remarked: "And there is a scheme of Agatha Christie's featuring M. Hercule Poirot, that ingenious Belgian who talks in a literal translation of schoolboy French. By duly messing around with his 'little gray cells' M. Poirot decides that since nobody on a certain through sleeper could have done the murder alone, everybody did it together, breaking the process down into a series of simple operations like assembling an egg beater. This is the type that is guaranteed to knock the keenest mind for a loop. Only a halfwit could guess it."

Charles Laughton, Marlene Dietrich, Tyrone Power, and Billy Wilder relaxing on break during the filming of *Witness for the Prosecution* (United Artists, 1957).
PHOTO COURTESY OF THE NATIONAL FILM ARCHIVE.

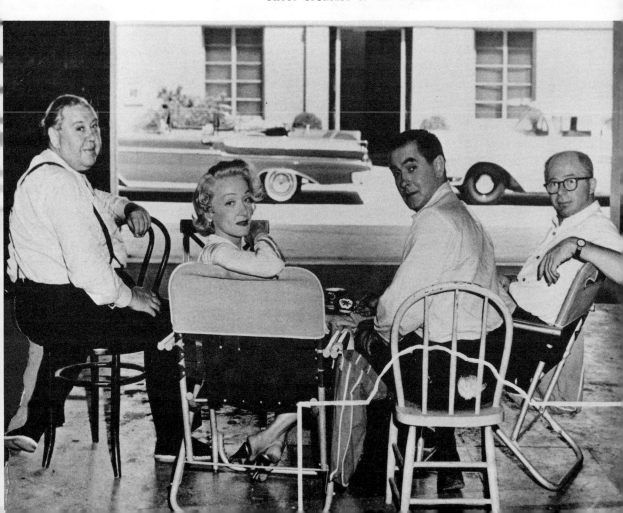

From left to right: Richard Widmark, John Gielgud, Tony Perkins, Lord Brabourne,
Albert Finney as Hercule Poirot, Sidney Lumet, Jean-Pierre Cassel, Martin Balsam,
in *Murder on the Orient Express* (Paramount, 1974).

PHOTO COURTESY OF THE NATIONAL FILM ARCHIVE.

It was this plot, *Murder on the Orient Express*, which EMI-British produced
in 1974 and Paramount Pictures released in the United States. Albert Finney
headed an international cast, playing Poirot, which included Lauren Bacall,
Ingrid Bergman, Jacqueline Bisset, Sean Connery, Sir John Gielgud, Anthony
Perkins, Vanessa Redgrave, Michael York, and, as the murder victim, Richard
Widmark. Sidney Lumet, veteran of exceptional films like *The Pawnbroker*
(Allied Artists, 1965) and the more recent *Network* (M-G-M, 1976), directed.
Ingrid Bergman won an Academy Award for her portrayal. The picture
opened to fabulous business all around the world. Even Agatha Christie, who
had formerly praised only *Witness for the Prosecution*, commented in the film's
favor.

"The only other Poirot I have ever met was Charles Laughton," Finney said
at the time, "who was introduced to Agatha Christie when he played the Belgian
detective on the stage. Being portly himself, Laughton was the right shape for
the role, but in order to get the short, solid look I needed as Agatha Christie's
elder statesman of criminologists, I wore body padding, a T-shirt draped with
cotton wool. I also had to have padded thighs to make me look wide so that my

height appeared less. Facially the transformation was achieved with a false nose and padded cheeks to achieve the egg-shaped look. By far the most important part of the make-up was the gleaming black hair and the meticulously trimmed, trained, and waxed period moustache."

The film was played straight, with a screenplay by Paul Dehn, which is to say it re-created the atmosphere and characters of the novel with no attempt at alteration. And it was a success! Perhaps it couldn't be done again, but it was done once.

The plot, Chandler's criticism to one side for a moment, did have one thing in common with René Clair's *And Then There Were None:* both dealt with universal guilt universally shared. It cut across the boundaries of one man at fault amid his righteous brethren. The British police are the most admired in the world, and not without cause. They walk into danger unarmed. They believe in fair play and practice it. The graft which characterizes both law enforcement and the judiciary in the United States is considerably less in the British Isles. This is one theme which Agatha Christie's novels stressed that makes them impressive. Universal guilt, as represented by *And Then There Were None* and *Murder on the Orient Express*, is another, and however time-bound the stories or films might be, it is a theme which has gained an increasing currency as detective films come of age, culminating in *Chinatown*. But the American detective film, sadly, I am afraid, cannot boast of the counter-principle, which ostensibly has been too British for export, the friendliness of the police which inspires both respect and trust, and the loftiness of the British court system where administration of the law is still advised by abstract precepts seemingly out of reach of the thoroughgoing corruption which has become the precedent on the other side of the Atlantic. I seriously wonder if the precept that a man is innocent until *proven* guilty can really exist without subscription to the philosophy of fair play before all else. The British are not above the American concept of guilt by association, but fortunately for them it would appear that in their own internal affairs it isn't quite so common as in the United States. However, Agatha Christie does seem to agree with Alfred Hitchcock that what British law enforcement does lack is imagination.

On January 12, 1976, Agatha Christie died peacefully. She had been made a Commander of the British Empire and she had received the equivalent of knighthood. In her eighties, as captured in photographs by Lord Snowden, she had attained a peculiar attractiveness denied her in earlier years by that curiosity of nature which sometimes rights in old age what it neglected to do in youth or middle age. She requested at her funeral service that these lines of Edmund Spenser be quoted:

> *Is not short paine well borne, that brings long ease,*
> *And layes the soule to sleepe in quiet grave?*
> *Sleepe after toyle, port after stormie seas,*
> *Ease after warre, death after life does greatly please.*

Her books and plays were earning her $10,000 a week in royalties, more money than she literally knew what to do with, and with which she provided for others. She had lived all her life in a world created by her own imagination, and she lived long enough for that world to seize and hold the attention of the generations for whom she wrote.

IV

The titles of Ross Macdonald's detective novels remind me of places I have been. *The Chill* (Knopf, 1964) brings to mind the many hours I was fogged in at the St. Louis airport. *The Far Side of the Dollar* (Knopf, 1965) reminds me of another long wait, this time at the air terminal in Boston. *Black Money* (Knopf, 1966), which I finished on a flight out of Washington, D.C., had me ranting to a college student seated next to me on the improbabilities of the plot. *The Zebra-Striped Hearse* (Knopf, 1962) I read as I flew over the Rocky Mountains. *The Way Some People Die* (Knopf, 1951) found me stranded in Tulsa, Oklahoma. *The Ivory Grin* (Knopf, 1952) recalls the sunlight slanting against the buildings at dusk outside a hotel room in the ancient part of Rome.

I have read all the Macdonald novels while in transit. I wouldn't bring it up at all, save I once mentioned it to Macdonald. It prompted him to say, "The public eye is always on California. People are fascinated by it. That's what makes it so interesting. California is the center of world culture." He then went on to say, as I quoted him in the Prologue, that everything good and bad begins in California. "I hope my novels are critical of California. And of Los Angeles. I want them to be."

Macdonald, using this as his rationale, has centered all of his Lew Archer detective stories in California. The farthest Archer ever gets is Michigan, while investigating a case (that is where Macdonald studied for an advanced degree), or to Canada (which is where Macdonald was raised). He gets to these places in *The Galton Case* (Knopf, 1959), which, according to Macdonald, is the novel which marks the changes he wrought in his detective and the kind of fiction he intended, from then on, to write. I suppose it is comforting, if you're going to focus so exclusively on California as a setting, that you think it the center of the world.

Despite this, Macdonald has became a favorite of critics and reviewers, especially those in the Eastern United States who are impressed by his wealth of literary allusions and the *mysterium* of modern psychology with which his tales are invested. The late Anthony Boucher, writing for the New York *Times Book Review*, even went so far as to declare Macdonald a better novelist than either Hammett or Chandler.

Very little biographical information on Macdonald has been printed, not unintentionally. He is a quiet and retiring man. He was born in 1915 near San Francisco. His father, apparently, was a sea captain who abandoned his mother and himself when he was about five. His real name is Kenneth Millar, and his early novels were published under this name. He may have resided in as many as fifty different houses while growing up. In 1938 he married a Canadian woman who has written novels under her married name, Margaret Millar. Harvard turned him down for a graduate fellowship; Ann Arbor didn't. He hasn't forgotten that. For thirty years, he has lived in Santa Barbara, about ninety miles up the coast from Los Angeles. He told me that he had seven different houses there before finally coming to live in a moderately large home on the Hope Ranch. He and his wife have a number of dogs which announce your presence long before you manage to get out of your car.

During the Second World War, Macdonald served as a communications officer aboard an escort carrier in the Pacific. Originally, in Canada, he taught high school, and, until his first Archer book was made into a film by Warner Brothers in 1966 and his novels began selling well, he taught creative writing and world literature at the college level in the evenings.

The Underground Man (Knopf, 1971) is generally considered Macdonald's finest novel. Eudora Welty, the gracious gentlewoman of American letters, called it "a stunning achievement" in a review for the New York *Times*. The plot is typically intricate to the point of absurdity. Macdonald's detective Lew Archer (named after Sam Spade's murdered associate Miles Archer) discovers the body of Leo Broadhurst buried for fifteen years in an automobile a short distance from Broadhurst's mountain cabin. Everyone thought he had disappeared but no one suspected foul play. Present at the scene of the crime the night Broadhurst was murdered was Martha Crandell, who was in the midst of sexual congress with him when he was struck in the head by a bullet fired by his wife from outside the cabin. In the loft of the cabin was Martha's daughter, Susan. With Broadhurst's wife was their small son Stanley. Nearby was Fritz Snow and his criminally inclined friend Al Sweetner. They bury the body in the car through use of a bulldozer, but not before Mrs. Snow, Fritz's mother, knifes Broadhurst for good measure since the bullet only grazed him. Also present is Brian Kilpatrick, whose wife has run away to Reno to divorce him and thus be free to marry Leo. Kilpatrick sets about blackmailing Mrs. Broadhurst for all her property and money. Eight people inside of two hours know what happened and still it has been kept a secret for fifteen years.

Reviewers appear to have formed a pact to ignore Macdonald's plots. They are more concerned with what they feel to be his perceptive portrait of American life, or they champion his vision of the degeneration of the family unit in the United States. (Unlike his detective, Macdonald had a child, who died at the age of thirty-one.) These overriding elements in his fiction, according to Macdonald, stem from the fact that he has put to literary use the sense of loneliness and deprivation caused through being raised without a father.

Macdonald admitted to me that he was deeply influenced by Freud and the theories of psychoanalysis. The myth of Oedipus is as central to his work as the California setting. In *The Goodbye Look* (Knopf, 1969), one character, when he was a boy of eight, actually murdered his father. A crime some fifteen years hence re-creates this same trauma and sends him off the deep end. In *The Underground Man*, when Susan, present at Leo Broadhurst's murder, witnessess the similar murder fifteen years later of Stanley Broadhurst, Leo's son who is searching for his father, the event has an identical effect on her. The theme is scarcely new with Macdonald. He used it as early as *The Three Roads* (Knopf, 1948). A man murders his wife, then suffers from amnesia; and, upon release from a mental hospital, undertakes to find his wife's killer, eventually tracing the crime to himself.

I don't know how the critics can feel that the repeated use of this plot, in all deference to Freud, can really be said to have something new and challenging about it as a perspective on American society. And whatever may be your opinion of California, I personally have been in a lot more depressing places where the quality of life has left far more to be desired.

"An honest critic is always an optimist," Macdonald told me, "or he wouldn't write."

"But that's my trouble," I said. "I can't really say your novels are particularly optimistic."

He smiled benignly.

"You're misled by my themes," he rejoined. "I deal with concealment, self-concealment. That is always depressing."

The past, in Macdonald's books, is usually not something pleasant. You will frequently find Archer describing people in terms of their attitudes toward the past. "His eyes and voice were faintly drowsy with the past." "She looked as if she were dying under the soft bombardment of the past." "Her voice had a rueful pride which seemed to belong entirely to the past." "Her whole body was dreaming of the past." " 'What's hurting, Jean?' 'My whole life.' " I haven't been stacking the deck, either. These lines are all from one book, *The Goodbye Look*. You can find them in any of the novels Macdonald wrote after *The Galton Case*.

Macdonald was raised in poverty. He wants to preserve what it taught him. None of his characters demonstrate a comparable enthusiasm about their early years; most of them want to remove themselves as far as they can from all memory of them.

Although he rarely leaves Santa Barbara, Macdonald has chosen to concentrate nearly all of his novels in one of two cities, Santa Teresa or Pacific Point. He alternates between them, book by book, so that neither grows stale.

He feels that the great threat to American liberty does not come from the apparently hopeless corruption of the judicial system or law enforcement agencies. Beyond these, and at the root, he finds that the American class system is being effectively replaced by bureaucracy. Because the free enterprise system has lost its ability to generate its own power, it has surrendered to the superimposition of power by the bureaucracy. Raymond Chandler said of bureaucrats in *The Little Sister:* "They are what human beings turn into when they trade life for existence and ambition for security."

Macdonald would never make so outspoken a comment, nor would his detective. In an essay on "The Writer as Detective Hero," reprinted in a pamphlet *On Crime Writing* (Capra Press, 1975), Macdonald observed that "a less encumbered narrator permits greater flexibility, and fidelity to the intricate truths of life. I don't have to celebrate Archer's physical or sexual prowess, or work at making him consistently funny or charming." Archer, unlike an avenging angel from the Old Testament, pleads for mercy, not justice. But he does it quietly.

It hurt Macdonald deeply that Raymond Chandler, whom he very much admired, thought very little of Macdonald's writing and said so. Yet, for all his admiration for both Hammett and Chandler, Macdonald felt that, to be true to himself, he had to take the detective novel in a new direction. "While he is a man of action," he said of Archer in the same essay I have made reference to, "his actions are largely directed to putting together the stories of other people's lives and discovering their significance. . . . This gradually developed conception of the detective hero as the mind of the novel is not wholly new, but it is probably my main contribution to this special branch of fiction." For Macdonald, since the beginnings of the detective story with Poe, reason is necessarily complemented by guilt and horror.

Macdonald went with Alfred A. Knopf because Knopf was Chandler's publisher.

"Chandler was a classic stylist," Macdonald told me. "I have learned a lot more from him now than I ever did in the beginning."

For Macdonald staying with one publisher has paid off. It seems when you choose to write genre fiction it takes longer for any uniqueness to be acknowledged. Here, motion pictures helped Macdonald.

When Paul Newman was cast as Lew Archer in the film to be based on Macdonald's initial Archer novel, *The Moving Target* (Knopf, 1949), Newman had already achieved the status of a superstar. It was Newman's idea to change the name of the detective to Harper. Newman's reasoning was based on the fact that pictures like *Hud* (Paramount, 1963) and *The Hustler* (20th-Fox, 1961), which had been very successful for him, featured the letter H in their titles. The film was issued as *Harper* (Warner's, 1966).

Harper proved popular. Elliott Kastner, who was subsequently involved in the production of both *The Long Goodbye* (United Artists, 1969) and *Farewell, My Lovely* (Avco Embassy, 1975), was the co-producer. Jack Smight was the director. William Goldman did the screenplay. The novel certainly presented a challenge. Macdonald in the books had emphasized not dialogue but plot. On the other hand, Paul Newman's most inspired performances on the screen derive from those circumstances when he can interject into his own personality the psychology of the character he is playing. This required that Archer, or Harper, had to be fleshed out more than the sketchy existence Macdonald provides him in the novel. Archer comments here and there over the years that his wife left him because she objected to detective work.

It may have been that Dashiell Hammett was the only writer of detective novels who could effectively marry his detective-narrator. Macdonald tried it, without so much good fortune, in *The Ferguson Affair* (Knopf, 1960), maybe the best of the non-Archer books. Goldman, after some discussion, wrote in Harper's wife, Susan, as a character. Susan was played by Janet Leigh, well cast as a woman frantically determined to divorce the reality of her husband rather than abandon her girlish dream of marital bliss. This situation made for one of the more humanly touching scenes in the film, when Harper, beaten and exhausted, comes home only to leave again because the job of knowing the truth is more important to him than a false sense of happiness.

When *Harper* was released, critics immediately found a parallel between it and *The Big Sleep* (Warner's, 1946) and insisted that in Paul Newman the screen had found a successor to Humphrey Bogart. Such a posture prohibits an appreciation of the film on its own merits or the perception of how completely different it is, and Newman with it, from any Bogart vehicle. Paul Newman's Harper is a mature personality. He's neither a tough guy who loses everything including love, the way Sam Spade did, nor is he a Philip Marlowe wisecracking his way through a case where everyone including the detective is endemically confused. Harper is scarred by life, but he retains his integrity, not by talking tough, not by being tough, but instead by understanding what it's all about. There is no wounded cynicism, nor is there sequested romanticism behind his stance. At the end, when he exposes his best friend, with a gun pointed at him, he walks away, ostensibly to turn him in, but he can no more do that than the friend can shoot him to save himself. The picture has to conclude with a freeze-frame of Newman throwing up his hands at the folly of it all.

This is possible because the scenarist did keep one aspect of Macdonald's world view, namely that everyone to a greater or lesser extent is guilty; there are no good guys and no bad guys. Lauren Bacall is cast as the murdered man's embittered wife, who, if anything, is relieved by his death. His daughter doesn't love him. His mistress, capably played by Shelley Winters, is only conning him. Strother Martin, as a religious mystic who founds a temple on a mountain given to him by Sampson, the murdered man, uses it as a blind for the smuggling of itinerant workers illegally across the border from Mexico. Half the characters Harper meets are directly involved in a plot to kidnap Sampson and hold him for ransom.

"Tell him that, lawyer," Janet Leigh shouts at her attorney. "Tell him, he *is not* loved."

Sampson's daughter, trying to seduce Harper, comments to him, "Harper, you work hard, do you know that?"

He calls her bluff and then resumes working.

When Robert Wagner, who was in on the kidnap plot, is shot, Harper has to tell Julie Harris, as Wagner's girl friend, the bad news. She prattles on about how profound their love for each other was. She asks Harper what Wagner's last words were.

"Yeah, you're right," Harper lies to her. "He died saying your name."

Neither Sam Spade nor Philip Marlowe would have been capable of such compassion. And compassion is what Paul Newman saw in the character. Harper can talk tough, as when he says, "The bottom is loaded with nice people —only cream and bastards rise." But it's a pose. Harper is a nice guy. He's a hard worker. He's the only character not out wholly for himself. So according to the way of things, he loses what all the other characters yearn after or clutch for, love, money, youth, power. But he has what none of them have, possibly because they don't even know it exists: freedom. Nor is he sorry for himself or his lot. He has no reason to be. He's shrewd enough to know what the alternatives cost.

"Newman is very, very good as Archer," Macdonald agreed.

It may not be accidental. Paul Newman was born on January 26, 1925. He was forty-one years old when he came to the part. He studied economics at Kenyon College, Ohio. He tried for two years to manage his father's sporting goods store, but fled from it. He was married in 1949 to Jackie Witte, but the marriage ended in divorce in 1956. His early years in stock and repertory companies were difficult. His first film, *The Silver Chalice* (Warner's, 1954), was a bomb. He returned to the stage to play the lead in Joseph Hayes's drama *The Desperate Hours*. Robert Montgomery was the director. Humphrey Bogart was dying when he played the part in the motion picture version. To many, it seemed the perfect role for Bogart. But Montgomery felt that Newman's clean-cut youthfulness would invest the character with an element of added terror. He was right.

Playing losers and bums, drifters and alienated loners became the Newman trademark when he returned to films. Although he was color-blind himself, the public effused over his blue eyes. All of which led Newman to comment, "I'd like to think that I could have been a successful actor if I'd had brown eyes."

On January 29, 1958, Paul Newman married Joanne Woodward, whom he had first met many years before when he was working on Broadway. The marriage has lasted. Some of Newman's best screen work has been with his wife. Therefore, it was not surprising that, when the time came for him once again to play Harper, Joanne Woodward should be in the cast as a former intimate of Harper's.

Ross Macdonald complained to me that he would prefer if Hollywood would select one of his later Archer novels for treatment. I cannot entirely agree. Archer is going soft as he progresses from book to book, or—should I say?—as he ages.

The Drowning Pool (Warner's, 1975) was based on Macdonald's second Archer novel. It was produced by Lawrence Turman and David Foster. Tracy Keenan Wynn, Lorenzo Semple, Jr., and Walter Hill did the screenplay. Stuart Rosenberg was the director.

I suspect that Warner Brothers made a mistake in not reissuing *Harper* prior to the release of *The Drowning Pool*. Almost ten years had elapsed since the first film. Paul Newman's performance, if anything, was better than it was in the earlier picture. The dialogue matched the increased depth of character he brought to the role, but here the intricate Macdonald plot worked against the film. The viewer is so busy trying to figure out what happened, who lost what, who was involved, who is after what, that attention is distracted from where it should be placed.

"I've got no idea what justice is," Harper remarks at one point. "But I am interested in the truth." He adds, "Fired or not, I'm sticking it through to the end. And people might not like what I find."

Again, all of the characters, this time including Harper, are guilty of something. The setting is Louisiana. The police are corrupt, but corruption is rela-

A scene between Joanne Woodward and Paul Newman in *The Drowning Pool*
(Warner's, 1975).   PHOTO COURTESY OF WARNER BROTHERS.

tive. *Everyone* is corrupt. Flawed as he may be, Harper at least still serves, as
impartially as he can, the function of a truth-seeker. The loneliness that is imposed on him as a result is all the more terrifying. Richard Jaeckel, who won an
Academy nomination for his role with Newman in *Sometimes a Great Notion*
(Universal, 1971), is back, this time as a tough and crooked cop.

The reader may recall Dick Richards' comment that he had difficulty in de-
ciding just how to put over Marlowe's gift of money to an innocent widow at
the conclusion of *Farewell, My Lovely*. Despite his reassurances, I don't think
the incident was brought off with half the aplomb Newman manages at the end
of *The Drowning Pool*. He gives a hooker $10,000 blood money, less his ex-

penses. The hooker quips, "Harper? You're not so tough." I think the success of the effect lies in the fact that Newman's Harper embodies a degree of inner strength and fortitude of character somehow lacking in Bob Mitchum's sardonic but world-weary Philip Marlowe. You feel rather sorry for Marlowe because he appears seedy enough to need the money. Newman's characterization is of a man more in control of himself and his destiny, no matter how capricious may be the circumstances of his life.

Lew Archer, after years of promoting the notion, finally got his own television series, but it didn't work out. Ross Macdonald attributes the show's demise to the twenty-seven other private eye programs against which it was competing. In part, he may be right, but perhaps there is more to it. The television audience may be ill-prepared for an outlook even approximating that which Paul Newman has brought to his screen portrayals.

Given a more streamlined plot which would permit further character development than any plot from a Ross Macdonald novel can provide, Paul Newman's Harper is to my mind one of the healthiest screen manifestations of a detective in the history of the genre.

A motion picture is not dependent on quite so many whimsical turns of fate as a television series. In any case, however, the second Harper movie was no more successful than the Archer TV series. There was talk at the time of the release of *The Drowning Pool* of doing *The Instant Enemy* (Knopf, 1968) as a film. Now it may not happen. But then, no matter how much I may like Newman in the role, it is no longer feasible for an actor to identify himself so closely with a screen characterization.

If by some of the things I have had to say about Ross Macdonald I have given the impression that I do not enjoy reading his novels, in my own defense I have to point out that I have read them all, some more than once. It is just that I prefer what Paul Newman has done with the character. Macdonald has his reasons, both psychological and literary, for emphasizing lives in his narratives other than that of his detective. He wants, for one thing, to get away from the necessity of having a hero, or even an antihero. In his view of life, he is well aware that there are no heroes. I cannot disagree with him.

However, there are stronger forces at work than all this philosophizing admits. Arguing one way or the other about Archer, or about Newman's Harper, is somewhat pointless. Hero and antihero are being replaced by a Titan, a central character whose methods are no different from those of the villains. John Wayne, to an extent, and Clint Eastwood have brought the violence of the Western to the detective story. The detective, whether policeman or private, forsakes his profession. He is only nominally a truth-seeker. In actuality, he is an avenger, working outside the law, above it and beyond it. Despair over the hopeless corruption in political leadership and law enforcement has given birth to a new wave of vigilantism. Since justice cannot and will not be meted out by the judicial system, the detective, by means of superior firepower, killing and maiming his way toward some obscure, mystical idea of justice, determines to set right with a bullet the evil forces which long ago paid off and retired due process.

V

While it is always difficult to pinpoint where a certain tradition begins, it is made even more complex in the present case by the fact that this tradition, more or less, has always been a part of American history. One of its extreme proponents is surely Mickey Spillane. He was born in Brooklyn in 1918 and started his career writing for slick magazines. After some success he turned to pulp magazines and comic books. He was paid twelve dollars apiece for a block of copy and could do as many as forty or fifty blocks of copy a day. He helped create Captain America and Captain Marvel. During the Second World War, Spillane, born Frank Morrison Spillane, trained pilots and flew combat missions for the Air Corps.

After the war, Spillane returned to comic books. He also worked as a trampoline performer with the Ringling Bros., Barnum and Bailey Circus. He had a short stint as a federal agent during which he helped smash a narcotics ring (he still carries the scars of two bullets and a knife wound to prove it). He was converted to Jehovah's Witnesses in 1952. In 1965, he married his second wife, a beautiful model whom he had pose in the nude for the cover of his 1972 book *The Erection Set*. For a time he was one of the most popular authors in the United States, with seven titles among the ten best-selling American books of this century. His first detective novel was *I, The Jury* (New American Library, 1947). He wrote the book in a tent while he built his first house, trowel in one hand and a how-to book in the other.

I, The Jury introduced Spillane's tough detective Mike Hammer. Hammer has no patience with judges and juries; he knows better. He can knock out teeth, break arms, gouge eyes, and get what he wants. When a pal of his is killed, Hammer in the novel sets out to find the culprit. When he corners the murderess, she strips off her clothes to entice him with her body. He shoots her low in the belly. When she asks Mike, "How could you?" he replies, "It was easy."

Spillane made violence more overt than it had ever been in the detective story. His books, while tame today, had more than their competitors in terms of sexual episodes. "I lived only to kill the scum and the lice that wanted to kill themselves. I lived to kill so that others could live. . . ." This is Hammer's philosophy.

United Artists was quite anxious to bring Mike Hammer to the screen, impressed by the sales figures the books racked up. A four-picture contract was signed with Spillane. *I, The Jury* (United Artists, 1953) was first, filmed in 3-D, featuring Biff Elliot as Hammer, with Preston Foster and Peggie Castle. The plot was somewhat toned down for the film version. The picture grossed only $1,299,000. United Artists couldn't discern what was wrong.

Kiss Me Deadly (United Artists, 1955) came next. Robert Aldrich was contracted to direct. The emphasis was more than ever on individualistic violence.

Ralph Meeker was cast as Mike Hammer, Maxine Cooper portraying Hammer's sexy secretary/companion. When Mike gives a ride to Cloris Leachman, whom he picks up on a lonely country road and who is in trouble, thugs waylay them, force the car over a cliff, and kill the girl. Mike declares vengeance and sets out to even the score, one by one. The picture grossed only $726,000 in the States and a total of $226 overseas.

United Artists was losing its enthusiasm rapidly, but the firm went ahead anyhow and made *My Gun Is Quick* (United Artists, 1957) based on one of Spillane's most popular novels. Robert Bray was cast as Hammer, doing more investigating and with more murders orginated by the villain than by Hammer. The gross sank again, this time to only $308,000, with a foreign worldwide gross of $602.

Spillane had a chance to play himself as a detective in *Ring of Fear* (Warner's, 1954). James Edward Grant, one of John Wayne's favorite screenwriters, was the director. In order to capture a psychopathic killer who is sabotaging his circus, Clyde Beatty asks his old friend Mickey Spillane to take on the case. Spillane solves it. Having been the first detective story author to play himself in pictures, Spillane was cast as his own detective, Mike Hammer, in the fourth and last film on the United Artists contract, *The Girl Hunters*, farmed out to Colorama in England, where it was filmed, although the setting was supposed to be New York. Shirley Eaton and Lloyd Nolan were also in the cast. Hammer manages to come off a seven-year drunk when he learns that his secretary/companion Velda may not have met her death at the hands of the Dragon, a Red agent, but might still be alive. Hammer takes on the Reds. Despite an elaborate promotional campaign, the picture grossed less than a million dollars.

Spillane may have come to the screen too early, but I honestly don't think that was the problem. In *I, The Jury* Biff Elliot was perhaps too inexperienced as an actor to make much of the role. By the time Spillane himself took over the lead, even assisting on the screenplay, the story had a little more of the real flavor, such as nailing the villain's hand to the floor so he'll be there when Lloyd Nolan, representing the police, arrives, or rigging a gun so Shirley Eaton can blow her head off, but the millions of readers who bought Spillane's books just weren't buying movie tickets.

Nevertheless, I suspect it is the *literary* tradition (if it can be called literary) embodied in Spillane's books which acts as a harbinger of the detective films of the Seventies. John Wayne, when he had a four-picture contract at Warner Brothers, was offered *Dirty Harry* (Warner's, 1971) but turned it down. He didn't feel the character was right for him; more likely, there were too many physical demands in the role. Harry Julian Fink, R. M. Fink, and Dean Riesner did the screenplay. Don Siegel was contracted to produce and direct the picture. Clint Eastwood took the part of Dirty Harry. It was, in many ways, a stirring and provocative film.

Eastwood's performance was wholly consistent with the image he had been projecting in Westerns of a man who is, above all, fast with a gun, but a character who has no depth, who is satisfied with physical action alone. That would be sufficient to get patrons into the theaters. But, fortunately, once there the plot could unwind and present the viewer with the bleak, hopeless state the courts have reduced law enforcement to in the United States, especially in the big cities. The film opens to a girl getting shot by a powerful, long-range rifle while swimming in a pool on top of a high-rise apartment building. The Mayor of San Francisco is served with notice that the city will either pay a bribe of $100,000 to the killer or another shooting will take place. The mayor stalls for time. Eastwood, playing Inspector Harry Callahan, is assigned to the case. They call him "Dirty" Harry because he gets all the dirty jobs. Harry stops an armed robbery with his .44 magnum during an interlude in the search for the psychopath.

A ten-year-old Negro boy is shot because the mayor couldn't make up his mind. The killer is almost caught but machine-guns his way to freedom. A fourteen-year-old girl is kidnaped and the ransom goes up to $200,000. Harry is elected to deliver the money. The killer and Harry finally meet. The killer decides to murder the girl and to shoot Harry. Harry stabs him in the leg. The killer gets away, but he is traced by the police when he enters a hospital for

Clint Eastwood as a brand new detective for a brand new age of realism on the screen in *Dirty Harry* (Warner's, 1971).   PHOTO COURTESY OF WARNER BROTHERS.

treatment. Harry captures him in a football stadium. Harry is summoned to the district attorney's office. The DA has his expert, an appellate judge, sitting in on his conference with Harry. The man will be released. Because Harry broke into the killer's room without a warrant, despite all of the evidence, including the rifle Harry found, including the girl's dead body, which was found where the killer confessed having secreted it, the man is the victim of violation of his civil liberties and so cannot be prosecuted.

When he is released, the killer hires a black man to beat him up. Harry has been shadowing him. Now the killer announces to the press that Harry beat him up. Harry is told by the chief of police to lay off.

The killer commandeers a school bus and threatens the mayor that he will shoot all the school children unless he is paid the $200,000 and a chartered jet must be waiting for him at the airport. Harry is asked to deliver the money. The mayor promises the killer he will do nothing to stop him. Harry refuses. He goes out and sets free the school children, finally shooting the killer. At the fade, we see Inspector Harry Callahan throwing his badge in a pool of water where the killer's body is floating. It was the ending, of course, that concluded *High Noon* (United Artists, 1952) and *The Chase* (Columbia, 1966), an ending that John Wayne thought un-American but fitting nonetheless.

Magnum Force (Warner's, 1974) is a continuation of Harry Callahan's story. Harry Julian Fink and R. M. Fink are credited for the original story, John Milius and Michael Cimino for the screenplay. Ted Post directed. The picture begins with a mobster being acquitted on the basis of insufficient evidence. "Fuck the courts," he boasts to the newspaper reporters as he is leaving the San Francisco Hall of Justice. The mobster murdered an informer and his entire family. Now he is safe, or so it would seem. His car is stopped by a traffic cop on a motorcycle. The mobster declares that he'll have the officer kicked off the force. Then the cop pulls a .44 magnum and everyone in the car is shot to death.

Hal Holbrook is a police lieutenant. Harry Callahan works for him. During an interlude, Harry prevents a plane from being hijacked at the airport. Holbrook assigns him to the mobster's murder. When a group of gangsters and their women are machine-gunned at a private, seminude bathing party, Holbrook really becomes concerned. "Someone's trying to put the courts out of business," he remarks. But he's aware that it is a stupid comment, since the courts defend criminals and protect their rights, while no one, not even the police, are able to protect the rights of the victims. Holbrook suspects the entire affair may be the result of a new generation of vigilantes who are willing to do what the courts no longer are able to do.

The police are assigned to protect known criminals and gang leaders. One of them, just as he gets out of his bathrobe and is about to join a pair of heroin addicts, a beautiful boy and a beautiful girl who want him sexually between them, finds a uniformed policeman entering the room. They're all shot to death. It turns out that Holbrook and four new police recruits are at the back of it. The third picture in the series, *The Enforcer* (Warner's, 1976), the Christmas picture for the Bicentennial, continues the saga into the drug racket.

Harry Callahan is depicted as steering a middle course between being a good cop and yet being frustrated by the near collusion of the court system in promoting criminal activity.

"Crime isn't just organized. It's institutionalized." This sentiment is expressed in *McQ* (Warner's, 1974). It was John Wayne's last film on his four-picture contract, and it proved a box-office disaster, but its problems were only peripherally concerned with its plot. The truth of the matter, put bluntly, is that John Wayne has been much too old for the hero parts he has played for the last decade and, increasingly, it was catching up with him.

I was invited to the set to interview Wayne for my book *The Filming of the West* while *McQ* was in production in Seattle. The first day of my visit the unit was shooting the hospital sequence where Wayne first learns that his good friend has been shot, and comforts the widow who is sexually interested in Wayne. He was short-winded and still smoking at the time; but you have to see the picture before you become aware just how short of breath he is on camera. He seems to be constantly gasping for air. Years of intense drinking have clouded his memory of the past to an amazing extent, while his status as the last of the great superstars prompts him to forget everyone whom he once admired and worked with in the masterful Westerns he made for John Ford and Howard Hawks. John Sturges was the director. Wayne had his part of Lon McQ tailored to illustrate his own attitudes toward social and political issues.

The story begins with a series of murders committed by McQ's friend on the police force. The friend is killed by the forces who hired him to act as a hit man. Eddie Albert is McQ's superior officer. "Lon. I know you," he tells McQ. "I'm not going to stand for you making your own rules." "Seriously hurt a hoodlum," McQ snaps back, "and lawyers scream about his civil rights."

McQ finally is forced to quit the force. Albert is satisfied with interrogating young college revolutionaries rather than going after the Syndicate leaders who are doubtless behind the murders. McQ borrows $5,000 from his ex-wife's second husband and sets out after the Syndicate. He lives on his boat. "How do you do it," his friend's widow asks him, "this living in solitary?" "You get used to it," McQ replies. He visits his daughter on Sundays. But she's getting older now and has less time for him. It's the politicians who mastermind a drug heist from the police cache of seized narcotics. McQ is told by the Syndicate boss, "Certain officials are my competitors. See what the law has become." McQ bribes a female informer and then goes to bed with her. Later she is murdered. McQ finally cracks the case, shoots down the Syndicate boys, and brings the crooked politician at the head of the narcotics swindle—he's sleeping with the widow who's been after McQ—to justice.

Some of the premises of this film are accurate, but certainly not the Wayne character. He is outmoded and impossible in the modern world. One man alone, the solitary hero, isn't up to taking on the courts, city hall, and the Syndicate, and viewers of the film, to their despair perhaps, are only too keenly conscious of it.

Brannigan (United Artists, 1975) was filmed in London. Douglas Hickox, the assistant director on the first Miss Marple film, was the director. Brannigan is the Wayne character playing a Chicago policeman. He is sent to England to ex-

John Wayne as he looked on the set of *McQ* (Warner's, 1974). He was perhaps too old for such roles. PHOTO COURTESY OF WARNER BROTHERS.

tradite a mobster who has taken refuge there. Judy Geeson, representing Scotland Yard, meets Brannigan at the airport. "My father," she tells Wayne, "thought there were three things wrong with the Yanks. Overpaid, oversexed, and over here." I suppose part of the fun was supposed to derive from putting the Wayne character of the sagebrush in the middle of contemporary London, but the comedy really doesn't work. A contract is taken out on Brannigan. The mobster is kidnaped and £350,000 is demanded of the Syndicate for his return. Wayne as Brannigan has his hands full between the contract man, tracing the mobster played by Michael Larkin, and clashing with Scotland Yard's less violent approach to matters of law enforcement. Roughing up a London bookie, Wayne asks him, "Do you want to qualify for England's free dental care?" The end result is that the mobster and his lawyer plotted the kidnaping scheme themselves. It backfires and Brannigan makes his capture. The contract man is shot up.

If the Wayne character in a detective role is strictly a fantasy, James Garner symbolizes a different kind of fantasy in *They Only Kill Their Masters* (M-G-M, 1972). Here the slick yet homespun Garner character is cast as a small town chief of police. The setting permits one to forget all the big city graft. Garner can remark, "I heard once that Harry Truman used to have a triple Bourbon for lunch. When I heard that, I voted for him." That might have worked during even the Eisenhower years, but the nation since has had Kennedy, Johnson, and Nixon. Garner is rather out of place. James Goldstone directed with the screenplay by Lane Slate. A Doberman pinscher is accused of having killed its owner, Peter Lawford's ex-wife. Katharine Ross works for the local veterinarian, Hal Holbrook. She starts sleeping with Garner. But she gets turned off when Garner suspects her. The murderer turns out to be sweet June Allyson, now many years older than she was in those romantic M-G-M fantasies of two decades ago. She and the murdered woman were lovers. Edmund O'Brien, himself the star of several detective films in the Forties and Fifties at Columbia, has a part as a liquor store owner.

Negroes have long agitated that Hollywood has dealt unfairly with them. Why can't films be made with black men as lead heroes? Hollywood's answer to this was *Shaft* (M-G-M, 1971). When you think of Stepin Fetchit, Mantan Moreland, Willie Best, Snowflake, and the many other blacks who appeared in detective films of previous decades, you are inclined to wonder what they would make of Richard Roundtree as a "black Sam Spade," to paraphrase the screenplay. Shaft is a private detective working in Manhattan. He has two major beefs: "I was born black and I was born poor."

Shaft is the creation of screenwriter Ernest Tidyman. The blurb on the Bantam Books edition of *Shaft* tells the reader that "Shaft has no prejudices. He'll kill anyone—black or white." The film altered the central scene of the novel where Shaft sets fire to an entire street to rescue the daughter of a black hoodlum who manages narcotics in Harlem and whom the Mafia wants to turn over his district to them. Shaft runs crazily down the street, firing his gun and shouting, "The niggers are coming!"

In the film, Roundtree's characterization leaves no question that Shaft maims or kills what gets in his way. And both black girls and white girls know that Shaft's other gun can give them so much pleasure that they'll leave his bed bow-legged. In the film, as in the novel, Shaft throws a black hoodlum out of his fourth-story-office window when he feels insulted by him. When a Mafia man spits at Shaft, Shaft breaks a whiskey bottle on his face. Gordon Parks directed. The film showed Shaft getting the girl free from her captors by organizing black revolutionaries and declaring war on the mob, with time out for swaggering and screwing. The picture cost $1,543,000 to make and grossed $7,080,000 on release. Metro knew it had a winner, primarily because of white crossover at the box office.

Shaft's Big Score (M-G-M, 1972) was the sequel. Gordon Parks again directed and Ernest Tidyman once more supplied the screenplay. Issac Hayes had won an Oscar for Best Song for the original film, but he proved unavailable, so Parks, the director, did the score himself. Production standards were improved to the tune of $1,978,000, but the picture grossed only $3,936,000.

Metro followed it immediately with *Shaft in Africa* (M-G-M, 1973). John Guillermin directed and Stirling Silliphant did the screenplay. The idea is that Shaft should get to the bottom of the slave trade in Europe. The cost went up to $2,142,000, but the gross fell to $1,458,000. Metro quickly sold the property to television, but it barely survived its first complement of shows.

In the Coffin Ed Johnson/Grave Digger Jones team and the Virgil Tibbs series for United Artists, the black detectives are policemen and not private investigators. Tibbs was directed primarily at the white theatergoing public, whereas the Johnson/Jones team were black exploitation films like the Shaft series at Metro. *Cotton Comes to Harlem* (United Artists, 1970) was the first of two films to feature Raymond St. Jacques and Godfrey Cambridge as black cops in New York City. The French literary critics became effusive over Chester Himes's original novel and compared his two detectives to Inspector Maigret and Sam Spade *en noir*. Samuel Goldwyn, Jr., produced and Ossie Davis directed. The plot has to do with $87,000 hidden in a bale of cotton, taken from the back-to-Africa racket of black preacher Calvin Lockhart. The film gets hopelessly bogged down in sociological platitudes which seem to emphasize that black dissatisfaction leads principally to black exploitation of black. But the film proved popular and grossed $5,122,000, better than four times its cost.

Mark Warren directed the sequel picture, *Come Back Charleston Blue* (Warner's, 1972). The plot involved a presumed return from the grave of a Harlem black hoodlum supposedly done in by Dutch Schultz during the Depression. He liked to cut his victim's throat with a blue razor. Coffin Ed and Grave Digger find the real culprit to be Peter De Anda, who is a Nam vet running a youth center as a front for his attempt to wrench Harlem dope traffic from the Mafia and place it in black hands, where it belongs. There was no white crossover for the film at all and, even with a $2,235,346 gross, it died.

John Ball was born in 1911 in Schenectady, New York. He grew up in Milwaukee and attended Carroll College in Waukesha, Wisconsin. He became a commercial pilot and during the Second World War was a flight instructor and pilot in the Army. He reviewed music and wrote features for the Brooklyn

Eagle and then became a columnist for the New York *World-Telegram* before going to Washington, D.C., where he worked as a broadcaster in a radio station. He served on the science staff of *Fortune* magazine and became director of public relations for the Institute of Aerospace Sciences in Los Angeles. He now writes mystery stories. His first book having Virgil Tibbs as its central character was published in 1965, *In the Heat of the Night.*

I was introduced to Ball at a recent Bouchercon, a meeting of detective fans honoring the memory of the late reviewer of detective and crime fiction for the New York *Times,* Anthony Boucher. Ball is a quiet, retiring Caucasian. He is profoundly interested in Chinese artifacts, Sherlock Holmes, and Oriental martial arts. A demure man, he has a nervous habit of flitting about constantly. He imbued his black police detective Tibbs with many of his hobbies and interests, placing him in the Pasadena Police Department. Anthony Boucher said of Tibbs that he was "a remarkable individual who may well end up in the great detective category."

That judgment turned out to be a bit premature. But there is no doubt that *In the Heat of the Night* (United Artists, 1967) proved a most successful picture. It grossed $10,907,000, won an Academy Award for Best Picture, and Rod Steiger was voted Best Actor. Ball wrote the book well in keeping with the changing sentiment toward the blacks and probably had Sidney Poitier in mind all along. Norman Jewison directed. Tibbs is on his way through a small Southern town. A prominent citizen is murdered. Rod Steiger plays the red-necked police captain who suspects Tibbs primarily because of his color. How could such a plot miss in 1967? The film changed Tibbs's affiliation to the Philadelphia Police Department. Eventually, he and Steiger join forces to solve the case. Steiger's growing admiration for Tibbs was effectively projected on the screen and, certainly, deserved the recognition bestowed by the Academy.

Gordon Douglas directed *They Call Me Mister Tibbs!* (United Artists, 1970). The plot showed Tibbs with the San Francisco Police Department called on by a friend, who is a minister, to help prove him innocent of murdering a prostitute when all the evidence is against him.

"Poitier was great," Douglas told me, "a real pro. But we didn't have the ingredients in the second picture that *In the Heat of the Night* had. That first picture, why, they fought the Civil War all over again. We just had another police story, with a black as a cop; that was the only difference."

The Organization (United Artists, 1971) was directed by Don Medford. It had a more engaging plot. A group of young revolutionaries, seen at the beginning pulling a daring robbery, have set themselves up in opposition to the Syndicate. They ask Tibbs to help them in their fight against organized crime. They tell him—and he cannot deny it—that the police and courts are totally powerless

Sidney Poitier and Rod Steiger in the highly successful Academy Award-winning *In the Heat of the Night* (United Artists, 1967).

PHOTO COURTESY OF UNITED ARTISTS TELEVISION.

to battle the Mafia. Tibbs gets in trouble with the force and is suspended. Barbara McNair plays Tibbs's wife. This gives Tibbs substance as a character, meaning as a person, and, together, the two represent a humane outpost in a world that increasingly has become a jungle.

Bullitt (Warner's, 1968), starring Steve McQueen, brought realism to the screen by presenting a cop who is neither hero nor villain. San Francisco—for some reason a favorite setting—is again the city. Hospitals in their mechanized inhumanity, the pressures on the police and the graft within the force, the ambitions of young politicians, and the suave confidence of the gangsters are all there. But what made the picture a blockbuster at the box office was the suspenseful, frantic chase. Peter Yates directed.

Chases are as old as the movies. There's a chase in *The Great Train Robbery* (Edison, 1903), in *The Birth of a Nation* (Epoch, 1915), in *Stagecoach* (United Artists, 1939), and in *What's Up Doc?* (Warner's, 1972), among countless others. William Friedkin, director of *The French Connection* (20th-Fox, 1971) and Philip D'Antoni, who produced it, were walking along Lexington Avenue in New York City. They knew their story was interesting and the characters engaging, but the picture still needed something. The idea came to them in a flash during their walk: a chase. But it had to be an unusual chase, between a car racing after a subway train overhead with a murderer on board. Ernest Tidyman, who had been associated with the Shaft property, listened to their idea and put it into screenplay form, some twenty pages. All told, the picture was in various stages of production for two years. The fantastic chase, which made it a box-office winner, was shot over two weeks in New York on the Stillwell Avenue Line from Bay Fiftieth Street to Sixty-second Street. It was broken down into fragments, each one filmed out of sequence, generally with three cameras going. The crash of the trains was simulated by shooting one train pulling away from another, and then running the film in reverse.

"But at least 50 per cent of the effectiveness of the sequence comes from the sound and editing," Friedkin recalled. "I can't say too much about the importance of editing. When I looked at the first rough cut of the chase, it was terrible. It didn't play. It was formless, in spite of the fact that I had a very careful shooting plan which I followed in detail. It became a matter of removing a shot here or adding a shot there, or changing the sequence of shots, or dropping one frame, or adding one or two frames. And here's where I had enormous help from Jerry Greenberg, the editor."

The plot of the film was nothing special. It consisted of Gene Hackman, as "Popeye" Jimmy Doyle of the New York Police Department, frustrating Fernando Rey's sale to the Mafia of a large shipment of heroin. Rey gets away at the end and Doyle shoots an innocent man, mistaking him for Rey. *The French Connection II* (20th-Fox, 1975) showed Doyle going to Marseilles in search of Rey, working not always harmoniously with the French police. Rey is done in by the end. But without a spectacular chase, the picture had nothing to offer.

.The last film I wish to speak about in this connection is the one that contradicts any stereotype whatsoever of the superhuman, *Serpico* (Paramount, 1973). Directed by Sidney Lumet, the story tells of Frank Serpico, a New York cop who loves opera and ballet, whose pets include an English sheepdog, a Guatemalan macaw, and a white mouse. He has an apartment in Greenwich Village. He looks like a hippie and he wears one gold earring. But what makes him different from the Waynes and the Eastwoods and the Roundtrees, and his story one of tragic suspense, is that he is an honest cop who objects to the corruption within the department and the corruption in the streets, but realistically, as one man alone, he cannot singlehandedly overcome it. Serpico is a central figure, a protagonist, rather than a hero or an antihero. He is willing to sacrifice everything for his integrity, but American society, the law enforcement agencies, the courts, the legal system ordain that when a man takes this stance he doesn't come out a winner: instead he inevitably loses everything. With *Serpico*, the detective film is seen at last to have reversed itself from its beginnings: no one wants to learn the truth; the detective who is honest is at once an enemy of society and its victim.

VI

Federico Fellini, Michaelangelo Antonioni, and Pier-Paolo Pasolini represent one thrust of the European cinema. Roman Polanski represents a different thrust, to my way of thinking preferable to the other. He, like they, was applauded by the intellectuals, but he went to Hollywood and his films began making money; inevitably perhaps, under the circumstances, his former critical champions began turning on him.

Roman Polanski was born of Polish parents in Paris on August 18, 1933. Three years later his family returned to Poland and settled in Cracow. During the war, when he was eight years old, Polanski's parents were put in a concentration camp by the Nazis. Roman was left entirely on his own. He survived as best he could, living with a succession of Polish families. The movies proved an escape and refuge for him. His mother died in the concentration camp. His father, who lived, remarried after he was released. Roman had no desire to live with his father again. His father understood and financed him until he was able to support himself. When Roman was fourteen he began acting on the stage, and then in films. At the same time, he attended art school in Cracow, studying sculpture, painting, and graphics. After graduation, he spent five years at the State Film College at Lodz. His first completed short film was *Rozbijemy Zabawe* (*Break Up the Dance*) in 1957, for which he wrote the screenplay and in which he used real juvenile delinquents to disrupt a dance. Like his next film in 1959, *Lampa* (*The Lamp*), it has never been seen outside Poland. In 1960, he went to France for eighteen months, where he directed and played in *Le Gros et le Maigre* (Claude Joudioux/A.P.E.C., 1961), which had a running time of sixteen minutes. His eleven-minute film *Ssaki* (*Mammals*) in 1962 won him the Grand Prix at the International Film Festival at Tours. His first and only Polish feature, *Noz w Wodzie* (*Knife in the Water*) (Contemporary, 1962), won acclaim at the Venice Film Festival and led to an Academy Award nomination in Hollywood. "I woke up famous," he commented.

Knife in the Water began that fantastic series of motion pictures which more firmly established Polanski with an international audience and both critical and popular recognition. *Rosemary's Baby* (Paramount, 1968) was a joint enterprise between Paramount Pictures and William Castle Enterprises. I have already mentioned Castle in connection with the Boston Blackie, Crime Doctor, and Whistler films for Columbia release. Castle sweated it out on the picture because Polanski was such a perfectionist; the film excited much controversy, but it proved popular.

Polanski married Polish film actress Barbara Lass, but the marriage ended in divorce in 1962. He loved her but she left him. He met Sharon Tate during the summer of 1966, while she was in London featured in *Eye of the Devil* (M-G-M, 1966). Polanski felt Tate less promiscuous than he was. He would flip through his address book and remark, "Who shall I gratify tonight?" It wasn't really arrogance, as so many who met him thought; it was insulation. "I'm not pessimistic," Polanski had once said, "only serious."

"I remember I spent a night—I lost a key—and I spent a night in her house in the same bed, you know," Polanski told police of his relationship with Sharon Tate. "And I knew there was no question of making love with her. That's the type of girl she was. I mean, that rarely happens to me! And then we went on location—it was two or three months later."

Martin Ransohoff, the producer on *Eye of the Devil*, had asked Polanski to see if he could use Sharon Tate in his film *The Fearless Vampire Killers* (M-G-M, 1967).

"When we were on location shooting the film, I asked her, 'Would you like to make love with me?' and she said, very sweetly, 'Yes.' And then for the first time I was somewhat touched by her, you know. And we started sleeping regularly together. And she was so sweet and so lovely that I didn't believe it, you know. I'd had bad experiences and I didn't believe that people like that existed, and I was waiting a long time for her to show the color, right? But she was *beautiful*, without this phoniness. She was fantastic. She loved me." They were married on January 20, 1968.

Sharon Tate, another woman, and three men were slaughtered by Charles Manson's "family." Sharon was pregnant, and for that reason she had stayed behind when Polanski had to go to Europe. The baby was slaughtered. The word PIG was scrawled in blood on Polanski's front door.

William Castle rushed to the Paramount lot when he heard the news. *Rosemary's Baby* was in release. "Alone and stunned, Roman stared at me," Castle recalled. "Handing me a piece of paper, he spoke in a monotone. 'Print "PIG." '

"Confused, I looked at him. 'Why, Roman?'

Roman Polanski as a hit man in *Chinatown* (Paramount, 1974).

PHOTO COURTESY OF ROMAN POLANSKI.

" 'Do as I ask . . . please!' I printed the word. 'Again . . . please, Bill, again!' Pausing, I looked at him. Then his eyes welled with tears. 'Sharon, my poor Sharon . . . And our baby.' "

After the murders, Polanski returned again and again to the home which he had shared with Sharon. It appeared strange to him. All he could ask was the question: "Why?"

As could only be expected, law enforcement and the courts could do very little about the tragedy, and the trial dragged on for years. The death penalty was gone, as were several witnesses and an attorney the defendants didn't like. Parole eligibility for those convicted begins in 1978.

Chinatown (Paramount, 1974) cast Jack Nicholson as J. J. Gittes, whose name every character pronounces differently. He is a retired cop who was once on the Chinatown beat but quit the force because he got sick of hearing every time a crime was committed, and the police chose to do nothing, "Forget it. It's Chinatown." Now Gittes has a successful matrimonial detective agency. Unwittingly, he is used as a dupe to find a girl who is supposedly the water commissioner's mistress but who is anything but that. When Nicholson gets too close to the truth, Polanski himself appears in the picture as one of the hit men who are charged with the cover-up of a phony irrigation swindle. He places his switchblade knife in Nicholson's nose and yanks the knife out sideways. "Next time you lose the whole thing," Polanski warns Nicholson. "I cut it off and feed it to my goldfish."

The picture is told from the first person, with the camera, not through narration. The camera sees very little that Nicholson doesn't see. The viewer comes to know the truth no more quickly than Nicholson does. And the truth, in contradiction to those philosophers who once imputed it with the mystical ability of making us free, is discovered to do nothing at all. The truth is unimportant. More than ever, it is a simple case of the inexorable fact that when someone wins someone has to lose.

When I came upon Roman Polanski at the Studios de Boulogne, he was in the midst of dubbing *Locotaire* (*The Tenant*) (Paramount, 1976) into English. The scene was where Polanski climbs the stairs alongside Melvyn Douglas and he is told how one must properly act. Up the stairs, backwards, up the stairs, backwards, up the stairs—each time some new sound was added; each time the bands indicating the sound track running on the screen beneath the picture took on different markings. Polanski was giving directions in French. Up the stairs, backwards . . .

After a long time, Polanski walked over to where I was sitting opposite the control panel.

"This is my new picture," he said. "It is about a man who comes to live in France. He becomes a naturalized citizen. But the French, they don't accept him. He is made to feel an outsider. He is a French citizen, but he is not French. And his mind, he is beginning to lose his mind. I call it *The Tenant*."

He resumed working. Up the stairs, backwards. I began to think Polanski and Douglas would never make it. Then they did. Douglas opened the door to his apartment. Suddenly, backwards, up the stairs, backwards, up the stairs.

Time passed. The editors exclaimed satisfaction when finally it went right.

"Have you ever had *couscous?*" Polanski asked me, appearing beside me again.

"No."

"It's a dish from Northern Africa. Come, I know a restaurant nearby. Try some."

We walked out of the editing booth.

"Posters all over Paris are announcing the opening of *The Tenant*," I said as we walked along a passageway.

"Yes, but the critics didn't like it. It was entered at Cannes, one of the two French entries. I don't give interviews. That was a mistake. In France, you must give interviews, or you'll pay for it. I'm paying for it now."

We descended a long flight of stairs and were in the light of the street.

"This way," Polanski directed. "It isn't far."

We walked down the street.

"Did you ever interview Adolph Zukor?" Polanski asked.

"Yes," I said. "When I was doing *The Filming of the West.* The man was a hundred and his memory was incredible. He died recently."

"I know. I will tell you a story. When I was at Paramount in New York, I would see him every day at lunchtime. He always hid his mouth with his hand, as if he didn't want anyone to see that he was shoveling the food in, you know? When he had a mouthful, he would take his hand away. Every day one of the publicity people would take me over to his table and introduce me. 'Mr. Zukor, this is Roman Polanski. He is directing a picture for us.' "

Polanski laughed.

"And every day he would nod at me as if we were meeting for the first time. 'Good,' he would say, 'that's good.' "

We were at the restaurant. Polanski held the door. We were shown to a booth. He ordered. I had whiskey; he had wine.

"What did you think of *Chinatown?*" he asked.

"That's what I came here to talk about."

I had with me a book consisting of screenplays from three of Polanski's early films. There were many illustrations of him directing the pictures.

"Have you seen this?"

"No," he said, taking the book and paging through it, dwelling on the illustrations. After a time he said, "You know, it is strange, I was so unhappy when I made these pictures, but when I look at these illustrations, I feel nostalgic."

"I understand from John Huston that you were responsible for changing the ending of *Chinatown.*"

"Yes. When I was given the script, it was about two hundred fifty pages. Many of the characters were unfilmable. I worked on the script for eight weeks just to get rid of unnecessary characters. The script had it that Huston died at the end. I didn't want that. I wanted him to live."

"Why?"

"Because there is no justice in the story. You want the audience to be perturbed because justice *isn't* done. Hollywood likes to tease the audience, but the hero always comes along at the end and kills the bad guy. It's not that way, and I didn't want to film it that way. I wanted Huston for the role of Dunaway's father. He was perfect. And Nicholson. The script was rewritten with him in mind. Ask Bobby Evans at Paramount to show you the original script I was first handed. You wouldn't believe it."

*Couscou*s was brought. Polanski gave instructions on how it was best seasoned.

"Now, what do you think?"

I nodded my accord.

"Don't go anywhere else in Paris but here. They know how to make it here."

"The detective loses in the end," I said, changing the subject.

"Well, he had to lose, didn't he? Detectives are losers to begin with. Theirs is a dirty business, peeping and spying, getting photographs of what people do in hotel rooms. That's not a profession. A detective is a loser."

"What amazes me about the film is how little violence there is in it."

"Yes, and the critics attacked it, saying it was full of violence. But there is none really. Violence shouldn't be drawn out. It's there in the scene where I cut Nicholson's nose. It happens so fast, you aren't aware of it; then it's over. That's how violence is. They want to cut that scene when they release the film to television. Even when Dunaway gets shot, the violence is quick. Audiences like sensations. So if you have to include violence, if it's quick, it is also sensational."

Polanski stretched out in his booth seat.

"From what your secretary tells me, you'll be busy for the rest of the year."

"Yes. When I finish editing *The Tenant*, I have to go to Munich, where I'm directing an opera."

"Which one?"

"*Rigoletto*. Then I fly to Hong Kong to be a judge in a beauty contest. Then I go to California. Then, in January, I start a new picture in London."

"*Chinatown* didn't have a very happy ending," I said, abruptly changing the subject again.

"Happy endings make me puke, don't they you?"

"But audiences like happy endings."

"I don't believe in giving people what they want, or what they think they want. When I was little I saw *Of Mice and Men* [United Artists, 1939]. That didn't have a happy ending, did it?"

But he knew I was only teasing him.

"Think about successful stories. They're usually unhappy. Happiness doesn't give you intrigue, no suspense; and if you don't have conflict, you don't have a movie."

We talked some more over our Moroccan tea. It was light, served in glasses from a samovar which had been brought to our table. Then it came time to return to the studio.

"How are you going to end your book?" Polanski asked as we walked out of the restaurant and into the street.

"I don't know," I confessed.

Polanski's spirits were jubilant. He began to whistle. I was reminded of an incident that had occurred some twenty years previously.

Howard Hawks once went hunting with Ernest Hemingway. He wanted Hemingway to come to Hollywood and work on a screenplay for him. Hemingway demurred. He told Hawks that he knew nothing about screenwriting and he thought it unwise for a man to try something about which he knew so little. Hawks then surprised Hemingway by telling him he would turn Hemingway's worst book into a successful motion picture. *To Have and Have Not* (Scribner's, 1937) was the book Hawks had in mind.

"But you didn't use Hemingway's story," I said to Hawks during one of our talks.

"I did," he said. "I told him I wanted to tell the story of Harry Morgan and Marie, the prostitute he'd married. We spent days together and I kept asking Hemingway about Harry Morgan, how he'd been when he first met Marie, how she'd been, what was their first meeting like. I took the story back ten years from when Hemingway had started it in his novel."

"And the film you updated by ten years, putting it during the Second World War."

"That made the story more contemporary," Hawks responded. "The audience could follow it more easily."

I thought about that conversation as we walked along the sidewalk in Boulogne; or, I should say, while I walked and Roman Polanski skipped along the curb.

Howard Hawks knew what he was about, and he knew his stars, Humphrey Bogart and Lauren Bacall. He gave the story a happy ending. He allowed Bogart, one man alone, to triumph over his circumstances. If it were done today, possibly Harry Morgan's story could be told the way Hemingway wrote it.

> "A man," Harry Morgan said, looking at them both. "One man alone ain't got. No man alone now." He stopped. "No matter how a man alone ain't got no bloody f——ing chance."
>
> He shut his eyes. It had taken him a long time to get it out and it had taken him all of his life to learn it.

That was how Hemingway wrote it. He told how Harry Morgan loved his boat, and his freedom, and his self-reliance. Harry Morgan lost his boat, because in life, when somebody wins, somebody else has got to lose. And lying on the deck of his boat, gut-shot, bleeding to death, Harry Morgan had lost his freedom and his self-reliance. And now he was losing his life.

Hammett had recorded how corruption infested everyone, how it made them blood simple. There was no way out. Ned Beaumont thought he was getting away but he was only leaving town, if in fact he ever left.

John Huston directed *Key Largo* (Warner's, 1948). He had some of the dialogue altered from the stage play. Edward G. Robinson played a gangster who was holding Humphrey Bogart, Lauren Bacall, Lionel Barrymore, and Claire Trevor prisoner in a hotel in the Florida Keys. At one point, Barrymore asks

Jack Nicholson and John Huston in *Chinatown* (Paramount, 1974).

PHOTO COURTESY OF PARAMOUNT PICTURES.

Robinson what it is he wants. "He wants more," Bogart says. "Yeah," Robinson agrees. "That's what I want. I want more. *More!*"

"Will you ever get enough?" Barrymore asks him.

Robinson is perplexed.

"I don't think so," Robinson says. "I haven't yet."

In *Chinatown*, Jack Nicholson confronts John Huston. The bond issue has gone through. The people of Los Angeles will be paying to irrigate land in the Valley owned by Huston. It will bring him another fortune.

"How much money do you have?" Nicholson asks Huston.

Huston shrugs his shoulders.

"A million dollars?"

Huston nods agreement.

"Ten million?"

Huston again agrees.

"Well, then," Nicholson asks in exasperation, "why are you doing it?"

"Because," says Huston, "you have to think of the future."

Criminal corruption can at long last be ignored successfully because it has finally thoroughly integrated itself into the American political, judicial, and law enforcement systems; criminal corruption is now synonymous with the American way of life.

Huston in *Chinatown* wants one last thing, the young daughter he bore incestuously through his daughter Faye Dunaway. Jack Nicholson would prevent it from happening; he would have Huston brought to justice for his crimes.

Faye Dunaway is about to escape from her hiding place in Chinatown with her daughter. Huston arrives there with Nicholson. Nicholson's men were waiting for him to show up, but the police showed up first and handcuffed them. When Faye Dunaway makes a break for it, she is shot through the eye by a plainclothes policeman. Huston holds his daughter/granddaughter to him and leads her away from the terrible scene.

"He owns the police," Nicholson is warned when he tries to struggle and object.

"As little as possible," he mutters then, under his breath.

"C'mon, Jake," his men comfort him. "It's Chinatown."

As I watched Roman Polanski skipping along, I could not help recalling that at that very moment in the States the story of his wife's brutal murder was being televised for the entertainment of the viewing audience.

"*Chinatown* didn't have a very happy ending," I said again.

Polanski moved back onto the sidewalk and walked beside me.

"When people leave a theater, they shouldn't be allowed to think that everything is all right with the world. It isn't. And very little in life has a happy ending."

I couldn't help reflecting on those critics who have such faith in the power of the written word that they seem actually to believe that merely by condemning a film or a book for having a bleak if realistic perspective they can dissipate its accuracy and substitute in its place the same old reassuring fantasies. Fantasies are like theological tenets. A man is made to feel righteous for believing them.

"And," said Polanski, stopping in his tracks and facing me, with the beginnings of a smile on his somber features, "*Chinatown* was a popular film, wasn't it?"

"You needn't be so smug about it," I returned. "All you're saying is that you were lucky—once—and got away with telling the truth."

We were outside the Studios de Boulogne. Polanski put his arm around me.

"Let's go back inside and work on *The Tenant*, shall we?"

In early 1977, Polanski was scheduled to begin work on a new film that was to be a Columbia Pictures/Electrical and Musical Industries, Ltd., joint venture, and we agreed to visit again after the first of the year. In March of 1977, Polanski came to Hollywood to prepare the screenplay while staying at the Beverly-Wilshire Hotel. On the night of March 11, 1977, he was arrested in his hotel suite and charged with rape and on March 29, 1977, the Los Angeles Superior Court indicted him on six felony charges for drug abuse and rape of a thirteen-year-old girl. Suddenly it seemed that the caprice of the American judicial system which Polanski had attacked in *Chinatown* might be the only thing standing between him and imprisonment or deportation, or both. Columbia Pictures canceled his contract for the film.

Robert Altman, when we spoke in Palm Springs about *The Long Goodbye*, urged me to see *The Late Show* (Warner's, 1977), which was then still being edited. It starred Art Carney as an aging retired detective and Lily Tomlin as his kooky client. Bob Benton, Altman's assistant director on several films, directed it, with Altman as the picture's producer. Altman told me that *The Late Show* attempted to put across everything *The Long Goodbye* had failed to do, and, screening it, I had to agree with him. It involves the audience with the characters, presents a graphic portrait of contemporary Southern California, restores mirth to a murder mystery, and most of all depicts the classic fictional detective of the Forties as older, by now anachronistic, but charming in his sense of personal integrity and, despite his years and a debilitating heart condition, more than a match for the corruption surrounding him. *The Late Show* may be the swan song of the private detective genre, but if it is, it is also witty, delightful, and touchingly human.

Faye Dunaway, whose sexuality in *Chinatown* (Paramount, 1974) has a desperate and forbidding aspect.　　　　PHOTO COURTESY OF PARAMOUNT PICTURES.

INDEX